CW01643019

Dear Dawn

Thank you for [illegible] of my journey. I hope my story brings you value.

All the best.

Matt :)

Matt Sims

Entrepreneur. Leader. Continuous Improvement Practitioner. Author. Speaker.

Anxiety Tamer.

High Performance Starts with People.

Respect. Authenticity. Engagement. Empowerment.

Continuous Improvement Isn't Something You Do.

It's How You Think.

TABLE OF CONTENTS

ACKNOWLEDGMENTS

Writing this book has been an incredible journey of reflection, and even growth, and there are so many people who deserve my deepest gratitude.

First and foremost, to my three remarkable children. You have been my source of strength when the days were long, my belief when doubt crept in, and my motivation when the work demanded more. You may not have seen every late night or wrestled with every draft alongside me, but your presence has always been there in the background, steady and powerful.

Knowing that you were watching, learning, and forming your own standards has driven me to hold mine higher. You remind me daily why resilience matters, why integrity matters, and why finishing what you start matters. Everything I have built, and continue to build, is rooted in the responsibility and pride I feel in being your Dad (Bubba). I'm not perfect, far from it, but I love you beyond words.

To my late Grandad, Mick Sidwell, whose solid reputation, unwavering pride, and the deep respect he earned provided me with the greatest platform from which to build my own journey. His encouragement and wisdom still guide me today. Although he's no longer with us, his impact remains, a legend in Croydon, South London. Gone from this dimension, but never forgotten.

To all the incredible people who have invested in me over the years, thank you for believing in my potential, for opening doors of opportunity, and for being the role models who helped shape the leader I've become. I am forever grateful for your trust, guidance, and belief in my journey.

To those that doubted me, I told you I'd make it.

I want to extend a heartfelt thanks to everyone who has taken the time to listen to and engage with my content, your support means the world to me.

To the wonderful guests of the ***Ever-So-Lean Podcast***, thank you for sharing your wisdom, insights, and experiences. You have not only enriched my own knowledge but have also helped inspire so many others through our conversations.

To my friends, colleagues, and mentors throughout the years, your influence on my personal and professional growth cannot be overstated. Your belief in me has given me the confidence to pursue new challenges, and your leadership has helped shape me, and develop my own path as an unexpected leader.

To the teachers who told me I wouldn't amount to anything, and to the schoolyard bullies, thank you. You lit the fire. You unknowingly gave me the drive and resilience to push harder, to strive for excellence, and to prove that limits are only what you put on yourself. Without your doubt and your knocks, I may not have had the fire to achieve what I have today. If you do fall into this category, and you're reading this, what brought you here? I'd love to know.

A special thank you to the one and only Paul Akers for doing me the honour of providing the foreword for this book, and for inspiring countless leaders and practitioners, myself included, right from the beginning of my Continuous Improvement journey. Your kind words of encouragement and unwavering support are something I will always be grateful for. Also, your brilliant, passion and energy infused voice messages that spur me on!

Finally, to all the readers of this book, thank you for joining me on this journey. I hope you find inspiration and value in the lessons I share, just as I have in living them. Now, it's your turn, get yourself across that bridge. You've got this!

Foreword

Matt is a masterful storyteller and skilled communicator.

Interesting, funny, well written, and a compelling life story from insecurity to massive success. Another necessary book to fill in all the questions that many of us have, about how to become an effective leader, and a great Lean Thinker!

Fantastic read!

Paul Akers
President FastCap, and Author of "2 Second Lean"

Introduction

Welcome to my story, authentically shared in my own words, it's a story from a career that has spanned over twenty-five years.

My journey has profoundly shaped me into a better human, devoted father, accomplished communicator, and a dedicated leader of high performing, highly engaged teams. I hope that my words and experiences resonate with you, igniting a spark of inspiration and motivation as you progress along your own path, just as they have done for me.

This book traces the story of a low-grade student who to say struggled academically would be an understatement. Someone who faced bullying (both in childhood and as a young adult), and has lived with lifelong anxiety, only to emerge as an unlikely yet deeply impactful leader.

My journey is woven together through moments of growth, discovery, heartache, self-acceptance, and failure, culminating in the creation of ***The Bridge to Inspirational Leadership***™, a leadership framework born from my own transformation from setbacks to inspirational leader.

My story begins as the eldest of five children, often feeling "different" to everyone else. At school I faced challenges, where I often felt lost and uncertain about the present, never mind the future. Uncomfortable in my own skin, I was labelled as someone with "no potential" and was put into the "disruptor" category. But I found a way, I hid behind a persona, the joker or the entertainer.

At sixteen I left school, but many of these struggles followed me into my working life, where I juggled frontline roles and the complexities of my personal mental health battles. Amid the daily grind of work, I began, unknowingly, identifying inefficiencies and driving continuous improvement in my work, always striving for excellence in myself. Fuelled by a hyper focus to accept nothing less than exceptional in everything that I do.

As I grew and learned, I uncovered invaluable lessons about respect for people, the need for collaboration, and the human elements of leadership. I came to understand that true leadership isn't about status, money or a fancy title, it's about being genuine, and respecting and supporting others to achieve their goals.

Leadership, I learned, is shaped by our challenges, victories, and the relationships we forge along the way.

Each experience, whether triumph or setback (mostly setback), was simply a change of direction, becoming a building block in my understanding of what it truly means to lead. I didn't know this at the time, but when I reflect it's obvious to me that this was the case.

As I transitioned into roles with greater profile and responsibility, my passion for continuous improvement got greater and greater. For the first time in my life, finding a way of learning that worked for me and provided the structure and creative freedom that my brain craved to grow.

The result? ***The Bridge to Inspirational Leadership***™, my recipe for high performance. A framework built upon four fundamental pillars: Respect for People, Authenticity, Engagement, and Empowerment. These pillars are not abstract concepts, they are core principles for creating high performing teams. They are there to remind us to value people not just for their contributions but for who they are as human beings. When leaders prioritise respect, they earn trust and inspire others to go the extra mile.

The Bridge to Inspirational Leadership™, also highlights the vital role of continuous learning and continuous improvement as stabilising forces that support our collective journey towards excellence. The bridge symbolises not a final destination, but an ongoing commitment, something that we cross frequently, where progress is valued over perfection.

As you journey through this book, I invite you to reflect on your own experiences. Through shared stories and lessons, I hope you find the inspiration to build your own bridge, creating a culture that embraces vulnerability, promotes collaboration, and empowers people to take ownership of their work. Let's embark on this transformative journey together and unlock the potential for true excellence that lies within each of us.

Share your experiences with the hashtag **#UnexpectedLeader** for me and others to learn from.

Before we begin, I want to note that while the stories and experiences I share in this book are drawn from my real life, some of the names of people have been changed to protect their privacy. The lessons, challenges, and triumphs remain true, but any resemblance to real persons is purely coincidental.

CHAPTER 1: THE EARLY YEARS

Am I ahead, am I behind, or am I actually where I should be? It's a question I've asked myself more times than I can remember.

Wisdom tells me that each of us is running our own race, a journey filled with triumphs, challenges, and self discovery.

Yet, as we navigate this, it's hard not to glance around and feel that everyone else seems to be miles ahead. They seem to radiate success, wealth, happiness, and an unwavering confidence that feels elusive to us.

“Why can’t I be like them?”

“They’re so much better than me”

“I wish I could be like that”

These thoughts echoed in my mind throughout my early years, and continued like a dripping tap well into my early thirties.

Whether at school, work, socially, or even with strangers passing in the street, or in a shop, I’d subconsciously label these people as ‘successful’, and I'd long to be just like them.

I’d think

"If only I could do what they do, look like them, sound like them, or have what they’ve got"

Rather than embracing who I was and the unique blend of strengths and vulnerabilities that makes me, well, me.

During my childhood, my family was incredibly close on my mother's side. She was the eldest of four, and we would often find ourselves in and out of each other's homes, with much of our time spent at my grandparents' house in Croydon, which truly felt like the heart of our family.

My grandparents were the glue that held us all together, creating a strong sense of unity and pride in being part of something so special. It felt unbreakable.

However, everything changed unexpectedly one Christmas when my Nan, the life and soul of the party fell gravely ill. She suffered a brain aneurism, it was sudden, severe, and although she fought to recover, she never fully regained her health.

That period was especially difficult for me (as I'm sure it was for everyone). I was at the difficult age of sixteen, and grappling with anxiety at the time, and seeing her in the hospital, unconscious with a huge stapled wound on her head, looking so fragile was both heart-breaking and terrifying. It shook the foundation of the family that had always felt so solid, and left a lasting impact on all of us. For me personally, from memory, I was the only grandchild to see her like that, and that image haunts me to this very day.

She was left physically disabled, and it totally changed her personality too. She was a different person. I really struggled. When I saw her, I could still see what I saw when I saw her in that hospital bed. I avoided her if I could as I didn't know what to say. I hate myself for it, and if I could change that I would. I was young, but I should have done more, I didn't and I have to live with that.

When she passed away some years later, the family dynamic began to deteriorate. Literally crumbling like a sandcastle. A divide formed down the middle of the family, and relationships that once felt so strong started to weaken.

Throughout my late teens and early adulthood, I often found myself as the only one traversing both sides of the family, trying to stay neutral and avoid the conflict. It wasn't easy, and the emotional strain took its toll on me over time. Years later, when my Grandad passed away, the division became permanent, set in stone and unrecoverable. When he died so did any hope of the family reuniting.

It's heart-breaking to think about how close we all once were and how different things are now. I often reflect on what my Nan and Grandad would think about the divide if they were still here. I'm certain they would be deeply saddened by how things have turned out.

I'm the eldest of five children, separated by only eleven years between oldest and youngest. Four boys and one girl (right in the middle). Growing up we also were very close. But today we don't really have a relationship. They are all still really close, and I speak to my sister now and again, but I am very much an outsider.

As I got older, I often felt that I didn't fit in with them. That I was different. Things happen and people change. In recent years I've actually found out that there is name for this, it's called "Family Detachment".

It's basically where someone becomes emotionally, physically, or psychologically distant from their family.

It can happen for many reasons. Sometimes it is intentional, where a person chooses to step back from family relationships because they feel those relationships are unhealthy, draining, or preventing them from growing as an individual. In other cases it happens more gradually, where people simply grow apart as their lives, values, or priorities move in different directions. I think I fall in to the latter category.

Family detachment does not always mean conflict or rejection. Sometimes it is about creating space and independence, establishing boundaries, or protecting your own personal wellbeing. It can be part of becoming your own person, learning to make decisions without relying on family influence.

It happens when people create distance in the relationship, whether emotional, physical, or both, often as someone navigates their own identity, responsibilities, and path in life.

I have nothing official to confirm this, but everything I read about it feels like it describes me and how I feel exactly.

But, as much as it pains me to say, it is what it is. Sometimes, despite our best efforts, things remain beyond our control.

Relationships with those we grew up with and shared so many special memories can fade as we move into adulthood, take our own paths, and experience life in different ways. Our values change, we grow, and sometimes that growth takes us in directions that distance us from those we once held so close.

It's a bittersweet reality, knowing that while the bond was strong in our youth, time, experience, and life's many twists have a way of shifting those connections.

On my father's side, my grandparents lived some distance away, but they would come to stay with us for weeks at a time, several times a year. Their visits were always special for my siblings and I. We'd eagerly wait by the window, scanning the road for any sign of their arrival. We'd watch them pull onto the drive; our excitement was electric. They'd walk through the door, laden with the normal suitcases and belongings, they also carried something else, a flask of liquid gold, the most amazing coffee that they had brewed for the journey. My brother and I always waited excitedly because they'd save some for us. It was the best tasting coffee I've ever had, sweet, silky, and hot. Just thinking about it now brings a warm and mellow feeling over me.

Their visits were filled with love, laughter, and cherished moments. We'd talk about football, share our sticker books, hear stories of players like Bryan Robson, Charlton, and other greats. Pop would tell us stories about his time as the foreman of the Power Station. My Nan would talk away to my Dad about his sister and her children. We'd play games, and take walks to the paper shop down the road. Those simple routines became treasured memories.

It didn't seem odd at the time, but on reflection it's a bit gross. Pop was an early riser; he'd sit quietly with a cup of tea until we got up extra early to hear his stories before school. That's not the gross bit, that bit was that he'd have a wet shave every day in the kitchen sink. I don't know why. I'm wondering now why my Mum or Dad didn't tell him to use the bloody sink in the bathroom! But they didn't, and it was just the way it was. Special times.

One of the most special gifts from my Pop was my first car, a bright red, G reg, Nissan Bluebird 1.6. He had always said he'd pass it down to me, and true to his word, he did. The insurance was probably worth more than the car, but it didn't matter. That car became my gateway into the world. I learned to drive in it, and it symbolised both freedom and a lasting connection to my Pop. I regret selling it, but at the time it wasn't doing much for my street cred! I sold it and bought a Ford Fiesta with a subwoofer in the boot. What a wally!

Both my Nan and Pop have long since well passed on, but the love, wisdom, and warmth they shared with us are deeply missed and fondly remembered every day.

Nursery and First School were wonderful times for me. I hold nothing but happy memories from that period of my life.

One moment stands out clearly. I remember standing on stage in the school nativity play with a stuffed lamb tucked under my arm, a tea towel on my head held in place by a ring of straw. I was playing the role of a shepherd. A key role, of course.

Without the shepherd it would have been complete chaos with all those sheep wandering across the stage.

It was when I moved into Primary School that things began to change.

The Primary School I attended also had its own First School attached. Most of the children simply moved up together, surrounded by the same classmates they had known for years. I was one of only a few who arrived from somewhere else.

That made me an outsider from the very beginning.

I struggled to find my place. I would look for any excuse not to go to school. It was during this time that my troubles with anxiety began. In fact, I can trace it back to one very specific moment.

One day I pretended I had a stomach ache so I would not have to go to school.

My mum took me to the doctor, and as she examined me, I timed my "oww" and "ouch" responses perfectly. I must have been very convincing. A few hours later we were sitting in A&E at the local hospital. The doctors believed my appendix was about to burst and prepared to remove it.

That was the moment the plan fell apart.

I told them I had been pretending. But they did not believe me. They assumed I was just saying it because I was frightened of the operation. After several more tests it finally became clear that I was, in fact, completely fine. We were sent home.

But the experience shook me far more than anyone realised.

From that moment something changed. Anxiety crept in and began to take hold. Every small ache or symptom suddenly felt serious. My mind would run straight to the worst possible outcome. Hospitals, illness, danger. It consumed my thinking.

Over time it spread. What began as health anxiety turned into health anxiety, plus social anxiety and a fear of many everyday situations. It drained the joy out of things that should have been simple and carefree.

Looking back now, it is striking how quickly something small can escalate and shape the path that follows.

Senior School was particularly tough for me; I really struggled academically and found it increasingly difficult to grasp any form of concept or retain any information that wasn't rude (French and German specific). But there's a good reason behind this, which I'll come back too.

I spent a significant amount of lesson time standing in the corridors peering through a heavily scratched, dark wood classroom door with a glass pane near the top. It had wire inside that went horizontally and vertically – creating lots of squares. I would count the squares, I can tell you that there was 750 in total, apart from the door to the third Science room, that only had 620 (it must have been replaced).

The words "Sims, out!" could often be heard echoing through the halls. You see, I know now that sending me out at the start of the lesson was the easy option for the teacher. With me outside they didn't need to worry about trying to engage and inspire me, they could focus on the easier task of teaching the people who could retain the information presented on the blackboard. Also, with me trotting up and down the corridor counting squares, they didn't have any competition for the attention of the audience. Something I would if given the opportunity steal away in a heartbeat.

Now, to close off my remembering of the "rude words" in language classes. With the wisdom and experience I have today, I know that the reason that I could (and still can) retain and recite them, is because I emotionally connected with them. Granted, it doesn't say a lot about the state of my mind, but the logic, and the science is there.

If we emotionally connect with something, we engage with it, and we remember it. If I asked you what your favourite line from a movie was, or even for your favourite joke that you heard from a comedian, or a guy down the pub. You may have only heard it once, but you remember it word for word because it connected with you on an emotional level.

This is the key to learning, to truly learn, we must first create a pull for learning, a desire, a want and a need. If we don't do this, the learning becomes a push, its forced onto us, we disengage, we emotionally switch off or disregard, and guess what, we don't remember it! Think health and safety training at work, or the safety briefing on an aeroplane, do you remember it, did it engage you? I doubt it.

Despite my best efforts, I wasn't sporty (well I was if it was a non-contact sport like tennis). I laugh now, but I was in the school football team throughout senior school. I played as a striker. I'm the only striker that has never had a single shot on goal. Not a sniff. I blame the service.

The truth is that even with a satnav I'd have struggled to find the goal! I just wasn't physical enough back then. It was too dangerous, if the wind would have picked up, I could have blown away, never to be seen again.

I remember vividly taking part in a five a side football tournament for my school. We had an A-team (the best players), and a B-team (the rest). I was the captain of the B-team, I'm not sure how that came about. I'm guessing the other four players were all busy at chess club when the vote was made to lead the team.

Anyway, at this tournament we were awarded a penalty kick. As the captain I saw this as my moment. This was the time to become a hero, or so I thought.

All the other schools' teams were sitting around the edge of the indoor pitch, watching with interest. I put the ball on the spot, took two steps back, and time seemed to slow right down, as if the world was operating in slow motion.

I stepped forward and pea rolled the ball so gently to the goalkeeper for him to pick up with ease. Honestly, it couldn't have been easier for him. It wasn't a shot (hence this not counting towards my tally). It could never have been classed as a shot by any stretch the imagination. The penalty spot was at most 3-yards out from the goal. Once I took the shot the goalkeeper had time to pop home, do his homework, eat his dinner, watch Newsround, and them come back to pick the ball up. It was embarrassing!

The next day in assembly the Headmaster called out that Year 8 had two teams representing the school at this tournament. He asked us to stand for the rest of the school to applaud. As I stood up the PE teacher put his hand on my shoulder and said in a calm and directive voice "sit down Sims". At this point I decided that professional footballer wasn't a career path I would pursue.

I was never considered "cool" or popular. You could say I was the original "inbetweener." Bullied from the outset of primary school for my slim appearance and inability to perform academically, my confidence and self-belief took a significant hit. Teachers told me I wouldn't achieve anything, a voice that occasionally still calls out from darker corners of my mind. Mental health struggles have been a constant companion, both then and now.

My parents offered contrasting advice on how to deal with the bullies: my mother would say, "Tell the teacher, tell the teacher", while my father urged me to "fight back." The end result was a hybrid approach that left me feeling uncertain about how to handle the situation. This conflict often added to the confusion and complexity of my experiences as I tried to navigate a path between seeking help and standing up for myself. Both offered advice with good intentions, but in the thick of it, it was difficult to know what the best course of action was.

Telling the teacher had little impact; they seemed powerless or a lack of willingness to make change. I eventually did fight back physically, it felt unnatural to me, and provided only short-term relief, it then also came with repercussions from the school, I felt like I just couldn't win.

Amidst this turmoil, I discovered a natural talent for entertaining. Making people laugh came easily to me. Quick-witted and able to spin humour out of almost any scenario, I embraced the role of the "joker", the class clown. With the bullies, as opposed to a physical battle, in the grand arena of humour, I was the king of the castle, few could contend.

My weekends became a battleground, a delicate balancing act between savouring the fleeting freedom of Saturday and bracing myself for the inevitable return to school just a few days later. Saturday evenings and Sundays in particular felt like the main event, where my anxieties waged war against my young racing mind, leaving me drained and defeated before the week even began. It was a relentless onslaught, an unbroken cycle of dread that stretched on for eleven long years, and without realising it, I had begun a life under the constant, heavy shadow of anxiety.

These early experiences have profoundly shaped who I am today, fuelling my growth both personally and professionally. As an adult, I have zero tolerance for bullying, injustice, or discrimination. When I started out as a young manager, I constantly faced the uphill battle of being dismissed or mocked for being "young and lacking knowledge". I felt I had to constantly prove my right for a place at the table. Yet, rather than deter me, these challenges only strengthened my resolve.

I will challenge anyone on anything I believe to be wrong or unjust (though I must admit, my approach has become much more refined over the years!). In the past, I worried that this might be seen as "being difficult," but now I realise that my natural instinct to question the status quo is what has driven my achievements. It's doing it in the right way that is the art.

Equally, being told at school that I wouldn't amount to anything has been a powerful motivator. It fuels my relentless drive and passion for excellence. If someone tells me I can't do something, or that it's impossible, I'll do it twice, improve it, and plaster it all over social media to prove it! Then if you're really lucky I'll ask you for a testimonial.

My experiences with the education system as a young person, and most recently as a parent, have made one thing abundantly clear to me: our methods of educating and assessing knowledge are outdated and have scarcely evolved throughout history.

I once believed my struggles in the classroom stemmed from my own inadequacies, I thought I was incapable of absorbing information, the blackboard or a textbook may as well of been written in Martian for all the sense they made to me, I thought I was stupid!

It felt like my failings were the reason I couldn't pass exams that required me to simply regurgitate information. Other people could do it. Other people remembered the content. But not me.

The conventional approach of sitting students in classrooms, handing them textbooks, and testing them with exams before moving on to the next topic is far from the only way to learn or assess knowledge. Yet it's commonly the instinctive method that is used to assess.

When I was in school, students were divided into four sets: Set One for the top performers all the way down to Set Four for those at the lower end of the "performance spectrum."

Unsurprisingly, I found myself in Set Four for most subjects. Except Art, I was in Set Two for that. However, there was only two sets in this subject. But still, it broke the cycle!

The criteria for the four set groupings were based solely on exam performance, which when you think about it, really only identified those who could absorb and regurgitate information in a test environment, essentially about 25-50% of the students.

What makes this process even more baffling is that in any given year group, there could be up to a twelve-month age difference between the oldest and youngest students. I was summer born, so I was one of the youngest in my year.

As an adult, a twelve-month age gap feels largely irrelevant. However, in childhood, that difference is incredibly significant, not just in terms of attention span and concentration, but also in brain development. Yet, the education system measures every student in a year group against the same standard, regardless of these critical developmental differences. Unsurprisingly, many of my fellow set four classmates were also summer-born.

Also, think about it: for your entire school life, you're placed in groups with peers all within a twelve-month age range. You attend classes together, study together, eat, play sports, and maybe even socialise outside of school together, all with people of the same age. Then, when you leave the education system, bang, you enter a multigenerational workplace, filled with people of all ages, experiences, knowledge, talents and interests.

Imagine walking into your favourite restaurant and being told:

"The thirty-year-olds sit in this section, the thirty-one-year-olds over there, and the thirty-three-year-olds at the back. We don't mix age groups here, thanks, and enjoy your meal!".

I know that's a wild example, but what we accept as "normal" in education feels downright odd when you think about it in the cold light of day. And yet, this same system still persists today as it always has.

Even in the job market, many roles advertised on LinkedIn or on recruitment websites still list a university degree or equivalent as a critical requirement. On top of that, if you're lucky enough to get through the initial stages, you're often met with an online "aptitude test", featuring absurd questions like:

“Janet and John went swimming in the sea while eating twelve red apples. They ate one each, lost nine, sang a rendition of Bananarama’s ‘Venus’, sipped on a Manhattan, and watched reruns of ‘Homes Under the Hammer’ on Freeview. How many green apples did they have left after watching Eastenders?”

The panic and helplessness, it immediately transports me back to 1992, and I can only think, "WTAF!"

It puzzles me that we continue to rely on such outdated methods to assess knowledge, focusing primarily on retention and exam testing. It’s these experiences and thoughts that have inspired the development of ***Ever-So-Lean Rising Stars***™.

If you’re not familiar with it, I developed this programme for young minds aged eight and above, offering engaging, inspiring, and gamified learning experiences. The programmes provide exciting opportunities to develop critical skills in areas such as teamwork, Lean, continuous improvement (CI), problem-solving, leadership, and more. It’s even accredited by the British Quality Foundation (BQF), giving participants an accreditation with meaning for their achievement.

The key difference is that knowledge is not solely measured by tests; it’s gained through hands-on, learn-by-doing experiences. Equally important, is that young people are not measured against other young people, everyone is assessed individually, for their logic application, as it should be. It’s about building confidence and skillsets for life.

My children are home educated. It was a decision we made as a family when my son was in Year 1 at a school that, on paper, was rated excellent.

But we felt the system was not working for him, or for the kind of learning environment we believed in. So we made the choice to step in and take responsibility for providing an education that truly suited our children.

It has been one of the best decisions we have made.

He is absolutely flying now. More importantly, all of my children can hold a conversation with anyone. They are caring, compassionate, empathetic and curious about the world around them.

Learning for them is not something that is pushed. It is something that is pulled. At their pace, in a format that they decide, and for as long as they decide. When curiosity leads, learning follows.

It's astonishing to realise that despite being in my forties, having grown so much through experience, amassed decades of knowledge, learned invaluable lessons, travelled the world, and achieved significant success in business, I would still struggle to apply for many roles simply because I don't have a degree. I find this just mind-blowing!

And for me it highlights a major flaw in the typical hiring process, one that could cause employers to overlook exceptional candidates. I'm not saying I'm exceptional, but I bring twenty-five years of application and experience. At this point I'm not sure what value a degree would offer that I haven't encountered in the field.

Great leaders aren't born; they are made. Yet, at the very first hurdle, many employers focus almost exclusively on early academic achievements as a measure of knowledge, ignoring the valuable "making" that happens over years of real-world experience.

Ageing truly opens the door to self-discovery and a deeper understanding of your own strengths and weaknesses. Life experiences, both good and bad, and without knowing it, help to build resilience and a more authentic sense of self.

As we get older, we seem to become less influenced by the opinions of others and are more focused on embracing who we truly are. We start to care less about fitting in or being liked, and more about getting a good night's sleep, or choosing between brooklyn matt emulsion and melville silk for the living room.

I no longer feel the need to follow the crowd or do things I don't enjoy just because it's what everyone else is doing. In fact, I've reached a stage where, in the nicest possible way, I genuinely don't care if people like me or not. I'm comfortable with who I am, and I'm proud of that.

It's through embracing my authentic self, establishing and standing by my values, and developing a deep respect for others that I've been able to overcome the challenges of my early years.

This openness and vulnerability has unlocked immense personal growth and opportunity for me, bound only by my belief in myself, not by the limitations of a test designed for retentive brains.

Interestingly, recently I was having a conversation with Paul Akers, a legend in the world of Lean and the author of several bestselling books, including "2 Second Lean". Paul has helped people and organisations across the globe achieve excellence through Lean principles, an incredible guy.

During our chat, it became clear that Paul and I share similar struggles from our early years, particularly with exam testing. Paul mentioned that interestingly, he has found that many people who excel in Lean also faced difficulties in school. He attributes this to the fact that Lean operates within a creative framework, encouraging innovation through practical, hands-on learning. Many who struggled academically developed workarounds, feeding their creative minds, an approach that aligns perfectly with Lean Thinking.

It's a fascinating insight, and Paul delves deeper into this topic on an episode of the ***Ever-So-Lean Podcast*** titled

"*Lean Culture Exposed: What You Need to Know.*"

Worth a listen if you find this subject of interest. It's on all platforms, or at www.eversolean.com.

Chapter 1: Key Learnings:

Throughout this difficult and uncomfortable period of my life, I've come to understand that everyone's journey is unique. For years, I found myself comparing my path to others, often feeling inadequate; however, as I've grown into myself over the years, I've learned to embrace my individuality and recognise that my strengths and experiences set me apart.

The loss of both of my Nan's during this time, and witnessing my family drift apart just goes to show that nothing is forever, and the importance of being true to myself while cherishing time with loved ones. It served as a poignant reminder that time is finite and can change unexpectedly, urging me to make the most of the present.

My struggles in school, where I initially believed I lacked intelligence due to my challenges in traditional learning environments, revealed the necessity of inspiration and an emotional connection to create the engagement needed to truly learn.

Without knowing it at the time, this insight allowed me to discover my own learning style, leading to the realisation that we are all inherently different. We grow at different rates, our minds are unique, and our learning styles are variable.

The bullying and underestimation I faced during my formative years ignited a fierce desire to combat injustice and societal barriers, transforming those challenges into success, resilience, grit, and sheer determination. I used to conform to others' expectations, but now I focus on becoming the best version of myself.

The struggles I faced in my life, especially in school, have evolved into strengths in my career in Lean Leadership, where creativity and practical solutions are vital.

Ultimately, these experiences have shaped me into someone who chases excellence. Someone who is unafraid to challenge the status quo, and committed to continuous growth of myself and of others. Because whatever industry you are in, whatever organisation, if you are a leader your purpose is to grow people.

That’s it.

June 1983

Just a few hours old, meeting my Grandad for the very first time.

His first grandchild. A moment neither of us would have known then would lead to so many shared experiences.

***1983**: A clearly tired me with my Nan & Pop. Pop evidently had already been at the kitchen sink for his morning shave!*

1984

Simple times. A toy in hand, a cheeky grin, and the whole world still ahead.

***1984**: My 1st Birthday.*
Birthday cake in the bowl, and judging by the smile it clearly met the standard.

1984

My Nan and Grandad on their silver wedding anniversary.

Two people who built a life together and became the heart of our family. Just look at the happiness on their faces.

1984

Me with my Nan.

Always the life and soul of the party.

Warm, full of energy, and loved by everyone who knew her.

***1986**: My Nan & Grandad took me on holiday to Hastings, East Sussex. This is me on the beach with my Grandad, very much looking the tourist!*

1988

Happy times before anxiety began to take hold.

You can see the joy and innocence of childhood right there in that smile.

1988

A yearly tradition. Meeting Santa at the Croydon Post Office Social Club Christmas party.

One of those moments that made Christmas feel truly magical as a kid.

1989

Thunderbirds are go!

A time before phones, iPads, social media, and Netflix.

1990

NYE, we had a fancy dressed party. I went as Michelangelo from the Turtles!

My Nan made that costume, and one for my brother too. The face paint was glow in the dark green!

Spot the jukebox in the background.

1996

I was 13 years old, and for Christmas I got a drum kit and an Arsenal kit. Neither lasted.

I soon came to my senses and found the Palace!

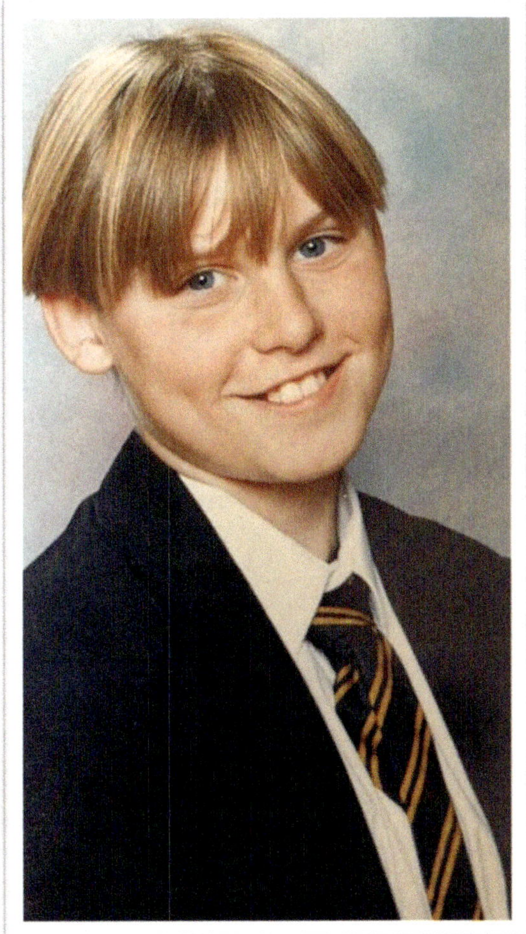

1994

This was my first year at Senior School. Fresh faced and not a pimple in sight!

1997

Away in the caravan. Teenager, full of attitude.

That haircut has an undercut too. If you lifted it up, it was cut down to a number one!

1998

I'm 14 years old in this school photo. The innocent smile had faded, and behind those eyes I was already carrying the weight of anxiety.

CHAPTER 2: ON THE FRONTLINE

It will by now come as no surprise to you that I left the education system at the first opportunity. At sixteen, I stepped into the working world with little more than a dodgy haircut that could've landed me in a '90s boyband, less facial hair than a new-born baby, confidence about as low as you can get, and a quick wit! What could go wrong!?

This is going to sound odd, but despite my lack of confidence, I spent a lot of time aspiring to entertain. This was my safe space; it was my costume and I knew how to wear it.

Fly-on-the-wall reality TV was just kicking off at this time. "Big Brother" was probably the biggest at that moment, and I would create and send in audition tapes every year. Once I had my driving license, I even drove an hour and a half each way to attend the live evictions as part of the audience (more than once! But less than ten times!). I loved being there, the buzz, the excitement, the production, the cameras, lights, and the deep bass of the music playing on the huge speakers. I felt so alive and at home in that environment. But would always come away feeling low. Feeling that it should be me on there. I really wanted it, perhaps too much.

There were other shows and experiences I applied for as well, but the entertainment industry is tough. You have to be able to take the knocks on the chin, pick yourself up, and keep going.

I found this difficult; it was hard not to take all the rejections personally. I'd get "Stage" which was a publication where producers would advertise auditions. This was before the internet really got going. I would take myself off to open auditions for films and soap operas, but it never came to anything other than a feeling of not being wanted. By the time I reached my early twenties, I stopped applying.

However, every year I would watch the opening night of "Big Brother", watching each housemate be announced and feel a mix of resentment and longing, thinking:

"I wish it was me."

Winning it for me wouldn't be about the money or the fanfare, it would be about knowing that people voted for "me", and that I had won by being my authentic self. Completely unrelated I promise, but I've had quite a few people say to me over the years that they think I'd make a good housemate, sadly they weren't producers though!

I also always had this fear that one day someone I knew would get out of one of the cars and make their way into the house as a housemate. I think that would have pushed me over the edge!

Looking back now, I realise I wasn't ready, mentally or physically. I was too fragile.

Fast forward to today, I believe I would be a great candidate for shows like "The Apprentice."

I watch the episodes, see the decisions that the candidates make and often think:

"What a prat, what are you doing!?"

As much as I'm tempted to apply, the weight of responsibility puts a quick stop to it.

Anyway, my Grandad had enjoyed a long and successful career on the Post. Even well after his retirement, he remained highly regarded and respected by both managers and frontline postal workers that he worked with.

Thanks to his lengthy career, our family maintained close ties with the company. I grew up attending annual events like children's Christmas parties and other seasonal events. He was loved by everyone, a proud man with a reputation for being "firm but fair," a quality that earned him widespread respect. He encouraged me to join the Post as soon as I was eighteen, but the idea of waking up at 3am didn't seem too appealing to me at the time!

On the other hand, my father, after a successful career with British Telecom (BT), had been self-employed for a number of years, still working in communications, installing all sorts of technology.

His work mostly involved running long lengths of cable through dusty, dirty, spider-infested lofts, basements, or required squeezing down into spaces so tight, that even a rabbit would struggle (ideal for my whippet like figure at the time).

He offered to train me up, get me out in a van and eventually hand over the business to me. He actually retired in 2026, but independent and strong-minded young Matt had other ideas, I wanted to work in a supermarket!

As I write this, I'm reminded of Cat Stevens', or in my era, Ronan Keating and Boyzone's 1995 cover of "Father & Son". It's like a musical heart-to-heart, where the father says:

"Learn from my mistakes, and life will treat you better."

But the son wants to do things his own way, find himself, and live life on his terms. The lyrics resonate with me, capturing the emotions of this time, and my search for self. It's a timeless story that, I imagine, parents and children could still relate to in another hundred years.

So that was it, I went off to work in a local supermarket, my shift was 2–7pm, Monday to Friday. I was allocated to the grocery department, and given responsible for an aisle split between pet products and laundry supplies.

So, there I was, working twenty-five hours a week to fund my trips to "Big Brother" eviction nights, managing my own stock orders, stacking shelves, and occasionally jumping on the checkout during busy periods. Sounds straightforward, right?

Well, not exactly. With undiagnosed dyslexia and a less than stellar grasp of maths, and despite trying to hide it, working the checkout became quite a challenge, especially when it came to giving change! It also led to a few blunders when ordering stock for my aisle. I'd often find myself summoned to the "grown-ups office", for a stern talking-to for things like ordering fifty-six boxes of rabbit and turkey, flavoured Christmas dog chews... on January 10th!

Eventually, I moved on to the fresh food counters and became a "fish specialist," responsible for stock rotation, ordering, sales, and even preparing the fish.

This turned out to be a fantastic experience, and I still use my fish-filleting skills today! But what I really loved about the role was the creative aspect, setting up the fish displays every morning.

I had creative licence to build grand, colourful displays upon a bed of crystal white ice, and could measure their success and impact through sales. Each day I challenged myself to raise the bar, using every ounce of imagination I had to attract customers to the counter where I would charm them with my fishy banter.

It wasn't just the displays that allowed my creativity to shine; the customer interaction was something I thoroughly enjoyed too. The sales banter and the relationships I built with both customers and colleagues made the job so much fun. Over time, we developed inside jokes.

One customer, whom we nicknamed "cat lady," didn't earn the title because she bought fish for her cat, or even because she liked cats, it was because she actually looked like one!

She wore this big, silver, furry coat that resembled a cat, and she had actual, long whisker-like features from her cheeks! She looked like a villain from the 1960's Batman TV show!

Of course, she had no idea about her alter-ego.

That was, until one fateful day. I had my back to the store whilst chatting with two colleagues who were working on the deli counter which was right next to the fish counter. For reasons I can't quite recall, I found myself doing a rather spot-on impression of "cat lady" ordering her usual whole filleted Scottish salmon, two dover-sole and 100g of calamari.

It was a great performance, so good in fact that one of my colleagues, laughing so intently, dropped a rather large pack of chicken satays she was preparing, sending them tumbling across the cream tiled floor. Her laughter stopped suddenly as I was in full flow. It was a masterpiece. But she didn't stop because of the spillage.

I turned around, and to my horror, there stood "cat lady," just two metres away, patiently waiting to order her whole filleted Scottish salmon... two dover sole and 100g of calamari. Whether she realised she'd just been the star of the show or not, I'll never know. She didn't mention it, she just purred contently. I, on the other hand, wanted the ground to swallow me whole!

Lesson learned: always be aware of your audience Robin!

By the summer of 2002 (kudos if your brain automatically read that in Anne-Marie's voice!), after three years at the supermarket, I decided it was time to submit and follow in my Grandad's footsteps and join the Post.

Attending the interview became a bit of a nightmare. The supermarket wouldn't give me the time off to attend. The Store Manager even came to me to tell me categorically that I couldn't go. So I had to go sick.

It didn't go down well, and when I returned the next day and handed in my notice, they immediately took me off of the counters and put me on the checkouts for my full two-week notice period.

The Store Manager was livid that I had gone after he forbid me. He pulled me into his office and went bananas. I do think this was rather dramatic, I was a part-time sales assistant who did the odd impression of Batman villains. I was hardly a great irreplaceable loss!

Anyway halfway through my dressing down he got called out for a few minutes, before coming back in and continuing to dismantle my career path. Strangely this same day apparently his keys went missing and he had all sorts of problems getting home. One of the section leaders pulled me to one side and asked

"off the record, do you know anything about these keys going missing?"

"Keys? What keys?" I said before trotting off back to my checkout.

So, at nineteen, I became a postal worker, working in the most traditional, stereotypical way, up and out early, riding a red-branded pushbike with a black tray strapped to the front, and a pouch of mail slung over one shoulder.

Dressed head to toe in a traditional iconic blue uniform, I rocked the full look: navy blue shorts, sturdy black, polished boots, a denim style, sky blue shirt with an attachment for my brass badge which had my number on it (807), and that unmistakable navy-blue fleece body warmer with a brass buckle on the left side of the chest for a torch. I was the very picture of a postal worker, ready to take on the rounds, come rain or shine (mostly rain)!

I'm not sure what it's like today, but back then everything at the Post was decided based on seniority. The longer you'd been working for the organisation, the higher up the list you were. Basically, the higher you were on the seniority list the better the job was. A higher seniority meant you got to pick your delivery round and your holiday first. Which as you can imagine, would give you the easiest and best rounds, and the prime holiday periods, like August and January.

This system always felt unfair to me, as it essentially punished you for being young!

By default, newer employees were left with the toughest rounds and the least desirable holiday weeks. This must be illegal right?

Also, from a business perspective it must be a challenge to prevent high attrition. This was definitely a pattern I saw in those early days. New starters would join, but be gone within a month.

I made no secret of my disapproval to this seemingly, medieval practice, but my dulcet tones went unheard.

Honestly, it was a tough time. I've never been a morning person, and this was beyond morning, well beyond, it was literally getting up in the middle of the night, up to six days a week, to walk miles in all kinds of weather!

It was a real culture shock, but without realising it at the time, it taught me a lot about efficiency, empathy and respect for people. I cannot tell you just how strong the temptation was to call in sick when your alarm went off at 4am, and then as you slowly became conscious you could hear the wind and rain beating against the window. You just knew you were in for a tough day!

For the first year, I was what they called a "floater" (yes, I know!), meaning I'd float from round to round, covering for people who were on holiday or off sick. Sometimes even being send to other Sorting Offices if they were short staffed. This was a nightmare as you would be so late to start by the time you got to the location that needed you, and you didn't know the sorting frames, or how to tie it up (meaning what order to create bundles of mail in for when you were out on the street). It left you rushing and feeling stressed all day.

Over that year, I got to know nearly every round in my base Sorting Office and, just as importantly, the sorting frames for each one. The sorting frame is where you organise all the mail for each delivery point on your round, and trust me, the overall process is so much smoother if you're familiar with the frame!

Each road and delivery point were sorted in order, either by number (1, 3, 5 – odds; and 2, 4, 6 – evens) or, if you were really unlucky, by house name (those rounds were dreaded, and naturally, they always fell to the most junior, me)!

These tended to be more affluent areas, normally narrow country lanes with barely enough width to get the van down it.

You'd be driving down, in the dark, traffic queuing behind you, traffic coming towards you, and you're looking for "Tumbleweed" or "Crinkly Bottom".

Many of the houses would have long drives, and the only indication of what house it was would be the name plate actually on the front of the house. Which unless you had bionic eyes you couldn't see from the road. The best way to describe the first few days on these types of rounds is "living hell!".

If you didn't know the sorting frame well, prepping your round for delivery was slow, frustrating, and laborious. I'd watch everyone else leave the Sorting Office knowing they'd be done in three hours, while I'd still be standing there, staring at piles of letters, endless Saga magazines, and packages of all shapes and sizes scattered everywhere. I knew I'd be the last one out and the last one back, it was a pretty depressing situation, particularly when you could hear your old friend the rain, beating on the corrugated office roof above. But it taught me an invaluable lesson in perseverance and self-focus.

After twelve months of floating between rounds, the Sorting Office had what's known as a "re-pick." This is when all the rounds are up for grabs again, and starting with the most senior postal worker and going down the list (naturally!), everyone gets to pick which round will become theirs. Back then, the Post was essentially a job for life. People joined right out of school as “telegram” folks, and didn’t leave the role until they either became managers, union-reps, retired, or, well, passed on!

Out of about fifty postal workers in my delivery office, I was number forty-six in seniority. In twelve months, I had moved up a grand total of four places! As everyone loved reminding me, I was doomed to float for the next century at least.

The picking process was anonymous: each postal worker submitted their bid for their preferred round, and the Sorting Office Manager assigned the rounds based on seniority. One of the four spots I had moved up came from one of the most senior workers retiring, and he had one of the best rounds in the office, "Windermere Road."

It was right on the doorstep of the Sorting Office mostly flat, no hills, and best of all, no named houses, no flats, and no apartments (which were always a headache to deliver to!)

I had covered that round several times as a floater, and it quickly became one of my favourites. On a good day, you could be done by midday, yet still get paid until two in the afternoon. It was the dream round, and one I looked forward to calling my own when I was sixty!

Still, I submitted my preference for "Windermere Road," even though I knew it was a waste of time. Everyone took great joy in teasing me, rubbing in the fact that I was bottom of the barrel.

A few days later, I arrived at the Sorting Office at 5am as normal, all ready for another day of floating. Usually, the radio would be playing Johnny Cash or other "oldies," the choice of those with the most seniority (naturally!). But today, there was no music. Instead, it was replaced with a murmur that filled the air, low voices, mumbling, some groaning, and the occasional random shout of a lyric from a Westlife song, or a football team chant.

As I turned the corner, I saw a crowd gathered around the noticeboard, and people were looking at me, shaking their heads. I had no idea what was going on. Curious, I made my way over to see what all the fuss was about. And there it was, the shock of my life! Written in black and white was the results of the re-pick: "Windermere Road: Duty Holder: Matt Sims".

In a bizarre twist of fate worthy of a box office movie, all forty-five postal workers with more seniority than me assumed that someone higher up would claim "Windermere Road." So, they each opted for a round they felt more confident in getting!

I was utterly shell shocked. With just twelve months of service, an insignificant amount of time compared to the others, I had managed to land one of the best rounds in the Sorting Office! This was the stuff of legend.

In true British fashion, most people congratulated me, shook my hand, and wished me well, before immediately making their way to the coffee machine to call me a prat, put me down, and moan and complain about how unfair and unjust it was for someone like me to land "Windermere Road."

But they could complain all they liked. I'd played by their "seniority" rules and won fair and square. It was nothing short of a miracle!

Lesson number two; Never say never, anything is possible.

What I failed to mention is that "Windermere Road" came with a catch; a rotating night-shift one night per week. This meant doing sorting duties through the night, followed by my usual round in the morning.

Having experienced this a few times during my time as a "floater," I wasn't exactly thrilled. It totally wrecked my sleep pattern, even worse than the 4am starts. I'd already noticed that lack of sleep was a big trigger for my anxiety, although at the time, I wasn't ready to admit that openly, let alone make it a "thing" at work.

To complicate matters, I was now working two jobs, Monday to Friday, just to afford the rent on a small, damp flat above a newsagent, a hovel is the best way to describe it. Really it was.

Most days, I'd start work at 5am, do my round, and then head to a local pub where I worked behind the bar from midday until six in the evening. Factor in the night shift once a week, and I was sometimes working from midnight until 6pm the next day!

Despite the gruelling hours, I really thrived behind the bar. Being the centre of attention, interacting with customers, and using my quick wit to entertain, it was all right up my street. The problem was that throughout the afternoon, regulars would say, "and one for yourself Matt" every time they bought a drink, meaning I had a growing tab of drinks waiting for me by the end of my shift. You couldn't save them for later, and wasn't allowed to take the cash sum; it was a "use them or lose them" situation.

So, come 6pm, I'd have a line-up of drinks to down before heading home! This combination of a lack of sleep, alcohol, and anxiety was a cocktail that fed a negative cycle.

I didn't see it at the time, but looking back now I know that this was possibly the worst scenario for my mental health. But I just kept my head down and got on with it. It was just about getting through each day.

But there was another way to boost my income that I discovered while working at the pub. I noticed that customers frequently played on the two fruit machines near the bar. Often changing up the best part of twenty-pounds into pound-coins to feed the machines.

As time went by, I found that I could gauge how much money had been put in to each machine, and estimate when the machine was due to pay out a jackpot. So, at the end of my shift, if the machine hadn't paid out and I knew a lot of cash had gone in, I'd take my chance. More often than not, I'd walk away with the jackpot in my pocket! This could be as much as thirty-pounds several times a week. Not a bad return for just paying attention and spotting patterns.

For the next three months or so, I continued doing the rotating night shift as part of my postal duties, but it really began to mess with my mental health. My anxiety outside of work grew worse, affecting my ability to enjoy the social life that most twenty-year-olds take for granted. I wasn't living, I was just about surviving. Just walking the twenty-minutes to the pub to meet my friends would result in sometimes two anxiety attacks. I'd be physically sick in a bush or behind a tree.

If it involved getting a train or a bus, then it could be game-over and I just wouldn't turn up. The feeling of being trapped, and unable to control when I could leave and go home was unbearable. I'd feel like everyone was looking at me, judging me, mocking me, and thinking I was weak and pathetic because I was so underweight and had a face covered in acne.

By then, I was on medication to manage the anxiety, but even with that, the long hours, the physicality of the job, the lack of sleep, and the erratic nature of what sleep I could get was taking its toll. It was becoming clear that the way I was living wasn't sustainable for me.

On the odd occasion, if my anxiety allowed me to make it out on a Friday night to a club with my mates, I would go straight to work on the Saturday morning. Changing from my clubbing clothes into my uniform in the locker room. It was awful. I never enjoyed it. It would destroy me both mentally and physically. But I did it through a combination of peer pressure, and believing that this is what someone of my age is meant to do. It wasn't serving me in any way, but I chose to fit in rather than listen to my own body.

I knew I had to make a change before things spiralled further out of control. One thing I noticed was that Carl, the Sorting Office Manager, wasn't exactly the most "computer savvy" person, a fact I'm sure he would have admitted himself; he was just a different generation.

Some evenings after work, Carl and I would meet to play snooker at a local social club. And during those games, I got to know him well. Carl had this incredibly dry sense of humour, and would make me laugh so much without even trying. He was just so deadpan in his delivery of everything that came out of his mouth, like an older, real-life Karl Pilkington (if you've seen his work with Ricky Gervais, you'll know exactly what I mean).

Carl must have been in his late fifties and had worked on the Post forever. He was a master on the snooker table too, effortlessly making the cue-ball glide around the table as if it were remote-controlled.

I, on the other hand, had earned the nickname "The Grinder," because my playing style was far from flashy. Instead, I'd slowly wear down my opponents by frustrating them methodically, until they made fouls that gave me points, or they would surrender out of boredom. It wasn't glamorous, but it was effective, and I'd usually end up winning by sheer persistence.

I managed to convince Carl that he needed me to take on some of the admin tasks that required computer work, freeing him up to focus more on managing the Sorting Office.

I made a proposal: once I returned from my round each day, how about I spend an hour in the manager's office handling non-sensitive admin? Conveniently, this added up to exactly the five-hours-per-week that my night shift was, Funny that!

To my surprise (and relief), after some consideration, Carl agreed to my proposal. He allowed me to take over the non-sensitive admin tasks in exchange for my much loved, rotating night shift, backfilling that responsibility in another way.

Suddenly, I had landed one of the best rounds in the office, without the dreaded night shift attachment!

You can only imagine how this went down with the other postal workers, many of whom were already disgruntled. Some admired my initiative and hustle, but most, well, let's just say they weren't thrilled. The gossip by the coffee machine was alive and well, and while some were genuinely supportive, a lot of others weren't shy about their resentment! The toilet doors were like a newspaper print room, full of headlines!

Beyond the obvious benefits, this new element of my role offered me an invaluable insight into the inner workings of the Sorting Office. Carl was fantastic; he often shared knowledge and greatly improved my understanding of how things operated behind the scenes, the mechanisms, processes and system etc.

I also became so proficient with my round on "Windermere Road" that I redesigned the sorting frame layout to improve efficiency. With these changes to the flow of the layout, and my now familiarity with the frame, I could prep my entire round in just over an hour if the mail was available.

When out on delivery, I found and utilised every possible shortcut through rat runs, and efficiency tricks to reduce my delivery time. As a result, I managed to cut the planned five-hour route down to two-and-a-half-hours on most days. With my reduced prep time and the added admin hour, my total working day was now about five hours, yet I was still being paid for eight.

As I continued to optimise, I restructured my day to further improve efficiency. Instead of sticking to the traditional "prep, then deliver" format, I would prep a bit, nip out to deliver a road or two, come back, prep the packages and remaining mail, and then head out again to finish my round. This reduced the weight of mail that I was carrying, meaning that I could move faster. This tweak and a few others, on a good day shaved up to an hour off my day, leaving me effectively working only four hours while still on the clock for eight!

Because I was finishing my round so early, I began getting asked to cover parts of other people's rounds if they were falling behind or if absences left rounds uncovered.

The best part was that this was considered "paid overtime," even though I was technically completing the work during my scheduled hours. My official shift was from six in the morning until two in the afternoon. But with the overtime, I was often being paid until four or five in the evening. In reality, though, I was home by lunchtime, pocketing the extra pay along the way.

This practice, known as "job and knock," was common, it was the way things worked. But from a business perspective, it's a serious loss. It essentially meant that once you completed your job, you could clock out and go home. Even if you still had hours of your shift still to go.

Any additional tasks turned into a negotiation over the rate, and as a postal worker, you had the business over a barrel. It was a game of nerves, who could hold out the longest. Crazy, right?

Anyway, this happened so often that I was eventually able to give up my second job at the pub and cover the difference in overtime.

I continued my now supercharged "Windermere Road" round for another two-years before moving into the mail processing side of the business.

My time in the Sorting Office had its ups and downs, but it gave me a solid foundation for the rest of my career. I learned great lessons about the challenges of frontline work, out in all weathers, battling hills, stairs, and carrying heavy loads.

These conditions could contribute to low mood, willingness to engage and emotional outbursts. At peak periods especially, being stressed and tired was common, an ask or a word in the wrong tone, at the wrong time, or if it was misunderstood could cause friction and discontent really quickly.

Being at the coalface, in the last mile element of the business we would experience the symptoms of upstream failures, defects, and issues the hardest. This would frequently leave us with a difficult and strenuous job to do.

The dynamics within the Sorting Office were eye-opening too. Everyone was out for themselves, with little collaboration or teamwork. People would "stitch you up" for a pound, there was definitely no loyalty, even within the micro-groups that had formed.

Other than Carl, there was really only one other person that I felt I could trust, James. He was about ten years older than me, but we worked well together and often helped each other get rounds delivered.

My time there was a crash-course in negotiation and holding my nerve, great training for poker!

I also learned a lot about engagement and winning hearts and minds to achieve goals. Seeing the behind-the-scenes operations of the Sorting Office was a unique experience for someone so young, and I will always be grateful to Carl for that. The time he invested in me was more than he needed to. I will always have great respect for him for that.

Carl was great, and watching him in action, whether it was during conference calls or handling various situations, was nothing short of enlightening. His ability to manage people and navigate challenges left a lasting impression on me, good and not so good.

Looking back today, my time on "Windermere Road," where I streamlined processes, eliminated inefficiencies, and maximised value, was my first real encounter with Lean principles, even if I didn't realise it at the time. My eyes were being opened to the concept of identifying waste long before I formally understood it.

It reminds me of a quote from Arthur Conan Doyle's Sherlock Holmes:

"The world is full of obvious things which nobody by any chance ever observes."

It's a perfect analogy for my experience, often, the most evident opportunities for improvement are hidden in plain sight, simply because people aren't paying close enough attention.

Moving over to the mail processing side of the business was one of the best decisions I ever made. Those years were some of the best of my life.

Even in the new setting, I was still known as "Mick's Grandson" and took great pride in living off of the solid reputation he'd built.

My cousin, who also worked in the Mail Centre, drove the 7.5-ton vehicles. He had quite high seniority due to his length of service, again since school, I think. He played a pivotal role in securing my transfer to the Mail Centre. Getting in wasn't easy, as it was a popular department, but thanks to his influence, he made it happen, and for that I'm very grateful.

The culture in the Mail Centre was almost identical to that of the Sorting Office still very much a "job and knock" environment, but the work itself was so much better! I worked in the collections department, where our main task was to empty post-boxes throughout the Croydon catchment area, and collect mail and packages from post offices, business, and schools/colleges etc.

Once collected, the mail was processed and dispatched to Sorting Offices' overnight for next-day delivery. This change in role felt like a breath of fresh air compared to my time in the Sorting Office. To me, it felt like the Post, but without the bad bits!

Although I carried my "three years seniority" over with me when I transferred, I was back to "floating" again due to the long-standing "job for life" culture. But the difference here was significant: no more early mornings, no more walking miles in all weather conditions, and no more lugging heavy weights across long distances.

Each week, I was assigned a different route to cover holidays and absences, which came with its perks: a van, a scanner to track actual vs planned collection times, and a red folder with all the necessary information, locations of collection points, maps, access codes, etc. That was it: the same route three times a day, collecting mail and bringing it back to be processed, simple!

The hours were much more manageable, typically ten in the morning until seven in the evening, though some shifts started earlier or ran slightly later. But, like in the Sorting Office I'd usually finish at least an hour before my scheduled end time.

Overtime worked the same way: if you covered an extra route, you'd usually get three-hours of overtime for it, even if it only took you an additional thirty minutes! As I became more familiar with the processes, routes, and time-saving tricks (like shortcuts avoiding bottlenecks, and where to park to avoid traffic), I could complete my route and an overtime route by six-thirty if it was close in proximity to my regular one. That meant I'd be home by seven but paid until ten in the evening!

Working in collections was also Monday to Friday, which gave me my weekends back, a massive plus. But it also opened up the opportunity to work Saturday mornings from eight until one, handling smaller routes. This was a perfect setup: I could still enjoy most of my weekend while earning a little extra on the side. It was a win, win situation all around!

I really enjoyed working in my new environment. I fell in with a group of colleagues who were around my age, shared similar interests, and had similar shift patterns. We bonded quickly and had some great times together.

Whether it was playing snooker or table tennis, having a laugh in the canteen, or meeting up at weekends to go for drinks or even to nightclubs, I felt a sense of belonging. Despite still hiding behind my "joker" persona, I felt comfortable with the group and settled right in.

Some of us were drivers (out collecting the mail), and some of the group worked in the Mail Centre on the machines (processing the mail).

When we got back from our collections, we would get a coffee from the Klix machine, and go and sit on the processing machines chatting until we had to go back out. We would be constantly dodging the work area managers who would send us on our way as we were seen as a distraction. It was like living in a soap opera. We would just talk and playout the daily dramas. Sadly we're not in touch anymore, but I still often think of them all today.

Around that time there was a significant change in my mental health. I felt more like being around other people. I had started spending time in a pub not far from where I lived. It was actually the most comfortable I'd felt being out since I could remember.

I haven't had many serious relationships, but one afternoon I got chatting with one of the bar staff. Her name was Danielle and she had recently started working there. She had moved down to London from Scotland and was staying with her mum and younger siblings while she got herself settled.

I told my friends back at the Mail Centre all about her, and they encouraged me to get to know her. I really needed that nudge back then, and they were great and giving me some confidence.

Danielle had a brilliant accent. I could happily listen to her talk all day. She had also recently come out of a long-term relationship, so in many ways we were both finding our feet at the same time. We got on straight away. She had this way of making me smile just by looking at me. She was absolutely stunning, not just in appearance but in the way she carried herself too. Everyone wanted to talk to her. But for some reason she wanted to talk to me.

She made me feel normal. Better than that, she made me feel that I was living again rather than the dark place I had been recently (all will become clear).

What caught me off guard was how quickly she got under my skin. At that point in my life I wasn't looking for anything at all. Yet there we were, spending lots of time together and really enjoying each other's company. Danielle was just great to be around. She made me feel like I mattered, like I was worth something. It was probably the first time in my life that I had truly felt that way.

One afternoon I was out on collections in Croydon when my phone rang. It turned out to be her ex-boyfriend from Scotland. To this day I have no idea how he managed to get my number. We exchanged a few words, although it quickly became clear that the reason for the unexpected call wasn't to share DIY tips, it was to warn me off. He spoke about Danielle as if she were his possession, "she is mine" was one term used. It didn't sit well with me. Let's just say I didn't receive a Christmas card from him that year.

As it turned out, that wasn't the last time I'd receive an aggressive phone call from an angry Scotsman threatening me, but that's a story for a later chapter.

For Danielle it was a particularly difficult period. On top of the relationship breakdown she had been through, she was also dealing with some health issues. I wanted to be there for her and support her as best I could. I remember wanting to be at the hospital with her every day, doing whatever I could to help.

Unfortunately things didn't work out between us and we went our separate ways not long afterwards. I was really upset when it ended because I genuinely cared about her. Looking back now, I think the timing was simply wrong for both of us. I also suspect that I probably came across far more intense than I realised at the time.

Back then I lacked confidence in myself. I honestly felt that she was far too good for me, completely out of my league. Because of that mindset I probably tried too hard to prove myself.

Not long after we split, I remember being on the bus heading into town with a friend for a night out. We sat near the front and were chatting away about football and who we were meeting later. Suddenly this guy behind us started shouting and mouthing off. At first, we paid no attention, assuming it had nothing to do with us. But then I realised he was directing it at me.

He started saying things like, "I can't believe he did that," and "Who does something like that?" Some of what he said became quite personal, mentioning things about Danielle and I that I couldn't understand how he knew.

Perhaps I was so paranoid that I was making what he was saying fit Danielle and I. But there was no doubt in my mind that it was directed at me. I didn't even know this bloke, and he certainly didn't know me.

It was a really strange and uncomfortable situation. This is exactly the sort of thing that was a trigger for me and my anxiety.

The truth is that at that time of my life I simply wasn't physically, mentally or emotionally equipped to deal with something like that. If the version of me today found myself in that situation it would play out very differently. But back then it just fed into the anxiety, feeding the voice that told me I wasn't good enough. The voice that was persistent in telling me that everyone hated me. I was still in a bad place, this just added to it and left me feeling ill.

Back at the Mail Centre, one of my closest friends was a guy called Marc. He was about ten years older than me, with slightly higher seniority, but we clicked immediately. Marc was married with two young children, but he still very much lived the life of someone younger, and we had a lot of fun together.

Despite being born with a disability that affected his hands, Marc never let it hold him back. He was a Black Belt Karate instructor and seemed capable of doing anything anyone else could. He was an inspiration to me, a powerful example of overcoming obstacles to achieve your goals.

Marc and I would often hang out at weekends, hitting the pubs and clubs or just driving around and listening to music. He became a real friend, someone who looked out for me, and we shared a lot of good times. But underneath, Marc was battling mental health struggles of his own, and his home life was tough.

I'd spend hours talking with him, trying to offer support and advice, but, unfortunately, three years later, when I was in my first managerial role, Marc didn't show up for work one day. I tried calling him multiple times, but I couldn't reach him. A few hours later, his wife called and delivered the news I could never have imagined: Marc had taken his own life.

I was devastated, shocked, and numb. It didn't feel real. As the manager, I knew I had to inform my superiors, so I went to the Mail Centre Manager's office. It was a big deal just going into the office, but in that moment, everything felt surreal. They told me they'd gather everyone together and deliver the news, but I refused. I insisted that I should be the one to tell the team. Marc had been my friend, and at that time, I was the manager responsible for the team. I owed it to him and the team to do it myself.

I walked back into the processing hall, turned off the music to a chorus of groans and abuse, and asked everyone to stop sorting and gather in the middle of the hall. It was, without a doubt, the hardest thing I've ever had to do. Even now, typing this brings tears to my eyes. I had to somehow not only find the words, but get them out of my mouth too!

I tried to switch off my emotions and be strong for everyone else, but it was overwhelming. I was in my early twenties, so young, and delivering such heart-wrenching news to a group of people, many of whom had known Marc for more years than me. It was utterly horrific. It was a tragedy.

That day, and that moment has stayed with me, forever etched deeply into my memory. It taught me profound lessons about leadership and ownership, but also about the weight of responsibility that comes with it, and the fragility of life.

Even after all these years, Marc's loss still hits me hard. I often find myself thinking about him, his laugh, his strength, his kindness, and most of all, his two children, who must all be grown up by now. I wonder what their lives are like and whether they remember the father they lost far too soon. Sometimes, I can't help but question if there was more that I could have done.

Recently, I stumbled upon a photo of Marc and I while rummaging through the attic, both looking young and dapper in our uniforms with customised accessories.

I stood there, staring at it for what felt like an eternity, my mind flooded with memories, our shared dramas, the laughs, all the good times. I could almost hear his voice again. But then, inevitably, my thoughts returned to that awful day. I tried to imagine what must have been going through his mind in those final moments, I'll never know, but it's something I'll always carry with me.

Marc's funeral was just as traumatic as the day I broke the news to our colleagues. Being there, alongside so many of our co-workers, his family, and his friends, it was gut-wrenching. Listening to his parents, his siblings, and those who knew him best speak about the man they loved was unbearably sad. Seeing his young children, their faces devastated with grief, was just so heart-breaking. It was all so unnecessary, and just so tragic.

That day was incredibly tough for me too. I wasn't very popular by this time (a story for a later chapter). I also felt this immense pressure to "be a leader," to stay strong for everyone else, to show no emotion through fear of looking "weak". I felt I had to maintain composure in the face of such overwhelming loss and not show any vulnerability.

But I was so young, so inexperienced, I needed a role model, I didn't have one, and I didn't really know what to do. I thought that leadership meant holding everything in and putting on a brave face, showing no weakness, so that's what I did. I buried my own emotions, thinking it was what people expected from me.

In hindsight, I realise I was doing the exact opposite of what true leadership requires. I wasn't being authentic, and I wasn't allowing myself to feel the loss fully. I wish I'd understood back then that real strength isn't about suppressing emotions; it's about being vulnerable, honest, and human. By doing so, I wonder how many others may have looked at me and been more confident to show emotion too? I'll never know, but I tried to be what I thought a leader should be, but in doing so, I wasn't being myself.

That's a lesson Marc has taught me, that I've carried with me ever since, that's lesson three, be yourself, be authentic and show vulnerability.

I also carry some guilt for not being there for the others that formed our close group. When I became a manager, I distanced myself from them. I was encouraged to do this, and I get there needed to be a line as I was a manager and not a postal worker anymore. But looking back now they all deserved so much better from me than that. I let them down, and should have been there for them during this time. I wasn't, and for that I am sorry.

About a year before Marc's death, I went through a relationship breakup that left me shattered. It was my first serious relationship and I felt like my entire world had fallen apart. I lost everything in what seemed like an instant, my home, my independence and my mental health.

I had to put all my belongings into storage and move back in with my parents, which felt like a massive step backward. I was devastated, and I spiralled into a deep mental breakdown. My body and mind just shut down. I couldn't cope. I was a complete mess.

During that time, I felt completely exposed and deeply shamed. The breakdown was very public, playing out both at work and within our social circle of mutual friends, as well as in pubs all around my hometown. The sense of shame and vulnerability was overwhelming. I was so poorly and I didn't know how to move forward. Just getting through each day took a monumental effort.

I remember the day the relationship broke down very clearly. I was at work, out on collection, and I can still picture exactly which post box I was emptying when my phone rang.

It was my aunty. She told me that my soon to be ex-girlfriend had called her and asked if she could stay there because she was leaving me. My aunty thought it was probably just a bit of a storm in a teacup and agreed.

I rushed home, but when I got there the house was empty. I sat down, trying to make sense of what was going on. Not long after that the front door opened and she walked in with her sister. At first everything seemed normal. She was calm, almost pleasant.

Then I said, "I hear you're leaving?"

In that moment everything changed. Her whole demeanour shifted. She became cold and distant and told me that she knew I had cheated on her and that she was done.

I hadn't. Not for a second. That's just not who I am. Loyalty and honesty are things I've always held very close to my heart.

But that was that. She had it away on her toes.

When I turned around, my parents were standing there behind me. I was a complete mess. Looking back, I don't actually think the pain in that moment was about losing her. I think it was the sudden realisation that I had lost everything I had worked for. My home, my independence, the life I thought I was building.

I'm not even sure I fully understood it at the time. I just remember my Dad holding me up and saying quietly, "Please don't, son."

This was the lowest point of my life.

I don't think I could have got any lower. They even dispatched mental health practitioners to my parent's house to see me.

It was like all of my anxiety and negative experiences had taken me over. This relationship coming to an end was the final nudge that pushed me over the edge. I didn't eat for months, and when I did, I would end up being sick. It was like I was punishing myself without the actual awareness of doing it.

I was put on medication, and this lifted me slightly, just enough for me to find myself in the pub causing all sort of dramas. I remember one time my uncle turning up in the bar unexpectedly and ushering me out and into the car. I was just looking for a fight that I had no chance of winning. I was broken. My life was out of control, and I couldn't see a future.

But Marc, he was there for me, he tried to help me pick up the pieces, encouraging me to take things one step at a time. He spent months trying to get me to see that I could move past it and rebuild my life.

Slowly but surely, with his encouragement and the presence of my family and a few other close friends, I began to find my way back. I started to believe that I could overcome the heartache and that life wasn't over just because one chapter had closed.

I knew deep down that this was actually for the best, but it took me a long time to realise that. I felt that I had shown myself to be so weak and pathetic during this time.

The vultures circled and some people took advantage. I let it happen. I couldn't stop it. At that point in my life I just wasn't strong enough, physically or mentally, to stand up to it or deal with it the way I would now. The people involved know exactly who they are. And at the end of the day, they're the ones who have to live with that and face themselves every day.

I really struggle going back to my home town now. I feel like time there has stood still, but I have grown and changed so much. It wouldn't happen now. But shame on those took the opportunity prey on someone so ill.

Although that period left me feeling raw and exposed, it also showed me the power of true friendship. Marc, my family, and the friends who stuck by me reminded me that even in the darkest moments, there's always a way forward. Even if it took me a while to see it.

That experience, though painful, taught me a lot about my own resilience, and how much strength can be drawn from the people around you.

Once I had managed to pull myself up from the place I'd been in, I started spending quite a bit of time in pubs. That became even more frequent after I bought my own flat. I'm not particularly proud of it, but during that period I probably turned into a bit of a Casanova.

It wasn't something I set out to do, and the last thing I would ever want to do is hurt anyone. But I'd meet lovely people through work or while I was out in the pub, we'd meet up or start seeing each other, and then as soon as things began to feel a little more serious, I'd panic and pull away. Very much a love them and leave them scenario. Then before long the same cycle would start all over again.

As you can imagine, that didn't exactly make me popular. Quite a few women understandably lost patience with me, and it's fair to say some of the blokes weren't overly friendly towards me either. Looking back, it was clearly a reflection of where my head was at the time. I was still figuring things out and probably not ready for anything real.

Without Marc and those who stood by me, I'm not sure how I would have made it through. It's crushing to think that I wasn't able to do the same for him.

Key Learnings Chapter 2:

Early rejections in the entertainment industry were tough at the time, but they taught me something I've carried ever since. Rejection is not the end of the road. It is part of the process. It forces you to reflect, reset, and go again. Sometimes the timing is not right, sometimes it is simply not meant to be. Either way, you dust yourself off and move forward.

My journey in the postal service began as a floater, covering unpredictable rounds and working long hours. It was not glamorous, but it built something important in me. Resilience. Adaptability. Over time, as I became more familiar with the work, I naturally started to see opportunities to improve how things were done. Adjusting the flow, improving the layout of the sorting frame, making small changes that added up. I did not realise it at the time, but that was the beginning of my interest in efficiency and continuous improvement. I found ways to reduce hours while maintaining performance, and something in me clicked. That drive for better had started.

I also learned the power of observation, creativity, and using facts to influence decisions. When I approached my manager about swapping night shifts for admin work, I built my case properly. I looked at the situation, understood the impact, and made a logical argument. It worked. That moment showed me that sometimes opportunity comes from thinking differently. If you do not ask, you do not get. I asked, and I got.

Building a relationship with Carl opened my eyes to a completely different side of the operation. It gave me a view behind the curtain and helped me understand what it takes to manage a complex environment with lots of moving parts. That experience expanded my thinking and gave me a broader perspective on how everything connects.

At the same time, I began to recognise the impact that poor sleep and working patterns were having on me, particularly on my mental health. That awareness became a turning point. It pushed me to start thinking differently about balance and sustainability, and marked the beginning of my efforts to better understand and manage my anxiety. Knowing a key trigger gave me the opportunity to be proactive rather than reactive.

The loss of my friend Marc brought with it some of the hardest lessons I have ever faced. It shaped how I see leadership in a way that no training course ever could. I came to understand that real leadership is grounded in authenticity, vulnerability, and emotional openness. It is not about hiding how you feel or distancing yourself from people. It is about connection, understanding, and being human.

Going through my own personal breakdown took me to a place I would never wish to revisit. But it also showed me something incredibly important. No matter how low things get, there is always a way back. Strength is not about never falling. It is about finding your way back when you do.

Marc's support during those difficult times also left a lasting mark on me. It taught me the true value of empathy and compassion. You never really know what someone else is dealing with. What might appear as someone being difficult or distant can often be something much deeper. Kindness costs nothing, and neither does taking the time to listen.

At that stage in my life, I did not have role models showing me what good leadership looked like. I was young, working on the frontline, figuring things out as I went. But those experiences, as tough as they were, became the foundation of how I lead today. Respect for people, emotional intelligence, resilience, and a focus on improvement.

Looking back, that period of my life brought some of the hardest moments I have ever faced. But it also gave me some of the most important lessons. Time and time again, when I reflect on it, I can see how those experiences shaped not just my professional development, but who I am as a person.

1985

Just home from a shift at the Sorting Office. Grandad taking a moment on the sofa, and me right there beside him.

2005

Early twenties, working as a floater at the Mail Centre at the time.

Here I am with a David Beckham inspired mohawk, still trying to figure out my place in the world.

***2006**: Taken in Lanzarote with two close mates who stood by me through my breakdown. I was struggling with anxiety at the time and know I made that holiday tough for them.*

2006

This is Marc and I in happy times. This was taken in the Mail Centre canteen. We were always larking about. A special image for me.

2008: *I was still working as a collections driver at the Mail Centre. It wasn't long after this that I got the Network & Distribution Managers role.*

Those tattoos are Japanese symbols. When I had them done, I was told they meant something inspiring. Years later, during a break at a WCM audit I showed them to the Professor. He took one look and chuckled.

Let's just say they were not quite as profound as I had been led to believe. I finally had them covered up in 2020.

***2009:** The year before I got married.*

When I look at these photos now, I can see the strain I was under. My anxiety still had a strong hold on me, and I just felt so uncomfortable in my own skin.

At the time I was the Workplace Organisation Pillar Lead at the Mail Centre. The aftermath of Network and Distribution was still being felt, and it had taken its toll.

On the outside everything probably looked fine. But inside, it was a very different story.

2011

Me and my Grandad at my sister's 21st birthday party. Exactly one year before he died. This might be the last photo that I had with him.

Just one of many memories I'm grateful for.

Chapter 3: A Baptism of Fire

I was still in my early to mid-twenties when I landed my first managerial position. By this time, I had pieced my life back together, bought my own flat through a shared ownership program. I'd thrown away or sold everything that I'd paid to have in storage for a few years (the irony), and was enjoying life again.

I had also now met my future wife, and quickly learned that adding the word "wedding" to anything seemed to double the price, a pattern I saw again a few years later with the word "baby"!

My frontline postal worker wages weren't going to cover all the costs of a wedding, and more than that, I felt ready for the next step in my journey.

The early shift Network & Distribution Manager role in the Mail Centre had been vacant for at least six months, and during that time it was being covered as a step-up opportunity by one of the other postal workers. The position came with significant responsibilities: overseeing the manual sorting of a particular mail stream, managing a fleet of 7.5-ton vehicles, and ensuring the dispatch of mail to Sorting Offices in the Croydon catchment area, ready for delivery that same day.

There were many positives to applying for this role. It would be a substantial step up, offer new challenges, and undoubtedly come with better pay. But there were a couple of big negatives to consider. First, it would mean returning to early starts and losing my weekends again, as the shift was Tuesday to Saturday, six in the morning until two in the afternoon. Second, I'd be managing people I'd worked alongside as a peer for several years, most of whom had far more seniority than me and several of them old enough to be my father, and I knew that this wouldn't go down well in the field.

And then there was the biggest issue of all: the postal worker who had been covering the role for the past six months just so happened to be my cousin. The very same cousin who had been instrumental in helping me get transferred into the Mail Centre in the first place.

Stepping into the role would mean potentially stepping over him, and I had no idea how that would go down. It was a complex situation, but I felt confident that this was a challenge I needed to take on, despite the complications. I had reached a point where I was ready to grow, take on more responsibility, and carve my own path.

I did the right thing and discussed my aspirations with my cousin. He was incredibly supportive and actively encouraged me to apply for the role. So, I made a CV and submitted my application!

Over the following anxious weeks (not unusual for me), the Mail Centre Manager, Adam, whittled down the candidates. I had seen Adam around the Mail Centre for years but had never mustered the courage to actually approach him; he always seemed so out of my league, what if I made a prat of myself? He reported directly to the Regional Director and had a grand office that I'd been told was more like a penthouse suite on the upper floor.

All the managers wore suits and ties. It was very traditional.

The more junior leaders had Nokia phones. The Senior Leaders carried Blackberrys. I remember seeing Adam sitting with other senior leaders in the canteen from time to time. Their Blackberrys would be laid out on the table in front of them, almost like a quiet badge of status.

To a young lad finding his way, that meant something. It represented responsibility. Influence. Respect. Or that was how I saw it at the time.

Eventually, the list of candidates for the role was narrowed down to just two candidates: me and, you guessed it, my cousin!

We were set to go head-to-head for the role, winner takes all, and the loser would return to the frontline as a postal worker, high stakes indeed!

News of our impending battle-royal spread quickly; it became the talk of the floor, and I wouldn't have been surprised at all if someone was running a betting pool on the outcome!

My cousin remained remarkably calm about the whole situation, exuding confidence from his six-months of experience in the role I expect. He must have taken some heat from the other postal workers about it, but if he did, he never let on to me.

Our assessments were scheduled for the same day. The process was straightforward but felt far more serious that anything I'd ever experienced before.

First, a face-to-face interview with Adam in his office. Then an exercise where we would each deliver a team briefing.

We would be given the topic on the spot, with twenty-minutes to understand what it was about and prepare our thoughts. After that, fifteen-minutes to stand up and deliver the briefing.

No slides. No safety net. Just you, your thinking, and how clearly you could communicate it.

In the build up to the big day, I committed myself to proper preparation. If I was going to fail, I was going to fail by giving it my everything.

I spent time researching what managers in similar roles actually do. The traits that matter. The importance of clear communication. I also spoke with existing managers to understand how they approached the role, the routines they followed, and the mechanisms they used to lead their teams.

And finally, I went to my Grandad. I wanted his perspective. His experience of people and work in this environment that he had built during his career. I knew there would be wisdom there that no book could offer.

"Just do your best boy", he said.

I rehearsed my delivery style countless times. I knew that if I didn't get the role, it wouldn't be for lack of effort; it would simply come down to my relative inexperience vs my cousins experience.

On the day of the assessment, I felt a wave of nerves wash over me. The pressure to perform well and not let anyone down was palpable. This had become such a huge event for more than just me. Everyone was talking about it, both at work and at home.

However, when I walked into Adam's office, and it was defiantly a penthouse suite by the way, it felt both imposing and impressive, my nerves began to dissipate, and I felt a surge of energy and confidence.

The interview portion seemed to go well; I answered Adam's questions with confidence and integrity. Now it was time for the presentation.

While I can't recall the exact topic, the scenario was clear: as the line manager, I was tasked with delivering a work-time learning session to frontline postal workers (who in this scenario was Adam). I maximised my twenty-minutes preparation time, using every second, and felt confident in my plan. I had bullet-pointed the key messages from the brief and outlined how I would convey them. All bases covered right? Well I thought so.

What I hadn't anticipated, however, was how Adam would quite literally embrace the role-play once the fifteen-minute timer started. It was like he was a trained stage actor!

He leaned back in his chair, propped his feet up on the desk, and began making comments like,

"This is boring" and "Who cares?".

At one point, he even pretended to take a phone call on his Blackberry and get up and walk out!

Initially, I was uncertain whether he was serious or just testing my composure. I couldn't decide if he was just rude or inline for a BAFTA.

But then it clicked. His role play was spot on.

This was exactly how many postal workers reacted during work time learning sessions. Often disengaged. Often uninterested. And never particularly trying to hide it.

In that moment I realised he was not being awkward. He was being realistic.

Rather than let his antics throw me off, I threw myself into the moment. I decided that I would role play how I thought a good manager would react. So I adapted my delivery on the fly, technically known as "winging it".

I challenged him on his comments, told him to take his feet off the table, get off the phone and listen to what I had to say, as there were elements within my brief that he needed to be aware of. When he tried to leave for a second time, I asked him what he was doing and suggested politely, that he sits down, and not to rush of at the end as I'd like to talk to him after the session. I got quite into it as you can tell!

I stressed the importance and relevance of the material, bringing in real world examples to help it land and show why it mattered.

Adam's role play became the catalyst. It forced me to step up, engage properly, and deal with the moment rather than the script I had in my head.

Something shifted. I could feel it.

The "anxious joker" version of me started to disappear. I quite like that phrase actually. Sounds more like a Bond villain than a nervous young lad in an assessment.

In its place came a more confident manager. Someone willing to take control of the room, read the situation, and deal with whatever Adam decided to throw my way.

Adam gave away no clues about how I had performed, but as I left the interview, I felt a sense of accomplishment. I had given the best representation of myself possible, I even surprised myself. Even if I wasn't successful in securing the role, the experience itself was invaluable.

The moment I challenged the Mail Centre Manager, told him to sit down and listen, even though it was a role-play scenario, would be etched in my memory for life. It wasn't just about the interview; it was a testament to my growth and finding my inner confidence, a pivotal step in my journey. Despite having no tangible experience of managing people, processes, or leading a work-time learning, I knew that I could do it, and I knew that I could do it well. But, the question on everyone's lips was, did Adam think so?

A few days later, I received a hand-written envelope in the post. My heart raced with a mix of excitement and terror; I knew it was about the role, and so much rested on what was inside.

I carefully opened it, my eyes scanning the words until I reached the bottom of the page, where it said,

"Congratulations, we would like to offer you the role of Early Shift Network & Distribution Manager."

I was stunned, completely blown away, I had actually done it!

One of the first people I shared the news with was my Grandad. He was incredibly proud that I was on the Post and would often drop by the Mail Centre to visit his old colleagues and have a cup of tea with me. During our visits to the canteen for a brew, I could see the pride radiating from him as he spoke to people about me.

People would call his name and smile, right from the other side of the room. You would also hear numerous cries of "eeeegles!", a reference to Crystal Palace Football Club who are known as the eagles. The local team that he had supported all his life. I too, felt a deep sense of pride in continuing his legacy and was determined not to let him down as I moved into management.

Our bond grew stronger through the work I was doing on the Post. It gave us something shared again.

That meant a lot, especially after some turbulent years when I was in my early teens and our relationship had all but collapsed. It was not really anyone's fault. It was simply the difficult reality of my anxiety at the time and the impact it had on things.

But, working on the Post brought us back together. Quietly, but meaningfully. Now we shared common ground, having known many of the same people, held similar roles, and spoken the same "post" language. It was genuinely special and something I'll always cherish.

He would frequently call me to share stories about his bowls matches or discuss the football results. I even endured calls about cricket, but this was where I had to draw the line!

Fast forward to a moment to 2011, my wife and I visited him to share the joyful news that we were expecting his first great-grandchild. He was ecstatic in his controlled way, and once again, pride was etched on his face.

Tragically, not long before my son was born, my Grandad passed away unexpectedly at home, alone.

I received a call from my Mum while I was working in the Mail Centre. Unusually, she couldn't reach him by phone, so called to tell me that she was going to check on him. Shortly after, one of my brothers called me to tell me they had found him. I left work immediately, feeling I needed to be there.

My Dad had climbed in through an open window and discovered him downstairs, while my mum waited outside, devastated. I went in to see him, and it's an image that haunts me to this day, a moment I wish I could erase. I miss him terribly and regret the years we lost.

I still have a voicemail saved on my phone that he left me a week before he died. I'd like to share it with you:

"Hello Matt, it's Grandad. Just to let you know that we managed a win today at bowls. We won on two rinks and drew on the other. We got nine points out of ten which was good. Freezing bloody cold it was! I had two jumpers and a fleece on. We played ten ends and then had a cup of tea. We were well down, but we came back and won, so that was good. So I'm back indoors now, back in the warm mate. Anyway take care, catch up with you later. Bye!"

I listen this frequently, it brings me a strange comfort. Although I must be honest, to this day I still haven't the foggiest what all the bowls stuff means!

Years later, when I left the Post for Amazon, I worried that he would feel let down by my decision to leave.

That period was incredibly tough, just as his funeral had been, again attended by so many from the Post. I couldn't relax or grieve properly, and to be honest, I still don't think I have. When you see pictures of him in his younger days, we were practically spitting images of each other, but just as in continuous improvement, each iteration gets better!

It's hard to believe there could be two such good-looking fellows in one family!

But now, back to my news.

News spread quickly around the Mail Centre of my impending baptism into management, and soon people began approaching me to congratulate me, on their way to the coffee machine to call me prat and complain about it. Despite that, I felt an immense sense of pride in this achievement.

Deep down, I knew that few would have backed me for this role, but I had believed in my own abilities and overcome the odds. This moment wasn't just a victory for me; it again demonstrated my resilience, self-belief and what's possible if you put yourself out there.

I had a two-week period between accepting the role and officially starting. During that time, I continued my frontline work, collecting mail on my regular route. The managers and staff at the post offices I visited several times a day were incredibly supportive. They made me feel genuinely special, offering encouragement and well-wishes for my new role. It was a real boost, especially since I was starting to notice a stark contrast back at the Mail Centre.

There, people had begun to distance themselves from me, almost as if I had betrayed them by getting promoted. The camaraderie I once had with many colleagues had shifted, and the relationship with my cousin felt noticeably colder. Some went so far as to say I had "stolen" his job.

That accusation stung, especially since I had been so upfront, honest, and discussed the situation with him beforehand. To make matters worse, even my close friendship group, including Marc, started to grow distant.

On some level, I understood it. Moving into management meant stepping into a different realm, one that naturally changed the dynamic between me and everyone else. But understanding it didn't make it any easier. It was a tough pill to swallow, seeing the people who had previously been by my side slowly pulling away, leaving me in a strange limbo between them and the managers.

The way I saw it, anyone could have applied for that role, or any managerial role for that matter. Anyone can choose to better themselves. But they didn't. I did, and I got it. It wasn't a matter of stealing anything; it was about taking initiative.

It's a very British thing, though, to quietly resent other people's success. In North America, if someone announces that they've won the lottery, people will scream, shake their hands, maybe even hug them and throw them into the air, genuinely thrilled for their good fortune. But in the UK, if they are lucky someone might say "Well done" to your face, but will then turn around to the next person and grumble, "He didn't deserve it, I picked much better numbers than he did. My numbers were much better. It must be rigged. It's a scandal!"

It's unfortunate how we often struggle to celebrate each other's victories, even when they're hard-earned. Oddly, in other situations, our reactions are completely different. Think about the joy that comes when your child achieves something like taking their first steps or saying their first words, you can't wait to share the moment and shower them with praise! But when someone wins the lottery or has a major personal success, the response can sometimes turn to envy or dismissal. Imagine seeing your child's first steps and responding with

"Well, I can walk further and better than that. And I did it well before you did. It's not a big deal. I prefer to crawl!"

It sounds absurd, right? Yet, that's how we sometimes react to the wins of others. Why can't we show the same joy and pride we do for those closest to us?

For me as a parent, and as a leader, I take great satisfaction in others achieving great things. I want them to do well, progress and achieve their goals. I see it as my role to support them to get there. Their success is my success. I certainly don't resent them for it.

And so it began. I suited up in a collection of cheap, shiny suits, paper-thin shirts and a multi-pack of purple value ties, and I stepped into my new role as the Early Shift Network & Distribution Manager.

I genuinely thought this new attire would change how others saw me, expecting newfound respect just because I was now "a manager."

It felt surreal reporting in this capacity to the early shift manager, but I was determined to give it everything I had. That role lasted just over a year, and it turned out to be the most intense, trial-by-fire experience I could ever have imagined. It was just horrific on so many levels.

Marc's passing during this time was gut-wrenching, and to make things worse, the lack of role model, guidance and support I received from my senior management team was abysmal.

On top of that, I was constantly pressed to reduce costs, clear workload, and eliminate overtime that wasn't being performed but was being paid. This wasn't just about efficiency, it felt like I was battling a workforce that had turned against me since day one. I was being asked to do things that I didn't really understand how to do. I had no idea about the complexities of handling such situations, all I knew was what I was being told, and that consisted of basically just get on with it.

The "job and knock" culture had devolved into a mindset focused almost entirely on the "knock" element, with people doing the bare minimum while still getting paid.

I was tasked with managing large volumes of work daily, all while my already shrinking team (who barely showed up) resented my very existence on this planet for daring to cross to the other side.

To add to the challenge, a powerful trade union fought against nearly every decision and change I tried to make/implement, even blocking any attempt to address absenteeism. Nothing I did was good enough. People could just do what they wanted and I was powerless to do anything about it. I was completely out of my depth, with nowhere to turn.

Looking back now, I wish I could mentor my younger self, offering the guidance and support I desperately needed at that time but never had. Though that's not possible, I've since committed myself to being the leader I once needed, providing that same support and mentorship to my teams, junior leaders and mentees. It doesn't take a lot, just word here and there, the knowledge that the door is open and modelled behaviours to learn from.

But for me without that, it was an uphill battle on every front, pushing me to my absolute limits. I was just cannon fodder.

At one point, things reached a boiling point when I was told to remove the overtime that wasn't being performed.

It was known as "scheduled attendance". This is overtime that is guaranteed and forms part of the duty. It could come before, during or after the core duty responsibilities, and was usually to perform sorting duties.

The problem with this was that the core responsibility of all of the people who worked in Network & Distribution was to drive. Shuttling mail out to Sorting Offices, other Mail Centres or network hubs. They were all professional drivers. So being asked to sort mail was seen by them as an added extra, and to be honest about it, something that was beneath them.

So I sat the postal workers down and made it clear: if they didn't turn up, the scheduled attendance would be cut, simple as that.

I was honest and told them straight. They had a choice, and they decided to continue to skip their shifts, so I followed through and removed it.

That's when things got nasty. Over the following week, I received what I believed to be serious death threats. It was terrifying for my family. It was early on a Sunday morning; we were in bed when my phone rang from a withheld number. I answered it and the abuse started, followed by the threats.

Upon reflection now, the perpetrator wasn't the greatest mastermind, the caller had a strong, unmistakeable Scottish accent, literally unmistakeable! Guess how many disgruntled Scotsmen who had just had their scheduled attendance removed were working at the Mail Centre? Genius!

I reported the threats to both the police and my Shift Manager, but the response from my manager was nothing short of a farce. I don't know why I was surprised to be honest. It felt like a pantomime, he could've been prancing around the Mail Centre dressed as Little Red Riding Hood while I shouted, "He's behind you!" and I wouldn't have been surprised.

The investigation dragged on for six long weeks, during which time the genius Scotsman responsible was suspended, but by then the damage was done. The atmosphere that was already resembling what I imagine the waiting room to hell being like, worsened. My team already resented me, but with one of their own suspended, the animosity skyrocketed.

Then, in a baffling move, the genius Scotsman was brought back and reinstated to his role, reporting to me, all whilst the investigation was still on-going.

To make matters worse, I was instructed not to communicate with him in any way until the investigation concluded. The pantomime continued. It was utterly absurd. I had no chance of establishing or maintaining any kind of authority or control, and the situation became a complete farce!

After all that, my manager concluded the investigation with "no further action." It was pathetic, a spineless, weak, integrity lacking display of leadership. I was left feeling completely abandoned, utterly alone, let-down and as though every effort I made was being undermined. This wasn't the organisation; this was incredibly poor leadership.

I had given my everything to this. I'd tried so hard, and I took so much (far more than any junior leader in their first managerial role should ever have to cope with). I don't think I've ever felt so let down as I did during this time. I was failed by so many on so many levels. At the time I felt like I had failed. That I wasn't good enough, and that my teachers who said I wouldn't achieve anything just a few years earlier were right.

Despite all this, that year taught me more than I could have imagined, about people, resilience, adversity, leadership, and most importantly, myself.

It was one of the worst times of my life, but looking back now, I wouldn't change it. Without that experience, I wouldn't be the person, or the leader I am today. They tried to break me, but what they really did was shape me into a strong, authentic, people-focused leader. I became someone who inspires others and supports growth and development, traits I desperately wish I had seen in my senior leadership at that time. That adversity was a crucible that forged my leadership style, one rooted in empathy, integrity, and resilience. For that I thank them all.

After pantomime season, I spent a couple of months on loan at a large Sorting Office as a first-line manager, overseeing a small geographical area. The Sorting Office Manager was a guy named Paul C. Although I'd never met him before this, I knew of him as he was one of my customers in distribution. From the very start, Paul C and his team were incredible. They made me feel like part of the team from the get-go, which was such a welcome change after the struggles I'd faced in the Mail Centre. For the first time in my managerial journey I felt part of a team, and not on my own.

This Sorting Office was large, with multiple operational floors, with about five or six other first-line managers, plus a backroom management team. My experience in the Sorting Office years ago came in handy, as I already understood the processes and structure.

Thanks to my time with Carl, I also had a good grasp of the backroom operations, the mechanisms, processes, and ways of working. Best of all I understood the terminology, abbreviations, and general language. This gave me a huge head start in getting stuck in and rebuilding my confidence.

Paul C was a true example of what leadership should be. He really looked after his people, showed them respect, supported their development, and genuinely cared for their well-being. I don't think I ever told Paul C this, but he went a long way toward restoring my faith in leadership. It wasn't just his words, but the way he consistently demonstrated care, empathy, and fairness in everything he did. I have so much respect for Paul C, and through LinkedIn, I'm really pleased to see that his career path has taken him onto some well-deserved opportunities.

I actually reached out to Paul C in late 2024 when I was in the early stages of establishing Ever-So-Lean. He invited me to pop into his site if ever I was passing. And a few weeks later I did. I turned up, we had a coffee, a really good catch-up, and I gave him a copy of this very book. It was great to see him again. It was also brilliant to see his development and growth as a leader too. His moral courage is inspiring, and I finally got to tell him what an impact he had, had on me during that time.

Anyways, in addition to my line management responsibilities, Paul C entrusted me with some project work. That was a real turning point for me. For the first time in a long time, I had the chance to express my innovative side again. It was a confidence boost, and I genuinely began enjoying work once more. I knew the role was only temporary, but I was determined to seize the opportunity and prove not only what I could do technically, but also show the resilience, heart, and the determination that had gotten me the Network & Distribution role in the first place. I had a point to prove, and I was going to prove it!

After two months, Paul C wanted me to stay. He had plans for me and tried to convince the Mail Centre to let me transfer to the Sorting Office on a permanent basis. However, things were changing significantly in the processing world.

At my Mail Centre, a new Mail Centre Manager had come in, and they wanted me to return. The organisation was about to embark on a new initiative called "continuous improvement (CI)," and they wanted me to be part of it. They wanted to assign me to work alongside another leader, the newly appointed "Mail Centre Champion" of CI. This role was to be taken by a senior leader from London, named Terry.

Little did I know, this new initiative, and working with Terry, would become the catalyst that transformed my entire career. It sparked a passion in me that went beyond just a role, it became a mission. Terry quickly became a mentor and role model, teaching me the intricacies of how to drive meaningful, lasting change. The experience opened my eyes to the power of improvement through people, processes, and leadership, laying the groundwork for everything that was to follow in my professional journey.

More than just a professional connection, Terry and I developed a friendship that has lasted throughout the years. In a full-circle moment that I could never have anticipated, many years later, Terry actually came to work for me at Amazon. It was like a classic "student, turned, sensei" situation, where the mentor who had once taught me so much ended up joining my team. It was a true testament to how our paths intertwined and how we both evolved as people and as leaders, continuing to inspire and support one another. This next chapter of my career taught me not just about leadership, but about how important it is to build a network, relationships and the lasting impact of great mentors and role models.

Key Learnings Chapter 3

Through my desire improve myself and secure the managerial position, I gleaned some important lessons that have shaped my approach to leadership and even changed me as a person.

First and foremost, I learned that embracing challenges, and putting yourself outside of your comfort zone is an absolute must for growth. The thought of taking on all this responsibility was daunting, and it certainly wasn't the easy option. However, I soon realised that stepping outside my safety net of the familiar was necessary for my professional development.

Being honest about my aspirations with my cousin not only eased potential tension but also made sure that I was acting authentically and with transparency. If I hadn't of done this, things could very easily become messy, fragmented, and I would have felt that I was lacking integrity. Equally, it would have given ammunition to the gossip mill, putting unwanted pressure on both my cousin and I.

I discovered that preparation significantly enhances confidence. The time and effort that I invested before my assessment was so critical to how I felt going into it. I think that the solid preparation I had also contributed to my ability to handle Adam's role play. If that would have happened without any preparation, I'm not sure how it would have gone.

The excitement and dreams I had about stepping into my first managerial role quickly turned into despair.

Looking back, placing a young and inexperienced lad into that situation without the right support was irresponsible. I am sure the intentions were good, but the reality is that my leaders failed me on a monumental scale.

The events that led up to the death threats could have been handled very differently. With the right guidance and support from my leadership, I could have built trust with the trade union and with the postal workers. Progress could have been achieved by doing things the right way, through respect, dialogue, and understanding the concerns on the ground.

Instead, I was left exposed.

Morally and professionally, I felt completely let down. When the death threats emerged, the way it was handled by my line manager was appalling. His inability to act placed me straight back into the lion's den. A situation that should have been taken seriously, addressed quickly, and managed with care was simply allowed to continue.

All of it was avoidable.

A proper leader would have stepped in immediately. They would have created a safe environment, taken the threats seriously, and ensured the appropriate protections were in place. They would have stood beside me, not behind me. They would have engaged with the union, opened honest conversations with the workforce, and helped me navigate the situation with experience and calm judgement.

Most importantly, they would have recognised that developing a young leader is not about throwing them into the deep end and hoping they swim. It is about guidance, protection, and helping them learn how to lead with confidence and integrity.

The lessons I took from that period are deeply woven into the person I've become.

As awful as it was at the time, those experiences shaped me in ways that are hard to fully explain. They tested me, stretched me, and forced me to grow. Without them, I would not be the person I am today.

One thing it did leave me with is a strong sense of responsibility to be there for others. I know how difficult things can feel when you are in the middle of it.

So if you are going through a tough time right now, remember that it will pass. Stay strong. Keep moving forward.

You will come out the other side, and the person who emerges will be stronger for it. I certainly did.

Losing my Grandad so unexpectedly was devastating.

There are still so many unanswered questions, and I carry regrets about the time we lost during my teenage years. But I also know that the past cannot be changed.

What I can do is give my absolute best every single day in everything that I do. In some small way, I hope that would make him proud.

1959

This is my Nan and Grandad on their wedding day.

Can you see the striking resemblance between my Grandad and I?

This is my original Post Office Issue ID badge and officer number.

I'm not sure that they do this anymore.

2024

This is Paul C and I when we met for the first time since I worked for him at the Sorting office.

Top man!

2008

I always looked after my van!

Returning to the Mail Centre felt like stepping into familiar yet challenging territory.

On one hand, there was comfort in being back in an environment I knew well, but on the other, the emotional and mental scars from my previous experiences were hard to ignore. Plus, I was still figuring high on the "most wanted" list with the postal workers, and I don't mean wanted in a good way.

Despite this, I walked back in with a steadfast sense of resilience, still wearing my cheap suit, transparent shirts, and value purple ties, determined not to let the past define me.

Many of the same faces were still there, including the Shift Manager who had bungled the investigation, but this time felt different. I had a new role to focus on, and with a role model like Paul C to inspire me, I was ready for a fresh start.

The company had introduced something new that they wanted me to be a part of, and I was eager to dive in and see what it was all about. This was my chance to rise above the past and not only embrace the future, but be a big part of it.

Upon arrival, I went straight up to what was when I was last there, Adam's office, the famous scene of the feet on the desk role play!

This time however, it was to meet the new Mail Centre Manager, Aaron. He had come from another part of the business, stepping into a role with greater responsibility, and from the moment we met, I got a positive vibe from him. We clicked immediately, Aaron was relaxed and confident, carrying an air of assurance with him, and he already had a sharp sense of the place. But what really cemented my first impression of him happened just a bit later.

Aaron's office had a private en suite toilet (and shower). After about half an hour of chatting, getting to know each other's backgrounds, I excused myself to use it (the toilet, not the shower), closing and locking the door behind me.

A few moments later, I heard a knock on the main office door followed by footsteps approaching. I couldn't believe my ears, it was the Shift Manager, the very one whose failure to support me and properly handle the investigation still stung. Hearing his voice made my stomach churn.

He was talking to Aaron about some workload issue for the day, but his voice was drowned out by the hum of the extractor fan in the en suite so it was difficult to hear exactly what he was saying.

Then, in a stern and no-nonsense tone, Aaron replied

"No, that's not acceptable. I suggest you find a solution; you've got four hours and more than enough people to clear it. I want an update every hour please."

At that moment, I debated whether to stay hidden in the en suite or make my presence known. The temptation was too much, I flushed the toilet, washed my hands, and emerged loud and proud.

Startled by the sudden noise of the door opening, he turned around, doing a double take when he saw me.

I just smiled and gave a subtle nod. He knew I'd have heard that, and I wanted him to know that I had too. Appearing slightly flustered by the instruction he'd just had from Aaron, he quickly "thanked Aaron" and scurried out of the office.

As he left, I looked at Aaron, and he gave me a knowing smile. In that moment, I knew that Aaron and I were going to get along just fine.

Terry then joined us, and over a mug of tea, the three of us gathered around the boardroom table as Terry began explaining what this "continuous improvement" initiative was all about.

I could feel a real sense of excitement in the room, this was big. He laid out the structure the organisation was adopting and what our next steps would be.

Terry was a breath of fresh air, injecting much-needed energy and an air of urgency into the leadership team. It was clear from the outset that he was driven and held high standards for himself and those around him. His passion was contagious, and I found myself eager to dive into this new venture.

He explained the concept of CI, a term I had never encountered before, and I found myself quickly swept up in the excitement of the task ahead.

Terry detailed the model the organisation was adopting, structured around ten technical pillars, each managed by a pillar lead (a leader from within the Mail Centre).

The pillars were:

Safety

Creating a workplace where hazards are systematically identified and eliminated so that every person goes home safe, every day.

Cost Deployment

Using data to clearly identify where losses exist in the operation so improvement efforts are focused on the areas that will deliver the greatest impact.

Focused Improvement

Structured problem solving that brings teams together to eliminate the root causes of losses and improve performance in a sustainable way.

Autonomous Maintenance

Developing operators to take ownership of their equipment through cleaning, inspection and basic care so problems are detected early and performance is protected.

Professional Maintenance

Applying planned and predictive maintenance techniques to ensure equipment reliability and prevent breakdowns before they occur.

Quality Control

Building quality into the process so defects are prevented at source rather than detected later through inspection.

Logistics

Designing the flow of materials and information so the right product arrives in the right place at the right time with minimal waste.

Workplace Organisation

Creating a clean, organised and visual workplace where everything has a clear place and abnormalities can be spotted and acted on quickly.

Early Equipment Management

Using the learning from existing operations to design new equipment and processes that are easier to operate, maintain and improve from day one.

People Development

Building the capability of every person through structured learning so teams have the skills and confidence to continuously improve their work.

Environment

Operating responsibly by reducing waste, energy use and environmental impact while protecting the communities we serve.

The visual that he had on the table, depicted a temple structure, with each of these categories represented as a pillar that was holding up the temple roof.

Similar to this:

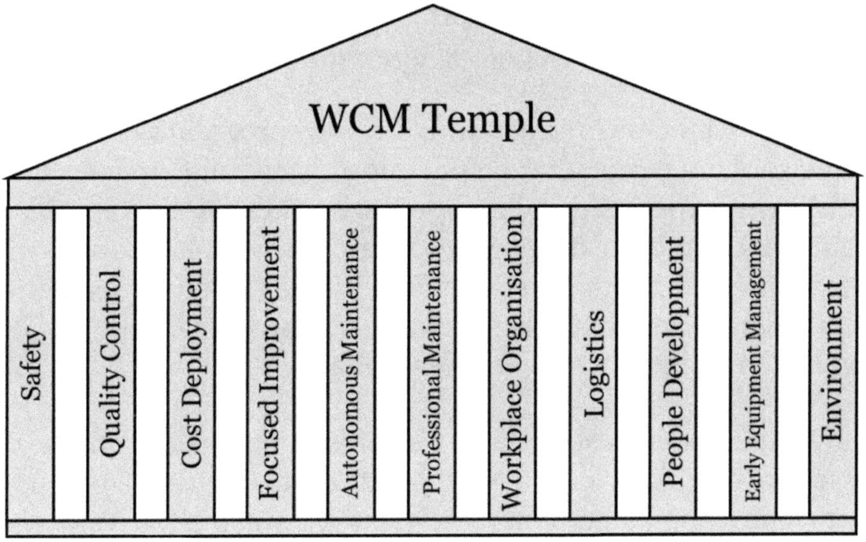

Each pillar would follow a clear, progressive framework with key milestones designed to achieve Bronze, Silver, and Gold status through points accumulation.

Terry shared that as the CI Champion, he would oversee the entire roadmap, working closely with the pillar leads to introduce logic and change to the Mail Centre. He would be reporting directly to Aaron, and together they would drive change, providing strategic oversight while Terry maintained a collaborative role without having direct line management of the pillar leads.

This partnership was set to create a dynamic environment for innovation and process improvement. The model had been implemented and tested in multiple other Mail Centres, and was now being rolled out in a phased approach around the country.

Quarterly Mail Centre audits would review progress against the framework criteria, with each pillar lead presenting updates on their specific roadmap and audit criteria. These audits typically included a Gemba visit (the place where the work happens) to a "model area", which was a designated space chosen for its high improvement potential based on an A-F Matrix exercise conducted by the Cost Deployment Pillar.

The matrices were a structured way of making sense of where losses are occurring and how they connect to the causes behind them. Once populated with real data, they would effectively guide you to where wastes existed in work areas and processes. These might include things like downtime, defects, scrap, rework, speed losses, or energy waste.

Each of these losses is then quantified so the business can see the true cost impact, rather than relying on assumptions, opinion, or anecdote.

Once the losses are visible, the A-F Matrix helps the other pillars link those losses to the processes, equipment, and underlying causes that create them. It's basically a structured map or WCM business plan, moving the culture away from trying to improve everything and instead targeting the few areas that create the greatest cost impact.

The model-area was to act as a focal point for CI initiatives, allowing frontline postal workers to contribute as part of a dedicated pillar team. These teams would consist of postal workers and management, creating a team that had a combined knowledge and understanding the existing processes.

This approach, known as World Class Manufacturing (WCM), is part of a broader industry agnostic framework that benchmarks its practices against global organisations such as, Fiat, Chrysler (now part of Stellantis), Nissan, Procter & Gamble, and Unilever.

The concept is the brainchild of Japanese Professor, Hajime Yamashina, although we affectionately referred to him as just "Professor" as time went on.

He was introduced as an expert in operations management and manufacturing systems, particularly known for his work on Just-in-Time (JIT) production and for bringing the WCM approach to the market.

His methodology focuses on improving efficiency and reducing waste through workforce involvement, aligning closely to the key tenets of Lean.

Terry gave me with a workbook that visualised everything he had explained, I've still got it actually, and the more I flipped through it as he spoke, the more excited about what was to come I became. The idea of a structured framework, a defined process that followed a logic, and the application of innovation and creative thinking to solve problems deeply appealed to me.

This was an opportunity to address many of the issues and opportunities that I had identified within the organisational operation. Problems that I didn't know how to fix during my time in processing, both as a frontline postal worker and as a frontline manager.

Aaron informed me that I would be working with Terry full-time to help get things up and running, while also leading the "Workplace Organisation Pillar".

This pillar focused on creating an efficient, safe, and tidy work environment, aimed at improving productivity and reducing waste.

Workplace Organisation was a great fit for me. As I delved deeper into the study materials, I could see that it incorporated some exciting strategies that were totally new to me, concepts like 5S, Flow, Ergonomic Study (Muri, Mura and Muda), Line Balancing, Visual Management, and Standard Work. All used to embed a standard that drove consistency and quality in processes.

In the early months of launching WCM, expectations weren't high, and the atmosphere was a mixture of relaxed, excitement and apprehension.

Terry and I spent day after day working on creating an infrastructure for the Mail Centre, identifying a large office space that was being underutilised by another department.

After a quick conversation between Terry and Aaron, the occupants promptly relocated to a smaller, shared office space, allowing us to move in. This change not only provided us with a functional workspace but also laid the groundwork for what we envisioned as our mini empire. Although, in hindsight and with the advantage of wisdom, having an office tucked away in the back was the first mistake we made.

You see, for continuous improvement to become "just the way we do things", and truly become rooted in the culture of an organisation, it needs to come from the shop floor.

It needs to be for the people, by the people. It can't be an additional thing to do. It can't be done by a specialised department. Having a dedicated team based away from the shop floor, who parachuted in to make changes to processes and then sweep out as quickly as they swept in, not only gave the complete wrong impression of the essence of continuous improvement, it also completely disrespects the people, which is the opposite of what we should have been doing!

But, like many organisations that pursue a continuous improvement culture, at the time we didn't understand this.

Terry and I quickly formed a strong bond, and he became a valued and trusted friend. Together, we didn't just build an infrastructure for continuous improvement, we created lasting memories, valuable experiences, and shared a vision of making a significant impact.

Aaron was incredibly supportive, actively involved in all our initiatives. He consistently backed us, removing operational barriers and, when necessary, delivering clear "rallying cries" to the Mail Centre leadership team. I cannot emphasise the importance of this, if senior leadership is not 100% behind you, and actively engaged in making continuous improvement part of everyday business, it will never become part of the organisational DNA.

If the situation is that the top leadership are not supportive, you may as well save your time and wasted effort. It will never work. They have to commit. They have to walk the talk.

Terry, however, was really tough on me. He held me to incredibly high standards and accepted nothing less. At times, I found this really challenging and couldn't understand why he was being so hard on me.

But as time went on, I began to see his intent. He was raising my bar, pushing me to develop into a leader with equally high standards. He was shaping me into someone who could operate in a high-performance environment.

One day, we talked about it, and he confirmed exactly what I had come to realise, that was his plan all along. And it worked.

The quality of my work soared, standing head and shoulders above the rest.

Terry taught me an invaluable lesson about leadership, coaching people to achieve high standards, not by dictating, or doing it for them, but by guiding and persistence. Yes, it often took longer, but in the long run, he had complete trust and confidence in me because he knew my standards were just as high as his. This philosophy has stuck with me ever since, and it's something I now pass on to those who follow me, and to my children.

As a leader, whether in my professional or personal life, my role is to coach and encourage. It's about passing on wisdom and maintaining a high bar, not because I demand it, but because the person understands its value and strives to achieve it.

That's the key. You can't make people high performers. They make themselves high performers. You coach and guide them, but the magic happens through their own action.

Aaron, Terry and I spent countless hours together, often working long days and late nights, but it was genuinely enjoyable and fulfilling. It felt as though we were building something truly special.

I felt really valued by both Terry and Aaron, gaining unprecedented exposure to strategic planning, decision-making, and interactions with directors and senior leadership team members, opportunities I could never even dreamed of.

Just over a year prior, I had been nervous about speaking to Adam, only entering his office for the first time during my interview for the Network & Distribution Manager role. Now, I found myself spending much of my day in that very same office, casually walking in without even knocking, tea in hand. I had been welcomed into a senior leadership circle, where a junior-levelled manager like me was rubbing shoulders with people of such high calibre, and it felt normal.

I was completely accepted into the circle of trust. And for the first time since moving into management, I felt like I belonged somewhere. It's mind-blowing really that someone so junior was within that group.

Everything was going incredibly well; I was learning a tremendous amount each day, and for the first time in my life, I was actively seeking knowledge rather than having it pushed upon me. I was pulling the learning. I now know that this pull is critical if we want to develop our knowledge and performance. We have to want it. We have to be hungry for it. If the pull is not there, we will disconnect, put it off, and eventually stop learning all together.

The concepts I was studying and then applying were sticking with me. I could understand the logic, and the tools, applying them practically, learning and then trying again, a stark contrast to my academic struggles in school.

With WCM, I felt like I was at the top of my game, Set One material! I loved what I was doing, and it was clear that my passion was being reciprocated.

When audit time approached, the mood shifted dramatically. What had been an exciting, collaborative environment between Aaron, Terry and I, suddenly became serious, tense, and focused.

The Mail Centre would be swarming with managers from across the country, all arriving to support us in preparing for the big day. In some ways, it was a fantastic opportunity to learn from others' experiences and expand my network, meeting people I'd likely never have encountered otherwise. Everyone had their own stories about past interactions with the Professor, sharing tips, advice, and cautionary tales about what he looked for, what he appreciated, and what he disapproved of.

Although mostly offered with the best of intent, this exchange of knowledge, sometimes bordering on scaremongering, only added to the growing anticipation and pressure that everyone was feeling.

In the weeks leading up to an audit, the days became incredibly long. We'd be meticulously preparing our PowerPoint presentations, crafting narratives that aligned with the WCM framework and highlighted our efforts, demonstrating that we understood the logic and was making progress.

A small group of postal workers would spend their time constructing elaborate cardboard storyboards to be presented to the Professor during the Gemba walk.

The stress was immense, with the weight of expectation felt heavily by every pillar lead. The Senior Leadership Team (SLT) would be present for these audits, and in some cases, even the company CEO would join. These events were a huge undertaking, requiring extensive planning, coordination, and execution. And the stakes were high. Prove to be a trailblazer in this arena and your stock rose considerably. Fall short and you could very quickly find yourself off of the Christmas card list of the Directors.

While the official responsibility for orchestrating the audits fell on Terry's shoulders, as his second-in-command, I did everything I could to support the preparations. Alongside my involvement in the overall planning, I also had to build my own presentation and storyboards for the Workplace Organisation pillar.

The problem, however, was that WCM was very much a top-down initiative within the organisation. Activity was pushed down onto people rather than being organically adopted from the ground up. The logic of WCM was sound, but the physical application across the organisation was missing the mark. There wasn't enough respect for the people, and no genuine engagement or involvement. This led to significant resistance across the board.

It felt as though the trade union largely viewed WCM and its objectives as a direct threat to both them and their members. There clearly was no trust either way. The trade union were acutely aware of the inefficiencies and waste within the system, and they didn't want the spotlight on these issues, let alone have their own members actively identifying and solving them.

For me this problem goes back to a lack of trust, lack of true alignment and shared purpose. For WCM to really have the impact that it was capable of, it required buy-in throughout the organisational leadership and from the trade-union. Without exception. But this simply wasn't the case.

On the management side, there were also significant challenges. Most of the pillar leads had been either voluntold by their line managers, or handpicked by Aaron. Few truly understood the initiative, and even fewer believed in it. And even less than that wanted to do it. To many, it was just "another task" tacked onto an already busy schedule, and there is a bigger problem as any!

The situation created a clear divide between WCM and the operation itself. While WCM focused on improving processes and driving efficiency, the operation was fixated on simply "getting the job done".

Often by any means necessary. The one and only metric being "did we clear the workload on time". If we did, great. If we didn't, who was to blame.

The principles of WCM, intended to become "the way we do things around here," as seen with Toyota's success, weren't being properly embedded. Instead, any attempt at doing things differently was seen as too difficult, we don't have time, or it's not my problem. There was a glaring lack of ownership.

The operational leadership appeared to be struggling. They lacked the urgency, direction, and leadership behaviours needed to inspire or encourage any type of change.

To be fair, the culture wasn't entirely their fault. They were simply following the patterns set by those who had come before them, replicating the behaviours that they'd seen in those around them. The general position was "let's just nod our heads and wait for it to pass".

In their eyes, if the system wasn't broken there was no reason to fix it. It was broken, but if it's all you know, and all you've ever known, how would you know what good looks like in reality?

Shift Managers only held people accountable (I use this term loosely) for clearing the workload, so there was little incentive for anyone to experiment with new ways of working. Taking risks seemed unnecessary, especially when it came with the potential for conflict. Even if some managers wanted to explore better methods, they could be met with bitter resistance from trade union representatives and postal workers.

The tension between management and the trade union is no secret, you see it in the news, and it often made trying new ways of working more trouble than it was worth for managers who were not bought in, and just wanted to get to the end of their shifts and then go home.

It was easier, and far less stressful, to maintain the status quo than to push for the changes WCM identified. Most of the managers were former postal workers who had eventually been promoted as they reached a time of their lives where they didn't want to be out and about on the front line anymore. However, many had fallen into a comfort zone, seeing management as the next natural step after years "on the tools."

There appeared to be three paths for postal workers who were either coming to the end of their time on the front line, or wanted an easier life:

1. You landed in a cushy duty with plenty of hidden inefficiencies to hide behind, alongside several "payment add-ons" such as shift allowance, or the lesser spotted scheduled attendance to boost earnings.

2. You moved into management with little in the way of motivation to show drive, passion, or a sense of ownership.

3. You became a trade union representative, with all the perks of option 1, but with fulltime release for trade union duties.

It was frustrating, not just for me, but for Terry and Aaron, and some of the newer pillar leads who had been parachuted in from other sites that wanted to deliver sustainable change.

It felt like many of the managers had run out of energy and needed new batteries, or perhaps even a "jump start" from another vehicle to get them moving again. The leadership ecosystem on site was stagnant, and it was obvious that without some major re-energising, and a significant culture change, no amount of WCM activity would make the impact it was intended to.

The result was a really high turnover of pillar leads, and eventually, managers from outside of the Mail Centre coming in to oversee pillars. This only further eroded the sense of ownership and engagement within the Mail Centre.

I, however, remained a constant presence throughout, loving every minute of it! I studied Workplace Organisation intently and threw myself into supporting both Aaron and Terry. While others were reluctant to embrace the change, I thrived on it, finding meaning and purpose in the very framework that so many resisted. I saw opportunity and potential, my eyes coming into focus more each day, and my knowledge expanding with every book that I read.

As our first audit day arrived, the atmosphere buzzed with nervous anticipation. Preparations were done, and now it was time for the pillar leads in the auditorium, and the postal workers at the Gemba to deliver their presentations.

Everyone had shown up bright and early, scattered across every corner of the Mail Centre, rehearsing in hushed tones, trying to perfect their message and demonstrate their "knowledge."

For most, the prospect of standing before a room packed with senior leadership, guests, and spectators was utterly terrifying. The scaremongering tales of the Professor's red laser pen pointed at the screen, and sharp scrutiny didn't help.

He was notorious for pulling out his red laser pointer, zeroing in on the presentation screen, and unravelling presenters with relentless, probing questions. If he didn't like it, he wouldn't hide it, and you would know in no uncertain terms that he didn't like it. Many feared they'd be tied up in knots, scrambling for answers they didn't have, but thought he wanted to hear.

It was really hard to watch sometimes, particularly when the presenter was trying their best and broadly understood the content, but couldn't articulate it under the pressure of countless eyes watching, and the sound of silence. The room waiting for you to fall over so that they could add a "I was there when" moment to their scaremongering tales.

Your heart would go out to them, but there was nothing you could do. Occasionally, if the Professor pressed too hard or lingered on a point for too long without accepting the answer that was being given, Terry, Aaron, or a senior leader would step in to save the day, steering the conversation back on track.

As time went on, and my confidence and knowledge in the pillars grew, I found myself stepping in more often to rescue my peers from the proverbial chopping block. Knowing when and how to intervene became a skill in itself, and in those moments, it felt like I was part of something bigger, I felt ownership, I felt like I was a leading player in making WCM a success.

Strangely, for me there was no nervous anticipation, just pure excitement. While others were dreading the spotlight, I couldn't wait to step into it.

I genuinely felt this was my moment, and I was ready to embrace it with confidence. I thrived on the energy, the high stakes, and the chance to demonstrate what I'd learned. Looking back at it now, I also think there was an air of "everyone is waiting for me to get torn apart, I'll prove them wrong" spurring me on.

While many around me were battling nerves, I was absolutely buzzing, eager to stand in front of the room and show that I not only understood WCM, but what I could do in this space.

It felt like everything I'd worked towards was building up to this, and I was ready to seize it. The only frustration was that I wasn't scheduled to present until immediately after lunch, it felt like I was waiting forever! I'd have presented them all if I could have done.

As my time neared and we broke for lunch, we all descended upon a room where a finger buffet was laid out across a table.

The Professor, as usual practice, was the first to help himself, followed by the rest of us in an apprehensive, somewhat tense bundle.

I have my own rule with finger buffets. If I'm not first (or perhaps second), then I'm not eating it. Not because I'm a diva, but because there's no way I'm eating anything from a plate where everyone else has had their grubby little mits in there before me. People don't wash their hands, then you see them grabbing handfuls of crisps, nuts, and sausage rolls from a bowl, or flicking through sandwiches with their fingertips checking fillings like their flicking through pages of a book.

Totally gross, no thank you! I'll stick with the pre-packaged high UPF items thanks.

Anyway, there was an unspoken rule, likely as a result of the scaremongering tales and the full autopsies that would occur with his red laser pen: keep your distance from the Professor, and defiantly don't make eye contact, least of all speak unless you're spoken too!

People actively avoided him, staying far out of his way, as if proximity to him might somehow invite an unwanted question that they couldn't answer. He usually sat alone, with the CEO, or a member of the senior leadership team.

But not today.

I spotted him sitting by himself in the far corner of the room, and without hesitation I made a beeline straight for him.

As I approached, he slowly looked up from his paper plate of carbs and gave me a stare that seemed to go straight through me. The Professor only seemed to move in slow motion, every movement seeming analysed for any waste and made with purpose.

Unfazed, I introduced myself, then before he could respond I immediately launched into a stream of compliments, telling him how fascinating I found his work and how I'd read everything I could find about it online. It was as if I was a starstruck teenager meeting my pop idol in the foyer of a concert hall, desperately seeking his attention and approval. Actually that was exactly what I was doing!

For the next twenty-five minutes, with very few breaths, I droned on about how much his ideas had inspired me, where I saw opportunity to remove waste, and which tools I thought would be good to evidence this, all while he silently worked his way through his pre fingered buffet delights.

The whole time he was impossible to read. His expression remained inscrutable, no nod, no smile, nothing to indicate if he was engaged or even remotely interested. I had no clue whether he was actually listening to anything I was saying or simply tolerating my presence in the most stoic way possible, kind of like when you're meeting a friend or colleague, and there's a big fly buzzing around your face. You know it's there, it's a mild irritant, but you ignore its presence and carry on as if it doesn't exist. You get the gist.

I was practically daring him to ask me a technical question so that I could impress him with my knowledge. But he didn't utter a word, not a sausage.

As we returned to the auditorium, the room was electric with a nervous tension, thick with anticipation for what was to unfold during the second half of the audit. People quietly filed back to their seats, the air heavy with whispered conversations and anxious glances.

Aaron stepped up to the front of the room, leant into the microphone that was mounted to the lectern, his voice breaking through the fading murmurs as he outlined the agenda for the second half of the audit.

Then, with the tiniest hint of excitement in his tone, he introduced me as the Workplace Organisation pillar lead.

This was it. This was my moment. Finally!

I walked onto the staging area and approached the lectern. As I settled in, I could feel the weight of the room's attention on me, it was completely silent. The Professor, who had been hunched over his notes throughout Aaron's interlude, slowly raised his head, his gaze locking directly onto mine. The silence was heavy, the entire room holding its breath as they waited for me to begin.

Then, to everyone's surprise, the Professor suddenly burst into life. His face lit up with an ear-to-ear smile, and in his unmistakable, broken English, he exclaimed

"Ahh, the one I've been waiting for!"

The tension broke as a ripple of shock and amusement spread through the audience. That one sentence, filled with unexpected enthusiasm, gave me all the energy I needed.

This was it. This was the moment I had been waiting for, as it was for the Professor by his own account.

One of the tales I'd been fed was that the Professor was frustrated with how slowly we were moving as an organisation. He wanted to see more rigor and pace.

The problem was that "pace" wasn't a word that fit with my experience of the culture; trying to instil it felt almost infeasible. Anticipating this challenge from him, I was determined to quash it early, hoping to remove any ammunition he might have for his infamous red laser pen.

During my preparations, I had stumbled upon an old black-and-white photo of the Mail Centre hanging in one of the upstairs corridors. To my astonishment, it was a photo of my model area taken nearly a hundred years ago. The scary part was he was right, little had changed! The process was virtually identical to what he was going to see later during our Gemba walk.

So, I decided to turn this finding into an opportunity.

I carefully scanned the old photo and saved it on my computer. Then I visited the Gemba during operation, surrounded by postal works sorting mail. I then took a similar photo from exactly the same angle as the historical one.

I created a slide with a side-by-side image that juxtaposed the two images, enhancing it with shaking effects and a time-traveling sound effect (fairly advanced effects for the time).

I knew no one had ever used audio and visuals like this in a presentation to the Professor before, and I was excited to be the first. It was a risk as I had no idea how it would be received. But I knew I had to engage him early on. If I got his attention and made him like me, I felt I had more chance of winning his favour.

As I began my presentation (I think it was the second or third slide), I displayed the old photo first, setting the stage for my dramatic reveal. Excitedly, I said

"Professor, you always say that we are too slow, that things don't change fast enough. You know what? You're right!"

Just as I hit the button to sync the audio and effects, the current photo appeared alongside the one-hundred-year-old version.

There was a moment of silence before the Professor burst into applause, literally laughing out loud and exclaiming

"Yes, yes, yes!"

The entire room erupted in laughter, their engagement surging to an all-time high. I felt like I had successfully disarmed him, reminiscent of Eminem's character "B-Rabbit" triumphing over "Papa Doc" in the final rap battle of the movie, 8 Mile.

If you haven't seen this movie, B-Rabbit had been bullied and harassed by Papa Doc's crew throughout the feature. Amongst other things he had been beaten up, and they knew that he lived in a trailer park with his mum.

When it came to the famous final rap battle at the end of the movie, B-Rabbit won the toss to go first. In his rap he threw it all out there, openly admitting that he had been beaten up, and that he lived in a trailer park with his mum. Then when he finished and Papa Doc took the mic, he had nothing to say as B-Rabbit has said it all.

B-Rabbit had totally disarmed Papa Doc of content. In a similar (perhaps less confrontational) way, I had disarmed the Professor of his “too slow” content.

After that, I breezed through the rest of my presentation, transitioning effortlessly from one slide to the next. I filled the room with logic, numbers, insights, and visuals.

I addressed the Professor directly, saying things like

“Professor, this is what we found”

and

“This is what we did, Professor, and this is why”

The minutes flew by, and when I finally reached the last slide, I invited questions from him. This is usually where the demolition starts. I’d witnessed many times before the Professor directing his recking ball at the presenter at this very moment.

His eyes had been locked on mine for the past forty-five minutes, and I don’t think he even blinked. Not once!

Finally, he mumbled in broken English

“No questions, thank you.”

The room erupted into applause, and I stepped down to return to my seat, riding the high of that moment. The audience looked completely stunned, almost in disbelief.

I was floating on air, relishing every second of it. If I could have crowd surfed my way back to my seat I would have done.

That moment marked the beginning of a "sensi and student" relationship with the Professor that would endure for the next three years.

From then on, he rarely asked me questions during presentations, let alone challenged me. I don't think I ever received the infamous red laser pen. Instead, he would challenge me to use advanced tools, and he began to engage with me during lunch breaks, whether at our Mail Centre or when I attended audits at others.

He generously shared his time with me, offering snippets of wisdom that extended far beyond the material we were working with. Some of these insights felt like seeds planted long ago, taking root in my mind. Over the years, I've found moments of clarity when I truly understood what he meant. It's as if it has taken decades for that understanding and appreciation to fully blossom within me. He even invited me to a leading Fiat plant in Italy, but that opportunity was quickly shut down by the powers that be.

The advanced tools and methods that he challenged me to utilise eclipsed anything other Mail Centres were implementing.

Whenever there was a business function that he was present at, that involved a sit-down meal, I found myself not only invited, but seated at his table. I was even parachuted into other Mail Centres to deliver their Workplace Organisation presentations because they recognised that I could effectively explain the logic behind initiatives and get the Professor excited about the activities.

People were acting like I was some kind of snake charmer!

The truth was, I was just embracing his offerings of wisdom and knowledge, applying it, then with fact and data showing him the impact. It wasn't rocket science.

I was so passionate about WCM that I became synonymous with it, and he could feel that energy, feeding off of it. He was known to literally fall asleep during some presentations, I even witnessed this once! But with me, it was different; he was too engaged, smiling and nodding throughout to fall asleep.

I soon established myself as the go-to person for Workplace Organisation guidance and support, with pillar leads from all over the UK reaching out to me for copies of my presentations, or inviting me to visit their Mail Centres, or even me inviting them to ours.

On occasion I attended small, benchmarking sessions where external leaders would visit our best Mail Centres to learn. It was an incredible opportunity to share knowledge and build a network of collaboration that spanned the organisation and beyond.

I felt valued and appreciated by Terry, Aaron and the Professor. Which if we are honest with ourselves is truly what everyone desires, to feel valued and appreciated. It's in this acknowledgment that the embers of respect for people begin to ignite.

Things continued much the same for the next year or so until one day, Terry informed me that he was leaving. He was moving to a higher-profile Mail Centre to lead WCM there.

I was genuinely pleased for him; it was closer to home, and he truly deserved it after all he had done to establish WCM in our Mail Centre. This was an amazing opportunity for him to take the lessons he had learned from both the challenges and successes he experienced and start afresh with that knowledge in mind.

However, inside, I was absolutely gutted. It felt like I was losing my best friend and mentor. Terry promised that he would find an opportunity for me to join him at the earliest possibility, which was incredibly generous of him, but at that moment, it felt like a long way off. It felt like everything had fallen apart. It felt like I was back to square one again.

Over the next four weeks leading up to his departure, Terry strongly advocated for me to be his replacement, strategically positioning me in front of Aaron and the Regional Director at every opportunity. He genuinely believed in me and wanted this opportunity for me. He even told Aaron that I was the right person to take over his role. He really couldn't have done any more to make it happen.

The challenge was that despite my exposure, and growing reputation, I was still a junior-levelled manager. The Mail

Centre Champion role was a senior management position, at least four levels above my current state. It was virtually unheard of for someone to make such a significant leap in one single step.

It just didn't happen.

After the agreed four-week transition period, Terry moved on to his new role and I was temporarily handed most of the Champion's responsibilities, with some of the more senior elements being managed by Aaron himself. There was no formal agreement, announcement putting me in charge, and certainly no pay increase, just a chance to take on elements the role.

I guess you could describe it as "keeping the lights on" until someone suitable was appointed.

I really threw myself into my new responsibilities over the months that followed, but without Terry's support, it became increasingly challenging to drive any movement among the other pillar leads.

I stood my ground, challenged appropriately, chaired pillar lead meetings, asked the right questions, and really tried hard to support others to make progress. I worked tirelessly to drive the roadmap, holding people accountable against it.

Knowledge wise and in terms of desire, there was no doubt that I was the right candidate. But trying to hold eleven pillar leads, who were all my seniors, accountable as a junior manager felt like an uphill battle that I just couldn't win. I simply didn't have the grade or the clout that went with it. I also didn't have the respect of the team.

You see, there were a few things that I didn't think about at the time, but looking back now I can see clearly:

1. I had never walked the walk. I had never proven myself in the live operation for a significant period of time.

2. I was still carrying the jack-the-lad postal worker turned traitor reputation within the Mail Centre.

3. The perception of my time in Network & Distribution was far from positive.

4. Perhaps most impactful. I was seen as a threat. I wasn't trusted. I had never earnt their trust. This is a deal breaker for any leader. You don't have to have a rank, seniority, or a huge pay packet to be a leader. You can be a leader regardless of any of these. Being a leader comes from your behaviours, the trust and relationships you build, and peoples wanting to follow you based on these. I had a big fat zero on all of these.

I was really the only manager that was taking WCM seriously. I wasn't just doing it; I was all over it. I was WCM. This made me different to them. It made them look bad, and it also made them worry that I was going to take their jobs.

A few weeks after the audit it was announced that Aaron was leaving too. He was being replaced by Dennis; a Bronze awarded WCM Champion.

I really enjoyed working with Aaron. I have huge respect for him, and had got to know him really well during his time at the Mail Centre. I saw him as a friend as much as the Mail Centre Manager.

He was even one of only a very small number of work-related people who came to my wedding. What made this even more special was that he lived in Woking, Surrey, and my wedding was in Canterbury, Kent. He travelled a long way to be there. This meant a lot.

Sadly we lost touch once he moved on. I often wonder what he's up to now. Would be great to catch-up. Maybe one day our paths will cross again. I do hope so.

I was still processing the shock of losing both Terry and Aaron when this news came about Dennis taking over. I understood why they had chosen him; with his experience of achieving a Bronze Award and his strong track record, he seemed like the perfect candidate to give the Mail Centre the kick-start and drive it so desperately needed. On paper, it made complete sense.

During the handover period, Dennis would either visit the Mail Centre or call me daily to check on how things were going. At that time, he was the golden boy of WCM, held in high regard for both his knowledge and results.

He had built a solid reputation, and working alongside him seemed like it would be an incredible learning opportunity for me. It was a chance to continue my own growth under the guidance of someone who had already achieved what our Mail Centre was striving for – a bronze award.

Despite the upheaval of losing Terry and Aaron, the prospect of working with Dennis injected a new sense of hope for me. It felt like there was still potential to push forward and get WCM on the right track, learning from the best in the business. It was exactly what the Mail Centre, and perhaps I, needed to regain momentum.

I had already sounded Dennis out about his plans for the Champion vacancy and my own future. He assured me that no matter what happened, I would definitely not be going back to early distribution. That lifted a huge weight off my shoulders.

However, when it came to the Champion vacancy, he was tight-lipped, which left me uneasy. I should have known from this that the writing was on the wall. But I was young and naive. A few compliments here and there, and a bit of responsibility and I was easy to string along.

Not long after, the announcement came that Dennis would be bringing in one of the pillar leads he had achieved Bronze with as the new Mail Centre Champion.

I was terribly disappointed. All the effort I had poured into the role, the isolation I felt, the months of unofficially filling in and pushing the WCM agenda, seemed to have been overlooked. It stung. But in all honesty, looking back now and putting myself in Dennis's position, I understand his decision.

If I were in his shoes, I'd probably have made the same choice. He needed to hit the ground running, and this was a critical opportunity for him. Bringing in someone he trusted, someone who had already proven their capability in the role, was the logical move. It wasn't just about knowledge; he needed someone who could immediately demand the respect of the pillar leads, someone with the credibility of "been there, done that", and push the initiative forward without missing a beat.

Although I was disheartened, I tried to look at it as an opportunity. Perhaps this was a chance to learn from someone who had already been through the Bronze element of the WCM journey successfully. There was still so much to gain from the experience, even if it wasn't in the way I had hoped.

Working with Dennis was brilliant. His style was utterly unique, super relaxed, very direct, and incredibly easy to get along with.

Unlike anyone of that level that I had ever seen before. Whilst everyone else was wearing full suits and a tie, Dennis would turn up in jogging bottoms, t-shirt and trainers. All designer label of course, he was very flashy. He had a Porsche that stood out in the carpark, he had presence and people noticed him.

He gave me an unprecedented amount of his time, coaching me and shielding me from the political challenges within the Mail Centre. He even handed me a key to the Mail Centre Manager's office, giving me full access and freedom to come and go as I pleased.

Dennis really took me under his wing, ensuring I felt valued and relevant, even as the new leadership team settled in. He had my back, and as time went on, we built a strong camaraderie. He gave me the same level of exposure that Aaron and Terry had, maybe even more. We had some great times, and I was happy for a while.

Meanwhile Terry had found me a role in his new site, but the travel was significant and my anxiety just couldn't cope with that. Things seemed to be going ok at the Mail Centre, so as grateful as I was, I decided to stay where I was.

But things weren't great for long, and soon became incredibly messy.

Since I was so close to Dennis, he would tell me one thing, guide me, and coach me in one direction, while the new Champion would say and instruct something completely different. It quickly became a case of too many chefs, with all of us treading on each other's toes.

I was fiercely independent by this time and confident in what I needed to do, particularly with the Professor's guidance. I was comfortable moving forward with the direction I had been provided by the man himself. The problem was, the new Champion wanted to be the one steering Workplace Organisation, offering direction, and taking overall ownership, just as he did with the other pillars.

The problem was that the other pillars were asking me for support with logic, they saw me an emerging leader in this space. I had been leading WCM for a number of months whilst the leadership changes took place. I was a known resource who'd they had seen the Professor accept. This was seen by the new Champion as a challenge to his authority.

This and the dynamic with Dennis created tension between us, and it became increasingly uncomfortable for both of us. Neither of us was happy, and it drove a wedge between us.

This dynamic created tension between us, and it became increasingly uncomfortable for both of us. Neither of us was happy, and it drove a wedge between us.

Dennis, through his own doing really, found himself stuck in the middle. Sparks were flying almost daily; it was clear to everyone within a one-hundred-mile radius that things weren't right. Apart from being uncomfortable, it gave the others an opportunity maximise on this clear weakness in the WCM agenda.

Before too long, I had achieved the required points in Workplace Organisation to qualify for a Bronze Award. But as a collective Mail Centre, we fell short.

Many of the other pillars had never recovered from the slow pace they'd been moving at previously. The gap between them and the leading pillars was vast.

In WCM, the framework requires all pillars to meet a standard, if one is weak, the entire Mail Centre falls short.

Around this time, I was invited to join a developmental program called "Elevate". This initiative, set up by one of the Regional Directors, aimed to identify and nurture up-and-coming talent who had demonstrated encouraging potential for future leadership.

This was the program's second year, and I, along with nine other candidates, participated in tasks reminiscent of the BBC's "The Apprentice", albeit without the sacking element, and without Alan Sugar. Instead, we had Alex, the Regional Director, who was a fantastic guy to work with; I could tell he genuinely believed in me too.

Some of the tasks we undertook were great fun. For one, I created an entire presentation inspired by "The Apprentice". I filmed scenes of myself coming down the stairs, answering the phone, and taking instructions on where to meet "Sir Alex" to give us our task. It was a blast to create, and when I presented it to the Directors at an away day, it brought big laughs. Secretly, I think it gave "Sir" Alex a bit of an ego boost too!

Interestingly, I bumped into Alex a couple of years ago at the zoo! He was visiting with his grandchildren while I was there with my young family. We had a brief conversation about where our career journeys had taken us, and he even made a joke about Amazon stealing the best talent, make of that what you will! It was a delightful reminder of our time together in the program and how far I had come since then.

Another memorable task had us split into two teams, each given a starting budget of £500 and tasked with raising as much money for our chosen charities as possible.

My team organised a "Bollywood" themed evening at the Post Office Social Club, which was packed with authentic music and Indian food. It turned out to be a fantastic night. I can't remember exactly how much we raised, but I do know we won the task! There was no official "winner" of the program, as it was more about exposure and learning for us all, but I was proud to be a part of it.

Anyways, Dennis had been my mentor for a few years, and I considered him a friend, I looked up to him and aspired to be just like him. He met my family and sometimes we would go for drinks after work, or he'd take me out in his Porsche. I believed he had my best interests at heart.

However, as time went on promises were missed, and my development stalled. I started to see a pattern of a lot of talk but nothing ever happening. Others had warned me about it, but I either chose to ignore it, or I simply didn't see it. I was under a kind of spell. Completely blinded to the reality being that after years of hard work, I was still at the same level with no path forward.

Without growth or promotion, the gap between my current level and the Champion's level would remain too vast to close. I started feeling like I was being used, for audits, rolled out like the best bone china whenever VIPs visited, only to be put back in the cupboard afterwards gathering dust next to the gravy boat until the next big occasion.

Eventually, it reached a point where it felt like I had to choose between WCM audits and my family. I understood his position, he needed me; the pressure was high, but my family needed me too and I was at work for long hours. And when it comes down to it, there was only ever going to be one winner. My family comes first, always.

As I grew in knowledge and confidence over the years, I realised I no longer needed someone's protection or constant mentorship. What I needed was support, encouragement, the space to find my way as a leader, and the freedom to carve out my own path.

I had learned so much from the experiences I'd been through, and from the people around me, even from the not-so-great people I'd worked alongside and for. They taught me how not to lead, showing me the importance of treating people with respect and supporting their development. I knew the kind of leader I wanted to be, and I was ready to fully embrace my authentic self, shedding the "joker" persona I had once relied on so heavily.

I was ready to stand on my own two feet and take the next step forward. But I also knew that it couldn't happen within the same environment. I needed a fresh start, a place where I could be seen as Matt the leader, without the baggage I'd accumulated at the Mail Centre.

I became concerned that Dennis was preventing this from happening, and I began to suspect the reasons were self-serving. He wasn't going to let go unless it was on his terms, and that didn't align with my values.

My time at the Mail Centre had naturally run its course.

Regrettably, it felt like Dennis and I parted ways on a sour note. I didn't like this, and still don't. My late Grandad once told me "Never leave on bad terms boy, always keep the door open".

I felt like I had failed that, and while it was disappointing, in my mind I was clear about my self-worth and the value I added. It was time to move on, and I hope that in the time that has passed since Dennis has realised that too, and that one day we can grab a beer together and talk about some of the good old times.

Key Learnings Chapter 4

This period saw me find a method of learning that worked so well for me. Everything about continuous improvement appealed to me. It gave me a passion and a desire to grow that I had never experienced before. I had found something that I was genuinely good at.

It was also a rollercoaster of emotion, with mighty highs and bitterly disappointing lows.

What began as a fresh start quickly became one of the most important periods of my development. Working alongside Aaron and Terry gave me belief, exposure, challenge and the sort of support every developing leader needs. For the first time, I felt trusted, valued and part of something that mattered.

Undoubtedly the greatest success of this period of my life was meeting Terry and forming the friendship that we have. It's stood the test of time and he is one of the few true friendships that I have in my life.

It was also the chapter where I found my voice. Through the audits, the pressure, and my interactions with Professor, I built confidence and credibility. I stopped being the young manager hoping to survive and started becoming someone who could hold a room, explain ideas clearly, and lead with conviction. In many ways, this was where I began to see and feel what I was capable of.

Resilience was again an overarching theme of my learning. Times were hard, the pace and volume of work was relentless, unlike anything I have ever experienced before. It was hard work too, all of it taking me outside of my comfort zone. But the key here was that I really loved what I was doing.

But beneath my growth sat a much bigger truth. The application of WCM in the organisation was flawed. The framework itself was strong, but the culture was not. It was introduced from the top down, pushed onto people rather than built with them. There was too little trust, too little engagement, and not enough respect for people. As a result, resistance was inevitable. What should have become part of the way the organisation thought and worked instead became, for many, just another task.

But if I'm honest, from a personal perspective it was incredibly fulfilling. I felt like I was playing a vital part in something important.

As time went on, the chapter also became one of loyalty, disappointment and political reality. Terry left. Aaron left. Dennis arrived. I was trusted with more, exposed to more, and continued to grow, but I also began to see how organisations can keep using someone's energy and talent without ever truly moving them forward. I gave everything to the work, but eventually realised that knowledge and passion alone are not enough. Trust, credibility, timing, relationships and environment matter just as much.

Courage plays a crucial role in career advancement; pursuing the next step in our journeys often requires bold steps, and risk taking. If it was easy, it wouldn't be a challenge right!

Going back to the Mail Centre was a risk for me, I was fragile and it wouldn't have taken a lot to push me over the edge. At times it almost did. I wasn't very popular with the management team or with the postal workers. The genius Scotsman was still there, and so was everyone else. We never spoke again. We'd frequently pass in the corridor where he would smirk at me or try to intimidate me with an aggressive stare. But I just ignored it.

I can't lie, it did bother me, and made me feel really uncomfortable. But that's what he wanted, he was a bully, and at that time I wasn't strong enough mentally of physically to deal with it. But I didn't let him drive me out. I stuck it out. I came back every day. I kept going. I was going somewhere, he wasn't. That was my victory.

In the end, this chapter is really about my own growth through contradiction. I was thriving and frustrated at the same time. Valued and held back. Inspired and disillusioned. It shaped me deeply.

It taught me what good leadership looks like, but just as importantly, what poor leadership, poor culture and poor deployment can destroy. And it left me knowing that if I was ever going to become the leader I wanted to be, I would need to do it somewhere I could step forward without the weight of the past hanging over me.

2009

Building a CI empire with Terry at the Mail Centre.

This WCM room quickly became our base, our space to think, plan, and drive projects forward.

2009

This is me preparing the Workplace Organisation Model Area for yellow line marking.

Back then it was common to be doing everything yourself.

2009

Taken outside Gatwick Mail Centre, I'm on the far right. This was during a benchmarking visit from Mopar, who came to see the WCM work we had in place.

2010

Me on my Wedding Day.

My Grandad looked at me and said "you could have shaved boy".

I took a short break after my son was born, but my anxiety returned with a vengeance almost immediately. I had managed to keep it mostly under control for years, only experiencing flare-ups during major life changes, like when we moved homes. In those moments, it was rush, rush, rush, and then, once everything settled down in the evening, anxiety attacks would strike. Day to day though, I was generally okay.

I guess your first child entering the world would count as a "life changing moment". The day he was born was magical. He arrived at lunchtime at a beautiful birthing centre, just as we had planned.

The atmosphere was calm and everything went smoothly; we were incredibly fortunate, as we were with all three of our children. After the birth, my wife asked me to grab some pizza from the takeaway just around the corner, apparently, she had built up quite an appetite!

Then she asked me to pop home to grab a couple of things that she needed. We had been up very early that day, so I was feeling tired, which I knew was a trigger for my anxiety.

While driving home, I felt an attack creeping in.

The symptoms were always the same for me. I would feel hot, uncomfortable and on edge, with that horrible sense that I was about to be sick. What made it even worse was how aware I was of it building.

The best way I can describe it is this. Imagine anxiety as a liquid inside my body. I could feel it starting in my stomach and then slowly rising higher and higher. First my stomach, then my chest, then my throat, until eventually I would be sick.

And strangely, being sick brought instant relief.

The moment it happened, it felt as though the anxiety had gone. Almost like I had flushed it out of my system. I became so tuned in to that pattern that sometimes I would make myself sick just to get it over with. That is how consuming it had become.

It was awful.

I got so used to dealing with it that I became a master at being sick without anyone noticing. I hid it incredibly well.

I have so many stories of anxiety getting the better of me. I can talk about them now and even laugh at some of them, but only because I hope that in sharing them they might help someone else feel a little less alone.

I remember one awful time after taking a girl out on a first date. I had dropped her home and was driving away in solid traffic when I felt it coming on. I knew the signs, but there was nowhere to go and nothing I could do.

Then bang. I was sick all over the inside of the car.

I rushed home, went straight to bed, and tried to forget about it. In fact, I did forget about it until I opened the car door the next day.

It was horrendous.

The car was never the same again. I ended up telling people I had spilt milk in there, which felt like a far more acceptable explanation than the truth.

Anyway on this occasion after my son was born. My wife sent me home to get some bits. I could feel it coming. I made it home before it hit fully, but when it did, it completely wiped me out. I began to panic about when I would be able to sleep again!

As the days and early weeks passed, my anxiety only worsened. The problem was, we were both trying to do everything. So, when he woke in the night for feeds, or even just stirred and grumbled, we would both get up, and I would just linger whilst my wife nursed him.

It wasn't until the penny dropped and we established a routine that ensured I got enough sleep that I finally started to calm down.

My poor wife must have felt the strain!

What was amusing during that period was the role of the "Health Visitor", someone who comes to check in on mum and baby in the first few weeks after the birth to offer support. After her first visit, our Health Visitor would walk in to our home, breeze right past my wife and the baby, and ask

“How are you, Matt? Are you doing, okay?”

We laugh about it now, but at the time it was difficult. I wasn’t eating anything. I was tired, weak, and fading away. Literally worrying myself away. I’d be better in the morning, but as the sun set and it got dark, I’d begin to panic.

Eventually I went to see my GP, who put me on a dose of Citalopram. This helped lift me enough to function.

I used to get really down about my anxiety, especially when it left me visibly underweight. It made me so self-conscious and weak. But as I got older, I learned to accept that anxiety is part of who I am, and I found ways to manage it, particularly physical exercise.

I’ve always been open about my struggles, and I make a point of discussing it with anyone dealing with similar challenges. I think it’s vital to talk openly about mental health, and even find ways to laugh at yourself.

By talking about it, I hope that it helps others who are dealing with their own struggles, to know that they are not alone and that how they feel is common, and that it doesn’t define you, it can and will get better.

I’d often joke that I’m the only person who could go to a nightclub, and get thrown out before I’d even touched a drink.

I'd be in the bathroom having an anxiety attack, throwing up, and the bouncers would just assume I'd had too much and kick me out! It would only be 7pm!

Still, I guess it made for a cheap night out!

My humour, along with being open about my struggles, has been key in helping me deal with anxiety. I've accepted that I'll never be free of it, but the key is that I control it, it doesn't control me.

Interestingly though, with my other children's early days, I was completely fine. I think that was because I had a sleep routine in place and was confident in our ability to manage. I also knew from experience that while the days and nights felt long, the weeks and months flew by quickly, and each stage would pass. With the others, I managed to enjoy the experience much more!

Becoming a father completely changed my perspective and priorities. I know it's a cliché, but it's true. Despite the lack of sleep, I felt like I could see things more clearly.

Shortly after my son was born, I left the Mail Centre and took a temporary role supporting a Sorting Office which had just begun rolling out WCM. I stepped in to support them, eventually taking on the Workplace Organisation pillar through their first audit.

The audit went well, despite some initial reservations from the senior regional leader, Ant. We had a minor clash beforehand; he didn't think there was enough to secure the point for Workplace Organisation, but I was confident I could explain away the criteria gaps and still pick up the point. After much debate, we agreed to disagree, and fortunately, things played out exactly as I had predicted. I think that earned me a bit of respect from Ant, who would later play a big role in my career, though at the time, this meeting was just a short, term assignment to help with the audit whilst keeping me closer to home.

For the six-month period leading up to my son's arrival I had been commuting back to Croydon from Kent where we had moved too. It was only about an hour each way, but it was gruelling day after day, particularly after a long day. Once he was born, I didn't want to be that far from home. So this worked nicely.

The build-up to the audit, however, was a bit prickly.

The Champion, someone I knew from her time in another Mail Centre close to ours, had a few misinterpretations of the framework logic and was giving some questionable advice to the pillar leads. I found it difficult not to step in since I knew the answers and felt I could solve the problems, but I didn't want to overstep the mark or cause friction, I was only there temporarily to help out after all.

Things got really awkward when in the run up to the audit, Ant arrived to review the progress that had been made. He sat with her and they went through each pillar, discussing the logic they had against the WCM criteria. I was working away on the other side of the room, but I could hear everything that they were saying. Ant was pointing out the same issues I had been "subtly" drawing her attention to over the previous week.

Now, we were all in this strange, uncomfortable situation: she knew she was a bit lost; I knew she was a bit lost; she knew I knew she was a bit lost, and Ant knew she was lost too. On top of that, Ant was probably wondering why I hadn't said anything, possibly assuming I was lost as well. All in all, it was a bit of a mess!

But we found our way through, and I was able to apply some of my leadership learnings that I'd acquired, in a new setting and that helped me grow in confidence.

However, one of the real highlights of my time at this Sorting Office was meeting a guy who would go on to be my sidekick, trusted right-hand man, and best mate to this day.

In the Sorting Office version of WCM, the Champion had a direct report, aptly named a "Champion Support."

On my first day, I was introduced to the Champion Support, Jamie. He was a slender chap, smartly dressed, with a pair of intelligent looking glasses perched on the bridge of his nose. Depending on your generation, think "Penfold" from the cartoon "Danger Mouse", this was Jamie.

Jamie had recently relocated from the other end of the country to take on this role. He had been with the organisation for several years, previously working as a postal worker in a Mail Centre.

From the moment we met, we hit it off. Jamie was the complete opposite of me, quiet, mellow, and a bit timid, he was a thinker, whereas I was a "get on with it" type of person. His character reminded me of Carl, my old Sorting Office Manager: dry, considered, but with a laid-back West Country twang. He was calming where as I was high energy.

We bounced off each other incredibly well and quickly formed a close friendship. Jamie appeared to trust me, valuing my insight, frequently sought my advice, acting on it without hesitation. He wasn't afraid to make mistakes, and he was always keen to listen and learn. While his attention to detail was impressive, it often came at the cost of urgency. Yet, when given a task, he'd always manage to do a solid job.

Our dynamic worked so well because we balanced each other out, and that connection became one of the most valuable relationships of my career.

In fact, I would later bring Jamie with me on three separate occasions, including to Amazon. Our early relationship reminded me very much of my time with Terry, but with the roles reversed. I was tough on Jamie, pushing him for excellence just as Terry had done with me. I could see his potential and knew he had it in him.

As time went on Jamie became one of the few people I could truly rely on. If I needed something done, I knew Jamie would deliver it to the standard, and always with integrity. When he attended meetings on my behalf, I had full confidence in his ability to speak for me. He understood what I needed, and I understood him. He was also incredibly loyal, a value that I share and respect greatly.

Through many years of working and socialising together with our families, I was able to encourage and support Jamie as I watched him grow in confidence and ability. Even during times of personal struggles, I made sure to be there for him in any way that I could, whether it was offering a homemade meal or simply being a shoulder to lean on. He knew he could count on me, just as I could count on him.

I vividly remember one instance when my son was a toddler, and both my wife and I came down with horrendous food poisoning. We were completely incapacitated, unable to move, let alone take care of our son. I called Jamie, and without hesitation, he was there within minutes. He spent the entire day playing with my son and taking care of him, without a single question asked.

That's true friendship, the kind of person you know will be there for you any time, night or day. Even in a house full of vomit!

I'm incredibly proud of how far Jamie has come and all he has accomplished. He's gone on to follow his own path, and earned every bit of success through his hard work and dedication. It's been a privilege to witness his journey develop first-hand.

Not just professionally either, privately he has done so well for himself. He got married in 2022 and my family and I were lucky enough to be invited along to share in their special day. They have both faced some really tough times over the past few years, but inspire me with their ability to stay strong and keep going.

After the audit, Ant offered me a substantive role as a Sorting Office Manager in a nearby Sorting Office. It was close to our new home and would finally get me away from the Mail Centre.

However, this particular Sorting Office had a reputation that preceded itself, it was known to be difficult.

There was a significant lack of engagement from the group, high absenteeism, and multiple performance issues. The office had been struggling for some time, under the oversight of a Senior Sorting Office Manager, Wilson, who also managed a larger mother site.

Wilson was a highly respected, no-nonsense leader with a track record of high performance. But the demands of overseeing both offices had left him overwhelmed due to a lack of on-site presence in the smaller Sorting Office.

The Sorting Office was currently being managed by two step-up postal workers. They were doing their best to keep the lights on, but with all due respect, the challenges were far beyond what they could handle.

The situation reminded me of when I first took on the early distribution role, stepping into chaos. The difference here, however, was that these two had the full backing of a strong leader in Wilson, who had an abundance of grit, backbone, and a solid understanding of processes. But even with that, the issues were still overwhelming.

I took the role, and genuinely enjoyed working with Wilson. He backed me 100% in everything I did, giving me the confidence, empowerment and authority to turn things around.

He taught me a lot about dealing with difficult people in a professional way, managing confrontation with tact, and thinking strategically about risk. His support helped me work through some challenging situations while keeping sight of the bigger picture.

The two step-up postal workers were also invaluable assets, fully buying into the changes I was introducing. They vocally supported the culture transformation I was driving, helping to set the tone.

I think they were relieved to have some onsite support.

Ant also had a significant impact on my development as a leader. He always backed my decisions publicly, but wasn't shy about giving me honest feedback behind closed doors, pointing out where I could improve. This was a touch of class, and I appreciated his approach.

One day, during my first week, once all of the rounds were out on delivery, I went down to a hardware store and bought multiple tins of white emulsion, brushes, rollers, masking tape etc. I brought it all back to the Sorting Office set it on the desk, and told the two step-ups

"Tomorrow, wear jeans and a t-shirt."

They looked confused and asked, “Why?”

I replied

“Because tomorrow, we’re clearing this office out, cleaning it up, repainting it, and making it a pleasant place to work.”

Their stunned expressions said it all, they were clearly thinking, “What is this guy on?!”

But there was method in my madness. I wanted them to see that I wasn’t afraid to get my hands dirty, and more importantly, I wanted to gauge their attention to detail.

You can tell a lot about someone’s standards by how they prep and paint a wall. I wanted to get a feel for their level of ownership and pride in their work.

At the same time, I wanted to send a strong, visual message to the frontline postal workers, that I was here to improve things, and to make their working conditions better. Plus, I wasn't about to work in that dirty, dusty office that looked more like a wartime bunker!

This particular office was used by the step-ups, and had a large glass window that looked out onto the sorting frames, and I was moving into it with them. I wanted to be at the Gemba, with the team, able to observe and learn. The official Sorting Office Manager's office was actually tucked away in the back, out of sight. I told them that from now on, that office was a red tag area, any junk left there unclaimed for five days would be going into the skip. One of the postal workers shouted

"What skip?"

I smiled and replied

"The big yellow one that's arriving first thing tomorrow!"

There were some tough days during my year as Sorting Office Manager at that office. I had to have some difficult conversations that simply couldn't be avoided.

It wasn't all smooth sailing either. I made plenty of quick decisions that turned out to be mistakes. But whenever I did, I was quick to admit it and take action to correct them.

You see, I didn't want anyone to be afraid of making mistakes. I wanted to create a culture of empowerment and innovation, where people weren't held back by fear of reprisal or consequences. I now know the term I was looking for at the time was "Scientific Thinking". I wanted everyone to think like a Scientist. To feel empowered to find solutions to problems by trying things. If it didn't work, what did you learn from it?

My hope was that by seeing me make mistakes, learning from them, and continually adjusting my approach, being agile, the team would begin to mirror those behaviours. I wanted them to understand that taking calculated risks was okay, as long as we learned and grew from the experience. Innovation thrives in an environment where people feel safe to experiment, and I was determined to create that culture. I was still young, but I was determined, and this role became my playground for growth.

I quickly learned how to carry myself, when to speak, and, more importantly, when to stay silent.

When I did speak, I made sure my message was clear and my expectations were precise, removing any room for confusion or game-playing. It wasn't easy. There were significant disagreements with the trade union, a few of which escalated to director level. But I stayed true to my values and beliefs, kept it professional, and trusting my gut instinct.

Most of my decisions were grounded in facts and data, stripping out any emotion from the debate. By simply referring back to the facts, I managed to stamp out much of the petty game-playing and ingrained behaviours that had become commonplace.

It wasn't just me driving this cultural shift; my two step-ups were also growing more confident in this approach. Together we began shaping a positive culture, a shared understanding of "the way we do things around here."

I'm proud of what we achieved in those twelve months. It wasn't perfect, but we transformed that Sorting Office leaving it in far better condition than when we started. I have no regrets and gained incredibly valuable experience in leadership, engagement, conflict resolution, and navigating trade union dynamics. I learn the art of replying, rather than reacting. This was significant and demonstrated a maturity that was brewing up inside of me.

By the end of it, I felt that I had earned some more of Ant's respect too, and I respected him in return. I think I proved a few doubters wrong during that period, there were those who expected me to crumble under the pressure.

Instead, I did the opposite: I grew in confidence and stature. I felt in control, finally emerging as an independent leader with a reputation built on my own actions and results, not my Grandad's incredible legacy, or under someone else's protection.

I was ready for the next step, becoming the Regional WCM Champion.

A neighbouring region was preparing to launch WCM, covering around twelve to fifteen Sorting Offices.

The main site, was an ex-mail centre facility that had since closed, and had then merged two Sorting Office's into one massive, sprawling facility. The building itself was in rough shape, run down, with a maze of long, narrow corridors with room after room across multiple floors.

The ground floor housed both sorting operations, and a collections hub in the afternoon/evening. There was a large "Callers Office" where customers could pick up missed deliveries. There was also a small canteen upstairs, a holdover from its Mail Centre days, that remained open in the mornings, perfect for grabbing a cheap cooked breakfast. All subsidised too, so it was exceptional value. Especially if you hid an extra rasher of bacon under the beans.

I applied for the WCM Champion role and passed the assessment without any issues. Since this was a Sorting Office based role, the model also required a WCM Support.

Negotiating with Ant, I managed to secure Jamie as my support, although it wasn't straightforward, we eventually came to an agreement. This was important to me, I wanted to hit the ground running and maintain the momentum I'd built over the past fifteen months. Having Jamie, someone I could trust, work well with, and continue to develop, was crucial to making that happen. Plus he had a lot of experience by now of launching this is his current Sorting Office. It really was a no brainer for me.

To support the rapid expansion of WCM across the Sorting Office function, the organisation had developed a "WCM Academy."

This was a ten-week program led by an academy coach, typically a former Sorting Office Manager (a read the manual type of guy in this case). Each cohort included newly appointed Champions and Supports, ensuring everyone started with the same foundational knowledge before launching WCM in their respective regions.

The academy's structure cantered around a comprehensive binder full of logic, methodologies, tools, and a detailed explanation of the WCM framework, audit process, and timeline expectations. Guest coaches from more advanced sites in all functions, usually Bronze Awarded pillar leads, were brought in to deliver training on their respective pillars. I had even coached Workplace Organisation to several academy cohorts in the past.

At the end of the programme, to my utter delight, there was a timed exam under full exam conditions to test everyone's knowledge. Yes, that was sarcasm.

What made the situation slightly unusual was that, as part of my new appointment, the organisation required me to attend the full ten-week academy as a delegate. This was despite the fact that I was already an experienced and well established WCM practitioner. And my Support had already been through the Academy and has been active in his Sorting Office for almost a year.

Then things became even more curious. During one of the weeks I was asked to deliver the Workplace Organisation module as a coach.

So the arrangement became a rather strange one. For nine weeks I sat in the room as a delegate going through stuff that I had been doing for several years. Then for one week I stood at the front of the room as the coach. It was an odd mix of roles to say the least.

It felt unnecessary, the academy was more targeted at people new to WCM. I believed that, given my experience, I would bring far more value by getting straight to work in my new region rather than wasting ten weeks sat in a room learning the basics again. Both my new Regional Manager, Gerry, and I tried to push back, but our efforts fell on deaf ears, and I had no choice but to attend.

Cards on the table time. One of my big concerns wasn't the content; it was the exam. I was genuinely worried that I would fail, not because I didn't know the material, but because I've always struggled with exams.

The very environment of an exam transports me back to school, causing my brain to freeze up. Even though I understood the content, I feared I'd be perceived as a fraud if I couldn't perform under test conditions. I put an incredible amount of stress and pressure upon myself. Classic imposter syndrome symptoms right there!

Imposter syndrome is the feeling that you're not as capable or skilled as others think you are, even though there's evidence that you're successful.

People with imposter syndrome often doubt their abilities and fear being "found out or exposed" as a fraud, even when they've earned their achievements or status through merit.

The term originated in the 1970s by two psychologists (Pauline Clance and Suzanne Imes). They did a study on successful women who felt they didn't deserve their accomplishments. As the study went on it became clear that imposter syndrome can, and does affect anyone, regardless of gender, experience, or profession.

I’ve suffered with this so many times in my life, as have most people. It's that nagging feeling of "I don’t belong here," even when all the facts say you do.

Anyway, I attended the academy, and to be honest, it was a frustrating experience for much of the ten weeks. During the pillar coaching sessions, I noticed that the delivery methods and explanations of the framework's logic often missed the mark. The essence of the Professor's logic, rooted in people development, involvement, and pace, was being diluted.

Instead, the focus seemed skewed towards cost-saving, rather than maintaining the human-centric principles at the core of WCM.

It felt like watching someone trying to explain the Big Bang and the birth of the universe but leaving out key details. Imagine asking Brian Cox to do it, and then swapping him out for John from number four. The basic message might still be there, but the critical depth and clarity are lost.

I didn't want to be "that guy," the one who jumps in constantly, correcting or showing off what he knows. I held back as much as I could. But there were moments where I felt compelled to intervene, not to undermine the coaches but to make sure the core principles weren’t lost. I tried to handle it tactfully, but I’m sure it was as uncomfortable for the coaches just as much as it was for me.

The whole experience led me to question the academy's true value. The concept is brilliant, but to get the best results, it needs a team of "Brian Cox's", experts who deeply understand the principles. Who have been there and done it. People who have credibility. People who can communicate with the right level of insight. Unfortunately, what we had felt more like a room full of "Johns," well, meaning but lacking the depth needed to deliver the true power of the message.

The soul-destroying approach of sitting in a classroom, staring at presentation after presentation, followed by "please refer to page 1139 of your binder," and then taking an exam, felt prehistoric, a carbon copy of the traditional education system.

I can just imagine the conversation that took place between the senior leaders in designing the academy:

"We need to train people to lead WCM."

"OK, let's get them in a classroom for ten weeks. Completely away from where the work actually happens so as not to get distracted."

"That is a great plan! To make it even better, lets remove the people essence of WCM and make it about saving money. That way it will pay for itself in no time."

"Yes, great idea, let's build some presentations for people to deliver, and follow it up with an exam."

"Ohh I like that. But people need stuff. Let's give them a ten-thousand-page blinder full of theory to carry around for the ten weeks."

"Brilliant! We've cracked this whole continuous improvement education thing!"

"Look at us, we've now got a continuous improvement culture!"

"Another scone anyone?"

I joke. But it was clear that this method didn't reflect a true understanding of continuous improvement or what the Professor was really trying to teach us.

The saying

"If you always do what you've always done, you'll always get what you've always got"

perfectly summed up the flawed thinking behind this approach.

Continuous improvement requires a people centric approach, on the shopfloor, encouraging innovation and hands-on learning. Not outdated training methods that failed to ignite any meaningful change.

What we should have been doing was heading to the Gemba, the place where the real work happens. We should have been speaking with postal workers directly involved in the processes, meeting with Line Managers and Sorting Office Managers who were living the transformation, learning from mistakes, making real shifts in culture, and driving results.

Observing, learning from people, understanding their behaviours, seeing the application of principles, and practicing empathy, that's where the true learning would have taken place.

Spending ten weeks in a classroom didn't feel like the right approach if we were serious about driving change and transformation. Continuous improvement is about evolution on the ground, in real time, through real-world scenarios and people, not through reading slides, or memorising the contents of heavy binders that we lugged back and forth for ten weeks.

If we wanted real, sustainable change, we needed to immerse ourselves in the environment we were trying to improve.

Rant over. I made it through the academy and, to my relief, passed the exam at the end! In fact, I ended up achieving the highest pass mark ever recorded at the time, 97.7%! I'll gladly take that; I probably spelled my name wrong somewhere along the way.

Launching WCM in my sector was an exhilarating experience, reminiscent of the time Terry and I worked together in the Mail Centre.

It involved a lot of creativity, as we sought innovative ways to engage both managers and frontline postal workers, sparking their interest and enthusiasm.

I was keen to ensure that I had the full backing of Gerry, as it was essential to establish a mutual understanding of what WCM was and, just as importantly, what it was not.

Strangely, senior leaders like Gerry hadn't undergone any WCM training; perhaps the academy would have been better suited for this demographic? I recognised that this knowledge gap, like a missing link in a chain, was critical for the success of WCM in our organisation.

I wasn't content with merely "doing WCM"; I was driven to achieve true operational excellence, and Jamie shared that same passion. For us, it was about implementing WCM properly, transforming the culture, and setting a benchmark for others to follow.

I had immersed myself in book after book on continuous improvement, reading brilliant works by leading experts like James P. Womack in Lean Thinking: Banish Waste and Create Wealth in Your Corporation, Jeffrey K. Liker with The Toyota Way, and Paul Akers' 2 Second Lean.

Each of these authors told the same story. They emphasised the necessity of a strong commitment to Lean principles from the top down. For us, Gerry represented that top leadership, and I felt it was crucial to test his understanding and commitment to these principles.

By engaging Gerry in conversation around the core principles of WCM and inviting him to share his views, I was really trying to understand where he stood. For something like this to succeed, leadership alignment matters. I needed to know whether he truly believed in the direction we were heading and whether he would be willing to stand behind it.

It was important to gauge not just his understanding, but his willingness to support the initiative and encourage others to move with it. Having that backing from the start would make a real difference in building momentum and giving the work the foundation it needed to deliver lasting operational excellence.

Unfortunately, I found it increasingly difficult to secure time with Gerry. Although we would agree on a meeting day and time, he often had to reschedule multiple times due to "operational issues". Often at the very last minute.

This was frustrating and led me to believe that his understanding and commitment to WCM weren't where I needed them to be. I would stress that if he could spare just a small amount of time, I could help him address these "operational issues" with solutions that fixed the root causes. However, he seemed to view WCM as an "extra" initiative, something that was bottom of the list, and could wait rather than an integral part of "the way we do things."

Classic mistake. Something that I see all too often in the organisations I visit now with Ever-So-Lean.

Over the following months, Jamie and I put forth our best efforts to advance the WCM agenda, but Gerry's actions frequently sent mixed messages to the region. His tendency to prioritise immediate operational concerns over long-term stability and goals undermined the progress we were striving to achieve.

When shortfalls occurred in any of the Sorting Office's within the region, Jamie and I often found ourselves dispatched to "support," which typically meant physically delivering the rounds ourselves. It felt like sheer firefighting in its purest form.

I didn't like it, and I certainly wasn't happy about it. But Jamie was on another level entirely. He absolutely hated it. Whenever we were told we had to go out on delivery he would be visibly fuming.

I tried to take a more balanced approach. I tried to stay positive about it. I tried to push back where I could. I even tried to argue the case against it. But every road led to the same place. We were going out on delivery.

I couldn't blame Jamie for being so angry. We both knew it wasn't right. The real issue was that Gerry didn't see it that way.

This disheartening reality highlighted the disconnect between our vision for WCM and the practical implications of Gerry's leadership approach. His inconsistent support not only affected team morale but also hindered our ability to implement meaningful change.

The constant back-and-forth between addressing urgent operational issues and pushing for a culture of continuous improvement created a challenging environment.

We were so eager to demonstrate how WCM could not only resolve these immediate problems but also lay a foundation for sustainable success. Yet, without Gerry's commitment to viewing WCM as an integral part of the operation rather than a secondary concern, we faced an uphill battle in aligning our efforts with the overarching goals of the organisation.

To shift this perception, I knew I needed to find a way to demonstrate the value of WCM in addressing the operational issues that Gerry prioritised. By illustrating how WCM could be a powerful tool for solving these problems rather than an additional burden, I hoped to change his viewpoint and secure his commitment to our vision.

As our first scheduled audit approached, I felt a growing concern about the lack of progress we had made and the potential implications for both Gerry and my own reputation.

Throughout my time in WCM, whether in the Mail Centre or the Sorting Office, I had consistently delivered results, raised the bar, and made a significant impact. I was a high performer, and with that success came increased pressure and expectations, both from others and from myself.

I knew we simply weren't ready to be audited properly. If it went ahead in that state, it would have been embarrassing for everyone involved and, frankly, a complete waste of time.

There was a small part of me that thought letting it happen might actually force a reality check. If the audit happened and they tore us apart, it might finally give Gerry the wakeup call he needed. And trust me, he really needed a size nine up the backside. But I couldn't take that risk, and I certainly couldn't sit back and watch my own reputation take the hit.

What we needed was time. Fortunately, I managed to negotiate a postponement by positioning it as a way to ease the pressure of a busy period on the auditors. It bought us some breathing space, which at that moment felt like a blessing.

But I also knew it was only a temporary reprieve.

The work still had to be done. We needed real progress, and we needed it quickly. The pressure to show movement weighed heavily on me because the standards I had set in previous roles mattered to me. If I didn't act decisively, we risked losing credibility and undoing the momentum we had worked hard to create.

Over the following months Jamie and I continued our charm offensive across the region. Jamie in particular did some fantastic work visualising risks and defects.

Take the junk mail that comes through your door. Things like leaflets from "Patty's Pizzas" offering a two for one deal, or those plain envelopes addressed to "The Homeowner" with a local estate agent fishing for business. In the postal world these are known as Door-to-Door items.

Customers pay for these items to be delivered within a specific catchment area. That could be national, regional, or even targeted down to a single street. Postal workers are paid per item delivered, on a sliding scale depending on the size and weight of the item. In my day it could range from around 0.1p up to as much as 0.5p per item.

It doesn't sound like much, but it quickly adds up. If you were paid 0.5p per item and had six hundred delivery points on your round, that was thirty pounds. It was rare to only have one Door-to-Door contract in a week as well. Usually there were two or three running at the same time. So it was quite easy to add thirty to fifty pounds a week to your earnings.

Sounds simple enough. But there was a complication.

Some households would contact the Post Office and say something along the lines of:

"Thank you for all these wonderful leaflets you're putting through my door every week. However, as amazing as they are we don't want them, so please stop delivering them."

That request would be captured centrally and passed down to the Sorting Office. A small card would then be placed into the Walk Log for that particular delivery round to notify the person delivering the mail that this household did not want them.

The problem was that although the information existed, it relied on someone actually finding it, reading it and acting on it for it to work.

The process said that before tying up their walk, the postal worker should check the walk log for any instructions specific to that round and then act on them before heading out. In reality, everyone was under pressure to get out on delivery. There was a lot going on in the morning, and that step was easily missed.

When that happened, defects occurred. Door-to-Door items would be delivered to people who had asked not to receive them, which then triggered customer complaints.

The default response from management was often to blame the postal worker. After all, the process hadn't been followed. But in a continuous improvement environment we go deeper than that. Blaming, coaching, or disciplining the person only treats the symptom. It doesn't address the root cause.

This is where Jamie did some brilliant work, first in our own Sorting Office and later across the wider region.

Visualisation is incredibly important in an operation because it removes the need to guess or go searching for information.

In many workplaces the information people need is buried in systems, reports, someone's head, or in this case a Walk Log sitting in a tray under the sorting frame gathering dust and coffee stains. When that happens people spend time asking questions, chasing answers, making decisions with incomplete information, or sometimes simply doing nothing at all.

Good, well placed visualisation changes that.

When the information is visible, the situation becomes obvious. You can immediately see what is happening, where the issue is, and what needs attention. It removes effort and creates clarity for everyone working in that process.

One principle I always come back to is this.

Put the answer where the question is.

If someone is asking “What should I do here?”, the instruction should be visible at that point.

If the question is “Is this correct?”, the standard should be visible.

If people want to know “How are we doing?”, performance should be visible where the work happens.

When the answer sits exactly where the question naturally arises, work flows better, decisions are quicker, quality improves, and people feel far more confident in what they are doing.

That’s the power of visualisation. It turns hidden information into shared understanding.

And that’s exactly the countermeasure Jamie introduced.

He identified every delivery point on a walk (delivery round) that had requested no Door-to-Door items and placed a simple symbol directly on the sorting frame to represent that request. With a bit of education around what the symbol meant, and a standard process for reviewing and updating the requests, the whole system became much easier to follow.

Now, when the postal worker was placing Door-to-Door items into the frame slots, if they saw the symbol, they would simply skip that address.

Simple. Clear. Effective.

It's a perfect example of what continuous improvement really looks like. Small, thoughtful changes that make the work easier to do right. Better for the customer, better for the employee, and better for the business.

Another example using a similar approach came after some analysis of dog attacks on postal workers, where effective visual countermeasures and clear processes were introduced that significantly reduced the number of incidents.

We pulled together the previous twelve months of incident reports and went through them carefully to look for trends and patterns.

Jamie did a brilliant job of combing through the detail, breaking the incidents down and stratifying them by things like location, type of dog, type of injury, and the underlying cause.

What quickly became clear was that one of the main root causes wasn't the dogs at all. It was human behaviour.

On many rounds there was a regular postal worker who knew the route well. When they were working the round, they would often carry dog treats in their pocket and give them to the dogs they saw every day. Over time the dogs came to expect it.

The issue came when that person was off and the round was covered by a floater. The replacement postal worker didn't have any treats. The dog, of course, didn't know that. It would run over excitedly expecting its usual reward. The postal worker, caught off guard, would panic and turn to run.

At that point the dog would give chase, thinking it was a game. Eventually the dog would catch up and jump up, often scratching or nipping the postal worker in the process.

The primary countermeasure was to educate postal workers on what we had discovered and encourage them to stop giving dogs treats on their rounds. That behaviour, while well intentioned, had unintentionally created the problem.

However, simply stopping the treats wouldn't immediately solve the issue. The dogs had already learned the behaviour and would still expect that interaction.

To help address this, we designed a simple visual system. We created small warning stickers that could be placed on the sorting frame to indicate that a particular address had a dog. The stickers were colour coded to give a quick visual cue, for example whether the dog was generally friendly or known to be a bit more boisterous.

These stickers were placed on the frame so that when the postal worker was preparing and tying up their round, they could clearly see which addresses required extra awareness. The indication would then be transferred to the bundle of mail, either with a small marking on an envelope or by using a laminated dog warning card that could be removed before delivery.

The aim of the countermeasure was simple. Increase awareness at the point of preparation so that postal workers approached those addresses more carefully, helping to prevent incidents before they happened.

I'm very aware that I've made this all sound quite straightforward. In reality, it was anything but. The work went into significant depth and took several months to complete.

What it really became was a bit of an eye opener into the quality of root cause analysis that was being carried out by managers at the time. Given the number of investigations they were completing each week, you might assume the standard would be fairly strong. Even more so when you consider that they had a very good template to work from. In theory, all they needed to do was follow the prompts, answer the questions, and complete the form.

But the reality was very different.

The quality was incredibly poor. Most of the reports we reviewed had symptoms recorded as the root cause, with very little real analysis taking place. The investigation often stopped at the first visible problem rather than digging deeper into why the issue had occurred in the first place. And the countermeasures that followed were rarely addressing the underlying cause.

Even I was surprised by just how weak the standard was, and my expectations going in were already fairly low.

What this discovery did do, however, was highlight another opportunity. It led us into a separate piece of work focused on raising the standard of root cause analysis across the management team.

We began defining what good looked like, strengthening the approach, and putting training and education in place to help managers develop the capability to investigate problems properly rather than just documenting them.

All of this became a clear example of the kind of results the WCM approach could deliver when it was applied properly. In truth, the work shouldn't really have been carried out by Jamie and I. Ideally, this sort of analysis and problem solving should sit with the operational teams themselves.

But that was a battle for another day.

At that moment the priority was to demonstrate what good looked like. To show, through a real operational problem, how the framework and tools could be used in the right way to understand the issue and put effective countermeasures in place. Once people could see it working in practice, it became much easier to start building momentum behind the approach.

In addition to the dog attack work, we managed to implement several small-scale improvements in other areas, and a site wide 5S application and education, that enhanced our visibility and overall impact.

5S is a great approach to organising the workplace so that everything has a clear place and unnecessary clutter is removed.

Sorting frames in particular have a habit of becoming magnets for collecting all sorts of rubbish. Under them, on top of them, down the sides. Before long there is clutter everywhere. I've even seen some postal workers turn their frame into something resembling a small kitchen larder, complete with tea, coffee, sugar and various food items tucked away.

When you strip away the fancy terminology, 5S is simply about getting back to what is actually needed to do the job. Sorting out what is required and what is not, putting the necessary items in the right place so they are easy to find and return, keeping the area clean and tidy, setting clear standards, and then maintaining those standards over time.

The real value is that it makes problems visible and removes a lot of the everyday frustrations people experience at work. It is also a brilliant place to start when introducing continuous improvement because people can see the difference very quickly.

This is why it was such a great approach for us to get active as quickly as possible.

Ultimately, we wanted people to improve their own workspace, take pride in it, and start to see that small, practical improvements can make a real impact. But let's not run before we can walk. For now I was happy to roll my sleeves up and help get it done.

I had also built a strong and positive relationship with the trade union, both on site and at regional level. As it happened, the regional representative was based upstairs in one of the offices, which meant we spoke regularly. Over time we developed a good level of trust, built on being open and straight with each other. From what I could see, that hadn't always been the case in the past between WCM and the union.

I was really pleased with how that relationship developed, because it created a solid foundation to work from. When there is honesty and mutual respect in the room, it becomes much easier to move forward together. It helped create a more constructive environment where we could focus on making improvements and working towards the same goals.

As we entered our rescheduled first audit, we were in a better place than we were the first time around. But I knew we barely had enough to demonstrate any real traction.

Fortunately, I had managed to warm up one of the auditors beforehand, whom I'd met once or twice at the Mail Centre. He knew my background and experience in this space which really helped.

I explained the issues we were facing with Gerry and outlined my plan for moving the agenda forward. I asked him to be honest and direct in his feedback, ensuring that he left a sense of urgency without causing anyone to become despondent, just enough to give me something to work with.

On the day of the audit, I crafted a positive narrative around our minor accomplishments, and the Sorting Office looked impressive following the 5S implementation.

The pillar leads somehow managed to get through their presentations with minimal setbacks. However, throughout the audit Gerry appeared uncomfortable and distant. I couldn't blame him; I would feel the same way too if I had invested so little time and commitment into something that was now demanding a full day's attention for an audit. It felt as though Jamie and I were the prime representatives of WCM, while Gerry was there more out of necessity than genuine enthusiasm.

Totally unrelated I'm sure, but not long after this, it was announced that Gerry would be leaving, and while Gerry was a nice guy, his departure was beneficial us; I needed a leader who would actively support our initiatives fully.

The new regional leader, Eddie, arrived from Scotland with a wealth of experience and a track record of delivering some of the best results in the country.

In stark contrast to my interactions with Gerry, I secured time with Eddie almost immediately, and during our first meeting, it was clear that we were on the right path.

My biggest challenge was going to be understanding a single word he said!

It was aye this, wee that, bonnie this, followed by a good old blether about how dreich the weather was. It used to get right up my bugle. I couldn't understand why he didn't just come down the apple and pears and speak in my shell in a way I could actually understand.

When he arrived on site for the first time, I saw him walking the Gemba, actively engaging with postal workers and managers alike. He was accompanied by the Regional Director, smiling and genuinely eager to meet everyone. This hands-on approach not only set a positive tone for his leadership but also indicated his commitment to developing a collaborative environment.

Eddie appeared different, and this is exactly what I was hoping for. In fact, he proved to be everything I could have dreamed of and more.

Not only did he fully back our WCM approach, ensuring it became "the way we do things," but he also became an inspirational force in my own growth and development.

Jamie and I partnered with a few folks from the central customer team to develop and implement a new search-and-store process in the Callers' Office. This is the counter you go to, to collected a parcel or letter that couldn't be delivered because you were not home.

Traditionally, each Callers' Office had its own method for storing the letters and packages, and most storage areas were pure chaos, leading to stressful searches, long wait times, and frustrated customers and postal workers alike.

The new system was nothing short of revolutionary, a radical transformation from the old practice of frantically searching through containers when a customer came to pick up their package.

In Japan, they call this kind of sweeping change Kaikaku, meaning "radical or breakthrough improvement."

It's different to Kaizen, which you may have heard of before. Where Kaizen focuses on small, continuous steps which drive incremental improvement, Kaikaku is about bold, dramatic shifts that deliver significant results in a short period of time. And that's exactly what we were doing.

We introduced new technology, restructured the processes, redesigned the system to improve efficiency, reduced waste, standardised the process, and boosted productivity.

It was brilliant.

The new process involved returned packages being catalogued by a postal worker, by scanning a barcode on the package. This would then prompt a label to be printed with a location reference and a unique item code. These packages were placed into smaller containers on space-optimising roller-racking, designed to minimise the time it took to retrieve an item when a customer arrived.

One of the major benefits was that the system provided a real-time overview of where each package was stored, how long it had been there, and how many packages were being held at any given time.

Packages are only held for a defined period, and if not collected, they were automatically routed to another team in a central location, streamlining and simplifying this process as well.

When customers arrived, their collection slip was scanned, or even just part of their name or address could be entered into the system to locate the package.

The new system was designed with security in mind too, requiring specific forms of ID, which were logged digitally. It would then give the postal worker an exact location and unique item code to locate, dramatically reducing retrieval time.

This new process scaled efficiently during peak periods too, when additional postal workers were needed due to higher volume. What's more, the system was simple enough that anyone could perform the task with minimal training or support.

What made this transformation even more special was that we had achieved it from start to finish with full engagement from line managers, trade union representatives, and the postal workers directly impacted.

It was exactly what I had envisioned when I took on the role, a benchmark example of WCM executed the right way. The initiative wasn't just about implementing a new system; it was about cross collaboration with other teams and involving the people who worked within it every day. Their input was critical in helping shape the process. They were part of the solution, making their own jobs easier and significantly improving the customer experience, they owned it!

Just brilliant.

This collective effort really captured what Lean is all about. People working together, respecting each other's contribution, and focusing on improving the work.

The project became a strong example of what can happen when everyone, from the frontline right through to leadership, pulls in the same direction. It showed the power of engaging people properly and raised the bar for what future initiatives could look like. When people are trusted to contribute and take ownership, the results can be remarkable.

Over the months that followed, the Callers' Office became something of an attraction. Visitors started coming from across the organisation, everyone from other Callers' Office teams to senior directors, executives, and even board members, all wanting to see what was happening.

The level of exposure that the Sorting Office received was incredible. More importantly, the energy it created was contagious. The positivity around what had been achieved started to spread, building real interest in continuous improvement throughout the building.

Eddie wasn't just stabilising the region since taking over; he was also garnering significant attention for leading the way with WCM initiatives. This, in turn, increased exposure for Jamie and I, with almost daily requests for support and site visits flooding in.

The momentum continued to build when we were invited to showcase our storyboard and impact on a trade stand at a national WCM convention in the Midlands. This event allowed us to further highlight the success of our work and generate more interest in our approach. Not to mention the exposure.

A few weeks later, the attention reached new heights when we were visited by a board member, Darren, a super senior, high-flyer in the organisation.

His visit centred around our work in the Callers' Office, where a postal worker took him on a full tour of the improvements we had made.

In a moment of spontaneity, I challenged him to serve a customer, despite his having no training or prior experience with the system. To my delight, he accepted the challenge, and to my relief, he was able to complete the entire process flawlessly.

It was the ultimate test of the system's simplicity and efficiency, and it worked perfectly.

At the end of his visit, he extended an unexpected invitation. He wanted the postal worker from the Callers' Office and me to join him at a leadership convention happening the following month at the NEC in Birmingham.

Initially, I thought this was just an opportunity to network and soak up the experience, but I was wrong. He wanted us to join him on stage to present our solution to a large audience of the organisation's leadership. It was an incredible honour, a true validation of the work we had done, and a clear signal of the impact we were making.

The NEC event was absolutely mind-blowing. I can't overstate the size and scale, it was massive, with tiered seating for the audience that appeared to disappear into the darkness!

The bass from the music was thunderous, literally rumbling through my bones, and the lighting was intense, transitioning between deep reds and purples. It felt like a full-scale production, and I loved every second of it. This was a bit of me.

A well-known BBC newsreader hosted the event, and the CEO kicked things off with an inspirational keynote talk, followed by several board members who shared insights and plans that normally would be reserved for only the most senior leadership circles.

During a break, the music dipped slightly, and then Darren's name, the postal worker from our project, and my name were called over the loudspeakers to report to "stage production."

“Bloody stage production” I thought. This is madness.

It reminded me of the setup that I saw at the Big Brother eviction nights all those years ago. It had the same buzz and excitement, only this time I would actually be on stage and not in the audience.

We eventually found the sound crew, where they wired us up with those sleek head worn microphones, the kind that wrap around your face and the wire hides under your shirt. They even dusted our faces with some powder to prevent any shine from the stage lights.

Then, before I knew it, the host introduced Darren, and then I heard my name and my colleagues, alongside some booming background music. It was Katy Perry's "Firework", just the instrumental version, without vocals. Every time I hear that song, it transports me right back to the NEC that very day and that walk to the stage.

The stage lighting was so intense and focused that I couldn't see anyone past the third row. The heat from the lights was pretty overwhelming too. Almost melting my cheap shiny suit!

We gave our twenty-minute presentation and ten-minute Q and A, with Darren leading the way, followed by the postal worker who walked through the process and its benefits.

I closed by explaining how we implemented the solution with such engagement, and was creating such a positive culture for change. Everything flowed perfectly, and Darren was clearly thrilled with how it all went.

I was absolutely buzzing, it was like presenting at an audit, but on a much grander scale, and I loved every minute of it! This was the moment I fell in love with the stage all over again. The energy, the bright lights, the chance to engage an audience and inspire them. It felt so natural, and I realised this was something I was meant to do. Connecting with people, and driving positive change, there is nothing else quite like it.

It took several weeks to come down from the high of the NEC event, and we continued to received visitor after visitor, all eager to see our Callers' Office in action. Even today, years after Jamie and I left the post, I still smile whenever I visit my local Callers' Office as a customer, and see the process we introduced being used. I'm sure it's evolved since then, but the core of it, the essence and the history, came from the hard work, innovation, and dedication of the team we had back then. It's a proud reminder of what we were able to achieve together, and it stands as a lasting legacy of that incredible period.

Eddie had been with us for about eight months, and during that time we continued to develop the CI culture within the region. While not everything worked perfectly, things were definitely moving in the right direction. Eddie and I had built a strong rapport, he frequently took the time to help me develop a deeper understanding of the senior levels of the organisation. He was also an incredible role model, consistently demonstrating the behaviours of a true leader with authenticity.

One afternoon, Eddie called me and invited me up to his office. His office was practically right above mine, and it wasn't unusual for us to float between the two.

I sat down as he made us both a cup of coffee, and we chatted casually about his upcoming two-week holiday with his family. He was heading somewhere warm and sunny to recharge, and after all his hard work since taking over, it was well-deserved. He had the full support and respect of everyone who reported to him within the region.

Then, out of the blue, in his deep, authoritative Scottish accent, he asked if I would be interested in stepping up to cover for him during his time away. He explained that he had already discussed it with the Regional Director, and they were both in agreement that I was the right person for the role. He then added, with a hint of encouragement, that if all went well, this wouldn't be a one-off opportunity, it could open the door to greater responsibility.

I was speechless, completely blindsided!

There were Sorting Office Managers in the region who were significantly higher graded than me, and far more experienced in terms of managing the operation, yet Eddie wanted me to lead the region.

Once I regained my composure, I enthusiastically accepted. Eddie told me that over the coming weeks, he wanted me to join his daily calls so I could get a feel for the format, the information flow, and how to handle the responsibilities.

I left his office, floating down the stairs back to mine, still trying to process what had just happened.

When I got back, I looked at Jamie and I casually asked

“Do you want a coffee? Oh, and by the way, when Eddie’s on holiday, you’ll be stepping up into the Champion’s role.”

Jamie looked at me with a shocked and concerned expression, before following up with

“What? Why? Where are you going?”

I replied with a smile

“Not far. In fact, I’ll still be sitting right there, I’ll just be leading the region while covering for Eddie.”

Jamie grinned, clearly thrilled for me, and I was equally excited to give him the opportunity to step up and lead the WCM activity. It was an exhilarating time for both of us!

I adapted to leading the region well and quickly found my rhythm with the cadence of reporting and daily calls. Eddie had prepared me so thoroughly that it all felt structured and well-planned.

It was important for me to get out to the all of the fifteen Sorting Offices within my region. I wanted to walk the Gemba at each location so that I could visualise the operations when on calls or reporting. Having a visible presence early on was also crucial, those who didn’t already know me needed to, and for those who did, I wanted them to feel comfortable with my new role, however long it might last.

The Sorting Office Managers were generally very supportive, with really only one or two that needed a bit of time to get used to the change, but it was nothing that caused any significant concern.

My new peers were also fantastic. They involved me in conversations during meetings, asked for my input, and spoke openly in front of me, even when the Regional Director wasn't present. It helped that Ant was now one of my peers as well. You might remember Ant, he was the one I had supported for a WCM audit at one of his his Sorting Offices shortly after my son was born, and he later gave me the opportunity to be a Sorting Office Manager at one of his sites.

Ant's support wasn't just professional; it felt personal too. He assured me that I could reach out to him anytime for advice or assistance, which was a gesture I deeply appreciated. His encouragement not only made the transition smoother but also reinforced the camaraderie I valued so much. I had immense respect for Ant, he was highly experienced, having been a trailblazer for WCM within the function, and he understood operations inside out.

Knowing that someone of his calibre was backing me gave me an extra boost of confidence and solidified the foundation of trust and support that I knew would help me succeed.

During the fortnight I covered for Eddie, I had to put a few fires out. A few of the smaller sites had failed to meet their workload targets for various reasons, and these needed to be reported to the Regional Director on one of the two daily calls.

Fortunately, there was an excellent mechanism in place for addressing safety incidents or workload failures, which I suspect had originated from Ant given its structure. In either occurrence, it was standard practice to present an A4 Root Cause Analysis (RCA) document during the daily call.

This process was highly effective and demonstrated that WCM was becoming embedded into the region's daily operations. This document was then used by the Regional Director as he fed up the chain of command.

Each morning, I had a call with the Sorting Office Managers at around 8am, during which they would inform me of any potential issues.

By 8:45am, just before my first call with my peers and the Regional Director, they would provide an update. Managing the level of detail I shared during these calls was crucial. But it was also an art that I had to learn. If I underplayed an issue, it could leave the Regional Director underprepared and potentially exposed. On the other hand, offering too much information could cause unnecessary panic and overreaction.

I had seen both scenarios play out in real time while sitting in with Eddie previously, and I knew it was essential to strike the right balance. This was probably Eddie's most valuable piece of advice before he went on holiday.

The first time I encountered a significant issue, I called Ant before the 9am call to seek his advice on how to frame it properly. His guidance was invaluable in helping me present the situation in a way that was neither alarming nor dismissive.

You could tell that he had been in the game for a long time, he helped me put a spin to it that JK Rowling would be delighted with. It wasn't being deceitful, or deceptive. It was about framing the information in the correct way. Very clever and it made a huge difference to how the information was received. This is a leadership skill that I have found priceless over the years since.

As the two weeks progressed, I became better at asking the right questions to my Sorting Office Managers to ensure there was a solid plan in place to recover from any potential setbacks. Some of them had a tendency to understate problems, while others were prone to exaggeration. Learning to navigate these differences became a key part of my role.

There were times, however, when I found myself uncomfortably exposed. On occasion, I had to attend a second, 2pm Regional Director's call and report a failure, only to find that the Sorting Office Manager hadn't provided the necessary RCA on time, or to the required standard. This left me without a full explanation, which didn't sit well with the Regional Director.

To say that he was quite an emotive character in difficult times would be an understatement. In situations of failure, his direct, rude, and sometimes outright aggressive style could make these calls quite challenging. After enduring a very public reprimand the first time this happened, I made it clear to my team that I would not tolerate being left exposed like that again. From then on, I was vigilant in ensuring that I had the right information at the right time to avoid further mishaps. It became just as much about managing him as it was managing my region.

I also had to deal with a serious disciplinary issue during that two-week period, which was a first for me. I'd dealt with minor bits during my time at the Mail Centre and in the Sorting Office Managers role, but nothing at dismissal level.

Thankfully, my strong relationship with the regional trade union helped to ease some of the friction and stress that could have otherwise escalated. However, as the situation unfolded, it became increasingly clear that I would have to dismiss the individual involved. It was a case of unauthorised absence and deception. The evidence was overwhelming. He had spun a web of lies and, with each conversation, only dug the hole deeper for himself. Had he simply been honest, held his hands up, and learnt from the mistake, the outcome may have been different. Instead, he chose a different path, and in the end there was no other decision to make.

This was my first experience having to make such a difficult decision, and I was determined to handle it thoroughly and by the book to ensure the person was treated with dignity, fairly and in line with procedure. Delivering the decision face-to-face made the task even more challenging, and I knew it wouldn't be easy.

As I drove to the Sorting Office for that meeting, I reflected on something my late Grandad once told me, he said

“Boy, if you ever have to dismiss someone in a disciplinary situation, never start by saying, ‘I regret to inform you’ or ‘I’m sorry to say.’”

He went on

“You shouldn’t apologise for delivering the decision because you’re not the one responsible for it; the individual made their choices, and you are simply following procedure”.

At the time he gave me that advice, I never imagined I’d actually need to use it, but now, it resonated deeply.

After all, you never hear a judge in a courtroom say

“I regret to inform you that you’re sentenced to ten-years in Wormwood Scrubs

Or

“With the deepest regret I sentence you to life without the possibility of parole. Reluctantly and with sorrow, please take him down to serve his sentence.”

It just wouldn’t happen.

The saying goes

“If you can’t do the time, don’t do the crime.”

I understood that it was my responsibility to conduct a thorough investigation, and that's precisely what I had done. I had all the facts, and this is what made the decision. This wasn't just about the decision itself; it was about upholding the integrity of the process and ensuring fairness for everyone involved.

When the moment came, I did it.

As expected, it wasn't easy. It was an emotional situation for the individual involved, and the trade union representative did their best to mitigate the consequences. But the facts were clear, and the decision had to be made. These situations are rare, but they certainly send a strong message. It demonstrated to everyone that I wasn't just a placeholder but someone willing to take difficult actions when necessary, reinforcing my leadership.

After the two weeks of covering for Eddie were over, I anticipated returning to my WCM Champion role, plenty of high fives, raised glasses, and a welcome home cake from Jamie.

However, that wasn't the case. For reasons I'm not entirely sure of, Eddie moved across to improve another part of the region (still under the same seemingly emotionally unstable Regional Director), while I remained in his role for about another three months.

Eventually, I transitioned to a different part of the region, and then again, several months after that, all again still under the same Regional Director. I did this for just over a year right across Kent and Sussex.

With this more permanent role came some valuable perks, including a company car, which was a nice touch. It was really the first time that I had ever experienced driving something nice and new. With the additional responsibility, the car, and the increased pay, I was really becoming quite the part. I even managed to get myself a nice selection of tailored, designer shirts.

With each role I would have my own private office. The office I had in one of the regions was quite impressive, featuring leather chairs and a stylish dark wood desk and conference table. Around this time, in a new way to combat my anxiety I became heavily invested in strength and fitness. I joined a gym around the corner from where I lived and was going three evenings a week. One of the instructors there met with me to understand what I wanted to achieve, and created me a personalised training plan to follow. I was even eating pre-prepared meals that I bought from a company that delivered them on a Sunday for the week.

After turning thirty, I discovered that I could not only gain weight for the first time in my life, but also maintain it. This, combined with my gym routine and healthy eating, meant I was looking great and feeling fantastic too!

While my anxiety symptoms were still present, but they were far more manageable than what they ever had been before.

However, there were occasions when self-doubt crept in more than I would have liked. There was a reason for this, which I'll address shortly. Before that, I want to share a memorable experience from my 30th birthday, an unforgettable celebration.

My wife had arranged for us to hire a boat on the River Medway for a few hours. I'd always wanted to drive a boat up and down the river. I imagined that it would be such a relaxing and calming experience.

My wife, my son who was still very young at the time, and I were provided with life jackets, and I was given a crash course in how to drive the thing. Then in the blink of an eye we set sail on the open waters!

Well that's a bit of an exaggeration, it was actually between the two locks as I didn't know how to open them. There was always a lot of people about and I didn't want to make a fool of myself. Or sink the boat we had hired!

It was still a good few miles in one direction though so plenty to see. I even had to manoeuvre multiple times to avoid other boats. Impressive stuff!

Although mooring at the end of our time came with a bit of a bump. Quite literally. But overall a fantastic experience.

After this we went for what I thought was to be a casual meal at a restaurant in town. With all that sailing I had developed quite the appetite.

I led the way as we approached the restaurant. I'm fairly sure I had my son strapped to my chest in a carrier as I pulled open the door and stepped inside. Before long a waiter came over and introduced himself, as they usually do. Then I happened to look up into the restaurant thinking

“It’s really busy in here, we might not get a table”.

However, after a little more focus I thought to myself

“I know him. What’s he doing here”

Then I noticed another face, and then another. Before long it dawned on me that every table was filled with people I knew. I was absolutely stunned. Friends and family had travelled from far and wide to be there and celebrate with me, including Terry and Jamie. Just incredible. I didn’t realise that I knew that many people!

That wasn’t the only surprise. During the meal, unbeknownst to me, a book had been circulating among the tables. It featured a photo of me on the cover, and guests had written heartfelt messages about their experiences and thoughts of me. A bit like a guestbook you’d see at a wedding, but focused entirely on me.

Later that day, when we returned home, my wife handed me the book. I was genuinely overwhelmed. As I read through it, I found myself choked up. Was this really how people perceived me?

The stark contrast between their perceptions and my own self-image was shocking. That book lifted my spirits more than I can describe, and do you know what? I still have it. It’s tucked away in my bedside cabinet, and whenever my confidence dips, I take it out and read through some of the messages.

Even after more than a decade, it serves as a reassuring reminder that perhaps I'm not doing so badly after all.

Anyway. During my time working under the before mentioned Regional Director, my confidence began to slowly dwindle. It was like it was being chipped away.

I was subjected to behaviours that I can only describe as bullying and aggressive. It wasn't a supportive or developmental relationship; it was more of a parent, child dynamic.

His leadership style, if you could even call it that, was based on ruling through fear and intimidation. It was classic command and control behaviours. Public verbal lashings, undermining, and demoralising behaviour were common.

He was far from approachable, and his region wasn't performing as well as it should have been. Instead of shielding the team from external pressures and working collaboratively to solve problems, he intensified the pressure on us and would snap into anger or emotive meltdowns at the flick of a switch.

This wasn't just limited to in-person encounters either; it happened frequently on calls and even in emails.

The work environment became toxic. Instead of focusing on leading our teams, much of the energy of my peers and I went into managing his behaviour. Often, we were literally treading on egg-shells. Tip-toeing around him in case he flared up like an angry bear.

I know I wasn't alone in feeling this way, it was a topic of conversation among my peers, and we all felt the strain. His behaviour reminded me of the school bullies I'd encountered earlier in life.

But here's the issue: I wasn't on a formal contract for the senior role I had been performing for the last year, so I relied on his approval, and good will to remain in the position. Basically I was completely stuck.

His unpredictability made the situation unbearable, but I hung on, hoping he would eventually move on. But it was becoming increasingly difficult to tolerate.

I remember one occasion when I was on a conference call with him and one of my Sorting Office Managers.

It was late in the day, so I took the call from home and had it on speaker so I could take notes as we talked through the topic. The discussion was around forecasted hours versus planned hours for one of my Sorting Offices for the following week.

The standardised spreadsheet we were reviewing had been completed by the Sorting Office Manager who was also on the call. Both she and I had already gone through it the day before, and I had approved the overall forecasted weekly spend.

Saturdays were usually the lightest day of the week in terms of volume, which should have been reflected in the hours shown in the spreadsheet. The issue was that she had made a simple mistake and placed Saturday's volume in Friday's column, and Friday's in Saturday's. We had both spotted it during our review the previous day. It didn't affect the overall weekly total, so I had approved the figures knowing the total spend would remain exactly the same. She fixed the problem on her local version, but the SharePoint version still had the error.

You would have thought we had committed some sort of serious offence the way he reacted. He completely exploded. Shouting and making both of us feel incredibly small.

I tried to calm the situation down, explaining that it was simply an error and that the total figures hadn't changed. But he wouldn't accept it. He just couldn't see past it having zero impact to the spend. He then went into a tirade about being unable to have any confidence in our numbers. Adding that we had let him down.

When he eventually paused to draw breath, we just sat there in silence. I don't know what the Sorting Office Manager was thinking at that moment, but I was completely taken aback. I was trying to make sense of what had just happened.

Part of me thought I must have missed something. Surely there had to be a more serious issue behind such a reaction. But there wasn't. When I played it back in my mind, the whole outburst had come down to one simple thing. The numbers had been put in the wrong column.

In the end I politely asked the manager to leave the call. Once she had done so, I asked him directly what on earth was wrong with him. Apparently, I was being disrespectful for making such a remark.

I remember telling one of my peers about this the following day. The worst part was, he acted like it was normal, like he wasn't surprised at all! We joked about it and I tried to draw a line under it, but it really concerned me.

Another time we were both on site at one of my Sorting Offices. We were in the large conference room at the former Mail Centre where I had been based when I was the WCM Champion. It was just the two of us in the room when, once again, he started directing that same bullying behaviour towards me.

By this point I'd had enough. I challenged him directly and we exchanged a few words. I kept it professional, but I was very clear about how disappointed I was with the way he was behaving. I told him that his actions weren't just affecting me, they were affecting the whole team, and worse still they were damaging the region's performance. I found his conduct shocking and far below what I expected from someone in a leadership position.

His response was almost childish. Like a kid on a playground taking his ball and storming off, he told me that from the following week someone else would be stepping into my role and I would be returning to my previous position as WCM Champion. When I asked him for the reasoning behind that decision, he ignored the question, sat down, and started heavy handily typing away on his laptop.

I wasn't prepared to just leave it there though. I explained that stepping back into a peer role after leading the team for so long would be difficult, particularly as I had spent a lot of time holding many of them accountable for performance. That change in dynamic would create real problems and, in my view, it wasn't fair.

Despite his declaration, the following week came and went and I was still in the role. My suspicion was that he simply couldn't find anyone willing or able to replace me rather than having any change of heart. By that point though it didn't really matter to me. I knew my own value, and I had already begun to realise that it was time to take control of my own future.

I applied for several Senior Operations Manager roles that I found advertised on the internal intranet. One of which was dedicated to leading a cluster of Sorting Offices in London with performance issues. I really liked the sound of this as it aligned well with my WCM skillset. It was also the same level that I had been a step-up at for the past twelve months.

Within weeks I was panelled, passed the board and was offered the role.

I held off accepting the position because I had also panelled for a project role focused on efficiency and workload planning. It was technically a step down from the level I had been working at, but the nature of the work really appealed to me.

Another big factor was the senior leader the role reported into, Harry. I had met him a few times previously and we had always got on well. There was a natural connection there, and I felt confident that working with him would be a good experience and great for my development.

In the end I was offered both roles. Strangely, they were offering exactly the same salary. I challenged that given the difference in grading, but it was made clear that this was the offer on the table.

While the Senior Operations Manager role was tempting, the opportunity to work on meaningful projects, combined with the chance to work directly with Harry, convinced me to go in that direction.

So that was that. I turned down the Senior Operations Manager position and prepared to move into the programme role.

But it didn't quite unfold the way I had been led to believe.

In the lead up to the panel I had spent quite a bit of time speaking with Harry about his vision. He painted a very exciting picture of what we would achieve together. He talked about the impact we could make and how he wanted me to bring my experience and thinking into the team.

However, when the contract arrived, something immediately stood out. My line manager wasn't listed as Harry. Instead, it showed Mike, a mid-level Programme Manager who reported into him.

I tried to get hold of Harry to understand what had happened, but he was suddenly nowhere to be found. My calls and messages went unanswered. I then spoke to Mike who brushed it off, saying it was just a temporary arrangement while Harry worked through some structural changes.

At that point I didn't really have much choice but to go along with it. I had already turned down the Senior Operations Manager role, and my position in Kent and Sussex had become pretty fragile.

I stuck it out for a couple of months, but... nothing was changing and I realised that I has been sold a tale.

Strangely enough, Amazon Logistics had approached me twice in the previous nine months, and then again the week before. They wanted to speak with me about a Regional Continuous Improvement Manager role.

This time the timing felt right, so I agreed to have an initial conversation with the recruiter who had reached out.

The call itself was very structured. After a few initial pleasantries, I was asked to give an example of a time when I had used continuous improvement methods to improve a process. I had no trouble answering that and talked through the Callers' Office project.

We then moved on to the next question, where I was asked to describe a time that I had influenced a stakeholder in order to achieve a goal. I spoke confidently about some of the work I had delivered in the Mail Centre, and it all seemed to land well.

At the end of the conversation the recruiter told me the next step would be a discussion with the hiring manager, which was arranged for two days later.

That conversation also went really well too, and I came away with a strong feeling about what the opportunity could become. At that time Amazon Logistics was still very early in its development. They only had a handful of sites across the UK. The role would involve leading a team across the South East, helping to define standard ways of working and driving operational excellence as the network grew.

They made it clear that they really wanted me for the role, which made me feel valued and wanted. All in all the opportunity sounded incredibly exciting.

The panel process was unlike anything I had ever experienced before. It consisted of four onsite interviews, one after another. It felt a bit like the final stage of The Apprentice. I sat through interview after interview, and as soon as one interviewer finished their hour, they left the room and the next person walked straight in.

Each interview lasted around an hour, and each interviewer asked two competency-based questions that required examples from my past experience. What struck me was how different each person was in their approach. Some were very serious and direct, others more relaxed and conversational. Despite the different personalities, the structure and depth of the questioning remained consistent throughout.

The whole experience was fascinating. It was intense and quite exhausting by the end, but it was also incredibly well organised. From start to finish the process felt professional, polished, and exactly what I would have expected from a company like Amazon. At the end they even took me out onto the operational floor to see what it was all about. It immediately felt like home to me.

After a few nervous days waiting to hear my fate, I received the news that I was hoping for.

I was offered the position, and at that point I made the difficult and emotional decision to leave the Post.

Leaving the Post wasn't easy. My mind was full of mixed emotions. There was a strong sense of loyalty, and part of me felt like I was letting my late Grandad down by leaving a company he had always been so proud of. At the same time, there was also the excitement of what the opportunity with Amazon might bring.

The Post will always feel like home to me. It holds a special place in my heart because of the incredible people I had the privilege to work with and the personal growth I experienced during my time there. I joined when I was nineteen and by the time I left I was approaching my mid-thirties. In those years I had grown up. I achieved so much. I bought my first home, I got married, had two wonderful children, and worked my way up from a frontline postal worker to a Senior Operations Manager.

In many ways I felt like I was the Post through and through. Walking away was one of the hardest decisions I have ever made, but deep down I knew it was the right one.

I will always care deeply about that organisation and the people who keep it going. Perhaps one day I'll return in some capacity and repay it for everything it gave me. Not least the friendships and relationships that came from my time there.

Yes there were some very low moments along the way, but there were also some incredible ones that I will always remember.

There is undoubtedly enormous potential within the Post if it can work through some of its cultural challenges and become the best version of itself. At its heart it remains a very special organisation, built on the dedication, pride, and hard work of the people who deliver letters and parcels to every corner of the UK, six days a week.

Key Learnings Chapter 5

This chapter tells the story of a period of huge growth for me, both personally and professionally.

After the birth of my son, I faced another difficult battle with anxiety, something that had followed me for much of my life. Through support, routine, exercise, and learning to accept it rather than fight it, I gradually regained control. At the same time, I continued developing my leadership career within the Post.

I took on a challenging Sorting Office that was struggling with engagement, performance, and culture. With the support of strong leaders like Wilson and Ant, and alongside two committed step-up postal workers, we began to turn things around. It was during this period that I also formed a close friendship and professional partnership with Jamie, someone who would go on to become one of the most important people in my career.

Later, as a WCM Champion, Jamie and I implemented several impactful improvements across the region, including the breakthrough redesign of the Callers' Office process that gained national attention and even led to me having the opportunity to present the work we had done on stage at a major leadership event at the NEC. It was an incredible moment and helped cement my passion for engaging people and driving change.

During this time I also stepped into senior leadership for the first time, which gave me valuable experience and helped build my confidence as an independent leader. However, working under a Regional Director whose leadership style was poor began to chip away at that confidence and fuelled seeds of self-doubt.

However, I remained positive and resilient throughout. I refused to let someone else's behaviour pull me away from my goals. Instead, I focused on controlling how I responded, staying professional and remaining true to my values.

During that period I learnt to recognise my own self-worth and how to challenge behaviour like that in the right way. Experiencing that kind of emotional leadership also gave me an important perspective that has shaped my own style ever since. It taught me the difference between reacting and responding.

A reaction is driven by emotion in the moment. A response is shaped by thought and intention. From that point on, I made a commitment to myself to always try to respond to situations with clarity and respect, rather than react in a way that blames others or leaves people feeling small.

It was also during this period that I developed a vital leadership skill, the art of storytelling. Being able to frame a message in a way that resonates with different audiences requires a good level of emotional intelligence. Over the years, that ability to shape a narrative with clarity and purpose has proven incredibly valuable.

Eventually I decided it was time to take control of my own future. And after being approached by Amazon Logistics and going through a rigorous interview process, I was offered the role of Regional Continuous Improvement Manager.

Leaving the Post was one of the hardest decisions of my life. I had spent almost fifteen years there, starting as a postal worker at nineteen and working my way up to senior leadership roles. The Post gave me friendships, experiences, and opportunities that shaped who I am today.

But sometimes growth means drawing a line and moving on. While I was excited for the new chapter ahead, I left with deep respect and gratitude for the organisation and the people who make it what it is.

2013

My 30th birthday, celebrating on the boat we hired for the day. Look closely and you'll spot the book everyone wrote in, sharing their memories, stories, and thoughts about me. A really special thing to have.

2013

Terry and I with my son. Terry kindly traveled so far to celebrate my 30th Birthday with me.

Moya Greene

CHALLENGE AND OPPORTUNITY

2014

Our work in the Caller's Office drew widespread attention.

This an article from "The Courier". A central, internal publication that went to every postal worker in the UK (past and present).

The photo is Jamie and I alongside the amazing postal workers who

2014

One of the no door-to-door stickers being applied to a sorting frame. Simply but really effective solution.

2014

Our first WCM Audit

Here I am opening our first WCM Audit. Setting the scene in an attempt to limit the damage.

2014

Here the postal workers from the Callers' Office are presenting their project storyboard to the Auditors.

They were nothing short of incredible!

2015

Taken at a children's play center near my base sorting office during a lunch break with my family.

You can see in my face that I was starting to burn out.

Amazon was everything I had imagined, and more. It prides itself on being "peculiar," and that's exactly what it was, but in the best way possible!

The open-plan offices and casual dress code were both intentional, designed to break down barriers between management levels. The sheer scale of the organisation is almost beyond comprehension, and its embrace of innovation is second to none.

One of the first things that really struck me when I joined Amazon was being introduced to the Leadership Principles. They were not presented as a poster on the wall or something nice to reference now and again. They were introduced as the standard that guided how decisions were made and how all Amazonians (employees) were expected to behave every single day.

Very quickly it became clear that these principles were deeply embedded in the culture, and were a huge part of what had made the organisation grow at the pace it had.

Conversations, meetings, hiring decisions, and performance discussions were all anchored around them. People would openly reference them when challenging ideas or explaining their thinking.

What stood out most was the consistency. In such a large organisation, the Leadership Principles created a shared understanding of what good leadership looked like. They provided a common language that connected people across completely different parts of the business.

That experience left a lasting impression on me. It showed me what can be achieved when there are clearly defined leadership expectations, not just written down, but genuinely lived through the culture of every single function and department across the organisation. I found that they largely aligned with my own person values too. This made adopting them feel very natural.

Championed right from the very top, they reflect Jeff Bezos' vision of a fast moving, customer focused, and innovative organisation.

Let's take a brief look at the principles as they were during my tenure.

Customer Obsession

This is one of the cornerstones of Amazon. Everything begins with the customer. There are no exceptions and no shortcuts. The expectation is so simple: start with the customer and work backwards from there.

What this does is feed a culture where the customer experience is the ultimate measure of whether something is working or not. In many ways it reminds me of organisations like John Lewis, where customer satisfaction is treated as a serious performance indicator rather than a nice idea on a poster.

Feedback from customers is not seen as an inconvenience, which is something I have seen in other organisations in the past. It is treated as valuable information that helps shape better products, better services, and better decision making. This supports people to grow and develop through fact and data led decisions.

What really impressed me right from the start was how deeply this thinking runs through the organisation. Decisions are constantly tested against a simple question: does this make the experience better for the customer?

I genuinely struggle to think of anyone who has told me they received poor service from Amazon. Even when something goes wrong, people often come away saying they were looked after and that the issue was resolved quickly and fairly. That is not by chance. It is the result of a very deliberate and consistent commitment to customer satisfaction.

It is not just about keeping customers happy in the moment. The mindset goes further than that. It is about earning trust over time. It's the belief that when customers know that problems will be resolved and that their experience matters, loyalty will follow naturally.

Calling it customer focus almost understates it. It just doesn't do it justice. In reality it is much stronger than that. It is a genuine obsession with understanding what customers need and doing everything possible to meet those needs better than anyone else.

When everyone, in every role, in every department are pulling in that same direction, this becomes part of the culture, it influences how people think, how they make decisions, and how they approach their work every single day.

And when a whole organisation thinks that way, the results speak for themselves.

I know I am not alone in what I am about to say. I have heard many former colleagues describe exactly the same experience. Once you have operated in an environment where the bar for customer experience is set so high, your expectations of other businesses change dramatically.

What once felt like good service quickly begins to feel plain average. The standard you come to expect becomes much higher. The trouble is that not every organisation operates with that same mindset. As a consumer you often find yourself frustrated, wondering why something that seems so obvious is being handled so poorly. Simple things that should be easy suddenly feel unnecessarily difficult.

That said, there are organisations that clearly get it, and prove that the bar is raising across industries. John Lewis is a great example, as I mentioned earlier. Octopus Energy is another. These companies show that putting the customer genuinely at the centre of decision making is not limited to one industry or one type of business. It is a choice.

What it demonstrates is something Jeff Bezos understood a long time ago. When an organisation truly commits to putting the customer first, it changes how decisions are made, how problems are solved, and how people approach their work every day. Customer obsession is not a slogan. It is a standard. And when you have experienced what that looks like in practice, it becomes very difficult to accept anything less.

Ownership

This one is about taking genuine responsibility for the long-term success of the organisation. It asks people to think beyond their role, job title, their department, or the task they're focused on. Instead, the expectation is to think and act like an owner. Like you are the CEO of your process.

When you approach your work with that mindset, something changes. You begin to care so much more deeply about the outcomes, not just the immediate activity. Decisions are made with the long-term health of the business in mind rather than short term convenience. This applies to everyone.

In many ways it reminds me of how family run businesses operate. The people leading them see themselves as custodians rather than occupants of a role. They are responsible for protecting and strengthening the business so that it can continue to thrive for the next generation.

That same thinking sits behind this principle. Ownership means stepping in when something needs fixing, even if it sits outside your immediate remit. It means being willing to challenge poor standards, to raise problems rather than ignore them, and to follow things through until they are properly resolved.

It also means avoiding the classic trap of saying "that's not my job".

When people think like owners, that phrase disappears really quickly. Instead you see people taking accountability for the bigger picture, understanding that every action, every decision, and every standard contributes to the success of the organisation as a whole.

If you had asked me back in 2015 whether I believed that I, and the teams I was leading, demonstrated real ownership, I would have said yes without hesitation. And I would not have been lying. At that point in my career I genuinely believed we did.

But looking back now, having experienced what true ownership looks like in practice, I can see that the bar was far higher than I realised. What I thought was ownership at the time was really just people doing their jobs well and taking pride in their work. That is important, of course, but it is not quite the same thing.

But this level of ownership does not appear by accident. It only exists when the environment allows it to exist.

As leaders, I strongly believe that we carry a huge responsibility here. If we really want people to think and act like owners, they must feel trusted to make decisions. They must feel safe to speak up when something is not right. They must know that raising a problem will not lead to blame, but to support in fixing it.

If the environment is overly controlled, if every decision requires approval, or if people are criticised when things go wrong, ownership quickly disappears. In those environments people learn to stay in their lane, keep their heads down, and do only what they have been asked to do.

Ownership grows in a very different kind of culture. It happens when we set clear expectations, give people the autonomy to act, and encourage them to take responsibility for improving the work around them. When people know they are trusted, and when they see that their voice really does matter, they begin to care more.

Invent and Simplify

Innovation has always been a core part of Amazon's thinking, it's probably the thing that attracted me to the organisation more than anything else. But it does come with a very clear expectation.

That is that we do not innovate for the sake of it. It's not a tick box exercise. The goal is not to create something new or clever. The real aim is to make things better by making them simpler. Not more complicated.

In many organisations innovation can unintentionally create more complexity. New technology, new systems, new processes, new layers of work. Then before you know it something that was meant to improve things actually makes life harder for the people using it.

Invent and Simplify pushes hard in the opposite direction. The best ideas are the ones that remove friction, strip away unnecessary steps, and make things easier for the people that you are responsible for, employees and customers alike.

That kind of simplicity rarely comes easily. In fact, achieving it usually demands a lot of careful thought. Simplifying something usually means stepping back and challenging assumptions that may have been in place for years. It requires asking basic questions about why things are done the way they are, and having the courage to rethink processes that have simply been accepted over time.

A big part of making this work is involving the right people. The people who carry out the work every day hold insights that no process map or report can fully capture. They understand where the frustrations are, where time is lost, and where unnecessary complexity has crept in.

It sounds crazy, but this is so often not the case. We exclude these people, and try to change them, rather than them being part of the change.

The answers are often already there, sitting with the people closest to the work. When we actually take the time to listen, and give those people the opportunity to shape the solution, simplifying things becomes far more achievable.

In my experience the real discipline here is resisting the temptation to over engineer solutions. Sometimes the smartest thing you can do is remove something rather than add something. Fewer steps. Fewer handovers. Less confusion.

Are Right, A Lot

Here we are talking about judgement. Leaders are expected to make good decisions more often than not. That does not mean they are perfect, and it certainly does not mean they never get things wrong. It means they develop the ability to consistently land on the right side of decisions because their thinking is grounded in evidence, experience, and curiosity.

One thing that stood out to me was the emphasis on using data to inform decisions. Opinions and instincts still have their place, but they are not enough on their own. This was something that the Professor used to push too.

Decisions are expected to be supported by insight, by evidence, and by a genuine effort to understand what is really happening rather than what we assume is happening.

There is also a humility in this principle that I think is often overlooked. Being right a lot requires being willing to challenge your own thinking. It means actually seeking out different perspectives, listening to people who may see the problem differently, and being open to changing your mind when the evidence points you in a better direction.

In my experience, the leaders who make the best decisions are rarely the loudest voices in the room. They are the ones asking the most questions. They are curious. They dig into the detail, they look at the data, and they invite others to challenge their assumptions.

A key indicator for me of the maturity of an organisation who value Are Right, A Lot, is if decisions are less about hierarchy and more about understanding. It's usually pretty clear to me when I begin to observe, and ask questions.

This principle has to be lived. People need to see that decisions are grounded in reality (whatever that may be) rather than ego.

Learn and Be Curious

This principle speaks to something I believe sits firmly at the heart of personal and professional growth. No matter how experienced someone becomes, there should always be a willingness to keep learning. Curiosity is what keeps people moving forward. It stops us becoming comfortable with what we already know and encourages us to explore what we do not.

What I appreciate about this thinking is that learning is not reserved for certain roles or stages of a career. It is expected from absolutely everyone. Whether someone is just starting out or has been leading people and departments for years, the mindset is the same. Stay curious. Ask questions. Keep developing.

In reality, it's curiosity that drives improvement. When people ask why something works the way it does, or whether there might be a better way, new ideas begin to emerge. It creates an environment where learning becomes part of everyday work rather than something that only happens in a classroom (and you know where I stand on that).

I have heard from several people that Unilever has built a strong reputation in this area. There seems to be a genuine commitment to developing people over the long term rather than just focusing on the role they are doing today.

The thinking is that leadership and capability are not fixed qualities that some people have and others do not. They develop over time through experience, reflection, and a willingness to keep pushing yourself to grow.

Personally, I have always believed that the moment we think we have nothing left to learn is the moment we start to fall behind. The world moves quickly, industries change, and new ideas constantly emerge. The leaders who stay relevant are the ones who remain open minded enough to keep learning, curious enough to keep asking questions, and humble enough to accept that there is always more to discover.

Hire and Develop the Best

This principle is about recognising that the strength of any organisation ultimately comes down to its people. Leaders are expected not only to bring great people into the organisation, but to actively help them grow once they are there.

Hiring well is obviously important, but the real responsibility begins after someone joins. Bringing talented people into a team means very little if they are not given the opportunity to develop, stretch themselves, and move forward in their careers. Strong leaders see it as part of their role to help others grow, even if that growth eventually takes them beyond their current team.

I have always believed that developing people is one of the most rewarding parts of leadership. When someone joins a team with potential and, over time, grows in confidence, capability, and impact, it is incredibly satisfying to witness. Sometimes that development happens through coaching, sometimes through giving people opportunities they may not yet feel ready for, and sometimes simply through taking the time to listen and support them as they navigate new challenges.

What I also came to appreciate is that strong organisations do not hold onto talent too tightly. In fact, quite the opposite. When people develop well, they often move on to bigger roles, new teams, or entirely new opportunities. That is not a loss. It is a sign that the organisation is doing something right.

In Bellevue, just outside Seattle, you have three enormous organisations sitting almost side by side: Amazon, Microsoft, and Google. Over the years I have seen many incredibly talented people move between these companies. It is quite common to see someone leave one, gain new experience elsewhere, and then return later at a more senior level than before.

What struck me about this was the attitude towards it. People are not held back or made to feel guilty for exploring new opportunities. Quite the opposite. It is recognised that those experiences help people grow. When they return, they often bring broader thinking, new ideas, and a level of maturity that benefits everyone around them.

In many ways it creates a healthy cycle of development. People gain exposure to different environments, different leadership styles, and different ways of solving problems. As the weeks, months and years pass by, that experience compounds, and you see people come back stronger than when they left.

You start to realise that leadership is not really about the position you hold. It is about the number of people who grow because you were willing to invest time and belief in them.

When leaders consistently hire well and genuinely develop their people, the standard of the whole organisation begins to rise.

During my tenure, I worked incredibly hard and that paid off as earned substantive promotions twice. If I were to map that journey out, it would be marked by constant learning, growth, and opportunity. It wasn't easy, it was challenging for sure.

Each and every role brought its own hurdles to overcome, but those hurdles became some of the most valuable lessons I had.

With each promotion I was not just handed more responsibility. I was also given the mentorship, support, and space needed to grow into those roles. In many ways it was the "Hire and Develop the Best" principle brought to life.

That commitment to developing people played a huge part in shaping me as a leader, and it is something I remain incredibly grateful for to everyone who helped me along the way.

Bias for Action

Amazon is an incredibly fast paced environment. Anyone who has experienced it will tell you the same. To perform consistently in that kind of setting you have to become comfortable making decisions quickly.

This means that as leaders we need to act decisively. That thinking actually aligns closely with Lean principles, where progress is valued over waiting for perfection. The focus is on learning through action rather than endlessly debating what might happen.

You may have heard the phrase analysis paralysis. It is when people spend so long gathering information, weighing options, and debating possibilities that no decision is ever made. The intention is to get everything exactly right, but the result is that progress grinds to a halt. Instead of moving forward and learning through doing, people become stuck in endless thinking. It is surprisingly common.

For someone like me, who has always been a mega perfectionist and who naturally strives for excellence, adapting to this mindset was not easy at first. The idea of 80 percent now and 20 percent later felt uncomfortable. I had always been wired to try to get everything right before taking the next step.

It took me a few years to fully appreciate the value behind this principle. Once it clicked though, it genuinely changed the way I approach work. Now I struggle to imagine operating any other way.

A good example of this in my own world is the ***Ever-So-Lean Podcast***. The whole project has grown through hundreds, if not thousands, of small improvements over time. If I had waited for everything to be perfect before launching it, I would probably still be sitting on episode one.

Even today I still go back through the earlier episodes and improve things when I learn something new. Recently I redesigned artwork across the entire back catalogue after a breakthrough in my design skills. As my capability grows, my standards grow with it. It becomes a continuous cycle of learning and improvement.

Instead of waiting for perfection, I chose to start, learn along the way, and refine things as I went. Episode by episode the podcast has continued to evolve. Not only has that helped it move forward much faster, it has also made the journey far more enjoyable because I have developed so many new skills along the way.

Those same skills have even allowed me to help others launch and produce their own podcasts, applying the same thinking to support people who have the ideas but perhaps not the time or confidence to bring them to life themselves.

When I was leading teams at Amazon, I encouraged this exact mindset. I wanted people to feel confident making decisions based on the data and information we had available at the time. We were never reckless, but we also did not wait endlessly for perfect certainty. If the evidence pointed in a direction, we moved forward, tested it, and learned from the outcome.

More often than not, progress came from those small decisions made with confidence rather than from sitting around waiting for the perfect answer to appear.

Interestingly, over the years I have hired and worked closely with a large number of continuous improvement specialists, and I have noticed a pattern that comes up time and time again. Many of them have a natural tendency towards perfectionism.

It almost feels like part of the wiring that draws people into continuous improvement in the first place. When your role revolves around improving systems, reducing variation, and raising standards, it is easy to see how that mindset develops.

Of course, I am not saying that everyone in continuous improvement is built this way. But it is interesting how often I see it. There seems to be a strong instinct in many practitioners to want things to be exactly right before moving forward.

In many ways that attention to detail is a strength. It is what drives better processes, higher standards, and more thoughtful problem solving. But at the same time, it can also create a natural tension with the idea of moving quickly and learning through action. Balancing those two mindsets is often where the real growth happens.

As the saying goes, every day is a school day. And trust me, when you operate with a bias for action, you tend to learn a lot faster.

Frugality

Jeff Bezos has often spoken about the importance of doing more with less, an idea that closely mirrors the thinking Taiichi Ohno championed at Toyota all those years ago.

It is important to understand that frugality is not about cutting corners or lowering standards. It is about being resourceful. The focus is on making the very best use of what you have available, maximising value while minimising waste. That mindset becomes especially important during difficult economic periods, when careful use of resources can make the difference between survival and success.

One of the most well-known examples of this thinking comes from Jeff Bezos himself. The legendary story of how back in 1994 he walked away from a well-paid job on Wall Street to pursue an idea that many people at the time thought was risky at best. He believed the internet would change the way people bought and sold products, and he decided to act on that belief.

Amazon started life in his garage in Seattle as an online bookstore. In those early days money was tight and every decision mattered. Rather than buying expensive office furniture, he famously built his desk using an old door with lengths of timber as legs. It was simple, inexpensive, and perfectly functional. Rumour has it that he still owns and uses that desk today. I really hope that is true, because it captures the spirit of this principle perfectly.

Despite its materials, I bet it is worth a fortune now given its history!

Since leaving Amazon in late 2023 and stepping out on my own, I have found myself living this principle in a very real way. When you run your own business every decision about how you spend your time, money, and energy matters. Frugality stops being a concept and becomes a daily reality that you have to live by.

What I have learned is that frugality is not really about saving money. It is about thinking creatively. It pushes you to find smarter ways to work, to challenge unnecessary costs, and to achieve meaningful results without relying on large budgets or complicated solutions.

In many ways this is another principle that connects closely with Lean thinking. The discipline of removing waste, focusing on what truly adds value, and making the most of what you already have available.

The more you actively practice this, the more that mindset begins to shape how you approach problems and opportunities. You start to see constraints not as limitations, but as opportunities for better thinking. And often, some of the most effective solutions come from those moments when resources are limited but determination is not.

Earn Trust

It doesn't matter where you work or what role you hold, trust sits at the centre of everything. Whether it is with colleagues internally or customers externally, every strong relationship is built on it. Without trust, progress becomes slow and difficult. With it, almost anything becomes possible.

I hope some of the stories and experiences I have shared throughout this book have shown moments where things did not go quite to plan, particularly in situations where trust was missing. Those experiences were not always comfortable at the time, but they turned out to be some of the most valuable lessons I have learned along the way.

Over the years they have helped shape how I think about leadership and about working with people. This principle shines a big, bright spotlight on the importance of transparency, integrity, and building genuine relationships. When trust exists, it becomes one of the greatest strengths a person can have. When it is absent, it quickly becomes one of the biggest barriers to progress.

Earlier in my career there were times when, in my enthusiasm to solve problems and deliver results, I moved far too quickly. My focus was firmly on fixing the issue and implementing the solution. In doing so, I would overlook something equally important, bringing people with me and earning their trust along the way. Without exception, when I did this everything became so much more difficult. I would end up spending more time trying to fix problems created by the lack of trust than I would on anything else.

It was incredibly frustrating. Yet at the time I couldn't see that this was all of my own doing. Even when it was pointed out to me. I was completely blind to it!

As I have grown, I have come to understand that trust and respect for people are inseparable. You cannot truly have one without the other.

A real turning point for me came when I began to actually empower others. By giving people ownership and responsibility, something interesting happened. Work did not just move faster, it moved far more smoothly. There was less resistance, better alignment, and a much stronger sense of commitment from everyone involved.

By taking this approach, I found myself stepping back and looking at things from a much wider perspective. It gave me a far clearer view of what was really going on around the work. Something that I just never had before. From that vantage point it became much easier to see the strategic advantage of engaging people, departments, and teams much earlier in the process.

Those early conversations helped build relationships and understanding long before any change was introduced. Instead of constant resistance, there was far more alignment. Instead of closed doors, there were open ones. What once felt difficult and slow suddenly became far easier because the right people were already involved and supportive of what we were trying to achieve.

The best way I can describe it is the difference between trying to swim in treacle compared to swimming in water. I have never actually tried it, but I can imagine the feeling perfectly. One would be heavy, slow, and incredibly hard work. The other allows you to move freely and make real progress. That is exactly the difference trust makes.

It became clear to me that trust is not just important for relationships. It's the way to get meaningful work done in a way that supports long term success.

Throughout my journey I have also seen the other side of this. There have been many occasions where talented team members have taken ownership of significant projects and delivered impressive results. They hit the milestones, met the deadlines, and delivered strong performance improvements. On paper it looked fantastic.

But behind the scenes I found myself joking that I was following along with a dustpan and brush, clearing up the mess left behind.

What I mean by that, just as I once did, in their determination to deliver the result, they occasionally overlooked the importance of engaging with stakeholders and the people affected by the change.

When communication and relationships are overlooked, even successful outcomes can leave behind frustration, unhappy stakeholders, or damaged working relationships. Fixing those things afterwards can take just as much effort as the project itself, sometimes even requiring escalations or mediation to repair the situation.

With a little thought and care though, much of this can be avoided.

One of the habits I developed when I was delivering a program was to step back right at the start, and make sure I understood who was involved and who might be impacted by the work we were doing. In continuous improvement we often talk about systems, and systems are always made up of people.

A tool I have always found useful for this is a SIPOC. It's great because it provides a clear, high-level view of the process from end to end, helping you see not just the work itself but the wider system around it. It highlights who supplies the inputs, who carries out the work, and who ultimately receives the outputs.

More importantly, it helps bring visibility to the people connected to the process. When you take the time to see that bigger picture, it becomes much easier to engage the right people early, build trust along the way, and make sure that improvements strengthen relationships rather than unintentionally damaging them.

This is what a SIPOC looks like:

S	Suppliers	Who provides the inputs needed to start the process
I	Inputs	The materials, information, or resources required
P	Process	The high-level steps that turn inputs into outputs
O	Outputs	What the process produces when it is completed
C	Customers	Who receives and uses the outputs

Tip: Always start in the middle with the Process. Then work your way out either side.

By doing this exercise early, we can make sure that the right people are included, relationships can be built and maintained, and trust is strengthened throughout the journey.

Always remember that earning trust is not something that happens once and is then ticked off a list. It is built through consistent behaviour over time. It grows when people see honesty, humility, and a genuine respect for others in how we work.

Deliver Results

In any role, at any organisation there is of course always an expectation that people deliver results. And this is no different at Amazon. That mindset keeps people focused and accountable, making sure the work being done actually moves the business forward and supports the long-term direction of the company.

For me, to be an impactful leader and develop high performing teams, delivering results in the right way is just as important as delivering results itself. When we achieve results, we not only build credibility, but also gain the experience necessary to connect with others empathetically.

Let me give an example:

If I were to visit a doctor about some concerning symptoms, I might be impressed if the doctor provides a thorough explanation of the textbook definitions and theories.

Perhaps they even pull a copy of the textbook off of a shelf whilst I'm there and have a good read, or maybe even hop online. What they tell me may be technically factually correct, however, that wouldn't instil much of my confidence in their ability to diagnose my condition and find a solution.

Conversely, if I go to see the doctor and present the same set of symptoms, and they are able to draw upon real, practical experience in treating those symptoms effectively, maybe even with a few testimonials from past patients who have been magically healed by this doctor, my confidence skyrockets. I'm much more likely to trust their insights and commit to their action plan.

I understand this may seem like an extreme, unrealistic example, but the point remains clear:

I would much rather hear from someone who has "been there, done that, and has the t-shirt" over someone who merely read about it in a book, watched the DVD, or asked AI. It's that ability to draw upon real-world experience that builds trust, authenticity and credibility.

These leadership principles are the foundation of Amazon's distinctive approach to innovation, efficiency, and relentless customer focus.

Far from being just theory, they have evolved from Jeff Bezos' experiences, Lean methodologies, and a deep commitment to customer-centric business practices.

I still remember my first Peak season with Amazon Logistics. By that point I had only been with the organisation a little over two months. The site I was working at covered the ME postcode area around Maidstone in Kent.

It was Christmas Eve, approaching five in the evening, when a package was discovered with a NE postcode, meaning it belonged in Newcastle, Tyne and Wear, more than three hundred miles away.

I watched as the package was handed to the Shift Manager on duty. Naturally, I just assumed they would update the system, inform the customer of the delay, and hold the package until the first available delivery slot after Christmas.

What happened next completely took me by surprise, and at the same time made me incredibly proud to be part of the organisation.

The Shift Manager called a taxi.

Not to go home, but to drive the package all the way to Newcastle and deliver it to the customer.

At first you might think, that sounds ridiculous. But when you think about it from the customer's perspective, it starts to make perfect sense. That package almost certainly contained a Christmas gift. The impact of that customer not receiving it in time would likely have been far more damaging than the financial cost of sending it by taxi.

Just imagine the two very different stories that could follow.

Scenario One: The package doesn't arrive in time. The customer has no gift to give. They apologise to the intended recipient, everyone says it's fine, but really both people are disappointed. Later they both tell friends and family about the poor experience.

Scenario Two: A taxi drives the length of the country on Christmas Eve to deliver the package at a cost of say five hundred pounds. The story becomes one of amazement. Amazon went above and beyond to make sure the gift arrived. The customer and the intended recipient tell everyone about it. Those people then tell others.

Which story would you rather be told about your company?

The lesson for me was the everything comes back to the customer experience. Even when something goes wrong, the way you respond can turn the situation into something memorable for all the right reasons.

All of these principles keep the organisation agile and sharply focused on delivering value at scale. Amazon's rapid growth is a testament to how deeply embedded these principles are in its culture. Even to this day.

As great as it was, it wasn't easy adapting to my new environment. I had gone from knowing pretty much everything, all the analogies, products, processes and functions, into a new organisation where I had to start again. It was far more difficult that I imagined it would be.

I would be lying if I didn't admit that I had times in that first year where I felt lost, exposed and doubted if I had made the right decision. You could say that I was suffering from "imposter syndrome" again.

However, as time passed and I started making my mark, my confidence and knowledge grew, and those thoughts began to enter my head far less frequently.

With each achievement it became easier. As I continued to deliver results and build trust, my confidence grew. Over time I began to feel at home in the roles I held, comfortable in my abilities and clear about the contribution I was making. I was building my personal brand.

It's remarkable just how adaptable humans can be to their surroundings. Given time, we find ways to settle in and overcome hurdles that once seemed like insurmountable barriers, even things that felt completely out of reach at first.

During my incredible years at Amazon, I held a number of roles, each one increasing in scope and responsibility. From regional to national, European, and eventually global positions.

Each role provided me many valuable experiences and opportunities that helped me grow as a leader. There's truly no substitute for learning by doing. Although there's a role and a place for theoretical learning, practical experience outweighs theoretical learning, time after time in my view.

I was also able to see others grow and flourish as they progressed through their own careers. I had the privilege of seeing people develop in confidence, capability and belief in themselves over time.

On many occasions I was able to promote people who had worked incredibly hard and consistently delivered over a sustained period. Seeing them step into new roles, take on greater responsibility and realise their potential was a real source of pride for me.

In many ways, their success felt just as meaningful as my own.

One of the most valuable lessons I learnt came from travelling and working with people across different cultures. Early on, I made the mistake of trying to copy and paste solutions that had worked well in the UK, assuming they would land in the same way elsewhere. More often than not, they didn't. The ideas were sound, but the impact just wasn't the same.

I came to realise that no matter how strong a solution might be, simply lifting it from one environment and dropping it into another rarely works.

Different cultures interpret information, communicate, and approach work in very different ways. Each country has its own values, decision making styles, and ways of thinking. On top of that, there are different laws, regulations, expectations, and ethical considerations that shape how organisations operate. I was so naïve to all of this when I first started.

Looking back, it was a huge mistake to believe that a one size fits all solution would work everywhere. In many ways it can even come across as disrespectful.

But that was never my intention. The reality was that it just didn't even cross my mind. I simply lacked international experience at the time. It was something I had to learn through application, and those experiences helped shape a far more thoughtful and adaptable approach moving forward.

The same principle applies to leading people. Learning to understand and respect cultural differences, generational perspectives, and the different needs, beliefs, and working environments people bring with them takes time. It certainly did for me.

But once I took the time to slow down and really look at what I was doing, I began to truly appreciate those differences, then everything started to click.

Leading people became not only easier, but far more enjoyable. When you take the time to understand people and show genuine appreciation for who they are and what they bring, relationships grow stronger. People become more connected, more motivated, and far more aligned. That kind of environment is where high performance really begins.

Let me offer you some wisdom that has always stood the test of time. If you keep this in mind and shape your approach around it, you will find that your impact becomes far greater and your path far smoother.

We lead people and manage processes.

People are not things to be controlled or directed like a system. They need clarity, trust, encouragement, and the space to think and contribute. Leadership is about guiding, supporting, and helping people grow so that they can do their best work.

Processes, on the other hand are what we manage. They can be measured, improved, standardised, and refined. When a process is weak, the answer is not to blame the person working within it. The answer is to improve the process itself.

When you get that balance right, everything changes. People feel valued and motivated, and the work becomes more stable and predictable. Strong people and strong processes together are what create lasting high performance.

As you continue on your journey, it can be really easy to find yourself looking around and comparing your situation, your grade, status, pay, conditions, and achievements, with those of others. It's natural to look at others and compare ourselves.

But it's not healthy.

I know this because I've tortured myself in this way countless times over the years. The problem is that we often don't know the full story. Our minds tend to fill in the gaps, leading us to make assumptions. This can cause us to jump to conclusions and react emotionally, clouding our judgment and distracting us from our own unique paths.

It's important to remember that everyone is carrying their own struggles and successes, many of which we never see. Our most meaningful progress comes when we focus on our own journey rather than comparing ourselves with others.

When we focus on what we can actually control, our actions, our goals, and the direction we choose to take, we give ourselves the best chance to grow and make progress.

Speaking from experience, as someone who spent far too many years worrying about what other people were doing, I can tell you there is very little value in it. That energy is far better spent improving ourselves and moving forward. When we shift our attention back onto our own path, that's where real progress begins.

I'd been at Amazon for just over six months when I brought Jamie in from the Post. When I left, I'd promised him that as soon as I had the opportunity to bring him across to work with me, I'd make it happen. I had big ambitions for what we could achieve, and there was nobody I'd rather have had alongside me on that journey than Jamie.

The funny thing is, getting him in wasn't quite as straightforward as I'd hoped.

When I applied for my role about six months earlier, one of the steps in the process was an aptitude test. For me, that was almost a deal breaker. There was no way on earth I felt comfortable doing something like that. My brain just isn't wired that way, as we've already established.

I understand the idea behind aptitude tests in job applications. Employers use them as a quick way to see how people think and solve problems. Spotting patterns, working through numbers, logic questions, that sort of thing. From their perspective it's a standardised way of comparing lots of candidates and getting a sense of how someone's brain works.

The problem, at least in my view, is that it assumes everyone's brain works in the same way. And it simply doesn't.

Some people are brilliant at those kinds of tests. They can look at shapes, numbers, and patterns and solve them quickly. Fair play to them. But that doesn't automatically mean they'll be better in a real job.

For me, those tests never really played to my strengths. Sitting in front of a screen trying to decode puzzles under time pressure just isn't where I perform at my best. Give me a real situation, a real problem to solve, people to talk to, context to work with, and it's a completely different story. That's where I come alive. I can ask questions, connect the dots, see what's really going on, and work through a solution with people.

An aptitude test doesn't capture any of that.

That's why I've always felt the process is a bit flawed. It can filter out people who might actually bring huge value, simply because they don't think in the narrow way the test measures. In the real world, what often matters most is curiosity, judgement, experience, how you work with people, and how you approach real problems. None of that really shows up in a timed puzzle on a computer screen.

Jamie, however, was a different story. He had an excellent track record when it came to aptitude tests. So when I first applied, I asked him to give me a hand with it.

Problem solved.

Well... at least that's what I thought.

Six months later, when Jamie applied and had to complete the same test as part of his own application, he failed it!

I couldn't believe it. What a nightmare.

We had to find another route in. The workaround was to apply for a role in a slightly different job family so he could go through the process again. Thankfully it all worked out in the end, and before long he was back alongside me again as my number two.

We had some great times working together at Amazon. Together we led the work around standardisation, continuous improvement, and quality across the South East of the UK. A few months later I was promoted to lead the function across the whole of the UK, and Jamie stepped into the role to take over the South East.

Even now, years after I left Amazon and probably several years on top of that since we last worked side by side, I still don't feel like our story working together is finished. I've always had the feeling there's another chapter still to come.

One day I'd love to have him join me at Ever-So-Lean.

Let's see what happens.

I have to share a funny experience from around this time too.

In June 2023, one of my 40th birthday presents were tickets to the Eastbourne International Tennis Tournament at Devonshire Park. It was a beautiful day, one of the hottest of the year, and my son and I had an absolute blast.

What I loved most about it was the freedom once you were inside. Aside from Centre Court, where the top seeded players were, you could wander around and watch any match you liked. There were games happening everywhere, all at the same time. We got to see some brilliant players up close. Jannik Sinner, Liam Broady, Taylor Fritz, Coco Gauff, Harriet Dart, Heather Watson, just to name a few.

We bought a programme and my son spent the day collecting autographs. As the day started to wind down, we noticed where the players were coming in and out near the changing rooms. So we positioned ourselves nearby, hoping to catch a few more as they left.

After about ten minutes, a guy approached me and asked if I was playing.

Without thinking, I replied, "not today," as a bit of a joke. Then it hit me. He genuinely thought I was one of the players. To be fair, I was wearing a polo shirt, sunglasses, and a cap, I could see how he'd made the mistake.

At that point, I decided to have a bit of fun with it.

I thought, why not... I'll go with it.

He started asking me questions. Had I ever won a tournament? I said no, I've only made the semi-finals, which technically wasn't a lie. I told him it took determination and a bit of luck, but I got there in the end. What I didn't mention was that it was the Surrey Under 18s back in 1996.

After a bit more small talk, he pulled out his classic looking autograph book and handed it to me. I flicked through it and saw signatures from Andre Agassi, Tim Henman, Andy Murray, Roger Federer, Rafael Nadal, Pete Sampras, Björn Borg, John McEnroe, Boris Becker, even Stefan Edberg. This guy was a professional autograph collector!

As I went to hand it back, he said, "no, can you sign it as well?"

So I did what any creative minded person would do, I signed it.

I gave him a full blown, over the top, swirly autograph. The kind I imagine a professional tennis player might do. He thanked me like I had just made his day and hurried off.

My son looked up at me, completely confused, and said, "why did you sign that... you're not a tennis player."

I just smiled and said, "come on son, time to go."

Life lesson, you've got to fake it until you make it.

Throughout my career I have worked under a wide range of leaders. Some were truly exceptional, consistently demonstrating the right behaviours and offering genuine support. Others appeared convincing on the surface, but under pressure their true character showed through with impatience, stress, and a lack of authenticity.

Then there were those who were simply ineffective, lacking both the emotional awareness and technical capability required to lead people well.

Each of those experiences taught me something. The importance of respecting people, being authentic in how we lead, empowering others, and keeping our attention on what really matters, our own growth and development.

There were also times when my own self-perception didn't quite match reality. Hearing that you are not ready for the next step is never easy. In the moment it can feel frustrating and even unfair. But with the gift of time and reflection I have rarely looked back at those moments and thought my leader was wrong. More often than not they were right. I simply wasn't ready yet, even if I couldn't see it at the time.

As leaders, I believe that we carry a big responsibility to manage the expectations of others carefully. Particularly when people come to us looking for guidance around promotions or future opportunities. Being clear about development gaps, the milestones they need to reach, and realistic timelines is just a basic need if we want to build trust.

It isn't always easy, and it can certainly feel uncomfortable at times, but choosing authenticity, honesty, and transparency is always the right path. In the short term it might not make us popular, but it removes the uncertainty that so often leads to disappointment and frustration.

I've seen this from both sides. I've also been the person who was strung along and given false hope about opportunities that never materialised.

Experiencing that first hand taught me just how damaging it can be. It left me so frustrated, eroded any trust I had, and left me feeling misled and let down. That's exactly why honest and open conversations matter so much when we're leading others.

When people know where they stand, even when the message is difficult, it earns far more respect than avoiding the truth ever will. Clear and honest conversations create a healthier relationship, one built on understanding and trust. When people have that clarity and know what they need to focus on, progress and performance usually follow.

If you commit to something or make a promise and later realise you cannot deliver, perhaps because circumstances have changed, which of course happens from time to time, the most important thing you can do is address it openly and early. Speak with the people affected as soon as you can.

They may not like the news, but they will respect your honesty and integrity. Most people understand that things do not always go to plan. What matters is being straight with people rather than leaving them in the dark.

What really damages trust is the alternative. Avoiding the conversation, letting time drift by, and leaving people hanging only to disappoint them later. That approach erodes respect far more than an honest conversation ever will.

I've also worked under leaders who were power-hungry micromanagers, stripping away responsibility and accountability, removing autonomy and decision-making power. This left me with a great title, a decent pay check, but immense frustration, often draining my motivation and even causing me to disengage and withdraw.

Jeff Bezos provided some insightful analogies that resonate with me, and if you've heard me deliver keynotes you may be familiar with the concepts of one-way and two-way door decisions.

A one-way door decision is a decision that is very difficult to reverse. Once you step through it, you are committed, and if it turns out to be the wrong move it can be costly or even impossible to undo. These tend to be big strategic choices such as major technology investments, launching new products, restructuring parts of the business, or relocating operations.

Because of their scale and long-term impact, decisions like these should sit with senior leaders, executives, and boards.

A two-way door decision, on the other hand, is far easier to reverse. If it does not work out, you can step back through the door, learn from the experience, and try something different.

These types of decisions create space for experimentation, learning, and progress without carrying long term consequences. Because of that, they should sit with operational leaders, the people closest to the work and responsible for making things happen day to day. They are there to make decisions, test ideas, and move things forward, learning and adjusting as they go.

The thinking behind this is really simple. Leaders should encourage teams and people to take sensible, data led risks rather than slowing everything down with layers of approval and endless debate. Not every decision carries the same level of consequence, and treating them all the same only creates delay and frustration.

When organisations strike the right balance, they move far more quickly. Decisions are made closer to where the work actually happens, people feel trusted to act, and learning comes through doing rather than waiting for permission. This builds confidence and capability across the organisation, and innovation becomes part of the everyday way of working rather than something people are hesitant to attempt.

I frequently get asked

"How can we get our people to innovate."

This is how. No fancy systems. No grand gestures needed. Simply empower them to make two-way door decisions.

Understanding the difference between these types of decisions allows us to grow people. It creates an environment where people feel valued and engaged because they have the space to think, contribute, and take ownership of their work. When people are trusted to make decisions, even when it goes wrong, they grow in confidence, learn how to handle change, and develop the judgement that strong leaders need.

It also plays a huge role in retaining talent. Capable people want to contribute and make a difference. If we remove their ability to make decisions and constantly pull authority back up the chain, we risk disengaging them and eventually losing them altogether.

If we put our trust into people, support them, and give them freedom to act within clear boundaries without the fear of reprisal, we not only build stronger people today but also develop the next generation of leaders for tomorrow.

If we don't prioritise this development, when and how do we expect our future leaders to acquire these essential skills?

Throughout childhood, we are taught to categorise experiences in ways such as "correct or incorrect," "right or wrong," "true or false," "pass and fail," or "happy or sad".

These concepts are often presented as finite, binary, and black-and-white, conditioning our brains to see only two paths, one deemed good and the other bad.

Even the cartoons and movies of our youth subtly reinforce this binary thinking. Think about it: Batman and Robin are portrayed as good, while the Joker is bad, no in-between; Superman represents good, whereas Lex Luthor embodies evil; Spiderman is good, and the Goblin is bad. Here's an exam, the answers are right or wrong, you will pass or fail. It's all so binary!!

Now, many years later, as we step into the working world after all this social conditioning, what do you think our natural instincts are?

Do we gravitate toward freedom of creation, experimentation, learning, and scientific thinking?

Or do we find ourselves trapped in a mindset that insists, "I can't make a mistake or I'll get in trouble," or "If I get this wrong, I won't be promoted", or even "If I mess this up everyone will think I'm rubbish"?

This internal conflict can significantly hinder innovation and growth, making it so critical that we as leaders break free from restrictive mindsets and adopt a more dynamic approach to decision-making. To achieve this, we must create an environment where people feel safe, free from judgment, reprisal, or ridicule, and not chastised for things not going as planned.

Have you heard of psychological safety?

It is one of the most important ingredients when it comes to building a strong and high performing team. It's so obvious when you think about, but so easily missed. It means creating an environment where people feel comfortable speaking up, sharing ideas, and thinking differently without the fear of being criticised or punished if something does not go perfectly.

Mistakes will happen, that is part of learning. What really matters is how we respond to them. When people are encouraged to learn from mistakes rather than hide them, they grow stronger. Problems are surfaced earlier, ideas are shared more openly, and improvement becomes part of everyday work.

In an environment where people feel psychologically safe, they are far more willing to take sensible risks, challenge the status quo, and contribute their thinking. That is where innovation and continuous improvement truly begin.

This is respect for people.

It is about valuing their contribution, trusting their judgement, and creating the conditions where both people and performance can thrive.

Feeling valued and appreciated has always been so important to me. Earlier in my career it was probably something I felt more subconsciously, but in more recent years it has become something I recognise very clearly. It was only when I found myself in environments where I felt that I was not valued that I truly understood how important it is.

Because of that, as a leader I place a lot of importance on making sure the people around me feel recognised for their skills, their talents, and the contribution they make. Even if they don't work within my team.

Think about it.

When people feel valued, they naturally go the extra mile. When they feel overlooked or underappreciated, the opposite tends to happen. There is a lot of truth in the old saying that if you look after your people, they will look after the customer.

And it is not always about money or extra time off. More often than not it is the small things that have the greatest impact. A simple thank you for a hard week, a quick message to recognise someone's effort, or taking a moment to acknowledge an important day in their life can mean a great deal.

I always try to make a note of birthdays or significant moments for the people I work with. A short message wishing them a happy birthday or checking in to see how they are doing might seem small, but those gestures can genuinely make someone's day.

Let me share a personal experience with you.

One of my roles at Amazon required a great deal of international travel, and I found balancing that with family life a real challenge. There were long periods where my wife was left at home with our young children while I was away for work. Often in different time zones, making it challenging to even have a video call with the children.

I always tried to plan ahead as much as possible to minimise the disruption, but the reality was that sometimes travel came up at short notice and it wasn't always easy.

I never shied away from being open about that with my line manager. I felt it was important to be honest about the impact it had on my family life rather than pretend everything was fine.

One moment from that time has always stayed with me. It was the day before Christmas Eve during my first year working in that role when a courier arrived at our front door with a large, heavy box. My wife answered the door, slightly puzzled, as we weren't expecting any deliveries and for once I had actually managed to finish the Christmas shopping early.

After carrying the box inside and setting it down, she noticed it was actually addressed to her. Curious, she opened it to find a Christmas hamper inside.

It was a beautiful, suitcase sized wicker basket made from dark wood, secured with two sturdy brown leather straps and chunky brass buckles. It looked like something you would see in an old film where a family takes a picnic to the beach or park.

Inside, it was filled with a wide selection of festive food, wines, and snacks, all carefully arranged in soft hay.

Tucked inside was a card addressed to her.

The message read

"Dear Mrs Sims, thank you for letting Matt travel so much for us this year. His contribution has been invaluable in helping us achieve our goals. He has been amazing. Thank you, and have a wonderful Christmas. Dave."

Dave, my Line Manager, had demonstrated a serious touch of class here. Not only did this gesture make me feel deeply valued and appreciated, but it also made my wife feel recognised for the sacrifices she had made. This act of kindness significantly eased any apprehensions we had about the upheaval and strain that my travel might bring in the future.

While I'm sure Dave's intentions were genuine, there's a part of me that wonders if he was thinking it might make it easier to ask for even more travel the following year! Regardless, it was a class act that left a lasting impression on me. I took this valuable lesson to heart and have since made a concerted effort to do similar things for those who have worked hard for me every day.

I once had a Line Manager who, despite being a lovely person with good intentions, was fiercely focused on delivering results. He had his sights set firmly on success and would often forget about the people behind the employee number.

I don't think this was intentional; it was simply a by-product of his drive and focus. However, as an employee, this frequently left me feeling stretched and overwhelmed, torn between family commitments and work demands.

For instance, he would occasionally send a message at 4pm on a Friday afternoon, saying something like

"I need a quick whitepaper written for first thing Monday morning on the quantum mass of the deficit of the sun in proportion to Mercury against the pound per square inch of a black hole."

(I made that up, to sound important, of course!)

While he would sign it off with, "I don't expect you to work the weekend," it felt like a somewhat unachievable task without actually working over the weekend, and it put me in a really difficult position.

In my world at the time, weekends were filled with dirty nappies, scattered food on the floor, and mugs of half-drunk, cold coffee marooned around the house, making it incredibly difficult for me to focus on work at such short notice.

This situation is probably pretty recognisable for many, and demonstrates a real lack of empathy, something that is essential in leaders who want to inspire high performance.

Empathy is so much more than just recognising that someone is having a difficult time. It is about genuinely trying to understand how others feel and seeing things from their perspective. It requires listening properly, acknowledging their experience, and responding with care and consideration.

It's an art as much as it is a skill, and it doesn't come naturally to everyone. For some they have to make a conscious effort to pause and think from another's perspective. Often, they don't even realise that this perspective exists until they are made aware of it. It just doesn't even enter their thought process.

I had some truly wonderful experiences during my time at Amazon. I met incredible people who challenged my thinking, helped me channel my energy and enthusiasm, and supported my development in ways that shaped the leader I have become. Each experience added another layer to my understanding and helped me grow into someone I am not only comfortable with, but genuinely proud to be.

One of the most important lessons I learnt along the way is that leadership cannot be bought and there are no shortcuts to it. It is something that develops over time through experience, reflection, and growth.

Books such as this, frameworks, models, tools, and observations can support that journey, but leadership cannot be truly understood without the right blend of real experience, authenticity, and empathy.

By the time I left Amazon, I had a list of people longer than I could manage asking for mentorship, and there was never a shortage of people who wanted to join my team. That was not by luck or coincidence. It was the result of more than twenty-five years of learning, growing, and refining my approach to leadership.

For me, leadership has always been about inspiring people, empowering them, and helping them reach their potential. And even now, I know that the learning never stops.

In truth, I would not want it to.

Key Learnings Chapter 6

This chapter reflects a period where my world expanded significantly, not just in role scope and scale, but in how I understood leadership itself.

As my responsibilities grew, so did the complexity of the challenges I faced. That stretch brought valuable lessons that could only really be learnt through doing. It also gave me one of the most rewarding parts of leadership, seeing others develop, step forward, and succeed in their own right.

My time working across different countries also sharpened my thinking. It taught me that context matters, culture matters, and that great leadership is never about forcing the same answer into every situation. It is about understanding what is in front of you and adapting with respect.

More than anything, this chapter reinforced what I had been learning for years. leadership is about people. It is about trust, empathy, clarity, and creating the conditions for others to contribute at their best. When people feel safe, valued, and empowered, performance follows. When they do not, no amount of pressure or process will make up for it.

It also reminded me that leadership is not built overnight. It is shaped over time through experience, reflection, mistakes, growth, and the impact we have on others.

Looking back, I left that chapter not just with bigger roles behind me, but with a far deeper understanding of the kind of leader I wanted to be.

July 2016

Me with my first daughter in the carrier. We were visiting a farm in Kent. All three of my children all loved the carrier, a great way to calm them down.

You can see here by my appearance that my anxiety was more under control.

January 2017

This is Jamie and I at Old Trafford, home of Manchester United FC. This was the venue for our first (and last) Amazon Peak Party. They never did them again after this one.

July 2018

My first ever trip to the United States. I was there for an Amazon Standardisation event in Phoenix, Arizona. Here on my first night, I'm playing 'Top Golf' with my US colleague Andy. I gave him a right whoopin' in case you wondered! It was 110 degrees during the day!

June 2023

Eastbourne International Tennis Tournament, Devonshire Park Lawn Tennis Club.

This was a fantastic day with my son, and the scene of the famous autograph request!

For many years after a string of non-stop rejections in my late teens, I stayed well clear of auditions and anything similar. But that all changed when my wife spotted an advert in the local paper for a new community radio station that was about to launch. She encouraged me to give it a go, so I did.

Before long I found myself on air, sometimes several times a week. Even when Covid-19 came along, I built a home studio in a log cabin at the end of the garden so that I could continue to do shows remotely. The pandemic also gave me the opportunity to do more shows than normal as I now had the facilities to broadcast where others didn't.

From there I had the opportunity to be involved in some fantastic radio projects, ranging from community stations through to international internet radio. I've always loved the energy and creativity that radio brings. There is always an opportunity to try something new and create something entertaining. It really is a fine art. Not easy to master.

But what I value most is the people I've met along the way. I've had the chance to work with and learn from some brilliant individuals. Collectively, those experiences helped shape the skills and confidence I needed, both technically and personally, to eventually create the ***Ever-So-Lean Podcast***.

When we moved home in 2021, one thing that was non-negotiable for me was having a space to build a dedicated studio.

At the time I was presenting shows for an international radio station, so having a proper setup really mattered to me.

I started out hosting a Saturday evening show with a lively, party style vibe, before later moving for a short period to a weekday mid-morning slot. Over the years I gradually upgraded my equipment, piece by piece, improving the quality as I went.

Today I have what I would comfortably describe as a professional studio setup, something that has evolved over time through experience and a fair bit of trial and error along the way.

It's a special place for me. It's where the magic really happens. In many ways it's my Gemba. When I'm not travelling, this is where I work from.

The space is soundproofed, the lighting is just right, and everything is set up exactly how I like it. It's my own little corner of the world, a place where I can focus, create, and bring ideas to life. Just my space, doing what I love.

By late 2022 I was leading Content, Technology, Infrastructure & Lean Excellence for Europe within Fulfilment Centres at Amazon.

Using the skills I had gained from my radio work, I introduced podcasting to the organisation, and was producing internal podcasts for my departments for about twelve months. They had turned out to be a really effective way of engaging people across the organisation. Each episode was attracting lots of attention from all over the world.

What surprised me most was the level of interest it created. People from different departments began reaching out asking if they could feature their projects in an episode. That soon extended beyond project teams to operational leaders and frontline colleagues who simply wanted to share their stories with the wider organisation. It was clearly building real momentum.

That experience sparked an idea. Amazon has hundreds of thousands of employees across sites all over the world. Many people listen to music while they work, either through personal devices or through speakers in some locations. I started thinking about how powerful it could be to create something like "Amazon Radio", an internal broadcast platform connecting sites together.

In my mind it could be a live platform where employees could request songs, make dedications, recognise achievements, and share messages with colleagues across the business. From a company perspective it could also provide a clear communication channel when needed.

I even imagined feature shows hosted by Amazon employees themselves, giving people the opportunity to develop new skills while bringing a genuine and authentic voice to the platform. Given the success the podcasts were already having, I was convinced something like this could add real value.

So I did a bit of digging and eventually found the team that this type of idea might sit with, I believe they were based in France. I pitched the concept to them, but unfortunately the response was a polite thanks, but no thanks.

I was disappointed that I didn't even get the opportunity to explain what I was suggesting in any kind of detail. The more I thought about it the more I felt that it was a winning idea, and a step into the future. But it just wasn't to be at that time for one reason or another.

The following week, I was in one of my regular one-to-ones with one of my seniors, and I brought up the Amazon Radio topic.

I went on to explain my idea and how it felt like a natural segway from the internal podcast platform that I have created. She paused and looked at me intently, before saying

"Have you ever considered creating a podcast outside of Amazon?"

The honest truth is, I hadn't. It never even crossed my mind to do anything like this outside of the walls of Amazon.

I dismissed it as I really didn't know how to go about doing this. I knew how to produce a show and all that goes with it, but I had no clue about how and where to get it live, to make it visible, and to gain a following. It wasn't anything I had ever done before.

But that idea persisted in my head. It pestered me, and before too long I became hyper focused on it.

Let's just pause for a minute.

Let me introduce "hyper focus" to you.

When I look back over my life, one thing that has always been there is something I would describe as hyper focus. For me it means that when something captures my attention, it doesn't just get a bit of interest, it gets all of it. I naturally throw myself into it completely.

It's actually a symptom of autism I believe, and although undiagnosed I do suspect I fall on the spectrum somewhere.

Whether it was sports, a TV series I was watching, films, clothes, gadgets, computer games, cars, or even decorating the house, once something caught my interest it would get one hundred percent of my attention. I would dive into it, learn everything I could, refine it, tweak it, and keep going until I was genuinely happy with the outcome. I just fixate on things and don't stop. Literally.

In many ways that trait has contributed to the success I have had over the years. When I commit to something, I really commit. I immerse myself in it and keep pushing until I reach the standard I am aiming for. Which probably doesn't surprise you is exceptionally high. I expect a lot of myself.

However, it does have a downside.

When I become hyper focused on one thing, other areas of my life can sometimes take more of a back seat. My attention narrows, and while that focus can drive progress in one area, it can mean I need to make a conscious effort to keep everything else in balance. It's both a gift and curse that I think also plays a supporting role in my anxiety.

Now, back to that persisting idea of a podcast outside of Amazon.

I started looking into how I could actually make the idea work. The first question was where to host it, and how I would record conversations properly. I quickly discovered that there were some excellent platforms designed specifically for podcast recording that could produce really professional quality audio.

And there it was again, that familiar hyper focus. I couldn't accept the idea of doing it in a half decent way. If I was going to do it, it had to sound professional. That meant using the right tools and the right subscriptions.

The problem, of course, was that those tools cost money and I had absolutely no budget for the project. So I did what I often do when an idea starts taking shape. I sat down and wrote a business plan.

My thinking was that if I could build a solid plan, perhaps I could find a sponsor to support it.

As part of that process I did some research into how podcasts typically make money. The overwhelming message was that sponsorship usually comes once you have either an established brand or a large listener base that is attractive to advertisers. At that point I had neither.

Even so, writing the business plan turned out to be a really valuable exercise. It helped me get everything out of my head and onto paper. It was almost like telling the story of the idea, what I wanted to create, how I would go about it, and what it would realistically cost.

Once I had that together, I reached out to a friend who is the Executive Chair of a well-established consultancy company. I still remember the moment clearly. I was driving the kids up to the country park on the cliffs and called him from the car. I pitched the idea to him there and then.

After I had explained what I wanted to do and talked him through the plan, he paused for a moment and asked a simple question.

“What’s it going to be called?”

It was a brilliant question, and one I had somehow completely overlooked. I had gone into great detail on everything else but had never even thought about a name.

Without really thinking, straight off the cuff I replied, “Ever-So-Lean.”

To this day I have no idea where it came from. It just came out.

He immediately said, “I love it. How much do you need?”

I told him that to get started I would need about five hundred pounds to cover the subscription fees. Without even hesitating he replied, "No problem, let's do it."

And that was it. Just four weeks later I launched the trailer for the ***Ever-So-Lean Podcast***, feeling a mixture of excitement and uncertainty about what might come next.

At the start my fixation on getting everything "right" risked getting the project stuck in the mud. I analysed every detail, questioning the format, the sound, the structure, the art work, and how it should all come together. But after a while I realised something important. I didn't actually know what "right" looked like, or whether it even existed.

What I eventually understood was that perfection was never the goal. What really mattered was authenticity. The podcast needed to sound natural, feel genuine, and feature people with real experiences and stories worth sharing. Most importantly, I needed to show up as myself. The same person whose passion and enthusiasm had carried me this far.

That meant relaxing, dropping the idea that I had to perform or pretend, and simply being who I am. I needed to demonstrate a bias for action.

I truly believe that is what makes the ***Ever-So-Lean Podcast*** different. It's a relaxed space where people can talk openly, laugh, share their experiences, and learn from each other. It creates real connection because the conversations are genuine.

My role isn't to be perfect. My role is simply to be myself, and that is more than enough. Once I let go of trying to get everything right and focused instead on being authentic, everything began to fall into place and the path forward became much clearer.

I began searching for guests, mainly through LinkedIn. I reached out to a number of people, explaining the idea behind the show and what being a guest could represent. That is how the first handful of guests came about. The very first was the wonderful Anil Mathew from the Lean Enabled Group. In the episode he shared the story of how he had been involved in the development of the Covid-19 vaccine using continuous improvement methods.

It was a fascinating conversation and flowed very naturally. But when I sat down to do the post production edit, something struck me. As the podcast grew and more inspiring guests came on to share their stories, there was a risk that the listener might feel a disconnect. Someone listening might think, "That's incredible, but I just work in a warehouse," and struggle to see how it related to them.

I realised that if the podcast was going to connect with people in the way I hoped, I needed to close that gap. I needed to make every guest feel human and relatable, regardless of their role, responsibility, or achievements.

That is when I came up with the idea of the "Yes/No Game". It was something I remembered watching as a kid when the late Des O'Connor hosted the game show Take Your Pick!

The concept was simple, but surprisingly difficult. Contestants had to answer a rapid series of questions without saying the words “yes” or “no”.

Des O’Connor would deliberately ask questions designed to trip them up, and more often than not people would slip and say one of the forbidden words. It was brilliant entertainment because the audience could see the trap coming, but the pressure of the moment would usually catch the contestant out.

So I created a short segment for the podcast. I even produced some tense background music to ramp up the pressure, and challenged guests to survive sixty seconds without saying “yes” or “no”.

It had exactly the effect I hoped for. Even the most accomplished and impressive guests would eventually slip up, which instantly made them feel more human and relatable.

If you listen to the ***Ever-So-Lean Podcast***, you will notice that the Yes/No Game appears in every episode... apart from the very first one with Anil.

Since those first handful of episodes, I have rarely had to go searching for guests. Most people now approach me in some way, either directly or through recommendations. It’s now rare for me not to be sitting on a backlog of episodes that need editing and releasing. Now time is the issue, I am the bottleneck!

Since its launch in December 2022, the ***Ever-So-Lean Podcast*** has grown into one of the leading platforms for continuous improvement, leadership, and high performance.

Through it I have had the privilege of meeting some truly inspiring people. Many of them have helped shape the way I think about leadership, improvement, and personal development. Each episode becomes its own journey, exploring different ideas, experiences, and stories that reflect the many sides of the human experience.

My early learning in continuous improvement involved reading many of the classic books written by people like Jeffrey Liker, James K Franz, and Paul Akers. I spent hours absorbing their thinking, learning from their experiences, and trying to apply those lessons in my own work. So to then, many years later, find myself sitting down and talking with them on my very own podcast still feels slightly absurd. But that's exactly what happened.

One episode that still makes me smile was when Ian Annett, who at the time was Deputy CEO of the UK Space Agency, came on the show. The plan was simple. We were going to talk about the recent challenges surrounding a launch from a UK Spaceport in Cornwall.

I had done all the preparation, mapped out some guiding questions, and had a clear structure for the conversation. But within a few minutes of the recording starting, all of that went out of the window. Instead, I found myself asking things like, "Are there aliens?" and "Did we really go to the moon?"

I basically turned into a starstruck child, suddenly unloading all the questions that had clearly been sitting in my head for the last forty years.

To be fair to Ian, he was brilliant about it. He answered every question with good humour and patience. At one point he even joked that if he ever needed someone who knew absolutely nothing about going to space, he'd send me up there.

I've not had the call yet...

Another episode that took an unexpected turn was when Mark Gallagher joined me to talk about continuous improvement in Formula One Motorsport. Mark was fantastic. He shared some incredible insight into the world of motorsport and how relentless improvement is the difference between standing on the podium and finishing last.

One part of the conversation that really stuck with me was when he spoke about the development of the halo, the safety frame that now sits above the driver's head in every Formula One car. Hearing how teams across the sport came together to make that happen was genuinely inspiring.

Then, completely out of the blue, in his unmistakable accent, he said, "What I'd like to do, Matt, is kidnap you and take you to a Formula One garage so you can see it for yourself."

I couldn't resist having a bit of fun with that in the edit. I added the sound effect of frantic typing over the top of my reply, which was something along the lines of, "I'm just sending you my address now Mark so you can arrange that kidnapping. Maybe have a van pull up outside with a few blokes in balaclavas to take me to the garage."

It was all good fun, and moments like that are part of what makes the podcast so enjoyable. You never quite know where the conversation is going to go. There is no script, just an episode outline to stop scope creep. It's an honest and free flowing conversation.

On one of the early episodes I was still learning how to properly use the recording software. The only real way to learn was simply by getting stuck in and doing it.

My guest and I were recording late in the evening because they were in a different time zone. Before we started, we had a quick ten-minute chat about what to expect, how the show worked, and the general flow of the conversation. Everything felt relaxed and natural. I then rolled the intro and we got going.

About twenty-five minutes in we were deep into the conversation. There was a great chemistry between us and the discussion had been fascinating. There were even a few moments where I remember thinking to myself, this is going to be a brilliant episode.

I tend to glance down at the recording timer every so often to keep an eye on the time and make sure we cover the key topics before the sixty minutes are up. When I looked down this time though, my stomach dropped.

It said zero.

Like being hit by a speeding train, I suddenly realised I had never actually pressed record. My guest was happily chatting away, completely unaware, while inside I was slowly dying.

Trying to stay calm and professional, I managed to style it out and blamed the software. We had to start again from the beginning. Thankfully my guest was incredibly understanding about it, even though it meant repeating everything. I asked the same questions at the same points, and even found myself laughing in the same places as before just to try and recreate the flow. It was honestly a bit of a nightmare, and a relief when we finally got to a new bit!

I wish I could say that was my only disaster while producing the podcast, but unfortunately it was not.

On another occasion I had recorded an entire episode with a guest. The conversation had gone really well and all that remained was to tidy things up with a bit of editing before publishing. When I sat down about a week later to do the edits, I discovered that the guest audio was perfect but mine was completely distorted. So bad, in fact, that you could barely make out what I was saying. I sounded like a very angry robot.

After digging around in the settings I discovered the problem. For some reason the microphone input level had jumped up to one hundred percent. The audio was so blown out that no amount of editing could rescue it.

So I had to get creative.

I downloaded the full transcript of the episode and listened back to the recording. Then I re-recorded every single one of my lines from the transcript, carefully matching the timing of the original conversation. To make it work I had to replicate the same tone, pitch, and emotion I had used during the original recording so it blended naturally with my guest's responses.

It took a huge amount of time, but in the end it actually worked remarkably well. If you listened to the episode today you would never know.

In fact, I do not think I have ever even told the guest about it.

Learning from both of these disasters, you'll be relieved to know that I now conduct a thorough pre check on everything before we get going! Much like a pilot before take-off.

What has been most humbling is that while guests come from very different backgrounds, industries, and cultures, they often share the same drive to improve and to make a difference. They just go about it in their own unique ways.

These conversations have become a constant source of inspiration and energy for me. They remind me that learning never really stops. It continues to evolve with every conversation and every perspective shared.

The ***Ever-So-Lean Podcast*** has grown into far more than just a podcast too. It has become a global space for growth, not only for me, but for everyone who listens as we continue to learn, reflect, and improve together.

As time has gone on, it has attracted a number of well-known industry sponsors, and on several occasions, I have even been commissioned to cover live events such as the West Kent Business Exhibition, and the Rye Harvest Food and Wine Festival. Perhaps the most special of all has been the UK Excellence Awards.

2026 will be the third year I have covered this prestigious event. The 2025 ceremony, and again in 2026, takes place at Wembley Stadium. Not a bad venue for a podcast whose name was dreamt up in the car on the way to the country park on the cliffs!

In 2024 I was invited to appear on Ryan Tierney's Lean Made Simple Podcast. I have a huge amount of respect for Ryan and the work he has done, and continues to do, to bring Lean thinking to a wider audience. What I admire most is that he speaks from a place of real experience. He's not just talking about Lean, he's living it. His facilities operate exactly in the way he describes, and they really are a benchmark for any organisation that wants to build a healthy, thriving Lean culture.

So I flew out to Belfast, we recorded the episode, grabbed some lunch together afterwards, and then I flew home. It was a long day of travelling for a short visit, but it was absolutely worth it.

Joining us for lunch was my friend Tom Hughes from GembaDocs. Tom is a brilliant bloke. Always positive, always laughing, and genuinely passionate about continuous improvement. He's doing some fantastic things in the space as well.

I don't think I've ever actually told him this part of the story, but I can laugh about it now.

After lunch he kindly offered to drop me at the airport. I happily took him up on the offer. It saved me a few pounds on a taxi, he had a lovely car, and it gave us a bit more time to chat on the way. After about a forty-five-minute drive he dropped me off and I headed inside.

As I walked into the terminal, I remember thinking to myself, this looks a bit different to earlier. I brushed it off, assuming I had probably just come in through a different entrance or was at another part of the airport.

I wandered over to one of the departure screens to check my flight... and it wasn't there.

After a bit of confusion I eventually found a member of staff and asked what was going on.

That's when I discovered I was at the wrong airport.

Turns out Belfast has more than one.

That little mistake cost me a £75 taxi ride to get across to the correct one. Not exactly the ending to the day I had planned. But looking back now, it's one of those moments that just makes you laugh.

It's funny, when I'm recording an episode of the podcast, or even when I'm editing it afterwards, I have absolutely no idea who will end up watching or listening to it. Every episode takes a huge amount of time to plan, record, edit, and share, so I tend to become completely focused on just getting it finished and out into the world. Then once it's live, I very quickly move on to the next thing. In many ways I almost forget about it.

Yet it rarely fails that when I'm at a continuous improvement conference, running a workshop, attending an awards evening, or even guest lecturing at a university, which I do regularly, someone will come up to me and say they listen to the show. They'll tell me their favourite episode, mention that they listen to it in the car or on the train, or share how something they heard on it has inspired them in some way.

What's strange is that it almost feels like they're talking about someone else's podcast, or someone else entirely. It's a very odd feeling to have something out there in the world that people are engaging with, yet you know so little about these individuals.

I can see the statistics. I can see the countries people are listening from, and the times they tune in. I can even see how long people listen for. But the people behind those numbers remain largely invisible to me.

Whoever they are though, I'm incredibly grateful to them. Grateful that they take the time to listen, and grateful for the conversations and connections that the podcast continues to create.

I also discovered another unexpected use for my recording equipment: voice work. Over the past few years I have supported a number of different projects using my voice. Things like adverts, training content, audio books, and even characters in video games.

My kids find this particularly amusing. One of the video game roles I worked on involved voicing a character who mostly communicated through reactions rather than full sentences. So when the character interacted with others or got hit during gameplay, it was my job to provide all the sounds. Things like "ouch", "awww", "get off", "leave me alone", and a whole range of other noises and reactions.

The kids would often be downstairs listening and bursting into laughter while I was upstairs recording all these dramatic grunts and yelps into a microphone. At one point I even had to close the window because I suddenly realised the neighbours might be wondering what on earth was going on.

It was slightly ridiculous at times, but great fun all the same.

January 2020

Me on air for Maidstone Radio. This was taken in their studio only a month into me joining them.

2021

This is a social media promo from one station for one of my shows. Giving these tickets away was such a blast!

April 2021

The very first iteration of my home studio.

October 2022

This is me doing a live show from my home studio with my newborn daughter along for the ride.

I did this for about four weeks before it became too difficult.

July 2023

Outside Global in Leicester Square, London, meeting one of my radio heroes, Johnny Vaughan.

I cheekily asked Johnny to hold the phone... which made it look like he was the one asking for a selfie with me.

2023

Example 1 of my Hyper Focus:

I needed a racing rig for my steering wheel for e-sports. I couldn't find one that did what I wanted. So I made one from scrap wood.

2023

Example 2 of my Hyper Focus:

The pond was falling apart and needed some serious work. So I built a new one in its place.

2024

Example 3 of my Hyper Focus:

My girls wanted a tree house. So we collected free pallets from the local town, broke them up and I built one.

2024

Example 3 of my Hyper Focus:

Complete with built in furniture, fairy lights, and

There's even a ladder to get upstairs.

2024

Example 3 of my Hyper Focus:

Inclusive of a trap door, and sliding door that gives access to a role for a quick escape!

2024

Example 4 of my Hyper Focus:

We needed a stairgate to keep my daughter safe, and prevent the dog from coming up the stairs. I made one.

CHAPTER 8: A ROLL OF THE DICE

Leaving the comfort and security of a large organisation was undeniably daunting. I knew I would miss the people, my team, and those intense moments during peak when everyone pulls together and goes the extra mile for the customer.

What I didn't expect to miss was the infrastructure that sits behind an organisation. Things like IT, HR, marketing, finance, technical support, and legal services. They are all functions we tend to take for granted when they are simply there in the background doing their job.

It wasn't until I found myself sitting in my studio, just two days into this new chapter, staring at a to do list as long as my arm, filled with tasks I had never dealt with before, that the reality truly hit me.

Making the decision to walk away from everything I knew and invest my time fully into Ever-So-Lean was probably the biggest roll of the dice I have ever taken.

The first two years were incredibly tough. At one point I remember looking at my bank account and seeing minus eight hundred pounds. I was working tirelessly every single day, most of the time for fourteen hours, but nothing seemed to translate into any real financial return.

I'm not afraid to admit that I was worried. But in that moment, there was really only one thing I could do, keep moving forward. So that's exactly what I did.

Each new day brought with it the promise of new opportunity. I never knew what email might land in my inbox, who might be on the other end of the phone when it rang, or who I might meet at a networking event. That sense of the unknown is something that genuinely excites me. It's the possibility of what might happen next that gets me out of bed in the morning.

During those early years I experienced the fastest period of development in my entire life. Suddenly I had to learn new skills across almost every area of a business. It really was learning by doing.

I had to get to grips with the technical side of things, understand web hosting, work out marketing, handle administration, and everything else that comes with running a business. At times the practical side of it felt particularly overwhelming, especially building a functional website and developing a visual identity that felt right.

I decided to build the website myself. I do enjoy creative work and the freedom that comes with designing something from scratch. I'd love to say that was the reason I took on such a monumental task, but the truth is much simpler. I simply couldn't afford to pay someone else to do it. If it was going to happen, I had to make it happen myself.

In fact, I'm not afraid to say that everything that you see coming from Ever-So-Lean has been created by me. The website, the content, the programmes, the visuals, the ideas. I do it all. Not because I necessarily planned it that way, but because I had to.

I was very fortunate though. A former colleague of mine from Amazon had their own server and generously allowed me to build eversolean.com on it. That saved me a huge amount of money at a time when every penny mattered.

They also helped me with some of the more technical aspects of getting the site set up, which was a massive help. I remain incredibly grateful for their support and generosity. Twelve months later I was able to move this to my own server which matched the growth I had seen during that time

It took me six weeks to get the site built and live. During that time I was working around fourteen hours a day trying to figure it all out. It certainly wasn't easy. There were moments where it felt painfully slow and incredibly frustrating, and plenty of times when I felt completely out of my depth. Many times I'd spend days on an element, only to somehow delete it and have to start again.

Some days I would spend what felt like forever trying to fix the smallest things. I remember spending almost two full days just trying to get the spacing between sentences to look right. It was maddening.

Halfway through that whole experience my broadband provider let me down and I had to cancel the contract. The problem was the new connection wouldn't be installed for another two weeks. So during that period I spent my days working out of a local coffee shop just so I could get online and keep building the site.

But eventually I got there. The website went live.

It wasn't perfect. To be honest, it still isn't. But that doesn't really matter. What matters is that I built it, I understand it, and I can improve it whenever I need to. Over time it's become far more than just a website. It's now the platform that hosts the learning management system for the Ever-So-Lean online programmes as well.

Rarely does a week go by where I'm not improving something on it. As I learn more and develop new skills, I can continue refining it. Just like everything else in continuous improvement, it's all about those small, incremental steps that add up over time.

And don't even get me started on SEO! If anyone actually understands SEO, and has managed to actually do it right. Congratulations! You/they are an absolute genius!

But as the days and weeks went by, it all became part of a bigger lesson. Progress rarely happens in big leaps remember. In a similar pattern to continuous improvement, it comes from perseverance and from stacking up small wins, one after another, until something meaningful begins to take shape.

What started as a podcast project that I worked on in my spare time slowly grew into something much bigger.

One area of my work that I am particularly passionate about is ***Ever-So-Lean Rising Stars***™.

This is a project that means a great deal to me personally, as it focuses on something I believe is incredibly important, introducing continuous improvement thinking to young people at an early stage in their lives.

The programme is designed primarily for those aged eleven and above, although I have had children as young as eight fully engage with it and get real value from the experience. It combines interactive online learning with hands on workshops, all centred around making continuous improvement practical, relatable, and easy to understand.

The intention is not to overwhelm with theory, but to show how these ideas connect to everyday life. As young people begin to explore the concepts, they naturally start to develop important skills such as teamwork, problem solving, leadership, public speaking, and creative thinking.

For me, this goes far beyond preparing them for future careers. It is about helping them build confidence and develop a positive, growth mindset early on. Something I know I would have benefited from greatly during my own time at school.

What has been most rewarding so far is seeing just how capable young people are when you give them the space to think and explore. When they are not restricted by rigid ideas of right and wrong, their creativity and ability to solve problems is genuinely impressive.

This is how I believe learning should be. Engaging, practical, empowering, and something people actually enjoy being part of.

More broadly, today, Ever-So-Lean has grown into a modern consultancy and training practice that gives me the opportunity to work with organisations across a wide range of industries, both here in the UK and around the world. Through that work I support teams in developing better processes, better ways of working, and stronger, more capable leaders.

Ever-So-Lean is licensed by both the British Quality Foundation (BQF) and the Lean Competency System (LCS), which means our programmes provide recognised, premium accreditations.

Our Lean learning programmes, along with our Lean Six Sigma Yellow Belt, Green Belt, and Black Belt programmes, I designed myself to meet the high standards of both BQF and LCS.

I've built these programmes to be practical and easy to apply, not academic or theoretical. They can be delivered online, through virtual classrooms, or face to face with teams on site.

What I'm particularly proud of is how the learning is designed. We offer a version that works across any industry, which means anyone can learn the principles of Lean and continuous improvement.

But recognising that a one size fits all programme doesn't work for everyone, we also build bespoke programmes tailored to any specific industry or organisation. That way the language, the examples, and the problems we explore actually look like the world the learner works in.

That familiarity makes a big difference. People understand it quicker, and more importantly, they can apply it straight away. And for me that is the whole point. Knowledge is only useful when it turns into action.

Something else that has always been important to me is the level of support people receive when they reach the project stage of their accreditation. Every learner is different. People learn at different speeds, face different challenges, and need different levels of guidance along the way.

In many programmes in this space the support is fixed and rigid, often a set number of hours with a standard structure around it. In my experience that approach rarely goes far enough. If we genuinely want to build confidence in our practitioners and get the very best return from the investment in developing them, we have to do more than that.

For me it's about building a relationship with the learner and supporting them in a way that suits them. That might mean more regular check-ins, coaching through challenges, or simply being available when they need guidance. The goal is always the same, to give people the confidence, support, and encouragement they need to succeed and to apply what they have learned in the real world.

From an organisational perspective, it also makes complete sense for any continuous improvement programme to be tailored to the organisation it's being delivered within. If a business is investing in the development of its people, the programme should reflect that investment. It should feel relevant, aligned, and connected to the way that organisation operates. In many ways it should carry the identity of the organisation itself. That's simply the right way to approach it.

Another element of my work that has developed organically, is speaking.

Speaking at events, whether large conferences or smaller, more intimate gatherings, has always been a humbling experience for me.

Standing in front of people and sharing my experiences, the lessons I have learned along the way, and the thinking behind my leadership framework, ***The Bridge to Inspirational Leadership***™ is something I never take for granted.

Having the opportunity to offer practical insight that helps people think differently, build confidence, and lead meaningful change in their own environments is incredibly rewarding. For me, it is never just about delivering a talk. It is about creating a moment where ideas land, perspectives shift, and people leave feeling inspired and empowered to take action.

Each engagement gives me the chance to fine tune my message, inspire others, and just as importantly, be inspired by the people I meet along the way.

No two engagements are ever the same. Each brings its own atmosphere, different questions, different reactions, and different conversations afterwards. It is a constant reminder to me that a message can land in many different ways depending on the people in the room.

After every talk I take time to reflect. Usually performing a full autopsy in my mind back in the hotel room, or in the car on the way home. What resonated? What could be clearer next time? Where could I tell the story better?

Those small, incremental improvements matter. High performance rarely comes from one big leap. It comes from continuous learning and refining the craft, one step at a time. I can't help but do this. My burning fire for excellence just doesn't allow me to stand still and rest on anything, it's always about what could I improve? What can I be better at next time?

Over the past few years I've been fortunate to speak in some incredible environments.

Delivering a keynote at Agile Lean Ireland at the SuperValu Páirc Uí Chaoimh stadium in Cork in October 2024, speaking at the IHG Hotels & Resorts EU Finance Conference at the InterContinental Malta in March 2025, chairing a session on quality at CQI Quality Live in June 2025, and most recently speaking with the team at a Rolls Royce EU Conference in their hangar at East Midlands Airport in February 2026 are just a small sample of the incredible opportunities I've been given.

Each one has been unique in its own way and a real privilege to be part of.

CQI Quality Live was a particularly unique experience. BQF were a partner at the conference and invited me to chair a panel exploring the future of quality.

The central question we wanted to tackle was an interesting one. Is quality outdated? Are some of our methods old fashioned? And does the discipline need to evolve and modernise?

Joining me on the panel were three highly experienced practitioners, each bringing with them a huge amount of first-hand knowledge and insight from their own careers. Rather than running a traditional panel discussion though, we decided to approach it a little differently.

We knew we were the final session of the day, so energy in the room would naturally be dipping. The last thing we wanted was another slide heavy presentation that people simply sat through. We wanted it to be engaging, interactive, and most importantly a genuine two-way conversation with the audience.

So we came up with the idea of putting Quality on trial.

Each panel member took on a role. One acted as the prosecution, presenting the case that quality as a discipline had become outdated. Another took the role of the defence, arguing for its continued value and relevance. The third panel member played the key witness, offering perspective and evidence from their experience.

The audience became the jury. Their job was to listen to both sides, challenge the arguments, ask questions, and ultimately decide the outcome. At the end they had to choose which side of the room to stand on, guilty or not guilty.

You might be wondering what role I played in all of this.

Well, I was the Judge.

It was my courtroom. I opened proceedings, set the scene, explained everyone's roles, and kept order throughout the debate. As you can probably imagine, I got quite into the part. I even had a white curly judge's wig and a gavel to complete the look.

It was great fun, but more importantly it worked. The energy in the room was fantastic and the feedback afterwards was incredible. Several people told us it was the best session of the entire conference.

For me it reinforced something I strongly believe. Conversations about quality, improvement, and leadership don't have to be dry or overly academic. If we want people to truly engage with these ideas, we have to think differently about how we bring them to life. If we don't evolve how we connect with people, we risk losing their engagement altogether.

Alongside speaking, I've also had the privilege of hosting and presenting at some fantastic events. The Smiths Group Plc Global Excellence Awards in London in November 2023, the NHS Graduation Evening at the Union Jack Club in London in December 2025, and the Hypo Hounds Awards at the Ashford

International Hotel in March 2026 have all been memorable experiences.

Co-hosting the Hypo Hounds Awards alongside Hypo Hounds CEO Jane Pearman was an incredible experience. The theme for the evening was the circus, and when I arrived in the afternoon for the soundchecks I was genuinely blown away by the effort that had gone into transforming the venue. The room looked amazing. You could immediately feel the excitement building for the night ahead.

What made it even more special for me personally was the way the evening flowed. Of course the awards themselves followed a script, but much of what Jane and I did in between was completely natural and unscripted. We bounced off of each other throughout, which created a really relaxed and fun atmosphere throughout the evening. That freedom to be creative on the spot made it a real joy to host, and I know Jane enjoyed it just as much as I did.

But the real highlight of the evening was meeting the people behind the charity's work. Hypo Hounds is an incredible organisation that trains specialist assistance dogs to support children living with Type 1 diabetes. These remarkable dogs are trained to detect dangerous drops in blood sugar levels, alerting the child and their family before it becomes life threatening.

Meeting the families, the children, and of course the dogs themselves was incredibly moving. These dogs are not just companions. They quite literally help keep these children safe every single day.

It was a privilege to play a small part in celebrating the people and animals who make that possible.

After I had completed a handful of speaking engagements, I decided to reach out to a few talent agents who specialise in booking speakers for events. I contacted around ten agencies to begin with, but only one or two even responded.

The feedback they gave me was actually really helpful. The main issue was my profile. At that point I simply didn't have enough visible experience for them to confidently put me forward to clients. Although they didn't take me on, they pointed me in the right direction and told me what I needed to build.

So over the next eight months I focused on getting as much experience as I possibly could. I spoke anywhere I could. Conferences, workshops, panels, hosting events, presenting, anything that would allow me to develop my skills and become more comfortable on stage. In many cases I gave my time freely, simply because the experience itself was so valuable.

Whenever possible I also made sure the events were recorded. That effort gave me three really important things that the agents had told me I needed.

First, it gave me genuine experience speaking at different types of events and across different industries. Every audience is different, and those experiences helped me develop the confidence to adapt and connect with a wide range of people.

Second, it allowed me to gather strong testimonials. Clients were able to share their experience of working with me and talk about the impact the sessions had on their teams.

And third, it gave me the footage I needed to create a proper speaker showreel.

Once I had those three pieces in place, I reached out again. This time I contacted around ten to fifteen agencies, not just in the UK but internationally as well.

The response was completely different. Several of them agreed to represent me.

Having that association with recognised speaker agencies has been incredibly valuable. Of course they help secure speaking opportunities, but they also add credibility. Clients feel reassured when they see that you are represented by professional booking agents.

At first the bookings coming through the agencies were slow. But once I had delivered a couple of talks through them, more opportunities started to follow. One engagement often led to another.

So if you are someone who wants to share your experiences, tell your stories, and inspire others along the way, my advice is simple. You absolutely can.

Focus on building the experience. Gather genuine testimonials. Capture good footage that shows you doing what you do.

Then put yourself out there and see where it takes you. Because if you never try, you will never know where it might lead.

When I pause and think back to my early days working as an Early Network & Distribution Manager on the Post, these are experiences I could never have imagined being part of.

Whether it's through speaking, hosting events, or conversations on the podcast, one belief has only grown stronger for me over time. Real growth happens when we share our experiences with others. We all carry stories, lessons, and challenges that shape us. By being open about the journey, the successes and the setbacks, we find common ground with people we may never otherwise have met. In that shared space, we learn, we grow, and we move forward together.

And if I'm completely honest, the fact that I get paid to do this is simply the cherry on top. To be invited to share your experiences, your lessons, and your thinking, and then be paid for it, is something I never take for granted. It's incredibly humbling, and something I'm deeply grateful for.

And then in 2025 things began to get really mad!

In March I had the honour of being a finalist at the UK Excellence Awards, held at Wembley Stadium, in the category of Excellence in People Engagement & Development.

It was an incredible evening, full of those real "pinch me" moments that I know I will never forget.

To start with, just being in Wembley Stadium, a place synonymous with excellence, was a real buzz in itself. I spent much of the day there ahead of the ceremony, helping support the BQF team with preparations. Being inside the stadium while it was completely empty was something quite special. Standing there, looking out across the seats and the pitch, the view was simply breath-taking.

Then came the champagne reception in the Lionesses Bar. During the reception, BQF Patron HRH The Princess Royal arrived, accompanied by her security team and ladies in waiting. She was then escorted to a private reception with a small group of guests, sponsors and board members.

Here's where things became a little surreal for me. I was invited to join that reception too.

So there I was, having a conversation with HRH. Me. The guy who was the class clown at school. The guy who was once told he would achieve nothing. The guy who has spent much of his life battling anxiety. And yet there I was, standing face to face with a senior member of the Royal Family while she asked me about Ever-So-Lean.

It was honestly astonishing.

She was incredibly easy to talk to and took a genuine interest in the journey behind Ever-So-Lean. She asked thoughtful questions about my career path and about where I believe the opportunities lie for strengthening the UK excellence agenda. It was a moment I will always remember and one I will remain deeply grateful for.

You would think that would have been enough for one evening.

But there was more to come.

In the Excellence in People Engagement & Development category I was up against several large, well-established organisations. I didn't take the main award, but simply reaching the finals felt like a huge achievement and far more than I ever imagined when I first started this journey.

Then came one final surprise at the end of the evening. I was called to the stage and presented with an Excellenteer Award in recognition of my contribution to the UK excellence agenda.

What made that moment even more special was that the award was presented to me by HRH herself.

So not only had I been able to meet her earlier in the evening and share my story, I now found myself standing on a stage at Wembley Stadium, receiving an award from her.

Even now, it still feels a little surreal. I'm honestly lost for words.

Alongside that unforgettable evening at Wembley, I've also been incredibly fortunate to receive a couple of other recognitions that mean a great deal to me.

Also in 2025 I was honoured to receive the Lean Competency System Global Champion Award, presented at the Royal Welsh College of Music & Drama in Cardiff. This is a headline award that recognises individuals who demonstrate exceptional commitment to advancing continuous improvement on a global scale. To be acknowledged in that way by a community that cares so deeply about improvement, learning, and raising standards was something I felt genuinely humbled by.

This recognition came at the end of a wonderful conference in Cardiff where I had the privilege of delivering a talk on the main stage. The event brought together leaders, practitioners, and many others who share a genuine passion for continuous improvement. There is always something energising about being in a room full of people who care deeply about Lean and the difference it can make.

Between the sessions, people gathered in the refreshment area for tea, coffee, and a few nibbles, taking the chance to continue conversations sparked during the talks. On a couple of those breaks I was approached by some wonderful people who had read either The Emergence of an Unexpected Leader or Building the Bridge to Inspirational Leadership.

I have to say, that still feels completely surreal to me.

It's difficult to explain the feeling when someone asks you to sign a copy of your book. It never feels normal. Every time it happens, I find myself having to pause for a moment and take it in, because I'm genuinely humbled that people have taken the time to read and engage with something I've written.

What makes it even more special is when those conversations turn into thoughtful questions about the ideas, lessons, or approaches shared in the books. Those moments of curiosity and discussion are incredibly rewarding, because they show that the message is landing and that people are thinking about how they can apply it in their own worlds.

I still chuckle to myself when I think back to that moment of winning the award. I had completely forgotten that I was even an award finalist. The day had been so full, with conversations, the conference itself, and speaking on stage, that the thought genuinely never crossed my mind.

As the awards were being presented, I was simply enjoying watching the winners being announced and seeing them walk up to the stage for their moment. It was great to witness the recognition they were receiving.

Then it came to the Global Champion Award. A summary was being read out explaining why the winner had been chosen. It all sounded impressive, just as you would expect. You know the sort of thing... "this person has achieved this," and "this person has contributed that."

Then they mentioned Rising Stars.

Now Rising Stars is the programme I created to help young people engage with problem solving and continuous improvement. So my first reaction was actually annoyance. I remember thinking, hang on a minute... who else is using my programme name? I genuinely thought, that's a bit cheeky! Who's done that then?

And then, very slowly, it started to dawn on me that they were actually talking about me.

At that point I realised what was happening and thought to myself, you absolute wally!

Around the same time, I was also recognised with a Global Recognition Award 2025, an award that celebrates visionary leadership, bold thinking, and meaningful impact in business.

I'd never won anything before, then in the space of six months I won three prestigious awards!

If I'm honest though, it wasn't so much about titles or accolades. What mattered most was the recognition of the work I'd spent so many years pouring my focus into to help people and organisations think differently about leadership, improvement, and the role people play in high performing cultures.

When I step back and reflect on moments like these, it's hard not to feel grateful. None of this was ever part of some grand plan. I've simply tried to stay true to what I believe in: helping people grow, creating environments where improvement can thrive, and sharing what I've learned along the way.

To see that work resonate with others, both here in the UK and internationally, is something I'll never take for granted.

Sticking with awards for just a moment longer, I've also had the privilege of finding myself on the other side of the table.

I was incredibly proud to serve as a judge for the BQF UK Excellence Awards in both 2023 and 2025. Over those two years I've judged several different categories, and I have to say I've been completely blown away by the people and organisations doing truly exceptional work.

Reviewing those submissions gives you a real sense of the difference that continuous improvement is making in the world. When you see the impact these organisations are having on their people, their customers, and the communities they serve, it makes you incredibly proud to be part of this space.

I'm delighted that I'll be returning again as a judge for the 2026 awards, which I'm really looking forward to.

Alongside that, I was also invited by the Lean Competency System to serve as a judge for their 2026 programme. Of course I accepted their kind invitation, and I'm excited to see the same level of dedication, creativity, and excellence coming through in those submissions as well.

Judging is something I feel genuinely honoured to do. It's a chance to recognise the amazing work that people and organisations are doing, and to celebrate the positive impact that thoughtful leadership and continuous improvement can have on the world around us.

Do you remember the one to one I mentioned earlier, the conversation where one of my senior leaders suggested that I should consider starting a podcast outside of Amazon? Well, just before I left the business, I had one final one to one with that same person.

I remember the conversation clearly. I told her about my plans to put my full commitment into building Ever-So-Lean. As we talked through my hopes for it and the direction I wanted to take, she asked me a question that caught me completely off guard.

"What makes Ever-So-Lean different from any other platform, consultancy, or continuous improvement training provider?"

I paused for a moment to think about it. When I started answering, I began rambling about the content being engaging, about learning through doing, about creating something practical and accessible for people.

Then she stopped me.

She looked at me and said, "Matt, what makes Ever-So-Lean different is you. Matt Sims."

She went on to explain that without that, it would simply be another platform, another consultancy, just another training provider. What makes it different, she said, is what I bring to it.

I had never thought about it like that before.

But her words stayed with me. And the further I've gone on this journey, the more I've come to understand exactly what she meant.

Since starting Ever-So-Lean I have had to think a lot about marketing. I've experimented with a number of paid advertising platforms. Google, Facebook, LinkedIn and a few others. I spent time and money trying to promote what I was doing, but not once did any of those adverts lead to a real conversation, let alone a piece of work.

Eventually I came to the conclusion that I must have been doing something wrong. So I arranged a meeting with a marketing company and walked them through everything. I explained what the business did, how I worked with clients, the type of impact I was trying to create, and the way I had been approaching marketing.

The feedback they gave me was a real light bulb moment. One of those moments where something suddenly clicks in your head.

Their advice was simple. Stop trying to market to sell. Just be yourself. A very similar poke in the eye to the one I got in my last one-to-one.

They encouraged me to share my stories, my experiences, the lessons I had learned along the way. Talk about the work, talk about the challenges, talk about the thinking behind it all. Their point was that when people connect with those things, conversations naturally begin to happen. And it is those conversations that build awareness, relationships, and eventually opportunities.

From that day on I completely changed my approach.

Rather than trying to push a service or promote an advert, I focused on sharing what I genuinely care about. Continuous improvement, leadership, lessons from my own journey, and the experiences that have shaped my thinking over the years.

The difference was remarkable.

Not everyone likes my content, and that is perfectly fine. It is impossible to create something that resonates with everyone, and if someone does not connect with what I share then they probably were never the right fit for me anyway.

But since making that shift the growth has been incredible. as of March 2026, my LinkedIn following alone has grown by more than fifteen thousand people. More importantly, the engagement and conversations have been fantastic. I regularly hear from people all over the world who connect with the ideas, share their own experiences, or simply want to say that something resonated with them.

What that marketing conversation taught me was something very simple but very powerful.

People do not connect with adverts. They connect with people.

When you share honestly, when you speak about what you care about, and when you show up consistently as yourself, people begin to trust you. And over time that trust naturally turns into opportunity.

Another key part of my progress during the early years of Ever-So-Lean has been the unwavering support from BQF and LCS.

They backed me, encouraged me, opened doors, and gave me opportunities to grow. They even recognised the work I was doing, which meant a great deal, especially during the tougher periods.

There were days in those early years that felt incredibly heavy, and if I'm honest, without that support and belief from others, I'm not sure I would have got through them in the same way.

Believing in yourself is important, of course it is. But having people around you who believe in you as well can make all the difference. That support network becomes something you can lean on when your own energy dips. It helps steady you, refocus you, and keep you moving forward.

I will always be grateful for that.

Key Learnings Chapter 8

Leaving the security of a large organisation and stepping into the unknown to build Ever-So-Lean was one of the biggest decisions I have ever made. It was exciting, but also daunting. Not getting paid every month was also incredibly scary. What I quickly discovered was that when you step out on your own, you do not just leave a role behind. You also leave the entire infrastructure that once supported you. Suddenly everything becomes your responsibility.

The early years were tough. There were moments of real uncertainty and times when the financial reality felt uncomfortable. But those challenges also pushed me through the fastest period of growth I have experienced in my life. I had to learn everything from the ground up. Accounting, building a website, creating programmes, developing a brand, understanding marketing, and figuring out how to run a business properly.

Much like continuous improvement itself, progress did not arrive in big leaps. It came through persistence and hundreds of small steps forward. Gradually those improvements began to compound to move me forward and bring clarity around what I was doing.

What started as a small podcast project slowly evolved into something far bigger. Today Ever-So-Lean has become a consultancy and learning platform that allows me to work with organisations across different industries and around the world, helping them improve how they work and how they lead.

Along the way this chapter of my life has taken me into rooms and experiences I could never have imagined. Speaking at conferences, hosting events, meeting inspiring people, and even standing on a stage at Wembley receiving recognition from royalty for work I care deeply about.

But the biggest lesson from this journey has been a really simple one.

The thing that makes Ever-So-Lean what it is today is not just the programmes, the platform, or even the content. It is the authenticity behind it.

When I stopped trying to market services and instead started sharing my experiences, my stories, and the lessons I have learned along the way, everything began to change. People connected with it. Conversations followed. And from those conversations came relationships and opportunities.

Because at the end of the day people do not connect with advertisements. They connect with people.

And this chapter of my life has reinforced something I believe deeply. When you stay true to who you are, show up authentically, and keep learning along the way, the journey often leads you to places you never expected.

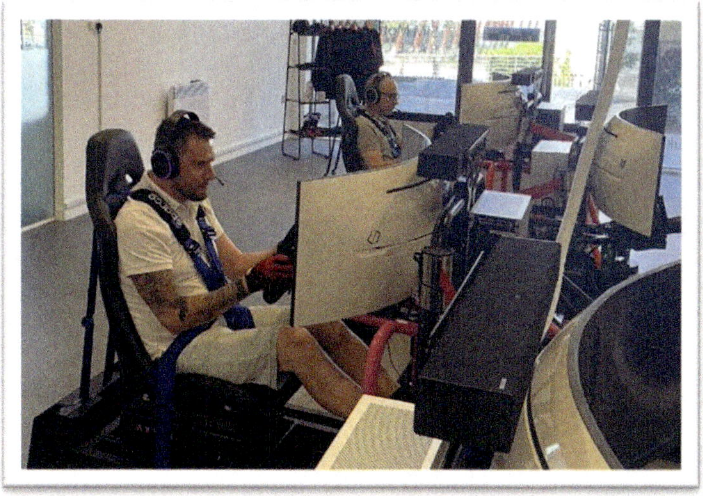

June 2023

My 40th birthday challenge. Jamie and I went head-to-head at Sim Motor Sport in Kent. What an experience. I beat him in every car category... he was clearly driving like a man true to his West Country roots.

October 2023

The UK Excellence Awards 2023. This was the first year that BQF commissioned me to cover the finals, held at the Hilton, Bankside in London.

November 2023

Hosting the Global Smiths Excellence Awards in London.

March 2024

IHG Hotels & Resorts EU Finance Conference, Malta.

Every delegate was given a copy of Building the Bridge to Inspirational Leadership.

I signed nearly all of them!

March 2024

The UK Excellence Awards 2024, Wembley Stadium, London.

Honored to have a meet and greet with HRH The Princess Royal before the ceremony.

March 2024

The UK Excellence Awards 2024. Being presented with an Excellenteer Award by HRH The Princess Royal. Wembley Stadium, London. One of the proudest moments of my career.

March 2024

The UK Excellence Awards 2024. Pitch side, Wembley Stadium before the awards, a strange and calming environment.

March 2024

The first edition of The Emergence of an Unexpected Leader is published.

So much work went into it, and the feedback was so positive.

April 2025

University of Roehampton, London. Delivering a guest lecture on Business and Entrepreneurship, sharing real world experiences and lessons from my journey so far.

June 2025

All rise for the right honorable judge, Matt Sims. Quality Live 25, London. The positive feedback we received from this session was extraordinary. Great fun too!

September 2025

Covering the Rye Harvest Food & Wine Festival, Rye, East Sussex.

September 2025

Delivering a keynote on the ***Bridge to Inspirational Leadership****™ at the LCS Conference & Awards, Cardiff.*

September 2025

Winning the LCS Global Champion Award at the LCS Conference & Awards in Cardiff. Presented by Cartin Archer, Head of LCS, this was a moment I will never forget.

December 2025

Hosting an awards night for the NHS, Union Jack Club, London.

March 2026

Co-hosting the Hypo Hounds Awards at the Ashford International Hotel, Kent.

Here I am with Jane Pearman, CEO of Hypo Hounds and co-host for the evening.

Have you ever been on a road trip where you've crossed a long bridge, maybe over a wide river or open stretch of sea? It's something we often take for granted. We drive across without a second thought. But when you really stop and think about it, that bridge didn't just appear overnight.

It took planning, expertise, experience, and strong foundations. It was designed to carry weight, withstand pressure, and hold firm in all conditions. Day after day it supports a constant flow of traffic, all relying on it without even realising. And it is not something that gets built and forgotten. It is maintained, checked, and improved over time to ensure it continues to do its job.

That idea has always resonated with me when I think about leadership.

Because leadership is not that different.

It is not something you simply arrive at. It has to be built. Thoughtfully. Carefully. With strong foundations. And then continuously developed.

Over the years, through my experiences, the lessons I have learned, and the mistakes I have made, I have come to see leadership in this way. As something that connects people, supports them, and helps them move forward, especially when things are challenging.

The ***Bridge to Inspirational Leadership***™ is my way of bringing all of this together.

It is supported by four key pillars: Respect for People, Authenticity, Engagement, and Empowerment.

These pillars are what hold everything together. When they are strong and in balance, they create the conditions for high performance, growth, and continuous improvement.

But if one is missing, or neglected, the whole structure begins to weaken. It may hold for a while, but under pressure it will start to show cracks.

Sustained success comes from maintaining strength across all four. It is that balance that gives the framework its resilience.

And just like any bridge, it is something that continues to evolve.

Now, let me introduce the ***Bridge to Inspirational Leadership***™ to you.

The Bridge to Inspirational Leadership Schematic

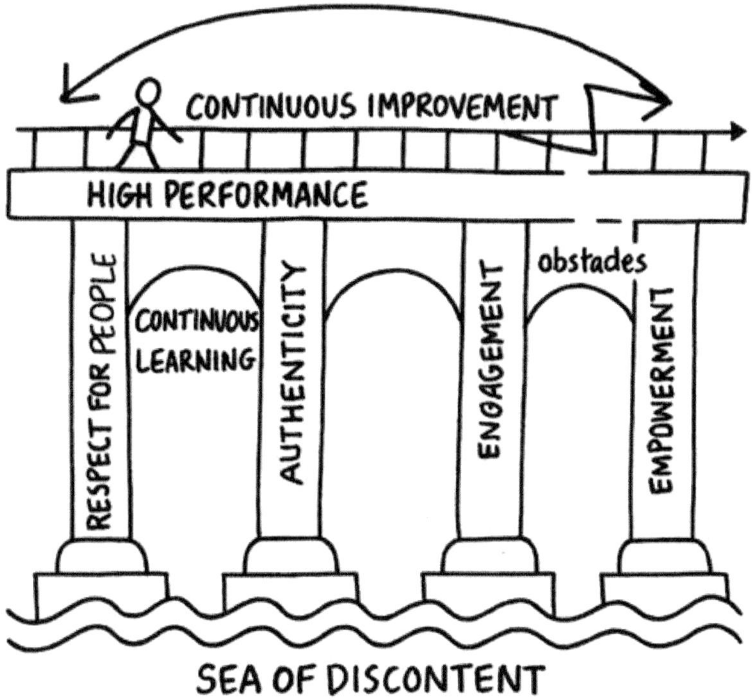

The Sea of Discontent:

Beneath the bridge sits what I call the Sea of Discontent. It is a place we need to stay aware of at all times, because it is where poor, or lack of leadership shows up most clearly.

This is where frustration builds, engagement drops, and people begin to feel disconnected from their work. The signs are often easy to spot. A lack of ownership. Low morale. Falling productivity. Complaints becoming the norm. Resistance to change. Not because people do not care, but because they no longer feel connected to what they are doing or valued for the part they play.

It is an environment where people feel unsupported. Where their contribution goes unnoticed. Where effort is given, but not recognised. And over time, that begins to wear people down.

The danger is that it does not happen overnight. It creeps in slowly. One decision at a time. One missed conversation. One moment where someone was not listened to or supported. Before long, what was once a motivated and capable team finds itself stuck, drifting in that sea.

Moving away from it takes conscious effort.

That is where the bridge comes in.

Leadership, in this context, is not about title or hierarchy. It is about the ability to lift people out of that environment. To create clarity, connection, and direction. To rebuild trust and give people a reason to care again.

It is about guiding people from those murky waters onto something more stable. A place where they feel valued, supported, and able to perform at their best.

Because when people feel that, everything changes.

The Four Core Pillars of Inspirational Leadership:

1. Respect for People

Respect for people starts with how we show up. It means being present, listening properly, and treating people like human beings rather than roles on an organisation chart.

It is about taking the time to understand their reality, their frustrations, their ideas, and their concerns. Leaders who do this well do not just hear words. They pay attention, ask better questions, and create space for honest dialogue. That is where trust begins.

It also means leading with empathy, honesty, and consistency.

People really need transparency, especially during change. They need to know why something is happening, what it means for them, and that their concerns will not be brushed aside.

Respect is shown when leaders acknowledge emotion, involve people early, and respond thoughtfully rather than defensively. It is not softness. It is strength shown in a human way.

Respect for people is also visible in what leaders choose to prioritise. It means giving time to those closest to the work, not just those highest in the hierarchy. It means recognising effort, celebrating contribution, and creating opportunities for people to shape solutions rather than being given instructions.

When people feel valued, trusted, and supported, engagement grows, ownership deepens, and performance follows.

Respect for people isn't complicated. It's about creating an environment where people can thrive. A place where they feel safe to speak up, able to contribute, and confident that what they do matters. When leaders consistently behave in that way, they do not just build better relationships. They build stronger people, healthier cultures, and far better results.

2. Authenticity

Being an authentic leader is about being real, consistent, and grounded in your values. It starts with clear, honest communication. Say what needs to be said without dressing it up. Share the reality, not just the highlights. When people understand the why, they are far more likely to engage with the how. Clarity reduces noise, and honesty builds trust.

It also requires vulnerability and integrity. Leaders do not need all the answers, but they do need the courage to admit when they do not know, to own mistakes, and to stay true to their principles.

That consistency between words and actions is what people watch for. It is what builds credibility over time. Trust is not created through statements, it is earned through behaviour, especially when things are difficult. People are not daft. They see through false, disingenuous, fake, fluffed up words.

Authentic leaders lead by example. They follow through on what they say, they face challenges head on, and they create alignment by making sure people understand the direction and their role within it.

They listen properly, not just to respond, but to understand. They create space for others to contribute, recognising that the best thinking rarely sits in one place.

Bring authentic is not about perfection. It is about ownership. It is about showing up as you, a real human being, making principled decisions, and responding thoughtfully rather than reacting emotionally.

It's these small, consistent actions that shape culture. They define the environment people work in, and ultimately, the level of performance that can be achieved.

3. Engagement

Engagement starts with presence. Leaders cannot build connection from a distance. You have to get out to where the work happens, see reality for yourself, and understand the pressures, frustrations, and opportunities people are dealing with every day.

Yes, reports and dashboards have their place, but they will never tell you what people on the ground are really experiencing.

When leaders show up consistently, listen properly, and take an interest in what is actually happening, trust and credibility grow.

It also relies on clear communication, regular feedback, and shared direction. People want to know where they stand, what matters most, and how their work contributes to something bigger. Confusion drains energy quickly. Clarity creates focus.

Engagement deepens when people understand the goal, feel involved in shaping the path, and receive feedback that helps them grow rather than simply be judged. One to ones, honest conversations, and meaningful recognition all play a big part in that.

Strong engagement also comes from involvement, not instruction. When people are encouraged to collaborate, contribute ideas, solve problems, and take ownership, they stop feeling like passengers on a bus, and start feeling like they have a real stake in the outcome. That is where innovation comes from too. The best ideas are often closest to the work, but they only surface when people feel safe enough to speak up and confident that their voice will be taken seriously.

Generating engagement is all about creating an environment where people feel seen, valued, and connected to purpose.

It is built through everyday leadership habits, being present, listening well, recognising effort, investing in development, and giving people the space to contribute in a meaningful way. When that happens, people do not just turn up for work. They care about work. They commit. And that is when high performance starts to become possible.

4. Empowerment

Empowerment is where leadership becomes real. It is not about control. It is about creating the conditions for people to take ownership, make decisions, and grow in confidence through doing meaningful work, learning, and going again.

It starts with trust. If you have brought someone into your team, trust that they are capable of contributing. When leaders show belief in people's ability, it changes how they show up. They step forward. They take responsibility. They care more about the outcome because they feel it is theirs.

Ownership does not happen by accident though. It comes from clarity. People need to understand what they are responsible for, what success looks like, and where the boundaries sit. Without that, what looks like empowerment quickly turns into confusion. Set the direction clearly, then step back and allow people the space to get there in their own way.

Delegation plays a big role here. Done poorly, it is just shifting workload. Done properly, it is developing capability.

Match responsibility to someone's strengths and stretch potential. Give them something that challenges them, support them through it, and allow them to learn. Over time, you move from directing every step to simply providing guidance when needed and removing barriers.

Support matters just as much as freedom. Empowerment is not about leaving people to figure everything out alone. You don't want people to feel abandoned. It is about making sure they have the tools, time, training, and access to information that allows them to succeed. When people are set up properly, their confidence grows quickly.

There is also a mindset shift required around decision making. Not every decision needs to be treated as critical or irreversible. Many are testable, adjustable, and low risk. When leaders recognise this, they can push decision making closer to where the work happens. People act faster, learn quicker, and build better judgement over time. I call this progress replacing hesitation.

The great thing about empowerment is that is creates accountability as a bi-product.

Giving ownership means trusting people to deliver, but also expecting them to own the outcome. When things go well, they take pride in it. When things do not go to plan, they take responsibility, reflect, and improve. That is where real growth happens, but only if we let it.

This is where Psychological Safety underpins all of this. People need to know they can speak up, challenge ideas, and try new approaches without fear of blame. When that environment exists, ideas can flow, innovation happens, and people become far more adaptable.

You can see when empowerment is working. Decisions are made closer to the work. Problems are solved without constant escalation. People contribute ideas rather than waiting to be told. The energy shifts from one of compliance to one of commitment.

In practical terms, strong empowerment comes down to four things working together.

1. **Clear direction** so people know where they are heading.
2. **Capability** so they have the skills to get there.
3. **Autonomy** so they have the freedom to act.
4. **Accountability** so they take responsibility for results.

Get that balance right and you do not just get more engaged people. You get a team that thinks, adapts, and drives performance without needing to be pushed every step of the way.

Here's a simple reflection to keep yourself honest.

Think about the decisions you made this week. How many of them could have been made by someone in your team with the right clarity and support?

That answer tells you a lot about how empowered your team really is.

The Supporting Arches: Continuous Learning

Continuous learning is what gives empowerment its backbone. Without it, ownership becomes fragile, confidence fades, and progress slows. With it, people grow into their roles, make better decisions, and build the capability to sustain performance over time.

Empowerment, Ownership and Learning go hand in hand. When someone is responsible for a piece of work, they are far more likely to reflect on it, improve it, and take pride in it. That is where development becomes real. Not in theory, but in practice.

The role of the leader is to make that growth possible. That means providing access to the right tools, training, and support. It means delegating work that stretches people, not just tasks that keep them busy. It means recognising that capability builds over time and adjusting support as confidence grows.

A big shift here is how mistakes are viewed. If failure is punished, learning stops. People play safe, avoid risk, and stick to what they know. If failure is treated as feedback, learning accelerates. People test ideas, reflect, and improve. Confidence grows because they know they are trusted to figure things out. This is a snowball effect, once it starts it builds momentum, it becomes bigger and bigger as it builds.

Learning also needs to be practical. Long courses and theory have their place (somewhere), but most growth happens in the flow of work. Solving real problems. Reflecting on outcomes.

Trying again. Short, focused learning that can be applied immediately will always have more impact than something that sits on a shelf, or takes people away from the Gemba.

Leaders have to set the tone. If you are not learning, your team will not either. When you are open about what you are working on, what you are improving, and what you have got wrong, it creates a non-verbalised permission for others to do the same. Learning becomes normal, not something people feel judged for.

When things ramp up and pressure builds, it's tempting to start cutting what feels non-essential. Learning time is often the first thing to go. Trust me, that's a huge mistake.

Cancelling your own development, or worse, other people's, sends a very clear message. Learning doesn't matter. And if that's the signal, don't be surprised when growth stalls and capability just plateaus.

Busy periods are exactly when learning matters most. That's when new challenges appear, when better thinking is needed, and when people need support to adapt and perform.

Protect that time. Treat it with the same importance as any operational priority. Because in reality, it is one.

If you want people that can handle pressure, solve problems, and keep improving, you cannot afford to switch learning off when things get tough. That is when it counts the most.

Reflection is a powerful habit, and for me it's something I've always done without really thinking about it.

But, taking a few minutes to step back and ask what worked, what didn't, and what we'd do differently next time keeps learning alive. It turns everyday experience into something useful. Try to encourage this in others too, you'd be surprised just how many people already do this without you ever knowing.

Without that pause, things just happen and move on. The opportunity to learn is there, but it's missed.

Learning is also social. Some of the best insights come from within the team. Creating space for people to share what they know, support each other, and build on each other's ideas strengthens both capability and connection amongst the group. It can quickly turn individual learning into collective progress.

Stretch is important too, but it needs to be balanced. Pushing people slightly beyond their comfort zone builds confidence. Pushing too far, and or too quickly, without support can create anxiety and hesitation. This is exactly how I felt in the Network & Distribution role at time. The difference is in how well the leader supports the journey. In my case it was hardly at all, leaving me swimming in the Sea of Discontent. Don't make the same mistake.

Feedback plays a critical role. It needs to be timely, specific, and useful. Not vague praise or blunt criticism, and certainly not a shit list. It needs to be clear guidance that helps someone understand what to continue and what to adjust. When done well, feedback becomes fuel for growth rather than something people avoid or become defensive against.

As the weeks drift by it's easy to see when this culture starts to take hold. People start seeking out challenges rather than avoiding them. They share ideas more freely. They reflect without being prompted. Learning becomes part of how people operate, not something that has to be enforced.

The connection is profound. Empowerment gives people the responsibility to act. Continuous learning gives them the capability to act well. You need both.

Let me share a practical way to ground this from my experience.

Look at your current team.

Where are people being given responsibility without the support to grow into it? And where are people being trained but not given the chance to apply it?

Closing that gap is where you will find that development happens.

Start small. Build learning into the rhythm of work. Keep it relevant. Keep it human. Keep it going by being consistent, it's that consistency that creates people that are capable, confident and adaptable.

The Path Across the Bridge: High Performance

The bridge represents high performance, not as a destination but as an ongoing journey. There is no finish line. It is about getting better, together, every single day.

High performance is not built on big moments or breakthroughs. It is built over time through consistent effort, reflection, and a willingness to improve. It is less about perfection and more about progression. Every task, every challenge, every result is an opportunity to learn, adjust, and go again.

Looking back, that mindset often shows up early. For me, it was in simple things, taking pride in my work, constantly thinking about how to improve it, and wanting to raise the standard each time. That drive stays with you. But over time, you learn to balance it. Perfectionism can push you forward, but it can also hold you back. Real high performance comes from shifting that focus towards continuous improvement, not chasing something that is unattainable. It's not an easy mindset shift, but I am living proof that it can be done.

It is something that can be developed. Not taught as a one-off, but built through mindset. A mindset that values learning, adapts to setbacks, and sees every challenge as a chance to improve.

It is not just about individuals either. High performance is a team game. The best teams are aligned, trust each other, and take ownership. When people believe in the mission, understand their role, and feel trusted to contribute, performance gets better. Not because people work harder, but because they work better.

Barriers will always exist. Fear of failure, lack of clarity, poor leadership, even burnout. The difference is how they are handled. High-performing environments face these head on. They create clarity, treat failure as learning, lead with consistency, and understand that sustainable performance requires balance.

Leadership makes such a difference. Not titles or credentials, but leadership behaviour. Being present. Making clear decisions. Creating an environment where people feel safe to contribute and improve. When that is in place, performance follows.

High performance is about building something that keeps evolving. Every result is not an end point, it is a new starting line. The focus is not on arriving, but on continuing to improve.

The Handrails: Continuous Improvement

Continuous improvement only works when it stops being treated like an initiative, a program, or a project, and starts becoming part of how the organisation thinks and operates every day.

The excuses people often lean on, such as "we've always done it this way" or "we don't have time", are not valid reasons to stand still. In truth, refusing to improve simply means accepting inefficiency, frustration, and wasted time as normal.

Continuous improvement is about people. It is not about box ticking, cost cutting, or looking good on a slide deck. It succeeds when people are involved, listened to, and trusted to help shape better ways of working. When people are treated as the source of ideas and improvement, rather than the problem, real momentum starts to build.

Leadership plays a huge role in this. Leaders need to be visible, consistent, and genuinely committed. They have to set the tone, create the right message from the start, and make it safe for people to experiment, learn, and improve without fear.

If leaders are not truly behind it, people will see through it immediately and the whole thing will struggle to take hold.

The most effective improvements are often not dramatic. They are small, practical, visible changes that make work easier, safer, and better. Those small wins matter because they build belief. They create energy. They show people that improvement is not just talk, it is something real that benefits them in their day-to-day work.

To make it stick, organisations need the right balance of freedom and structure. Improvement cannot be so tightly controlled that nothing happens, but it also cannot be so loose that things become chaotic or disconnected. A simple, clear framework helps people act, share learning, and build on success together.

The key lesson for me is this. Continuous improvement is not a programme to launch, revisit, or relaunch. It is a mindset, a rhythm, and a way of working. When it becomes part of the culture it simply becomes the way people do things.

Another trap organisations fall into is looking for an off the shelf model and assuming they can simply lift it from somewhere else and drop it into their own business.

What I mean by that is this. A company might look at the Toyota Production System (TPS) and think, that worked brilliantly for Toyota, let's use that here. Or they might look at Amazon and decide to copy the Amazon Customer Excellence System, or Royal Mail and WCM.

The problem is not that these systems are poor. Far from it. The problem is assuming that because something works well in one environment, it will automatically work in another.

There may well be elements of those systems that are useful. In fact, there usually are. But it is very unlikely that any model will be a perfect fit as it stands.

Every organisation is different. Different culture. Different operation. Different history. Different pressures. And most importantly, different people.

That matters.

One size does not fit all when it comes to continuous improvement. You cannot build something meaningful by copying and pasting another organisation's model and hoping for the best. What works is building something from within. Something shaped around your people, your environment, and the reality of how your organisation actually works.

If you try to force a model that does not fit, you do not create improvement. You create confusion, resistance, and frustration.

The real value is not in copying someone else's system word for word. It is in understanding the thinking behind it, taking what is useful, and then shaping something that is authentic to your own organisation. That is where lasting results come from.

Obstacles Along the Way

Obstacles are part of the journey, not something to avoid. If you're aiming for high performance, you're not walking a straight, predictable path. It's messy. There are setbacks, detours, and moments where it feels like you've gone backwards. That's not failure, that's just the reality.

What matters is how you respond.

Strong leaders expect challenges and prepare for them. They create environments where people feel safe to speak up when things go wrong, because hidden problems only get worse.

Instead of jumping in with answers, they ask the right questions, helping people think, solve, and grow. They keep people focused on what really matters, cutting through the noise when things feel overwhelming.

They also control the narrative through conscious framing. A setback is not something breaking, it is part of moving forward. When we frame challenges as learning, people build confidence rather than fear. And crucially, we don't take ownership away from people. We push it back to where it belongs, with the people closest to the work. It's a clever play on words and the mind, but it's really effective.

Having a structured way to solve problems makes all the difference. Whether it is simple questioning, root cause thinking, or more formal approaches, the goal is always the same, understand the real issue and deal with it properly, not just patch the symptoms.

You won't fix everything first time, and that's fine. The people and teams that perform at a high level are not the ones that avoid problems, they are the ones that learn quickly, adapt, and keep moving.

If you look at any success story, the pattern is the same. Obstacles were always there. The difference is that they were used as fuel, not excuses.

High performance is not about avoiding problems. It is about facing them head on, learning from them, and coming back stronger each time.

Call to Action: Embrace the Bridge to Inspirational Leadership: Your Pathway to High Performance

1. **Build Your Foundation**

Anchor your leadership in the fundamentals, Respect, Authenticity, Engagement, and Empowerment. When these are lived, not just spoken about, you create the conditions where high performance can take hold and grow.

2. **Demonstrate Respect**

See your people as more than the job they do. Take the time to understand them, listen properly, and recognise what they bring. When people feel understood and appreciated, they show up differently.

3. **Lead with Authenticity**

Be open, be real, and don't feel the need to have all the answers. When you're transparent and willing to show a bit of vulnerability, you create an environment where people feel safe to speak up, share openly, and grow.

4. **Prioritise Engagement**

Invite people into the decision, making process. Encourage their ideas and contributions to enhance ownership and commitment.

5. **Empower Your People**

Give people the space and support to take ownership of their work. Back them with the tools they need, and create an environment where trying new ideas feels safe and worthwhile, not risky.

6. **Commit to Continuous Learning**

Build learning into the way your team works. Create opportunities for people to develop, try new things, and grow, so they can adapt, build confidence, and handle challenges head on.

7. **Recognise High Performance as a Journey**

Recognise that high performance is never finished. Keep pushing the bar, focus on progress over perfection, and stay adaptable. What feels exceptional today will become the standard tomorrow, so keep improving, step by step, every day.

8. **Embrace Continuous Improvement**

Keep things moving by continually refining how the work gets done. Take learning from both wins and setbacks, and use it to drive steady, sustainable progress.

9. **Navigate Obstacles Together**

See challenges for what they are, opportunities to improve. Be open, communicate clearly, and lead your team through them so setbacks become stepping stones rather than sticking points.

10. **Adopt the Blueprint for Success**

Use the ***Bridge to Inspirational Leadership***™ as your foundation, not just a framework, but a way of thinking and leading.

Live the principles of respect, authenticity, engagement, and empowerment, underpinned by continuous learning and improvement, and let them guide how you show up every day.

11. **Take Action Today**

Now is the time to step onto the bridge with your people. Set the direction, move forward together, and bring others with you on a shared journey towards better leadership and high performance.

If you're looking for something practical to guide you through this, ***The Bridge to Inspirational Leadership™: A Guide to Leading for High Performance*** brings it all together.

It's built on real experience, not theory. What's worked, what hasn't, and the lessons learned along the way. You'll find examples you can relate to, tools you can actually use, and methods that help you take action, not just think about it.

More than anything, it's there to support you. To give you clarity when things feel messy, direction when you're unsure, and encouragement to keep moving forward.

This isn't about having all the answers. It's about helping you take the next step, build confidence, and lead in a way that works for you and your people.

As I bring this brain dump to a close, one thing is clear, this journey is still unfolding.

Ever-So-Lean has grown into far more than a podcast. It's now a platform for learning, development, and real conversations that support people and organisations in getting better every day. The podcast remains a big part of that, but so too are the programmes, the coaching, the speaking, and the work happening alongside teams on the ground.

I'm looking forward to continuing that journey, creating meaningful learning experiences, supporting leaders, and staying connected to the brilliant people I meet along the way. Because as much as I share, I'm learning just as much in return.

Where this goes next, I don't fully know. But what I do know is that the next opportunity usually sits just outside of comfort. It's there, waiting for a decision, a step forward, a bit of courage.

To everyone who has been part of this so far, listeners, clients, colleagues, friends, and family, thank you. Your support has meant more than I can put into words. If anything I've shared through the book, the podcast, the programmes, or our conversations has helped in some small way, whether that's sparked a thought, shifted perspective, or given a bit of confidence, then that means everything.

If you're finding things hard at the moment, I want you to know that it can get better.

Anxiety has been part of my journey for as long as I can remember. For a long time, I didn't really understand it, I just felt it. The physical sensations, the racing thoughts, that slow build that seemed to come from nowhere and take over everything. At times, it felt overwhelming, unpredictable, and difficult to control.

What I've come to learn is that anxiety isn't something you just switch off, and it doesn't define who you are. It's something you begin to understand over time. You learn what it feels like, what triggers it, and how to move through it, rather than fight against it.

There were periods where I genuinely thought it would always be that way. But it didn't stay that way.

Through experience, reflection, and a lot of trial and error, things started to shift. Small steps made a big difference. Being more aware of what was going on. Talking about it instead of hiding it. Giving myself a bit of space rather than piling on pressure.

Over time, it became quieter. More manageable. Less in control.

It hasn't disappeared completely, but it no longer defines how I live my life.

If you're in it right now, I know how heavy it can feel. But from my own experience, it doesn't have to stay like this. With the right support, understanding, and a bit of patience with yourself, things can change.

You're not alone in it. And you're not stuck with it.

There is a way forward, even if you can't quite see it yet. Just keep going.

Here's to continuing to learn, to grow, and to keep moving forward, together.

ADDITIONAL RESOURCES

In this section, you'll find quick links to additional resources that I believe will be valuable as you continue your journey. These carefully curated materials are designed to support your ongoing growth and development.

www.eversolean.com

Accreditations and Workshops for Adults

e-Learning and Workshops for 11yrs+

Library of useful templates, guides and checklists. Including video media support

Ever-So-Lean Podcast – Source of engaging, empowering and inspiring conversations

Printed in Dunstable, United Kingdom

80781048R00211

CW01643552

Warriors, Saints and Dreamers

Dragon-Slayers, Star-Chasers and Other Stories

Elizabeth Allen

Warriors, Saints and Dreamers:
Dragon-Slayers, Star-Chasers and Other Stories
ISBN: 978-1-917070-02-7

Published by Asterales Press
www.asteralespress.co.uk

Published 2024

Copyright © Elizabeth Allen

The author asserts the moral rights of this work.

All rights reserved. No part of this publication may be reproduced, stored in a retrieval system or transmitted, in any form, or by any means, electronic, mechanical, photocopying, recording or otherwise, without the prior permission of the publishers.

Scripture quotations taken from the King James Bible.

Dedication
To the warriors, saints and dreamers in my own life:

those who live faithful, quiet, unfamous lives for Christ,
those who carry the tiny candle of their faith against all odds
and those who adorn the darkness with their faith, hope and charity.

Elizabeth Allen is an author and illustrator, based in England, who tells stories in pictures and words in the midst of the beautiful ordinary of her everyday life.

Contents

As kingfishers catch fire, dragonflies draw flame;
As tumbled over rim in roundy wells
Stones ring; like each tucked string tells, each hung bell's
Bow swung finds tongue to fling out broad its name;
Each mortal thing does one thing and the same:
Deals out that being indoors each one dwells;
Selves – goes itself; *myself* it speaks and spells,
Crying *What I do is me: for that I came.*

I say more: the just man justices;
Keeps grace: that keeps all his goings graces;
Acts in God's eye what in God's eye he is -
Christ – for Christ plays in ten thousand places,
Lovely in limbs, and lovely in eyes not his
To the Father through the features of men's faces.

(Gerard Manley Hopkins)

Introduction

Many years ago Christianity came to a tiny archipelago of islands between Europe and the Atlantic Ocean. These small and insignificant islands were rocky, green and misty and today they're known and loved as the British Isles. No one knows how or when Christianity came here, exactly, but it was during the days of the Romans. The people of the British Isles weren't – and aren't – any more special than any other people in the world. They're just the people, born here or brought here by choice or circumstance, who breathed this air, loved this land and became part of this story as they loved, hated, studied, worked, made homes, had babies, laughed and cried here. Some were born here and stayed while others were born here and left for the four corners of the globe. Some came from around the world and stayed while others came and went. Regardless of their origins, however, the Christians of these islands have an extraordinary story of courage, kindness and hope which continues to this day. Some of them – like Eric Liddell or Amy Carmichael – are heroes and heroines who are still celebrated because they did memorable things for God. Most of history, legend and story, however, is about people who lived small but valuable lives and countless forgotten but faithful heroes and heroines who lived for Christ in the midst of their ordinary, difficult and beautiful lives. Their stories are part of our stories and our stories – written day by day as we live – are part of their stories, the story of Christianity in the British Isles and the eternal story of Christ. Some of their stories are in this book. Most of their stories are history. Some – specifically the stories of Jocelin of Wells, Lucius of Britain and Walter de Lud-Auk – are considered legend. Ohers, particularly those of the Dark Ages saints like Brendan the Navigator, Bega and Morwenna of Cornwall, are thought to be something between history and legend. Some of us, however, believe they are essentially true and lovely them dearly. All the stories in this book are about people who were part of the Christian story in the British Isles. Not all of them went to church every Sunday (although some of them did) but all of them were connected to Christ somehow or other. The people in this book are just some of the fathers, the mothers, the children, the rebels, the scholars, the warriors, the dreamers and the saints whose legacy of faithful, hidden lives for Christ we inherit today.

… for the growing good of the world is
partly dependent on unhistoric acts;
and that things are no so ill with you and me
as they might have been,
is half owing to the number who lived faithfully a hidden life,
and rest in unvisited tombs.

(George Elliot)

Adrian Batten

About 1591 - About 1637

A small boy was born and baptised in Salisbury in the years between the English Reformation and the English Civil War. He was called Adrian Batten and his whole life was about music. He had five older brothers and an older sister as well as one younger sister called Mary. The Batten children were all baptised in the parish church. The Batten home was busy and noisy – overflowing with children, school books and toys – and probably music too. Adrian was a chorister and organ scholar at Winchester Abbey where, one day when he was a bored teenager, he carved his name and the year into the wall of Bishop Gardiner's Chantry Chapel: "Adrian Battin: 1608". As he grew and matured as a musician, Adrian moved from Winchester to London, where he became "a singing man" at Westminster Cathedral. Later he became both "a singing man" and an organist at St Paul's Cathedral. He knew the cobbled streets of London well as he hurried back and forth between the abbey and the cathedral. He worked as a music copyist as well as a musician, and copied pages of music in neat and elegant handwriting. Sometimes, as he sat at a wooden desk with a quill pen, a bottle of ink and a pile of paper, he encountered a piece of beautiful and rare music. Carefully he copied and saved it for

future generations. Eventually he published a book called *The Adrian Batten Organ Book* which is the only place some of this music can be found today. Notes of music swirled around Adrian day and night and he was always scribbling tunes down to play or sing later. He published very little of his own music and many manuscript sheets of it are lost to time or tucked into books and drawers in cathedral libraries and archives. Adrian's music was considered serious with glimmers of joy which created a devotional atmosphere which helped people think about Christ. During his life his music became part of the early English and uniquely Anglican sacred music tradition. He always thought of music, however, not as a way to show off his own skill but as a form of worship.

Agnes Lewis and Margaret Gibson

1843 - 1926 and 1843 - 1920

Twin girls called Agnes and Margaret Smith were born in a little town by the sea in Scotland. Their mother died when they were babies and their father, who believed in education, independence and travel, gave them an extensive and robust education. The twins were linguistic, so he promised to take them to any country in the world, if they learned the language. Soon the Smith family visited France, Germany and Italy. Later the girls attended a finishing school and became beautiful and poised young ladies. When they were twenty-three, however, their father died and left them with nothing but each other and a lot of money. The girls visited Egypt and cruised along the River Nile. It was expensive, uncomfortable and wonderful and it changed everything for Agnes and Margaret. They knew that someday they'd return to Egypt and visit Mount Sinai. For now, however, they went home. Agnes wrote novels and travelogues and Margaret enjoyed a long courtship. Both the sisters married happily when they were over forty, but both their husbands died young, so Agnes and Margaret decided to visit Mount Sinai. The twins were Christians who worried about the new fashion for reading the Bible as a work of literature rather than the Word of God. They lived in Cambridge and had clever, educated friends

among the university professors. One of them mentioned St Catherine's Monastery on Mount Sinai, an ancient book he had found there and a dark and unexplored cupboard full of manuscripts. The twins spoke Hebrew and Greek and Agnes learned an ancient form of Aramaic called Syriac. It was related to the language that Jesus spoke and was one of the most important languages of the Early Church. After a long journey across sea and desert to Mount Sinai, the monks at the monastery welcomed the twins and Agnes explored the mysterious cupboard and its ancient manuscripts. One day, to her never-ending delight, she realised that she was holding a rare and precious book in her own hands. Her Syriac studies came to her rescue and she recognised an early copy of the Gospels. The discovery made an important contribution to the scholarly understanding of the Bible. It also launched Agnes and Margaret on a career of travel and scholarship and gave them the satisfaction of knowing that they had helped to strengthen Christianity in their generation and beyond.

Agnes Wilson

1672 - Unknown

Agnes Wilson was the youngest of seven boys and girls born to a Scottish farmer and his wife in Glenvernoch in Scotland. In those days, in the highlands and lowlands of Scotland, a group of Christians called Covenanters signed a covenant and pledged themselves to the continuation of the Protestant Reformation in Scotland and the freedom of the Scottish church from the control of the king in London. Covenanters met for secret church services called Conventicles, led by rebellious ministers who had been dismissed from their churches, in remote and hidden places where rocks and waterfalls hid their tracks and kept them safe. It was completely and utterly illegal and anyone who was caught at Conventicles was threatened with death. When Agnes was a little girl, her days were full of household chores with her mother and sisters and farmyard chores with her father and brothers, but then Agnes started growing up. Maybe no one really noticed at first. Before long, however, Agnes realised that her big brothers and sisters were up to something and followed them away from the farm to the wild countryside and the illegal Conventicles. Some say she lived as a religious fugitive with her brother Thomas and her sister Margaret after their law-abiding parents were forced to

disown them for their disobedience to the king. One day, however, Agnes and Margaret were arrested and thrown into the town gaol, "the thieves' hole", which was very little more than a dark, terrible hole in the ground. The girls were dragged before a judge with an older woman called Margaret McLachlan. The two Margarets – as they are known to this day – died for their right to worship Christ in freedom. In 1685, however, Agnes was a young girl of twelve or thirteen. She, too, refused to swear allegiance to the king and refute the covenant she had signed before God but the judge was merciful because she was so young. She was released to the care of her parents in return for the costly sum of one hundred pounds of precious Scottish gold. Margaret Wilson is still remembered and celebrated for her faith. Her little sister, Agnes Wilson, is all but forgotten by history. But she, too, believed in Christ and suffered for Him before she lived the rest of her life amid the glens and lochs of Scotland.

Albert Mahomet

1858 - After 1906

Albert Mahomet was born in one of the poorest and roughest parts of London at a time when the city was a bustling metropolis at the heart of a global empire. His father was an Indian seaman and his mother was an English girl. His father abandoned his family and died on his way home to India. His mother, left alone with four small children amid the crowded houses, narrow streets and noisy markets, struggled to cope. Albert was a street urchin – dirty, dressed in rags and roaming the streets to beg for coins – but he was a bright, tough little boy. Eventually he and his siblings were taken into the care of the state and Albert spent the next part of his childhood in a workhouse. At that time English workhouses were infamous for their harsh and unsympathetic regimes. Children received the most basic care, food and education and often experienced unkindness. Eventually, however, Albert was rescued by his uncle and given a family home in a seaside town. Among the flat fields, long beaches and big skies of East Anglia, in spite of his difficult start in life, Albert gained a basic education and grew into a handsome Victorian. As a young man he worked for a doctor, a farmer and a blacksmith. The farmer, a Methodist Sunday School superintendent, introduced Albert to the Gospel. Albert became a

Christian, a Sunday School teacher and a Methodist preacher. He campaigned for temperance but his heart was committed to Christ, evangelism and preaching. He married another evangelist, a girl called Paulina, then divided his time between his pastoral ministry and his job as a photographer. In 1894 he wrote a little autobiography called *From Street Arab to Pastor* in which he described the poverty of the London slums and explained how he broke free from its hopelessness. Albert also established at least one photographic studio in East Anglia. At that time photography was a complicated and lengthy process involving cameras, tripods, hoods, lenses, plates and a variety of chemicals. Albert fell in love with this art form and used it to support his family as well as his pastoral work. He took photographs of people and landscapes which survive to this day. Among the photograph is one of him with his signature written in Victorian copperplate handwriting below the words "Yours in Jesus".

Alfred Edersheim

1825 - 1889

A small boy called Alfred Edersheim grew up in the Austrian capital of Vienna. He was born into a family of modern, educated and cultured Jews who respected the ancient teaching and traditions of Judaism, but wanted to reform their faith and embrace contemporary life. Alfred's parents loved music and literature and sent him to a preparatory school for Austrian boys as well as the synagogue school for Jewish boys. Alfred developed a strong gift for languages at his day school – he spoke French, Italian and Hungarian as well as German, English and Latin – and learned Hebrew, *Torah* and *Talmud* as his Hebrew school. Over time, in the shadow of the Austrian mountains and the echo of the Strauss music which filled the salons and ballrooms of Vienna, Alfred grew into a quiet and thoughtful young man and went to the University of Vienna to complete his education. Later, because his family lost their money, he went to Hungary and worked as a language teacher. He met a Scottish preacher called John Duncan who talked about the Christian faith in such a way that Alfred, a faithful Jew with all the faith of the centuries in his heart, was captivated by the person and message of Jesus. He was baptised and went to Scotland with John Duncan. He studied theology, got married and became a

Presbyterian minister. Here in Britain, apart from a year he spent as a missionary in Romania, Alfred ministered faithfully for the rest of his life. He was ordained as a Church of England priest and become a beloved and respected theologian. He also became the father of seven children. He never forgot his Jewish birth and education and wrote a series of books to help Christians appreciate and understand the Jewish context of the life and work of Christ and the earliest days of the Christian church. One of his books, *The Life and Times of Jesus the Messiah*, is still published and read by students and scholars today. Alfred was a quiet man who people remembered for his tolerance and good-humour. He once said, “Christ is never in haste: least of all, on His errands of love. And He is never in haste, because He is always sure.”

Alice Driver

About 1528 - 1558

It was during the days of the Henry VIII and his six wives that a little girl called Alice was raised on an Essex farm. She grew from a tough and feisty girl into a tough and feisty woman behind her father's plough. She was a farmer's daughter and her life was shaped by the seasons of the year – spring, summer, autumn and winter every year – and the religious changes in England. The country was caught in a grim and gritty struggle between a Catholic past and a Protestant future. Kings and queens made decisions about theological ideals and religious practices, but a deep and earnest faith burned in the hearts of ordinary people. Change blew back and forth across the country and many people died in terrible ways rather than compromise their understanding of Christianity. Always, though, Alice drove her father's plough back and forth across the fields with her hair whipping in the wind, her nose burning in the sun, her hands guiding the leather reins of the oxen, her long skirt tucked up and her bare feet sinking into the fresh, soft soil. The birds sang, the oxen lumbered and Alice, the plough girl, ploughed the fields ready for the seeds to be scattered, grown and harvested for another year of bread. Once Alice married a young man called Edward Driver – and everyone called her Mistress

Driver until they forgot and called her Alice again – but he died and she was still the plough girl. And then, one day when she was thirty and old enough to know better than to think for herself, Alice found a Bible. It was a huge book full of words, but Alice the plough girl knew how to read, so she read about Abraham, Moses and Jesus, Peter and Paul. And everything changed forever. Alice decided that the local church – Catholic, at the time, like the queen – was wrong so she stopped going to church. The priest noticed and told the authorities. And the soldiers found Alice, not just reading the Bible, but hiding another rebel Protestant. The two of them were locked in prison, tried for heresy and condemned to death. Alice was funny, uncompromising and brave to the end.

Anne Bulkeley

1470 or 1475 - 1535

Many years ago, when the royalist families of red rose Lancaster and white rose York fought for the throne of England in the Wars of the Roses, a baby girl was born. Her family owned manor houses and farm land and her mother was cousin to a fugitive princess and future queen called Elizabeth of York. More importantly, however, the baby's family loved books. In those days almost all the books in England were written and illustrated by hand. Books were expensive and were meant to be treasured as well as enjoyed. The baby girl in her swaddling clothes and wooden cradle, however, didn't care about books at first. She was christened Anne and as she grew she learned all the things a girl needed to know in those days. She learned to pray, to bake bread and pies, to brew ale, to spin, weave and embroider cloth and to grow herbs and make medicines to doctor her family and servants when they were ill. Over time she filled her dower chest with beautiful and useful things for her future home. She also learned how to read and write in English and Latin. She married Thomas Bulkeley when she was a teenager and they had a family of boys and girls. One of her daughters was called Anne too. Her husband, who owned manors and land like her father, was a lawyer and a Member of Parliament so he could afford

books. Anne was a devout Christian and one day, when she was a young wife and mother, she commissioned a book of prayers. It was written by the monks of an abbey she liked to visit and was a unique collection of prayers which they thought would be helpful for a country lady. At the beginning of the book she wrote *domine Anne Bulkeley altinet liber ist* which is Latin and means "this book belongs to Lady Anne Bulkeley". Anne died in the early days of the English Reformation and it seems she left her prayer book to her daughter, Anne, who was a nun. The younger Anne also wrote her name in the front and added her own collection of prayers to the book. When her convent was dissolved by Henry VIII, in 1540, she lived and prayed in a little house with another nun and a servant. And so, somehow or other, Anne's prayer book survived the Reformation.

Ann Fanshawe

1625 - 1680

In the days of the English Civil War – when Royalists fought for King Charles I and Parliamentarians fought for Parliament – there lived a young lady called Ann Harrison. She had three older brothers and a younger sister and was raised in a country house where she learned music, singing, dancing, needlework and French. But, she confessed, she was "a hoyting girl" who liked riding horses and climbing trees better than anything. When the Civil War broke out, her father took her to Oxford, where he was serving the king. Here, amid the colleges, courtyards and spires of the university, Ann met and married her husband, a noble cavalier called Sir Richard Fanshawe. He was the love of her life and she said, "I more valued myself to be called by his name than born a princess." For the rest of the war Ann followed Richard around England and Europe, on horseback and by boat, as he served the king and the forlorn hope of the Royalist cause. One night their home was attacked while Richard was away and Ann hurried by candlelight to pack her husband's books, papers and bags of coins in a wooden trunk. She ran to get a travel pass from the soldiers at the gate of the city. She and their children escaped, at dead of night, just in time. Another day their ship was attacked by pirates and

all the women were locked in a cabin below decks for safety. Ann banged and shouted until a sailor came, and then she bribed him to obtain his rough coat and woolly hat. She crept onto the deck of the ship and joined Richard in the midst of the danger. Yet another time, when her husband was a prisoner of war for some reason, she and their children stayed in a strange city. Every day she prayed for Richard's release then stood in the street and called his name below his prison window until he looked out. In good or bad weather – sometimes with the rain running into the neck of her dress and filling her shoes – she cheered him up until he was free again. Ann was devastated when Richard died. She would rather endure cold, hunger, storms, pirates and wars with him than enjoy anything else without him. Now, however, she composed a heartbroken prayer in the midst of her grief. She later wrote that the two of them had lived day to day by begging God for bread and they often feared that they would die in storms or shipwrecks. In spite of everything, however, she – like her husband – had a deep and gallant faith in God which never doubted His watchful care over their travels and travails and she always tried to submit to His loving will. Ann lived to be an old lady but she never stopped missing Richard. When she died, she left a commonplace book full of recipes for medicines and sweetmeats, as well as an entertaining and touching memoir about her adventures, her babies and her conversations with the king.

Anthony Trollope

1815 - 1882

Anthony Trollope's life was a bit like a story in a book. His father was a crotchety lawyer, his mother was an idealistic novelist and his childhood was lonely and precarious. Anthony came from a family full of baronets, clergymen and lawyers. Unfortunately, however, his parents were terrible with money so Anthony was sent to very good schools, but as a charity pupil, so he was friendless and bullied. He worked for the Post Office in London and was miserable for seven long years. At the end of that time, though, he – and his boss – grabbed an opportunity for him to transfer and work for the Post Office in Ireland. Anthony found a new life in Ireland and fell in love with the land, the people and the culture. He was finally comfortable, happy and unstressed. He became a trusted civil servant, got married and had a family. He also decided, for some reason, to write a novel. Readers loved it, so for the rest of his working life, Anthony got up early to write for three hours before breakfast and then went to work for the Post Office. He did a lot of travelling for his job and he wrote in the train, too, as it wound through the countryside. When other writers talked about "imagination" and "inspiration", Anthony laughed, but said he was like a poor cobbler. He, like the cobbler, had a family to support so

he, like the cobbler, sat down and worked hard. He wrote a set number of words every day whether or not he felt like it – all about clergyman and politicians, muddy hunts and glittering balls, conscientious men and principled women – plus the odd rogue with a loaded pistol or adventuress with a diamond necklace! Anthony was a chatty, cheerful and loveable author. He was also a private man who didn't make a fuss about his faith in his novels, even though he called them as his "pulpit" and breezily lectured young men and women on the right and proper way of doing things. He was an advocate for free speech in almost every area, but refused to publish anything which denied or questioned "the divinity of Christ" in the magazine he edited. It seems that Anthony, like his much-beloved character of Septimus Harding, was simply "a good man without guile, believing humbly in the religion which he has striven to teach, and guided by the precepts which he has striven to learn". He is remembered, in the words of a contemporary, as a man who experienced life and feelings on a deep level and captured its gladness, sadness, charm, humour and meaning in words.

Barbara Wilberforce

1771 - 1847

It so happened that on a spring day in 1797 William Wilberforce, a Member of Parliament in the middle of a twenty-year political battle to abolish the British Slave Trade, married Barbara Ann Spooner. He was thirty-eight and walked with a stoop. She was twenty-five and wore a pretty dress, bonnet and flowers. They had known each other for about seven weeks. William's friends thought he – with his frail body, twinkling eyes and warm heart – was extraordinary. They weren't so sure about Barbara. But William, who had lost hope of getting married, was overjoyed with his pretty, sweet and unselfish bride. Barbara, a merchant's daughter and a committed Christian, was a young lady with a small fortune which meant she could marry for love rather than money. It seemed a perfect match and the young couple settled into a slightly chaotic but very happy life together near London and the Houses of Parliament. It turned out that Barbara was a terrible housekeeper but a fiercely committed and loving wife. She thought she didn't know a great deal about Christianity, compared to William, but they were equals and partners in their Christian faith. Although she prayed for him and his political work, William liked the fact that she was part of his private life, rather than his busy and stressful

public life. Barbara wasn't a society lady or a clever student, but she was always busy and happy at home. She did the housekeeping, raised her children, nursed her family and servants when they were ill, read, wrote letters, sewed baby clothes, visited and entertained friends, attended church and went shopping. She was always there when William got home from the Houses of Parliament or a meeting about one of his endless projects and societies. He struggled with a lot of health issues, which got worse as he got older, but Barbara cared for him and fussed over him for years. She also tended their babies rather than hiring a nanny and when they were older she played Puss-in-the-Corner with them, taught them to read and wrote them letters. The Wilberforces were rather poor when they were old but Barbara still adored and supported William. He said he was "captivated" by Barbara when they first met and later, after years of marriage, he said she was "so kind, so faithful a wife".

Bartholomew of Farne

Unknown - 1193

This is the story of a man who had three names. He was born in England to Viking parents who called him Tostig. He was a cheerful, friendly boy, but he got fed up with being teased about his unusual name, so he changed it to William. He was a bit wild as a teenager, but decided that he wanted to serve God. All was well until his parents suggested that he should get married. He didn't want to get married, so he ran away from England to Norway where he became a priest. He chose the name of Bartholomew – his third and last name – when he took his priestly vows. Although priests in England weren't allowed to get married, priests in Norway were, so before long a Norwegian man suggested that Bartholomew should marry his daughter. But poor old Bartholomew still didn't want to get married, so he ran away again, back to England. He worked as a parish priest then became a monk in Durham. He had a vision of Jesus turning His head towards him and opening His arms in an embrace. Bartholomew was deeply touched and decided to become a hermit, who lived on his own and devoted every moment of the rest of his life to Christ. He settled on the Isle of Farne where Cuthbert of Farne, before him, was a hermit. Bartholomew wasn't lonely because he had Jesus, a pet bird and a cow. He also had the

puffins that nested on the clifftops, the seals that lounged on the rocks and the seabirds that flew through the sky. He loved the island with its craggy rocks, rough grass and tiny flowers. And he loved the sea and the sky which had hundreds of colours, sounds and moods. The puffins made him laugh with their clownish waddle and rainbow beaks. He rescued baby seals which got separated from their mothers. He was fond of his pet bird and sang psalms at the top of his beautiful voice as his baked his bread, milked his cow and strode around the island in his simple robe. He was known far and wide as a friendly, generous hermit.

Bega

600s

It was said, long ago, that an Irish princess called Bega was the most beautiful maiden in the land and that her heart was as beautiful as her face. She was a committed Christian who wanted more than anything else to love and serve Christ, whom she called her Heavenly Bridegroom, for her whole life. Her father, however, was an Irish prince who ruled land and people and loved horses and dogs. He loved Bega very much and wanted her to be happy. He knew his duty and found a husband for his beautiful, saintly daughter. The groom was a prince who was handsome and strong. Bega, however, was horrified to learn of her proposed marriage. The prince who wanted to marry her was a pagan warrior who didn't know Christ. Bega bided her time and said her prayers and then, one night when everyone was asleep, she slipped away from her family home, deep in the hills and woods of Ireland, with a leather bottle of water from a spring and a cloth bundle of bread and cheese. She found a little boat by the sea and sailed across the Irish Sea. The wind flapped the sail back and forth and the waves lapped again and again against the little boat. Overhead the seabirds swooped and called. Finally, when Bega's lips and hair were salty and stiff with seawater and her eyes were weary of looking for

land, the little boat arrived in the safe embrace of a pebbly beach sheltered by red cliffs and green headlands and overlooked by colourful, waddling puffins. Here, in Northumbria in England, Bega lived in a little hut. Later, when fierce raiders from the sea attacked the coast with sword and fire, Bega moved from the beach to the woods and mountains beside the lake of Bassenthwaite. Here, surrounded by hills and woods, Bega prayed at night while an owl t'wit-t'wooed in a nearby tree, and by day while robins, blackbirds and thrushes sang in the surrounding woods. She vowed never to marry, but to love Christ with all her heart. Later she built a tiny chapel, out of stone, where she lived happily in peace and purity for the rest of her days. It is said that the nuns who followed in Bega's footsteps treasured her bracelet until the days of the English Reformation. The puffins still nest near her church in St Bees and in Bassenthwaite, along a twisting track and across a field full of sheep, the wild roses still scramble and nod around the little chapel beside the lake where Begs is remembered.

Billy Bray

1794 - 1868

William Trewartha Bray was a big name for a little boy and he was soon known as Billy Bray. He was born near Wheal Busy – an arsenic, tin and copper mine – in Cornwall. Here, for thousands of years, Cornishmen had mined metal and sent it throughout the country and around the world. Here, not long before Billy was born, John Wesley had given Cornish men, women and children hope for life and eternity. Cornwall was dotted with the mine shafts and Methodist chapels which kept body and soul together. Now, however, times were hard and Billy became a miner as soon as he was old enough. Every day he climbed down ladders, crept along passages and went to work in the depths of the earth by the light of a flickering candle. It was hard, dangerous work. The mine shafts were thousands of feet deep and some of the tunnels reached for miles under the bed of the sea. By day Billy worked underground with a mallet, a pickaxe and a shovel. By night he drank, cursed and fought. He lived with a dreadful fear of hell, but he was carefree, cheerful and clever, so he married a local girl, became the father of a big family and spent his hard-earned wages on beer. Later Billy said he was wild, daring and reckless, but one day in the dark of the mine, he had an accident. He almost died – or so he

believed – and he began to think about faith and desire a fresh start in life. He read the Bible, prayed and sang. Finally he found a sense of peace in Christ. Billy resolved to live like a real Christian now. He stopped drinking beer, raised his children plus two orphans and built three chapels in Cornwall. He also became a local preacher who was known for singing and dancing in the midst of his sermons. He was sometimes challenged about this. One time he said, "If they were to put me in a barrel, I would shout glory out through the bunghole!" Another time he said, "Why shouldn't I dance as well as David? David, you say, was a king; well, bless the Lord! I am a King's Son!" He was often called "The King's Son" and is still remembered as a small man with steady but twinkling eyes and "a desire to do good".

Brendan the Navigator

About 484 - About 577

Long ago an Irish boy was born and raised on the wild and beautiful west coast of Ireland where the cliffs seem to touch the sky before they tumble into the sea. His name was Brendan. He played and ran on the green hills when he was a boy. When he was a man, with clear eyes and strong muscles, he chose to be educated and ordained as a priest. But he wasn't an ordinary priest. He was, at heart, an explorer. He made a bold plan and then he made a little boat. One day he left Ireland and sailed west into the vast blue unknown of what we call the Atlantic Ocean. He took water in leather bottles, food in woven baskets and a pile of wool blankets and animal skins. He also took sixteen companions who were as adventurous – or, as their relations, friends and neighbours said, as foolish – as Brendan was. Together they wanted to find the Garden of Eden. For days and weeks and months the little boat was rocked by calm blue seas and tossed by wild white waves. Brendan and his companions didn't find the garden but they did have many adventures involving sea monsters that were bigger than their boat and icy pillars which rose out of the sea like the cliffs of Ireland. Maybe we would call them whales and icebergs. Once they lit a fire and cooked a meal on a tiny island that sank into the sea in the

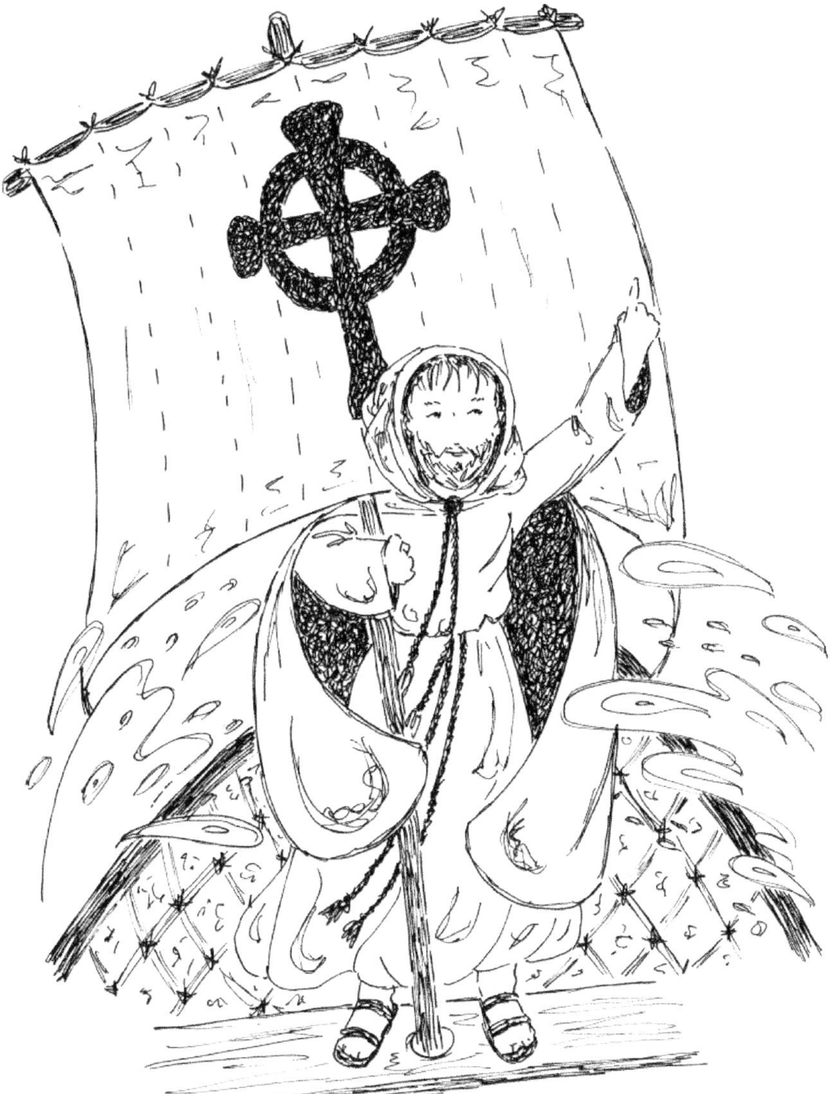

middle of their supper. And another time they found a beautiful goblet encased in crystal. Finally, with his heart full of all the wonderful things he'd seen, Brendan returned safe and sound to Ireland. Later he became a wise abbot with eyes full of mystery. His adventures were told and retold around the fire – remembered by children who liked to play at being Brendan – then recorded in a book called *The Voyage of St Brendan the Abbot*.

Brilliana Harley

1598 - 1643

In the days of the English Civil War, when Royalists supported King Charles I and Parliamentarians supported Parliament, there lived a Christian woman called Brilliana Harley who loved God and believed that the Parliamentarian cause was just and right. She and her husband, Sir Robert Harley, had a large and happy family of three boys and four girls and lived in a castle in the Herefordshire countryside. The Harley family had owned the land and the castle for hundreds of years, but all their neighbours were Royalists, so they began to feel like outcasts and strangers in their own home. Sir Robert Harley was busy in London with Parliament. He thought his family was safe at home and Brilliana thought so too. She wrote, "Thank God I am not afraid." When she began to feel anxious, she didn't run away, but prepared the castle for battle. She ordered muskets, gunpowder and shot. And then, being a devoted wife and mother, she sent her husband and son – both fighting for Parliament now – clean clothes and homemade cakes, pies and cider. The neighbours became more hostile and Brilliana heard stories of siege and war. She asked her husband if it would be better for her to leave the castle or "by God's help to stand it out". Not long after, hundreds of Royalist soldiers surrounded the

castle, which they laid siege to for seven weeks. The castle had a gatehouse with two stout towers and two strong portcullises and these kept the Royalists at bay while shots – and letters full of polite demands and refusals to surrender – were exchanged. Inside the castle, Brilliana supervised her tiny but brave garrison of fifty soldiers, servants and various friends and relations`, including little girls and elderly ladies. Resolutely she protested her ultimate loyalty to the king – in spite of the fact that she and her husband were Parliamentarians – and refused to open the castle gates to the Royalists because "my dear husband hath entrusted me with his house and children … and I do not know it is his pleasure that I should entertain soldiers in his house". Finally the Royalists were summoned by the king to leave the castle and support his cause at Gloucester. The "honourable and gallant Lady Harley", as she was called by her garrison, was triumphant at last.

Caradog of St Davids

Unknown - 1124

Once, many years ago, a young nobleman called Caradog left his home among the Welsh mountains and travelled to the court of King Rhys ap Tewdwr in what is now South Wales. Caradog was a skilled musician who played the harp and in the course of time – with a lot of patience and practice – he became the court harpist. Like King David in the Bible, Caradog was honoured with a seat at the king's table, where he plucked the strings of his harp and sang beautiful songs full of faith and legend and Wales. He also won the friendship of the king and all was well until the day when Caradog lost two of the king's favourite hunting dogs. Caradog loved animals, so he was probably upset and worried about the dogs, but the king lost his temper and threatened Caradog with all kinds of terrible punishments. Sadly, Caradog realised that his friendship with the king was over, so there was no reason for him to stay at the court any longer. Instead, he cut the blade off the end of his lance, which turned the warlike weapon into a walking stick. Boldly he said he would find a master who valued men more than dogs – and perhaps he also hoped to find a master who valued friendship more than hunting! Caradog escaped to what is now North Wales, took the solemn vows of a monk and began a new life of devotion to

Christ. He found a deserted shrine and built a tiny chapel in the middle of the countryside. He loved peace and quiet, but people knew he was a holy man who loved Christ, so they came to him for prayer and help. For the rest of his life, wherever he lived, worked and prayed, Caradog was known for playing the harp and loving all the animals – from the smallest to the biggest – which crossed his path.

Chad of Mercia

Unknown - 672

One day Chad – who wore a simple robe tucked into his belt but nothing at all on his feet – defied a bishop. He was one of four brothers who studied in Ireland and at the monastery of Lindisfarne under the monk and missionary Aidan of Lindisfarne. As a boy he read the Bible and learned many Psalms by heart. As a man he was known for his humility and kindness. At one time he was accused of not being fully consecrated for the role he held in the church. He explained that he was willing to resign because he had never considered himself worthy of the position and had only agreed to undertake it out of duty. The man who had accused him was so touched that he completed the consecration and Chad kept the job! Through it all, however, Chad followed the example of his hero Aidan: walking and sharing the Gospel of Jesus Christ with everyone who wanted to listen. And so it came about that he defied a bishop who didn't understand. Chad and his companions – his brothers and their fellow monks – were missionaries who travelled on foot, slow enough to notice people and have conversations, along the muddy roads of England. They settled in simple and humble communities – called monasteries – where they worked with the local people in the fields. They prayed with their feet in the

rich soil of the fields and told Bible stories with shovels, hoes and sickles in their hands. In rain and sun, at lambing and harvest, they worked and talked about Christ and laughed. It was a slow, good work for the land and the Gospel. The local people knew Chad and his companions were good men and they wanted to know why. Chad talked about Jesus and all He meant to him. People listened because he cared. But the local bishop didn't understand. Chad – with sun in his eyes, earth between his toes and wheat swaying all around him – looked at the bishop thoughtfully. But he was a small man and suddenly the bishop swung Chad up and onto his own horse. He urged the horse forward and told Chad to get on with making Christians as quickly as possible. Chad, humble and kind but with a mighty soul, defied the bishop and carried on sharing Christ with the local people in the fields day by day.

Charles Fraser-Smith

1904 - 1992

Charles Fraser-Smith was a boy with a talent for inventing and making things. He was orphaned when he was a little boy and was raised in a Christian home by a missionary family. At school he got into trouble for being better at making things with his hands than studying. When he grew up he worked as a teacher, a courier and a worker in an aeroplane factory. Later, because he was inspired by his foster family to be a missionary in Africa, he managed a farm for the royal family of Morocco. Finally, very much later in life, he became a dairy farmer in Devon and was known as a gentleman and a Christian. But between 1939 and 1945, when Britain and the Allies were locked in a life and death battle with the Nazi regime, Charles saved the lives of soldiers and spies with his talent for making things. It all started when, at the beginning of WWII, he preached a sermon at a local church. He talked about how hard it was to get certain things at his Moroccan farm – which was also his mission station – and how useful it was that he was good at making, finding and re-purposing the things he needed to live and serve as a good missionary. After the service Charles was approached and offered what he called “a funny job in London”. Officially he was “just” a civil servant working at a little desk in a dingy office for

the Ministry of Supply. His work was so important and so secret that even his boss and his secretary didn't know what he was doing, so he tried to talk like Winston Churchill, to make himself sound important. Secretly, however, Charles created a stream of clever and unique gadgets to help British soldiers and spies in their fight against the Nazi regime. He invented or made things like working pencils with detailed maps of the enemy territory hidden inside, golf balls with little compasses hidden inside and cigarette lighters with tiny cameras hidden inside. The pencils, for example, were made in the Derwent Pencil factory in Keswick, by trusted employees who were sworn to secrecy and returned after work to make the special pencils under cover of darkness. Later, when Charles was allowed to tell people what he did during the war, he called his inventions "Q Inventions".

Charles Taylor

1840 - 1908

Charles Taylor – a mathematician and a mountaineer – was a generous man who could see beyond his own world into the beautiful and rich world of others. He was born to a tea merchant in the early days of Queen Victoria and educated at a grammar school in London, then St John's College, which is part of the University of Cambridge. Here Charles studied mathematics and theology and rowed for Cambridge in the Oxford and Cambridge Boat Races on the River Thames. Charles wrote papers and books about mathematics, but he was ordained by the Church of England and became a theological lecturer at the University of Cambridge. He was fascinated by the work of the first Jewish professor of Jewish literature at the university, so he became an expert in Hebrew too. He produced a tremendous piece of work on a book of Jewish literature called *Pirqe Avot* or "Sayings of the Fathers", which was full of teachings which were passed from rabbi to rabbi for thousands of years. Later he studied and published *The Didache* or "The Teaching of the Twelve Apostles". It was an early Christian book, written by Jewish Christians in Greek for Gentile Christians, including some of the earliest prayers for Communion in Christianity. Later Charles worked with another professor of

Jewish literature, Solomon Schechter, who made a dramatic discovery in Egypt. Charles authorised and financed Schechter on a secret rescue mission to a synagogue full of ancient manuscripts which were being stolen and sold to tourists. Schechter brought a treasury of ancient Hebrew books, manuscripts and letters – a gift from the Jewish community of Cairo – back to Cambridge where he and Charles pored over the priceless documents and published their findings. Charles was a traditional Christian and faithful priest who loved the ceremony and tradition of the Church of England. In spite of his personal commitments and passions, however, he encouraged the University of Cambridge to admit non-Christian Jews and non-Church of England Christians to the university as students and staff. He understood and respected the value of other traditions and how they enriched the academic and social life of the university. Charles was an outdoors man who loved walking, hiking and mountaineering and was a member of the Alpine Club. The year before he died he married a young woman called Margaret and was rapturously happy. At St John's College in Cambridge, especially, Charles is still remembered fondly for his generous and inclusive spirit.

Charlotte Mason

1842 - 1923

Charlotte Mason was born near the sea in Wales. Her father was a merchant and her mother was a delicate lady who needed fresh air and sea breezes for her health. They adored Charlotte and took it in turns to give her lessons, but they both died while she was in her teens. She had no siblings or cousins, so she lived with friends until she went to London, at the age of eighteen. Here she trained to be a teacher at the Home and Colonial School Society, because she loved children and had happy memories of pencils, books and learning. Charlotte earned her teaching certificate, became the headmistress of an infant school and started a school for girls. Later she became a lecturer at a teacher training school. At this time, however, Charlotte's health was delicate. Victorian ladies with no family, little money and fail bodies were vulnerable to poverty, but it seems that Charlotte didn't panic. She took time off work, went for healthy and strengthening rambles through the countryside and made notes of everything she noticed along the way. She filled her notebooks with detailed observations and sketches of flowers, leaves and birds. From her notes, Charlotte wrote a series of books about the countryside for children, which enabled her to safely retire from teaching. But Charlotte still loved children and

everything about education. Her vicar asked her for a donation to parish work, but Charlotte gave a series of lectures about education instead, then turned her lecture notes into her first book about education. In the years to come, Charlotte wrote a series of books about education, then founded her very own teacher training school, the House of Education, in Ambleside in the Lake Distract. Charlotte was a deeply religious, profoundly compassionate woman who wanted children to grow and flourish. She respected children as small but real and whole people and she worked to give them beauty, goodness and truth. She believed in giving children real ideas and objects for learning rather than dry theories and textbooks. She stressed that children are supposed to "find out" all they can about everything they encounter. She encouraged them to memorise the great thoughts of others and create notebooks of their own ideas, observations and sources of inspiration. Charlotte also taught children to live by the dutiful principles of her own abundant and generous life: "I am. I can. I ought. I will." At the end of her life she was a soft and smiling woman, a busy educationalist to the last, living and working for children among the gentle hills, timeless rocks and mysterious lakes she loved. And some children, to this day, are still given the gift of "a Charlotte Mason education".

Christopher Chavasse and Noel Chavasse

1884 - 1962 and 1884 - 1917

Christopher and Noel Chavasse were identical twins born to a vicar and his wife in the Victorian era. The Chavasse family shared a deep love and reverence for the Bible and every morning, when they were little, the twins heard their father reciting Bible verses and praying before they, too, learned a Bible verse and recited it to their mother. Noel and Christopher were happy, clever, sporty boys who grew up with a lot of brothers and sisters, did well at school and were very creative. Once, remembering their years at Magdalen College School, they created a scrapbook full of stories, poems and paintings about Oxford, knights, ladies, faithfulness and heroism. The twins were inseparable and attended the University of Oxford together, where arts-minded Christopher studied Humanities and science-minded Noel studied Natural Sciences, before Noel became a doctor and Christopher became a vicar. The twins ran in races at university and both of them ran for Britain in the 1908 Olympic Games. Noel taught Bible classes and helped homeless boys then became a surgeon and joined the Royal Army Medical Corps. During WWI, he was awarded two Victoria Crosses, for bravery and gallantry in battle. He often tended wounded men in No Man's

Land between British and German trenches. Here, under enemy fire, he doctored and rescued as many wounded soldiers as he could. Towards the end of the war, on one of these medical rescue missions, he was wounded. He died of his wounds, after dictating one last letter to his fiancée, Gladys. Christopher, who was the first of the twins to go to war when he joined the Royal Army Chaplains' Department, survived but missed Noel for the rest of his life. As an army chaplain, he was promoted to a rank equivalent to Lieutenant Colonel and was awarded the Military Cross, for "conspicuous gallantry and devotion to duty" during WWI. After the war, Christopher married his fiancée, Beatrice. The couple raised a family while Christopher served as a vicar, rector and bishop in the Church of England. He was still known as a sportsman who respected Sunday as the sabbath day and his picture was once printed in a newspaper, alongside a picture of the runner and missionary Eric Liddell, as a "sports stalwart" who "reverenced God's Day". He also championed the importance of memorising the Bible. The twins' faith and heroism in the midst of battle is remembered to this day, but although they were caught up in a terrible war, they shared a strong faith in Christ and this shaped their entire lives: Noel's short, heroic life and Christopher's long, faithful life.

Christopher Trychay

1490s - 1574

Once, amid the green and pleasant countryside of Devon, a priest called Christopher Trychay shepherded his flock through the English Reformation. He was a Devon man and he didn't go to university, but he was ordained as a priest and sent to minister in a small village called Morebath. Here there were more sheep than people – or so it seemed – and here he was a faithful shepherd to his flock, not of sheep, but of people: squires, farmers, merchants, labourers and their wives and children. Christopher ministered in the church and lived in a small house nearby with a bed, a table and a stool. He worked to beautify the church and enrich the faith of his people by encouraging them to celebrate the church seasons and honour the local saints who, they believed, watched over them and prayed for them before Christ in heaven. Christopher kept a record of the life of the church. His church book still exists and is full of the details of his people: their births, marriages and deaths, the money they gave for a new robe and the way they started the new tradition of St Sidwell. When the Reformation came, Christopher grieved as images were burned and traditions were forbidden, but he knew his people hid some of their treasures in their homes: the wine chalice in this farmhouse, the bread plate in that farmhouse,

the beautiful and costly new church robe they gave him in the other farmhouse. Once the men of Devon and Cornwall, who were used to praying in Latin, rebelled against the *Book of Common Prayer* which was written in English. Christopher gave coins from the church coffer to some of the Morebath boys so that they, too, could go and fight in what was called the Prayerbook Rebellion. Probably they were killed by the king's soldiers near Exeter and never came home. Christopher didn't rebel – or encourage his people to rebel – again, but eased them out of the old ways of Catholicism and into the new ways of Protestantism like the caring and faithful shepherd he was. The table for Communion replaced the altar for Mass, but Christopher, first in Latin and then in English, still administered the Bread and Wine of Communion and preached the Gospel of Christ. When he died he was buried by his people at the heart of their church.

Cicely Mary Barker

1895 - 1973

Cicely Mary Barker was a young artist who had a secret sorrow. As a child she had epilepsy, a medical condition which still isn't totally understood today, but was even less understood in those days. She was kind, intelligent and pretty – she plaited her brown hair and wore it pinned around her head like a little crown – but she never knew when she might have an epileptic fit so she lived a quiet, reclusive life at home. Later Cicely grew better and stronger, but she was never totally well and never forgot the suffering she experienced and the love of beauty she learned. She was educated at home and took art classes by correspondence course. When she was seventeen, she decided to be an artist, like her father and many of her ancestors. She was strongly influenced by the artist and philosopher John Ruskin who believed art should be truthful and serve a high purpose. Cicely loved children and nature and was inspired to paint pictures of tiny little children, dressed as fairies and playing among flowers and leaves, by the children who attended the nursery school her sister ran. She made costumes out of gauze and wire for her friends' children and went to Kew Botanical Gardens to examine and paint plants in perfect detail. She always told children that the fairies she painted were "pretend"

but she created a whole world of these beautiful and tiny creatures. She imagined that they were born when the seeds of their plants sprouted and that they were responsible for the care for the plants which were their home. Cicely also painted pictures of Bible stories for greetings cards, children's books and church windows. The nativity story – showing the love of Mary for the baby Jesus and the beauty and innocence of the baby – was one of her favourite stories to paint. She was a faithful Christian and one of the most committed and generous members of her local church. To this day many people love her "Flower Fairies", but not many people know the story of the woman who carried a sorrow in her heart but trusted God in the midst of it and used her imagination and art to make the world more beautiful.

C.T. Studd

1860 - 1931

Once upon a time there were six brothers and three of them – Kynaston, George and Charles – were fabulously good at cricket. Together they dominated the cricket scene at Eton College and the University of Cambridge. And the best of them all was Charles Thomas Studd – known as C.T. – a medium-fast right-handed bowler who was the captain of his school team before earning cricket fame at university and playing in the first ever Ashes Test Match, alongside W.G. Grace, against Australia. His father had made a fortune in India and C.T. and his ten siblings were raised in luxury in England. When his father became a Christian, C.T. was not particularly interested, but eventually he committed his own life to Christ. He was a young man by now and he became convinced that cricket and fame were nothing compared to eternity with Christ. He gave his entire inheritance away and became one of "The Cambridge Seven": seven clever and educated young men from wealthy families, who were all born to privilege, but renounced everything to go to China as missionaries with the founder of the China Inland Mission: Hudson Taylor. C.T. and his wife Priscilla – a beautiful girl from Ireland – eventually served as missionaries in China, India and Africa. They had four little girls

called Salvation, Dorothy, Edith and Pauline. C.T. might have been one of the most famous cricketers of all time, but he gave that chance up for Christ. The Ashes Test Matches are still played between England and Australia for the Ashes Trophy in memory of a little urn of cricket ball ashes which still bears Studd's name:

When Ivo goes back with the urn, the urn;
Studds, Steel, Read and Tylecote return, return;
The welkin will ring loud,
The great crowd will feel proud,
Seeing Barlow and Bates with the urn, the urn;
And the rest coming home with the urn.

C.T., however, never regretted renouncing everything for Christ and living for Him and once said, "If Jesus Christ be God and died for me, then no sacrifice can be too great for me to make for Him."

David Lestourgeon

Before 1660 - After 1731

For many years, since the troubled days of the Protestant Reformation, Protestants and Catholics in France lived uneasily side by side. Huguenots were committed and serious French Protestants. Most of them lived quiet and useful lives, but they were considered dangerous and subversive by some of their Catholic neighbours. Eventually their rights, liberties and protection from persecution were revoked and a wave of immigrants escaped to England. Among them was a young man called David Lestourgeon. He was born in the Medieval city of Rouen. Here the *Gros-Horloge* or "Great-Clock", a Medieval clock built into a Renaissance arch over the Rue du Gros-Horloge, told the time plus the position of the sun, moon and stars. David must have seen it many times and maybe this is one reason why he became a clockmaker. To be a clockmaker, however, he needed more than inspiration. He needed skill and experience. He also needed good eyesight, careful, methodical and steady hands and endless patience to prepare and assemble the cogs and gears, rivets and screws, weights and balances which made the workings of the clocks. Apparently he had these things because he became an excellent clockmaker. David

moved to England, settled in London and started to attend one of the French churches in Spittlefields just before it was officially dangerous and illegal for him to be a Huguenot in France. In 1698 he became a member of the Worshipful Company of Clockmakers in London. One of his clocks can still be seen in the British Museum in London. It is a pocket watch with a delicate black and white face, showing Roman and Arabic numerals, in an intricately engraved silver case. It is easy to imagine David bent over his workbench – with delicate but strong hammers, pliers, plungers, saws, files and pliers nearby – making the watch, winding it up and leaving it to keep time for three hundred years or more. It seems that he made it to commemorate the death of William of Orange, William III of England, the Protestant king who ensured that England remained a Protestant country and a safe refuge for Huguenots like David.

David Richards

1822 - 1900

David Richards was a man who couldn't help but sing. He was born in a little farmhouse near the village of Brynberian, amid old chapels and ancient stones, between the Irish Sea and the Preseli Mountains. His father was a carpenter who sailed around the world on wooden ships with tall masts and billowing sails. He was also a singer with a good voice and it seems that David inherited his musical gifts. As a young man, David moved to the mining town of Blaina, where he worked in a coal mine. Blaina was nestled in a deep valley, surrounded by coal mines, iron workings and all the clatter and dust of industry, with a history of radical reform. Down the mine it was dark, dirty and dangerous. In his free time, however, David sat in the light of the rising sun or the flicker of a twinkling candle and worked through a little book called *Gramadeg Cerddorol* or "Musical Grammar". David could already read and write Welsh but now he could read and write music too. Soon he became the precentor of a tiny but beautiful Congregational chapel, built in the green and pleasant countryside, where he was responsible for leading the congregation in singing. Time passed and David became a schoolteacher. In his early

thirties, however, he made another change and attended the Congregational College to study theology. He also worked as the precentor of a nearby chapel alongside his studies. David served a number of chapels after his ordination as a Congregational minister but he also gave lectures and wrote articles about music and judged competitions at musical festivals. Wherever he went, he encouraged congregations to sing, worshipping God with the music of their voices. In 1862 he published a book called *Sŵn Addoli* or "The Sound of Worship": a collection of sacred Welsh tunes which he had collected from churches and chapels all over Wales.

David Thompson

1770 - 1857

David Thompson was a Welsh boy who was educated at a charity school in London. He was fabulously good at maths, became an apprentice in the Hudson Bay Company and sailed away from Britain forever when he was fourteen. He took a set of surveying tools, a brave heart and a strong faith with him to Canada. He called it a land of “the forest and the white water, the shadow and the silence, the evening fire, the stories and the singing and a high heart”. Here he became a fur-trader, explorer and naturalist but – first and foremost – a map-maker. The local people called him “The Stargazer” because of his technical skills of mapping using stars and the tools of his trade: the compass (to find the direction of things), the telescope (to identify objects and landmarks far away) and the sextant (to measure angles and calculate distances and locations) with paper, pen and ink. David left the Hudson Bay Company for the North West Trading Company and during the rest of his life he walked, rode or paddled over fifty-five thousand miles, making maps which were used for a hundred years or more. Along the way, he married a local girl called Charlotte Small, the beautiful and wise daughter of a Cree woman of Canada and a

Scottish member of the North West Trading Company. Charlotte, who was a young teenager when they got married in a make-shift ceremony, became the mother of their thirteen children. David called her“my lovely wife” and the local people called “The Woman of the Paddle Song”. She worked with everyone they encountered, found or snared and cooked food along the trail and kept her increasing family safe as they crossed rivers and climbed mountains. When one of their little girls got lost in the Rocky Mountains, David and Charlotte searched for her for hours alongside foaming water and sharp rocks, until they found her safe and sound. The couple were faithful to each other throughout the fifty-eight years of their marriage, which was formalised by a Christian minister when they moved back to the east of Canada, when they got all their children baptised too. In those days, life was hard and David and Charlotte were poor, but they used to go for long walks, sometimes at night, to look at the stars they knew and loved. David once wrote at the end of the day’s work that they “continued under the mercy of the Almighty … each of us thankful for our preservation” and he might well have said the same at the end of his long life.

Deborah Levy Alexander

1803 - 1872

Deborah Levy was born to a Jewish couple in Plymouth and raised amid the hustle and bustle of the city with the sea air blowing in from the English Channel. She learned about the faith and role of Jewish women in the tradition of biblical heroines like Sarah and Ruth. She watched her mother light the *shabbat* candles and maybe she dreamed of lighting the *shabbat* candles for her own husband and children in their own home someday. Everything changed, however, when Deborah met a young rabbi from Poland called Michael Solomon Alexander. She thought he was the most handsome and noble man she had ever known. It seems that the couple fell in love more or less at first sight so it wasn't long before Michael proposed and Deborah promised to be his wife. At first, everyone was delighted, but then Michael revealed that – in spite of his Jewish heritage and his rabbinical training – he felt a strong conviction that Jesus Christ was the Jewish Messiah. It was considered a betrayal of his faith and community and Deborah was pressured to break their engagement. She was shocked by his revelation, but she loved him and she was intrigued by his growing faith in Christ, so she kept their engagement even when he was

baptised as a Christian. Deborah and Michael were married under a wedding canopy as a Jewish couple. During the early months of their marriage, however, Deborah also felt an increasing conviction that Jesus was the Messiah and soon she was baptised too. Together, amid a happy marriage, Deborah and Michael had more than eight children and grieved the death of their eldest daughter, Sarah Jane, at the age of twelve. The family went to Ireland and Poland for Michael's work as a Hebrew teacher, an Anglican priest and a missionary to the Jewish community. Later, when he was consecrated as the Anglican Bishop of Jerusalem, they went to Jerusalem in the Holy Land too. Here, at Christchurch near Jaffa Gate, Deborah made a home for Michael and their children. Each day included morning and evening prayer with school lessons, family time and quiet rests during the heat of the day. Sometimes Deborah and Michael explored the ancient ruins of Jerusalem, read the Bible among the olive trees in the Garden of Gethsemane and sang Psalms in Hebrew together. Michael's role as Bishop of Jerusalem was stressful and he found it impossible to please both the Jewish and Christian communities. When he died of a heart attack while he was still a young man, Deborah took their children home to England, where she lived to be an old lady in Sussex. She was buried in the church where one of her sons was the vicar and it's said that her tomb is marked by a cross engraved with some words from Isaiah the Prophet: "Thine eyes shall see the king in his beauty".

Dorothy Dennison

1899 - 1978

It seems likely that Dorothy Dennison was a jolly schoolgirl like the heroines of her own novels for girls. She was educated at a girls' school and later worked for Scripture Union and served at a number of Christian camps for girls. Dorothy's faith in Christ was at the heart of everything she did, so although she wrote a lot of novels for girls about schoolgirls and friendship, study and "playing the game", many of her jolly heroines strive to live as Christians while doing the right thing even when it is difficult or painful. In the course of time, Dorothy met a Christian man. When she was in her early thirties, they married, set up home in an old house covered with roses, honeysuckle and clematis and had a little girl and a little boy. Dorothy's husband was a country doctor and general surgeon and Dorothy had a cook to help with the kitchen work and a nanny to help with the nursery work. She was able to keep writing for girls and encouraging them in their Christian faith, but a friend noted her "joy" at being a wife and mother and Dorothy considered herself blessed beyond measure by God. When WWII came, Dorothy had to cope with food rationing, blackout regulations and bombing raids, like millions of other housewives in England. Her

Exercise Book
Cocoa

husband's medical workload increased because of staff shortages and war casualties and Dorothy worried about him while their children grew up and their servants signed up to fight. Somehow or other, at this difficult time when enemy bombs fell around their home, she managed to write more books to help girls struggling with questions about God, suffering and faith, hope and love in the midst of war. By the time Dorothy was an old lady, the Victorian world of her birth had all but vanished, replaced by the modern world with all its worries. Doubtless, however, she still believed what she once wrote in a little book called *Jill Wants to Know*: "The Christian girl who is trusting in her Father's love … hasn't to fuss and worry about what the future holds. She has only to trust and be guided, for her loving Lord is silently planning for her – in love. And if she will be willing, He will unfold the plan at the right time and in the right way". Today Dorothy's schoolgirl heroines still live on in her books in dusty corners of antiquarian or online bookshops.

Dorothy Garrod

1892 - 1968

One day, in the Holy Land, an archaeologist called Dorothy Garrod oversaw a dig on Mount Carmel. Here, thousands of years ago, Elijah the Prophet defied the pagan priests of Queen Jezebel's idols. In the late 1920s and early 1930s, however, the sun shone out of a clear blue sky onto Mount Carmel which still overlooked the Mediterranean Sea and the Jezreel Valley on either side. Dorothy guided her colleagues and used her archaeological tools to explore the site, digging through centuries of earth and rock, looking for tiny clues – a human bone, a flint splinter, a pottery shard – of times gone by. Between them they found ten Neanderthal skeletons and tens of thousands of stone tools. It was dirty, exhausting and thrilling work and Dorothy loved it even though it was – perhaps – a bit of a surprise in some ways. She, like most Edwardian girls, was expected to be a prim and proper lady first and foremost. Her grandfather was Physician Extraordinary to Queen Victoria, her father was a doctor and a scholar and everyone expected her brothers to do interesting and useful things too. Dorothy was educated at home, but went to study at Newnham College, Cambridge, when she was twenty-one, where she became a

Roman Catholic. A year later WWI broke out and five years later all her brothers – and possibly, although no one knows for sure, her fiancé – were dead from war and disease. Dorothy, at less than thirty, was beautiful, clever and devout. She was also the only one of her family left to do interesting and useful things. At about this time Dorothy discovered archaeology and the ancient and mysterious "pre-history" of the world. She was fascinated by the age of the Neanderthal and the eras whose names are like the words of a poem: Paleolithic, Mesolithic and Neolithic. Dorothy worked as a field archaeologist – planning, digging, discovering, cleaning and recording – and oversaw her own digs and projects around the world. She also wrestled with her Christian faith and the scientific evidence for evolution she felt she discovered. She thought it through as she dug and studied and wrote. Eventually she found a way to keep her Christian faith and yet work with her discoveries and all they suggested about evolution. Later Dorothy worked as an academic at the University of Cambridge but her heart never really left the sites of her digs and discoveries.

Eadfrith of Lindisfarne

Unknown - 721

Long ago, when the light of art and learning in Europe nearly flickered into darkness because of the pagan raiders of the Dark Ages, a little man bent over his desk and created a masterpiece. His name was Eadfrith and he was the Bishop of Lindisfarne. Tradition says he was the scribe and illuminator – the writer and illustrator – of the Lindisfarne Gospels. The Isle of Lindisfarne was the perfect place to work. By day, the sun fell like a golden stream of light through the windows in the stone walls of the monastery. By night, the light of a candle twinkled like a little star in the darkness. But for years, as the sea swished back and forth around the island and he grew older, Eadfrith worked on his beautiful book. He was a Saxon boy who studied in Ireland and his work displays his skill as a scholar and an artist, and shows how people like Eadfrith brought the Celtic and Roman traditions of Christianity together in their writing and illustrating after the Synod of Whitby. But the work was delicate and Eadrith had to concentrate as he wrote the Latin words of the Gospels and designed and painted the illuminations. The designs, intricate and geometric, were created bit by bit. He invented a pencil and drew the outlines, with pens made from

feathers, in ink made from soot. He gathered his materials and mixed his paints – creating ninety different colours from six local vegetables and minerals – and then he applied the precious colours to the parchment using brushes made from quill shafts and squirrel hair. Last of all he added tiny touches of real gold. It was a personal act of devotion for God and the finished book of Gospels is as unique and beautiful today as when Eadfrith laid down his pen and brush over a thousand years ago. But between then and now, about a hundred years after Eadfrith wrote the Lindisfarne Gospels, a scribe called Aldred took pen and ink and opened Eadfrith's book. In the tiniest and neatest of writing, he wrote the very first English translation of the Gospels, threading his English words over Eadfrith's Latin words. Now his community of English Christians could, in their own language, read and understand the Christian story in this most beautiful of books.

Edith Brown

1864 - 1956

Edith Mary Brown was a little girl from Cumberland who had a dream. She was one of six brothers and sisters and one of her older sisters was a missionary. Gradually, as she grew and matured into adulthood, Edith's dream grew into something more serious and she felt called by God to serve Him as a medical missionary. First she studied at Girton College and passed the famously demanding Cambridge Tripos exams of the University of Cambridge. Next Edith trained to be a doctor at the London School of Medicine for Women. Finally she went to India as a pioneering medical missionary – she was the first one who was a woman – with the Baptist Missionary Society. She arrived in Bombay when she was twenty-seven and was enchanted with the beauty and colour of the culture that surrounded her with sunshine and spices. In time, however, Edith was concerned to discover that local women, who were very modest and religious, wouldn't accept the medical help of male doctors and were reliant on untrained women even when they had babies or were ill. Edith was heartbroken about the number of mothers and babies who died. She gathered a group of women missionaries in Ludhiana in Punjab, and when a lady at

home in England gave her a gift of £50, Edith rented an old school and started the first medical college for women in Asia: the North India School of Medicine for Christian Women. At first there were four members of staff and four students, but Edith was determined to train local women in medicine and the school flourished, as clever and compassionate Indian women learned how to diagnose and treat illness and how to help mothers deliver babies calmly and safely. The school was known as "Miss Brown's Hospital" and was beloved by local people and young students. The school trained over four hundred doctors and over one thousand midwives in its first fifty years. Today, as the Christian Medical College of Ludhiana or "CMC Ludhiana", it is still training men and woman, from any social or religious background, as doctors, nurses and midwives in India. Edith's motto is still the motto of the school: "My work is for a King".

Edith of Wilton

About 961 - About 984

Edith was a young princess and nun who loved animals and started the first zoo in England. Her father was a strong king and her mother was a gentle nun. She was born among the green hills and woods of Wiltshire and raised in a convent – surrounded by other nobly-born girls and nuns – so she, in time, became a nun too. Edith called called God "Father and Ruler of my life", but she was pretty, young and rebellious. She hated bathing in cold water – which was supposed to be good for her soul – and loved wearing beautiful clothes made of fine fabric and decorated with gorgeous embroidery. Once, in fact, she worried her fellow nuns when she risked her life by rushing into a burning building to rescue a wooden trunk full of her clothes. Another time she argued with a bishop. He suggested she ought to honour God by wearing the plain and simple black robes and white veils that other nuns wore. Edith retorted that God was interested in her mind and her heart and didn't care about her clothes. And so she carried on wearing bright colours and pretty dresses. Edith also studied and prayed as a good nun should. She was artistic, clever with needle and thread as well as pen and ink, so she embroidered church vestments and

illuminated prayer books. She also started a small zoo. Edith loved animals and tenderly looked after both the tame and wild animals which people gave her, and any ill or wounded animals she found in the countryside. She kept her pets in a special house next to the convent and visited them, to feed and pet them, as often as she could. She refused to be Queen of England when her step-brother died, but founded a church and designed the carvings and paintings that beautified it and helped worshippers enjoy their time with God. Edith lived the rest of her short life – she died when she was twenty-three – with great joy and zest.

Edmund the Martyr

841 - 869

It used to be said that Edmund was a true prince of England. He was born in the flat, empty lands in the east of the country – where the sky is the biggest thing you can see – and raised as a Christian. He was fourteen when he became king. He was young, but it didn't matter, so the royal crown was put on his head anyway. For another fourteen years he ruled his people bravely and fairly as a faithful and thoughtful Christian. But, from the lands of the north and east beyond England, trouble came over the sea. Long wooden boats with long wooden oars, huge cloth sails and fierce painted dragons as figureheads brought Vikings with violent ways and other gods. Men called them Norsemen. And priests – so it was said for generations to come – crossed themselves and prayed, "From the fury of the Norsemen, Good Lord, deliver us." To England, however, the Viking raiders came with the waves of the sea for a hundred years or more. Again and again and again they appeared like magic from the mist and the spray of the ocean with no warning, but great terror, to kill and pillage. And then, sometimes, they settled and built homes and married local girls. The Viking raiders and settlers worshipped their own gods, however, so

faithful Christians feared that England would become a pagan country again. Edmund led his men into battle and fought bravely for their freedom, but the battle was lost. Edmund was captured and given a choice: denounce his faith in Christ and share his power with the Vikings … or die. He didn't want to die, but he couldn't deny Christ. And so on a cold and murky day in November, deep in the woods, Edmund died for Christ. His body was guarded by a wise wolf until the warrior king was buried by his soldiers. People said he was "Edmund the Martyr" and called him the patron saint of England – the saint they thought had a special responsibility for England in heaven – for hundreds of years.

Edward Wilson

1872 - 1912

The big, empty whiteness of Antarctica drew a young man called Edward Wilson towards it like a magnet. He was a doctor's son who loved watching and drawing wildlife and studied Natural Sciences at the University of Cambridge. He became a Christian and then – inspired by his fervent faith – a doctor. He worked as a medical missionary in one of the poorest parts of London and almost died of a lung disease. His long recovery gave him time to develop as a nature artist, but Edward was working as a doctor again when adventure found him. One day someone suggested he should join an expedition to Antarctica with Commander Robert Falcon Scott. The International Geographical Congress wanted explorers and scientist to visit the *Terra Australis Incognita* or "Unknown Southern Land" and discover its mysteries. Scott's expedition was part of an international project and Edward was thrilled to be Expedition Artist, Zoologist and Junior Surgeon. He went to Antarctica on board the *Discovery* with Scott and Earnest Shackleton. He helped to map miles of coastline and made biological, geographical and meteorological records. Together, although they missed the South Pole, the explorers travelled

further south than anyone had before. Edward launched a campaign to save penguins from extinction, before he joined Scott in Antarctica again. He led a mad dash through snow and across rock to snatch five penguin eggs, which he hoped would provide the evolutionary link between dinosaurs and birds. They didn't, as it happened, but Edward was willing to brave immense suffering in the coldest place on earth in the exciting quest for truth and he saw no contradiction between science and faith or failure and success. He loved discovering the fingerprints of God which he saw all around him in the created world, so he set off cheerfully for the South Pole. The polar expedition was determined to reach the pole this time, which they did, after their rival Roald Amundsen. The men started to treck back to their ship, but never arrived. Edward and the rest of the poler expedition died of cold, starvation and exhaustion. When their comrades from their ship found them, they buried them in the snow, with a cross made out of skis on top. The men became heroes of exploration and science and Edward – who inspired the foundation of modern polar science and conservation – is still remembered for his joyous, inquisitive daring and faith.

Edwin and Ethelburga of Northumbria

584 - 633 and About 601 - About 647

Long ago, in the Dark Ages of history, King Edwin of Northumbria requested Princess Ethelburga of Kent's hand in marriage. He was a prince by birth, a warrior who had lost and regained his kingdom under dramatic circumstances and a man who bore a terrible scar down one side of his face. She was a gentle soul and a faithful Christian, the daughter of a Christian king and queen, who refused to deny her faith when her parents died and her brother returned to the pagan ways of the Anglo-Saxons. She didn't want to lose her Christian faith now. Happily, Edwin was a kind and wise man who would sit and think things through, rather than acting or speaking rashly. As part of their marriage settlement, therefore, Edwin promised religious freedom to Ethelburga and her Christian household. He also promised to consider the merits of Christianity and become a Christian if he found it a holy and worthy religion. The journey from Kent to Northumbria was long and hard for Ethelburga but Edwin was waiting for his royal bride. Here, surrounded by bleak moors and stark cliffs so different from the rolling hills and gentle beaches of Kent, Ethelburga practiced her Christian faith while Edwin watched and waited. On Easter Day,

however, Edwin's life was threatened by an enemy. He was saved by a loyal and courageous servant who died to save his king. That very night Ethelburga became the mother of a baby girl called Eanflaed. Edwin thanked his pagan gods for the safety of his little family, side by side with Ethelburga's Christian priests as they thanked Christ. Edwin baptised his baby daughter as a Christian and for a whole year he pondered the claims of the Gospel. One of his nobles said life was like the quick flight of a little sparrow through a king's hall. No one knew what came before or after life. If Christianity gave real hope, he said, then it was special. One of the pagan priests came to faith, took a weapon and destroyed his idols. Finally, on Easter Day the following year, Edwin was baptised as a Christian. From that day forward he ensured that his kingdom was a Christian realm. In those days it was said that a mother and her baby could walk from sea to sea without any threat of danger. All too soon, however, enemies and raiders threatened the peace of the realm and Edwin was killed in battle. Many of his people plunged back into the pagan ways of the Anglo-Saxons. Ethelburga and her children fled to safety in Kent. She took some of Edwin's treasures – a golden chalice and a cross – and her brother gave her a ruined villa between Canterbury and the sea. Here Ethelburga founded a community of study, charity and prayer for Christian woman and lived the rest of her days for Christ.

Elizabeth Elstob

1683 - 1756

Elizabeth Elstob was a girl who loved the Anglo-Saxon period of history. When she was a girl, the classical period of the Romans was idolised, but the English wanted to forget their Anglo-Saxon ancestors, history and literature. Elizabeth, however, was captivated by the stories of kings, saints and miracles. She was orphaned and raised by a clergyman uncle who didn't approve of education for girls, but Elizabeth had learned to read and write from her mother before she died and she wasn't going to stop learning now. Eventually she learned eight languages. When she was thirteen, she went to live with her clever and scholarly clergyman brother in Oxford, where he introduced her to a group of Anglo-Saxon scholars called "The Oxford Saxonists". Later Elizabeth helped him with his academic work and taught their servant boy to speak Old English. She also translated books from French and Latin and – encouraged and mentored by an Anglo-Saxon scholar – produced a scholarly edition of the Athanasius Creed and a book of Anglo-Saxon literature with a transcript of the Old English text plus introduction, translation and notes. Elizabeth argued that the Church of England was the true heir of the Anglo-Saxon church

and wrote about the history and heritage of the church in the tradition of a church historian. She also advocated for the education of women: "If Women may be said to have Souls, and if good Learning be one of the Soul's greatest Improvements … Where is the Fault in Women seeking after Learning?" Later Elizabeth published an Old English grammar book, which was unique, because it was by a woman who chose to write in English, not Latin, so other women could read her work. Elizabeth – sponsored by the Earl of Oxford – planned to transcribe and translate another book of Anglo-Saxon literature into English, but her academic career ended when her brother died. She was in her early thirties with no home or income, but many debts. Elizabeth ran away – abandoning her books and manuscripts – and started a small school, but she relied on the help of friends and didn't have time for books and study for many years. She was finally discovered by the Duchess of Portland, the granddaughter of the Earl of Oxford, who employed her as a governess. And so Elizabeth's old age was comfortable and happy among dust and books with her beloved Anglo-Saxons.

Elizabeth the Daughter of Rabbi Moses

Before 1400 - After 1414

In the days of chivalry, the daughter of a Jewish rabbi made a risky journey from her home in Europe to the *Domus Conversum* or "house of converts" in London in England. King Henry III, a good and gentle man, founded the *Domus Conversum* in 1232. It provided a home, a place to study and pray and a royal allowance for Jews who wanted to become Christians. King Edward I exiled the Jewish community from England in 1290 and now, a hundred years or so later, it was still illegal for Jews to live in England unless they wanted to become Christians. The *Domus Conversum* still welcomed them and Elizabeth the Daughter of Rabbi Moses heard of it in her home in Europe. Her Hebrew name is forgotten but she probably lived in France or Germany. She was presumably a devout Jewish woman who prayed in Hebrew, ate *kosher* food that was appropriate and fit for a Jewish girl and attended synagogue to pray and hear the *Torah* read aloud. Maybe she ran away from home to follow Christ. Maybe it was dangerous to be Jewish in Europe, so her family sent her to be Christian in England where she should be safe. At the *Domus Conversum* she was welcomed, given a home and taught about Christ. She took the

name of Elizabeth when she was baptised. In 1401, she was given a royal allowance and granted an extra penny per day because she was the daughter of a rabbi thought to be “a bishop of the Jews”. Elizabeth stayed at the *Domus Conversum* for seventeen years. In 1413, just before the Battle of Agincourt, her royal allowance was reaffirmed by King Henry V. Elizabeth was Mistress Elizabeth Pole now. She was married to a London tailor called David Pole. She kept house while her husband sewed clothes for the good people of London. Maybe she raised a family of little ones too. She was a devout Christian woman who prayed in Latin, ate whatever food the English garden and English market provided season by season and attended church to pray, light candles and hear Mass. For some reason Elizabeth the Daughter of Rabbi Moses chose to become part of the Christian story and is remembered for her mysterious name and the hint of grace, courage and faith in her story.

Elizabeth Tilley Howland

1607 - 1687

It was a blustery day in September 1620 when Elizabeth Tilley embarked upon a great adventure. She was born in a little village in England and baptised in the village church. Her parents, however, were very strict Puritans called Separatists who eventually "separated" from the Church of England for theological reasons. England was a difficult and dangerous place for Separatists at a time when church and state were so entangled. Elizabeth's parents moved to Leiden in Holland and here, in the Dutch city famous for its university and tulips, Elizabeth grew up amid windmills, tall, narrow houses and streets lined with canals, bridges and trees. She learned how to be a Christian woman and a good housewife, played with other little girls and went to church. The Separatist community in Holland, however, dreamed of finding religious and political freedom in America and became the Pilgrim Fathers. Elizabeth was thirteen when she boarded a wooden ship called the *Mayflower* that day in September 1620 and became a pilgrim girl. The rigging creaked, the sails filled and the wind blew the little ship across the Atlantic Ocean. The sea was stormy, the voyage was long and Elizabeth was dreadfully seasick and homesick. One day, Francis

Billington almost blew the ship and its passengers up when he played with his father's gun. Another day, John Howland almost drowned when he fell overboard in the middle of a storm. Everyone was exhausted, ill and weary by the time the *Mayflower* and the Pilgrim Fathers arrived in America. The sea around Cape Cod Bay mirrored the tattered ship and the shifting light and shadow of dawn and dusk. The hills and woods of the new land seemed to go on forever. They promised a thousand good things for the little band of pilgrims and all their sons and daughters to come. Everyone thanked God for the safe journey and the new land with hearts full of hope and gratitude. Elizabeth waited and watched while her father signed the Mayflower Compact. Finally everyone went ashore and Elizabeth worked side-by-side with her mother to build a new home in the new world. Sadly, both her parents died that first winter, but Elizabeth survived, was given a new home with the Carver family and celebrated the first Thanksgiving. Later she married John Howland and became the mother of ten children with good Puritan names like Desire, John, Hope, Jabez and Ruth. Elizabeth lived to be an old lady in America then made her last Will and Testament which confirmed her deep and ongoing faith through her confession of her sins, her statement of faith in the saving work of Christ and her solemn charge to her children to "walk in the fear of the Lord".

Elizabeth Wilson

About 1826 - After 1888

Elizabeth Wilson was raised in a Christian home and interested in faith from a young age and she cried when she realised that not everyone loved Christ as she did. Some years later, she met the famous missionary Hudson Taylor, when he was a young man training to be a doctor in London and dreaming of going to China. Elizabeth was inspired by his example and at the age of twenty she, too, pledged her life to mission for God. She wanted to go to China, but for thirty years she was needed at home to care for her ageing parents, after her siblings left home for careers or marriages of their own. Elizabeth never told her parents about her sacrifice for their sake. After they died, however, she volunteered to be a missionary with the China Inland Mission Society that Hudson Taylor had founded. In 1876 Elizabeth sailed to China and became the missionary she had longed to be for so many years. By now, at fifty or so, she had grey hair but Maria Taylor said she was "full of energy and brightness". She spent a year learning the language and customs, then started work, when she discovered that her grey hair made her irresistible to the local women. To them, her hair wasn't a sign of age and weakness, but of maturity and wisdom, so they

surrounded Elizabeth and overwhelmed her with their eager desire to hear her share the Gospel of Christ. Some of them travelled for miles to hear the woman they called The Elder Sister share the Gospel, even though her Chinese was imperfect. In 1880 Elizabeth and another missionary undertook a great adventure when they travelled over one thousand miles in three months by land and boat from Hankow, where Elizabeth was stationed, to Han-Chung where a missionary bride, Emily King, needed help and support. Together they rejoiced when eighteen women were baptised as Christians. Elizabeth comforted Emily's husband, George, when Emily died in 1881 and their baby son died in 1882. Elizabeth consistently went wherever she was needed until her health forced her to return to England in 1888. Hudson Taylor declared that her life in China was "an immense blessing". For Elizabeth it was a dream come true.

Ellen Lakshmi Goreh

1853 - 1937

Once, in the days of Queen Victoria, a baby girl called Ellen Lakshmi Goreh was born in India. She was born to a young couple, who might have been elite, influential and wealthy, but she was born in a little room in a missionary compound. Ellen's father, Nehemiah Goreh, was a Hindu theologian and writer who become a Christian theologian and writer as well as an Anglican priest. Ellen's mother, Lakshmi Goreh, was a Hindu who converted to Christianity after Ellen was born but died before her baby girl was three months old. Nehemiah was a young and heartbroken widower with a newborn baby, so according to the custom of the times, he lovingly arranged for Ellen to be raised in Christian foster families in India and England and educated at an English school. Ellen grew into a beautiful and gracious young woman who loved her foster family, her local church and her busy, faithful, happy life in England. She taught reading, writing and Scripture to children and Yorkshire mill girls. She also wrote poems and was encouraged to use her poetic gift for Christ. Ellen was a devoted Christian and she wanted to serve Him, but she assumed she would serve Him in England, where she intended to stay for the rest of her life.

One day as she was teaching a girl's Sunday School class, however, she sensed God tell her that she should be teaching her own people in India. It was a sorrowful decision for Ellen and her foster family and they grieved their parting together. In another way, however, it was a joyful decision. Ellen felt that God was calling her to go to India and she didn't hesitate. She went as a missionary to Punjab in India and served in schools, orphanages and churches as a teacher, a nurse and a deaconess in the Church of England. She also nursed her father in his last years of life. She was called a "happy-natured, well-educated and fully-consecrated daughter of India" at the time and when she was old she was noted for remaining calm and cheerful at all times. Ellen was very modest about herself but always said, "God has been so very good to me." Just before she died she wrote a poem ending with the words:

Oh, let Thy presence still
Remain with me
And be my stay.

After she died it was said, "She loved and was beloved."

Esther de Berdt Reed

1746 - 1780

The day Esther de Bert Reed boarded a sailing ship, watched the wind fill the sails and felt the sea carry her from England to America was thrilling. She was surrounded by the creak of the boat, the screech of the seabirds and the saltly, seaweedy smell of the sea. It already seemed a world away from the tall, thin house in the narrow, smoky street near St Paul's Cathedral where Esther had lived all her life. She was descended from Huguenots and her family called her Hettie and considered her a committed Christian as well as a sensible girl. She loved books, but one day she met a young American called Joseph Reed and began a real-life adventure of her own, which was much more interesting that anything she had read. Joseph was a law student who was studying at the Middle Temple in London. He and Esther fell in love, but although her father liked Joseph, he was reluctant for them to marry and go to America. So, for five years, Esther and Joseph waited, wrote love letters and waited some more. The relationship between Britain and America was uneasy and Esther – presumably influenced by her love for her dashing American, although he modestly attributed it to her own good sense – was already on America's side. When her

father died and left his family in financial difficulty, everything was chaotic and frightening, but then Joseph returned to England. He had come to claim his bride and settle near her family, but the couple changed their plans. They were married in 1770 and sailed for America with her mother. Seemingly Esther fell in love with America as quickly and as irrevocably as she had fallen in love with Joseph all those years ago. They settled in the little town of Philadelphia, within a hundred miles of the Indian frontier, where Joseph became a successful lawyer and Esther made a home and raised their children in the fresh air, open space and free world of the American colony. It was a harder, simpler life than Esther was used to, but she didn't mind. Then the American Revolution came and war broke out between Britain and America. Esther had no doubts about her loyalty, but threw herself heart and soul into the American cause with Joseph. She helped to organise the Ladies' Association of Philadelphia, raise more than three hundred thousand dollars and sew uniforms for the Patriot soldiers. For this she was called "A Daughter of Liberty". The war was dreadful but Esther and Joseph remained devoted to each other. Esther never forsook the Christian faith of her youth but found it a source of comfort and strength in those troubles days. She died while she was still a young wife and mother and her heartbroken husband died five years later. Esther, however, had never regretted the love, bravery and adventure which characterised her short life.

Ethelflaed of Mercia

About 870 - 918

Alfred the Great, King of Wessex, had a daughter called Ethelflaed. In those days Alfred was busy ruling the Anglo-Saxon kingdom of Wessex and fighting the Viking raiders who were attacking England with ferocity and fire. Alfred gave Ethelflaed the same education as her brothers so she learned to read and write, to think and negotiate, to use a sword and win a fight. One Christmas Day, Alfred and his family fled from their Royal Hall. They made their way through the forests and marshes and hid in an isolated fortress called Athelney, in the heart of a wilderness which is now called Somerset. Here Ethelflaed watched her father plan the unity and defence of his kingdom. Later she watched him rebuild the ruined and overgrown Roman forts and gather the Anglo-Saxon earls and serfs into a battle-ready army. Finally, when he won a hard-fought-for peace, she watched him organise trade and taxes, army and navy, church and state so that Wessex flourished. And then, when Ethelflaed was sixteen, Alfred arranged for her to marry King Ethelred of Mercia. Etheldred had admired her bravery and intelligence for a long time and he invited her to be his wife and the Queen of Mercia as the fellow ruler of his kingdom. Dutifully Ethelflaed left home and

travelled with her maids and guards into Mercia. Along the way, her party was attacked by Vikings, so she turned a ditch into a trench and led her servants in fighting and defeating the raiders. She and Ethelred were married and had a little girl called Elfwynn who Ethelflaed loved dearly and educated wisely. At Ethelred's side she campaigned, negotiated and rebuilt. Once she threw beehives full of sticky honey and angry bees over the battlements during a siege. She was a devout Christian like her father and built the minster church in Gloucester. Together – working with her father, brother and nephew in Wessex and Mercia – Ethelflaed defeated the Viking raiders, strengthened the Anglo-Saxon kingdoms and won the respect of everyone. She was beloved as "The Lady of the Mercians".

Etta Lemon

1860 - 1953

Once day Margaretta Louisa Lemon – known to her family and friends as Etta and her neighbours as Mrs Lemon – wrote a letter to a lady at church. In the letter Etta said that she had noticed the lady wearing a bird in a beautiful and fashionable hat. Kindly but firmly Etta explained that a real, live bird had been killed for the sake of the hat. Actually, Etta wrote more than one letter to more than one lady from girlhood onwards, because in those days it was the height of fashion for ladies to wear birds – or bits of birds, like wings or feathers – on their hats. The art of designing and making hats for ladies was called millinery, but Etta Lemon called it "murderous millinery", because it was responsible for killing thousands of birds around the world. She worked with a small group of other woman to found the RSPB – the Royal Society for the Protection of Birds – and not only campaigned to save the Snowy Egret from extinction, but persuaded Parliament to ban designers and milliners from importing rare and valuable feathers from dead birds. Etta was a steadfast Christian whose faith inspired her entire life. She was also a devoted wife and a faithful, generous aunt who virtually raised her nephew while his parents lived abroad. She had a

compassionate heart and good sense of humour. Eventually she became known as “the mother of the birds” and even, affectionately but seriously, as “the dragon”: once a director of the Natural History Museum hid when she was coming! But in time the RSPB became a serious and respected organisation which was run by ornithologists and scientists and supported by thousands of birdwatchers and bird-lovers across Britain. In the meantime Etta – who remained involved in the RSPB until she was eighty – was saddened that, despite her efforts, many of the rich and fashionable women who fought for Votes for Women still wore hats decorated with birds. She felt women could work for change in more constructive ways and was dismayed by the fact that the suffragettes cared more for Votes for Women than other social causes. During WWI, indeed, Etta cared for sick and wounded soldiers herself and was honoured by the king for her work. She was a faithful and intelligent woman who wasn’t afraid to use her voice and speak her mind because she was utterly convinced that her cause was good.

Fanny Coker

1767 - 1820

Fanny Coker was born into slavery on the island of Nevis in the West Indies. Her father was unknown and her mother was a young girl called Polly who had been enslaved in Nigeria and brought to Nevis in a slave ship as a child. Fanny grew into a beautiful, bright little girl and her owner, John Pinney of Bristol in England, arranged for her to be educated with some of his own children. In spite of this, however, Fanny was still a slave girl and she was taught how to be a dutiful and obedient maidservant and a good seamstress. In 1778, when she was about eleven, John Pinney gave Fanny her freedom but Fanny still worked for his wife, Jane Pinney, as her maid. Fanny went to England with John and Jane Pinney and settled with them in their new cream-coloured stone house in Great Georges Street in Bristol. Here, when Jane Pinney had another baby, Fanny worked as her nursemaid and tended Baby Charles carefully and lovingly. It was at about this time that Fanny joined Broadmead Baptist Church in Bristol. It was a tall, thin, ugly building but Fanny found a whole new life of faith inside. The church records that "Frances Coker the descd.t of African ancestors, gave a most intelligent and pleasing acc.t of the work of God upon

her soul, and was accepted as a candidate for Baptism". She was baptised in 1789 when she was about twenty-two. Later that year she paid a short visit to Nevis with John and Jane Pinney. She didn't want to go, but maybe she was glad she did, because she saw her mother and her step-brothers and step-sisters again. Later, back in Bristol, Fanny sent long and regular letters to her family in Nevis with presents and things she thought they might find useful in their work. For the rest of her life Fanny lived quietly and unremarkably. She served Jane Pinney. She received her wages and paid a tythe to Broadmead Baptist Church. John Pinney left her a yearly gift of money when he died. Fanny was about fifty-three when she died too. She left everything she owned to her family, a fellow-servant and the Baptist Missionary Society. She was buried by her friends at the church and they recorded that she 'lived honourably and died comfortably'.

Fanny Kemble

1809 - 1893

Fanny Kemble was twenty when she played Juliet in William Shakespeare's *Romeo and Juliet*. She was the niece of a famous actress called Sarah Siddons and was given an excellent education in England and France. She studied art and music, read the Bible until it became part of her and fell in love with poetry. Fanny was young, inexperienced and diffident when she played Juliet and she only rehearsed for three weeks. Her performance, however, was sincere and touching. In time, she played the leading ladies of all the famous plays by William Shakespeare and Richard Sheridan, but she hated being a theatrical star. On a theatre tour of America, she met a rich cotton plantation owner called Pierce Butler, who was admiring, charming and kind. He was also rich and Fanny knew that, as his wife, she could help her impoverished family. Fanny married Pierce and had two daughters, but the marriage wasn't happy and didn't last, partly because she was an ardent abolitionist who was horrified by the reality of slavery on her husband's cotton plantations. Fanny tried to give the slaves physical and spiritual help and later wrote a powerful and revealing memoir about her experience as a slave-owner's wife: "I have sometimes

been haunted with the idea that it was an imperative duty … to show the dangers and the evils of this frightful institution." Fanny and Pierce were divorced and Fanny was separated from her daughters for many years but neither she nor Pierce remarried. She earned her living by writing and giving public readings from plays. She lived in America for some time then returned to England with her younger daughter and her family. Fanny cultivated her gift for poetry and wrote with aching beauty and honesty about love and regret, trust and betrayal, sacrifice and suffering. She wrote a prayer about faith and loneliness which ended, "Be thou my fellow, glorious, gracious God! And fit me for such fellowship with thee!" In one of her poems she concluded:

But in my soul I heard a voice that said,
Be comforted – of what art thou afraid?
Nor for the hand she holds be thou dismayed,
The hand that holds her is the hand of God.

Francis Taylor

About 1550 - 1621

It is said that in those days, faithful Catholic families in Ireland would place a lit candle in their window, to let brave Catholic priests know that they were welcome to come in and say Mass. In that context Francis Taylor was, for many years, an important man who wore fine clothes, fur robes and a gold chain of office. He was born in a little town on the east coast of Ireland. In the course of time he grew up and became the faithful husband of a girl called Jennet and the loving father of five sons and one daughter. He also became a successful and wealthy merchant and eventually, after years of gaining experience and influence, he became Mayor of Dublin. He was interested in politics and in 1613 he was elected to become a Member of Parliament for Dublin in London. At that time, Ireland was racked with unrest between Catholics and Protestants, which caused division and sorrow. Francis was a faithful Catholic at a time when it was, frankly, dangerous. Maybe he heard the stories about his wife's grandmother, Margaret Ball, who died in prison as an old lady rather than renounce her Catholic understanding of Christ and her Catholic way of worship. Perhaps he never thought that such a thing might happen to him too. His

election to Parliament, however, provoked a fresh outburst of unrest and Francis was arrested and thrown into prison because of his Catholic faith. His captors told him that he would be free and welcome to return to his old life – his importance, his business, his house, his wife and his children – if he would take the Oath of Supremacy. With a heavy heart, however, Francis knew that if he took this oath then he would be obliged to embrace the Protestant way of worship. And for Francis this was impossible. For seven long years he clung with all his heart to his faith in Christ. Somehow or other he managed to provide for his wife and children in spite of his own troubles. Eventually, when he was a very old man by the standards of his time, he died in prison. His saintly faithfulness to Christ was soon whispered from person to person in Dublin. He is still remembered, by those who care about such things, as a man who loved Christ more than all the good things of life. He was like a candle in a window during a dark time.

Frank Foley

1884 - 1958

Frank Foley was a quiet little man who peered at the world from behind round glasses. He was a Somerset boy, the son of a railway worker in the days of steam trains, who originally wanted to be a Roman Catholic priest. For various reasons, however, he became a linguist and joined the army then joined the secret service and became a secret agent. Between WWI and WWII, Frank worked for MI6 in Germany, as the Director of Passport Control for Britain. At that time the Nazi regime was persecuting Jews who wanted more than anything to leave Germany and find a new home in Britain or some safe place in the British Empire. Every day, fathers and mothers with grandparents and children of all ages waited outside the British Embassy in Berlin with their passports, petitioning for visas. The British authorities underestimated the Nazi agenda and allowed themselves to be influenced by their anxiety about war with Germany and their confusion about the loyalties of German Jews in the British Isles. The order from London was clear: limit the number of visas to Britain and countries in the British Empire. Frank read the orders … and ignored the orders. He was horrified at the terrible things the Nazis regime did and heartbroken that the

persecution, fear and sadness Jews experienced was "in the name of Christianity". As a man and a Christian, Frank was incapable of turning all the people who wanted visas away from the British embassy without any hope. He didn't have diplomatic immunity and could have been arrested and executed as a spy at any moment, but he didn't care. Without making a fuss of any kind, he bent the official rules and issued as many visas as he could, giving thousands of Jews the chance of a new life in Britain, the British Empire or the Holy Land which was controlled by Britain at that time. Sometimes he went to a concentration camp to rescue someone, hid them in his home and gave them forged passports and visas to get them out of Germany. If there was no way he could give someone a British visa then he got one from the embassy of another safe country. Later some of the people he helped said that his brave and rebellious goodness and generosity made him "like a saint".

Geoffrey Luttrell

1276 - 1345

Sir Geoffrey Luttrell was a brave and mighty knight in the days when knights rode out from castles to rescue maidens. His sword was pledged to the king and he had manors – houses, land and tenants – all over England. Like most men of his era, Geoffrey was capable of being a ruthless and violent warrior, but he was also deeply religious. And one day he visited a book maker and ordered a Psalter – a Book of Psalms in Latin – which was illustrated with pictures of everyday life in Irnham in Lincolnshire. Maybe it was his favourite manor and village. It included a church and a mill as well as the peasants' cottages and his own house, the manor house, where he lived with his wife, their four children and their many servants for part of every year. Here, deep in the countryside, the peasants and servants worked the land to the rhythm of the seasons – lambing and sowing in spring, reaping and butchering in autumn – as spring flowers, summer grasses, autumn berries and winter frosts followed each other year after year. Geoffrey knew that everything would continue for his children and grandchildren as it had for his father and grandfather. And he knew that when he died, his family and priest would pray for his soul, which he hoped

would go to heaven to be with Christ and all His saints. Meanwhile, trusting God's mercy in life and in death, he said his prayers and recited the Psalms from his new Psalter. It was written by hand on sheets of vellum made from animals skins. The Psalms were surrounded with illuminations – painted by hand using precious pigments and priceless gold – showing Geoffrey's family, servants and peasants. In the margins of the book they still cook and eat meals, fight jousts and nurse babies, practice their archery and comb their hair, tend sheep and feed chickens, plough fields, sow seeds and harvest crops. Geoffrey could look at his Psalter at any time and see the familiar faces of those he knew and loved going about their daily business in the shadow of his care as he, their lord and master, went about his daily business in the shadow of God's care.

George and Grace Stott

1835 - 1889 and 1845 - 1922

For many years, in the Chinese city of Wenzhou, there lived a blunt, brusque, one-legged missionary and his wife. It all began when a Scottish crofter called George Stott lost a leg after an agricultural accident. He had been active, busy and thoughtless about the love of Christ as worked in the countryside with the seasons, the land and the animals. Now, however, George encountered the love of Christ in a new way and realised it was "precious". When he was better, he became a church member and a school teacher, but then, when he was thirty, he heard that Hudson Taylor was looking for pioneer missionaries to go and start new missions in the mysterious interior of China. George thought and prayed and wanted with all his heat to go and serve Christ in this way, but he wondered who would send a one-legged man to China. Apparently Hudson Taylor would. He believed that nothing was impossible with God, so he sent George to China with a brand-new wooden leg. Grace Cigie – who was ten years younger than George, had been raised by her grandmother and had wanted to be a missionary since she was sixteen – also hoped to go to China at this time. She fell ill,

however, so she was left in Britain. In China, far from the lochs and glens of Scotland, George learned the language and travelled through the beautiful but rugged Yandang Mountains to the coastal city of Wenzhou. He was the only British person in the city but he rented a little house, lived alongside the local people and travelled from village to village preaching and teaching the Gospel. George had a lot of patience and perseverance. Eventually he started a tiny church and a school for boys. Grace, at home in Scotland, worked with poor and vulnerable women in Glasgow. Some years later, however, George proposed to Grace by letter. She accepted his offer of marriage, packed her trunks and travelled to China. The couple got married and Grace promptly started a school for girls. Later they started a teacher-training school and a bookshop too! Together they invested love, prayer and years of slow, steady work in Wenzhou. For George – blunt and brusque to the end – it was the most wonderful thing in the world that God had used a so-called useless one-legged man to share the Gospel with hundreds of people who might never have heard it otherwise. When George died, still quite young, Grace returned to Wenzhou on her own and stayed, in spite of riots and epidemics, for another twenty years. The couple did not write essays or books about their work, but happily they did write a lot of letters to family and friends, which capture a tiny bit of their love and work for Christ in Wenzhou.

Georgiana Liddell

1822 - 1905

In 1841, when Queen Victoria was a young queen, Georgiana Liddell became one of the queen's maids of honour. It was an exciting time to be at the royal court. The queen was a happy wife and mother and had just survived an assassination attempt which made her subjects love her more than ever. She and her husband, Prince Albert, regularly invited the musician Felix Mendelssohn to Buckingham Palace and once they threw a Plantagenet ball which was attended by over two thousand courtiers and nobles wearing beautiful and imaginative Medieval costumes. Queen Victoria required all her ladies – including her maids of honour – to be ladylike, modest and cheerful. They had to be fluent in French and German and a little Latin and be able to play the piano, sing and dance as well as sketch or paint and embroider. The queen also liked her ladies to be good horsewomen. Georgiana was a well-brought-up young lady of her era who could fulfil the requirements of a maid of honour and she was a good artist and musician in her own right. Her mother advised her to please the queen by being obedient, punctual and discrete: being a maid of honour could be boring or fun, but in either case, Georgiana's duty was to serve

queen loyally and uncomplainingly. Eventually, when she was twenty-three, Georgiana resigned from court and married a rather dashing and handsome diplomat called Lord Bloomfield. The couple were married in the parish church near Georgiana's family home but then Georgiana and her husband travelled around Europe together on his diplomatic missions. As Lady Bloomfield, she saw the Winter Palace in St Petersburg and the Schönbrunn Palace in Vienna, before she and her husband settled at his family home in Ireland. Finally, when Lord Bloomfield died, Georgiana moved back to England. She lived near one of her sisters, where she interested herself in the life of the country, the village and the church, but she maintained her old friendship with Queen Victoria and wrote a book of reminiscences about her life at the royal court. Georgiana was known to be a religious woman – with an old-fashioned, solid and unfussy faith – who enjoyed the company and conversation of people from all walks of life and worked to provide poor old people with incomes and homes. She continued painting and left a lot of beautifully-drawn and delicately-coloured watercolours to illustrate her life.

Gilbert White

1720 - 1793

Everyone in Selborne knew that Gilbert White loved worms. He was a country curate during the days of powdered wigs, lace cuffs and buckled shoes, but he was more interested in the natural world than fashion, balls and duels. He was born in the country village of Selborne and lived there for most of his life in his grandparent's house: The Wakes. Gilbert spent hours, as a child, watching the development of plants and the behaviour of birds and animals. He became a gardener as a teenager. He grew cucumbers, raspberries, walnuts, peas, mushrooms, radishes and asparagus among other things. He was the first person in his part of Hampshire to grow potatoes and once, to cheer him up when he was recovering from a dangerous illness, a friend wrote a silly poem about Gilbert turning himself into a melon by accident! Gilbert was educated at Oriel College, which is part of the University of Oxford, then ordained as a Church of England minister. He divided his working life between a collection of country churches and Oriel College where he was a Fellow. His first love, however, was always and forever the natural world. Naturalists in those days tried to understand all of nature in one go. Gilbert, however, stayed close to home – not just because

he loved it, although he did, but also because he got terribly travel sick when riding on horses or in carriages. He therefore tried to understand the little bit of nature in his garden and in the fields and woods around his village bit by bit. With immense patience and concentration, he observed tiny changes in plants and tiny differences in birds and animals, noticing the modulating notes in a song or the varying feathers on a wing. He identified the harvest mouse and realised the bird called "the willow wren" was, in fact, three separate birds: chiff-chaff, willow-warbler and wood-warbler! And then, long before the essential role of the worm was fully understood, Gilbert observed its work and wrote, "Earthworms, though in appearance a small and despicable link in the chain of nature, yet, if lost, would make a lamentable chasm." He wrote long and detailed letters to other naturalists. Eventually his letters were collected and edited into a book called *The Natural History and Antiquities of Selborne*. Gilbert's book is still in print today and still transports its readers through history to a country garden seen through the eyes of a godly man who still seems to witness miracles everywhere.

Helen Gladstone

1849 - 1925

Helen Gladstone, the youngest daughter of Prime Minister William Gladstone, was a loving and loyal daughter. When she was twenty-eight, however, she became a student at Newnham Hall in Cambridge. It was less than ten years since it was founded and the idea of a university education for a women was still new and strange. Newnham Hall was an independent institution for young ladies attending university lectures. Young ladies sat university exams, too, but they were not allowed to graduate with degrees from the University of Cambridge until 1948. Helen didn't mind. She was simply thrilled to be studying at Cambridge. She was also worried that she was neglecting what she called her "home duties", especially because her father did not approve of education for women, although he made a special exception for her and she was there with his blessing. Helen, however, believed in education for women with all her heart. She was tall, graceful and beautiful and known for her good sense, good humour and sweet nature. She was a good advertisement for "a Newnham girl" at a time when girls at university were suspected of being ugly, rude and unladylike. Helen intended to study for one year but stayed and studied for three

years then took her final exams in Political Economy. She loved attending lectures, reading books and writing essays. She also loved the spirited community of students. There were skating parties in winter, boating parties in summer and cocoa parties by study fires at bedtime all year round. Helen became the secretary of the principal after her final exams. She was then invited to become the principal of the new Royal Holloway College for women in London and her father urged her to accept it and make it her vocation. Helen was a committed Christian and took her faith very seriously, but she decided to decline the invitation, because she felt her duty lay elsewhere. Later, however, she remembered her father's words and for four glorious years she was the vice- principal of Newnham Hall. At that point she resigned, because her elderly parents needed care, so she went home again. Later, after her parents died, Helen helped to found the Women's University Settlement which encouraged women with university educations to share the benefits of their education with others. She would probably be thrilled to know that Newnham Hall is now Newnham College and part of the University of Cambridge.

Henry Tidmarsh

1854 - 1939

One morning, as the sky above London faded from dark blue to light blue with a heavenly streak of pink and gold in the east, an artist sat and painted in a cobbled corner at the end of a street. His feet were cold and his nose was red, but he didn't notice. Quickly, as the light changed and the shadows shifted, his paintbrush flicked back and forth between his paintbox and his sketchbook and flew over the paper. The birds started chirping and the traffic started rumbling as, bit by bit, the scene the artist saw with his eyes sprang to life on his page. His name was Henry and the world knew him as H.E. Tidmarsh. He was a gentle soul, with keen eyes and nimble fingers, who worked as an illustrator for a newspaper. He travelled all over England sketching and painting pictures for a whole range of articles. In his private life, he also painted, filling sketchbooks and canvases with pictures of his beloved London from every angle and in every light. Gradually, over time, he created a beautiful record of a bygone world. He believed his art was a gift from God which he needed to use for His glory. Henry was a man of deep but quiet faith, a preacher and Sunday School teacher – to generations of boys – in the Methodist Church. He often painted pictures to

illustrate his Scripture lessons and during the week he taught his class woodcarving and metalwork. He was also a pacifist, a teetotaller and a vegetarian who embraced the socialist values of the Labour Party which supported things like Votes for Women and independence for Britain's foreign colonies. Henry married his cousin Nellie, the love of his life, when they were in their forties. Henry and Nellie didn't have any children of their own, but they were a loving uncle and aunt to their nephews and nieces and the neighbourhood children. Henry left a series of illustrated cards, telling the Gospel story, which he drew, scene by scene, for children to colour. He was remembered, by those who loved him, as a truly and unselfconsciously good man.

Isabella Gilmore

1842 - 1923

Isabella Gilmore was willing to do whatever Christ wanted. Such a thing is easy to say, of course, but hard to do. Whatever her joys and sorrows along the way, however, Isabella did it sweetly and wholeheartedly. She and her siblings had a happy upbringing in a Christian home. Isabella loved riding horses and having adventures with her brothers. One of her favourite things to do was to wake early and creep down the stairs and outside, without waking the nanny, to have a private adventure in the big garden while it was full of dew and early morning sunlight. She was sorry to leave school at seventeen, but came home and got married. She was a happy wife, but tragedy struck when her husband died and left her a young widow. In spite of her grief, however, Isabella didn't despair. She took responsibility for her eight orphaned nephews and nieces – who ranged from little children to young adults – and tried to give them a mother's love. The children did, in fact, call her "mother" and their children and grandchildren remembered her kindness too. And then, as busy as she was, Isabella also became a nurse. Her family disapproved, but Isabella knew that this was a way for her to love Christ and serve others in His name. She was a good nurse

and was happy in her job until the Bishop of Rochester approached her and invited her to be ordained as a deaconess in the Church of England. The church role of the deacon and deaconess is found in the Bible and is usually focused on teaching, pastoral work and service to others. The Church of England revived the role for Christian ladies in the Victorian era. When Isabella was invited to be a deaconess, however, it was less than fifteen years since the first Church of England deaconess had been ordained and it was a new venture. At first, Isabella was overwhelmed and worried about her lack of theological training, but then she felt that God was, indeed, calling her to be a deaconess: "it was just as if God's voice was calling me and the intense rest and joy were beyond words". She was ordained, welcomed by the clergy and assigned to a parish where she worked as a deaconess alongside the priest. Later, in her memoir, she confessed that wearing plain clothes and no jewellery – not even her wedding ring – was painful, but that she felt an enormous peace, at the moment of her ordination, which made her "strong and brave" for the task God had called her to do. She served for twenty years in the poorest parts of London. She was remembered as a gracious woman who was intensely loving and generous and unwaveringly serious about serving Christ and others in His name.

Isabella Pringle

1876 - 1963

In 1929, when she was fifty-three, Isabella Pringle – known as Ella to her family – was the first woman to become a Fellow (a honoured and senior administrative and academic member) of the Royal College of Physicians of Edinburgh. She was a Scottish girl, with big dark eyes and long dark hair which she wore plaited and woven around her head like a crown, who was born in Edinburgh during the Victorian era. She loved music and played the piano, but her father died while she was young, so Isabella lived with her mother and worked as an academic secretary at the University of Edinburgh. She typed countless theses for medical students and became interested in biology and medicine. In spite of that, however, she might have been a secretary all her working life if she hadn't heard a lecture about the Edinburgh Medical Missionary Society that changed everything. Isabella became a medical student when she was twenty-nine and completed her medical studies when she was thirty-three. At that time, women weren't granted degrees, but Dr I.F. Pringle completed her medical training and served as a medical missionary in Manchuria near China. It was a dangerous place to work due to war and plague. But here Isabella developed

an interest in and love for the medical care of mothers and children. She returned home to Scotland where she studied public health and developed a medical and welfare service for mothers and children which was ahead of its time. She was forty-five in 1921 when she finally received her MD degree. She went on to take the examinations to join the Royal College of Physicians of Edinburgh. Isabella never married or had any children of her own and was buried with her parents when she died. Her friends called her "Dr Ella" and remembered her as humble, honest and encouraging with a never-ending enthusiasm for medicine and being a doctor. She is still honoured by medics for pioneering the excellent and sensitive care of mothers and children.

Ivy Williams

1877 - 1966

Ivy Williams was a woman who loved the English law. She was a quiet and religious woman – wise, kind and funny with strong convictions and high ideals – but she also had the sort of brain that could argue clearly and logically. She could keep facts straight even when there were a lot of them and they were confusing. Pressure from other people didn't bother her or stop her thinking and speaking clearly. She made a perfect lawyer. Ivy, who had dark hair and blue eyes hidden shyly by round glasses, also loved tennis, gardening and travelling. She was born in Devon and her father, a solicitor, gave her and her brother a robust education. Together they learned French, German, Italian and Russian as well as the classical languages of Latin and Greek. Later they visited Europe and saw great wonders of nature and works of art. Ivy, who came from a family of staunchly non-conformist Christians who attended independent churches and chapels rather than the Church of England, grew into a graceful young woman with a quiet but deep faith. Her brother, Winter, trained to be a barrister at the University of Oxford and Ivy studied at Oxford too. She was the third woman in England to study law, but at that time women weren't allowed

to graduate from the University of Oxford with degrees. As a result Ivy did all the work for her bachelor and doctoral degrees in law, but wasn't qualified to work as a lawyer. Winter died during WWI and in 1920, when the university started awarding degrees to women, Ivy finally received her law degrees. In that same year, women were admitted to the Inns of Court, so Ivy applied to join the Inner Temple. She was determined to be recognised as a lawyer. She wanted to make a way for other women to practice law and she hoped to give free legal advice to people who couldn't afford to pay for it. She was the first woman in England to be called to the bar and she earned a certificate of honour in her final exams. Happily Ivy described her final victory as "the dream of my life" and described herself as a Barrister at Law ever after. She funded two law scholarships at the University of Oxford – one for women only – in memory of her brother and worked at the university, teaching law, for the rest of her working life. Later in life, Ivy went blind, so she taught herself to read and write Braille – a way of reading and writing by touch – and wrote a Braille textbook to help others too. She was remembered as shy but kind and brave.

James and Elizabeth Finn

1806 - 1872 and 1825 - 1921

James Finn was captivated when he discovered that Elizabeth Anne McCaul could speak fluent Hebrew. At the time, James was a dignified, portly and moustachioed diplomat who wasn't as young as he used to be. He was born to a Catholic father and a Methodist mother and educated at a parish school for poor children in London, until a generous nobleman noticed that he was clever and paid for him to have an excellent education. As a young man, James was a tutor and a linguist and somehow or other he fell in love with the Hebrew language and the Jewish people. Elizabeth, meanwhile, was a charming and intelligent young lady who was born in the Zamoyski Palace in Poland to a missionary couple who were sharing the Christian faith with the Jewish community. Later her father became Professor of Hebrew at King's College London and Elizabeth witnessed Queen Victoria's coronation procession to and from Westminster Abbey. She was educated at home and had a real love of homemaking and housework. She was, however, a natural linguist who learned Hebrew, German, Yiddish, Greek and Latin as well as Arabic and Ladino. After that first meeting, when they discovered their mutual love of Hebrew, James and Elizabeth

discovered that they also shared their Christian faith. They married and had three children and in 1846 James was appointed Her Britannic Majesty's Consul at Jerusalem. Although he did not work as a missionary, he was a committed member of the Society for Promoting Christianity Amongst the Jews, who believed that the Holy Land was the perfect homeland for the Jewish people. With Elizabeth at his side, he not only fulfilled his diplomatic duties, but explored and fell in love with the land of the Bible. Together the couple founded what is now called *Kerem Avraham* or "Abraham's Vineyard", a training farm for Jewish agricultural students, on a barren and unloved piece of land outside the walls of Jerusalem. At the time they built houses, workshops and cisterns. Today it is a beautiful and bustling neighbourhood in Jerusalem. James and Elizabeth were beloved by the Jewish community in Jerusalem, but James' superiors decided that he was too personally involved, so he was recalled to England in 1863. James died less than ten years later. Elizabeth founded two societies to help those less fortunate than herself, worked as a translator for the Church of England when the Patriarch of the Ancient Syrian Church visited England and lived to be an old lady of ninety-five who was busy and generous to the very end.

James Bonar

1801 - 1867

It is said that James Bonar was one of five brothers and three sisters born into a Christian family in Scotland. In those days, Sir Walter Scott was writing his poems and novels featuring knights, princes and ladies amid the heather and hills of Scotland during the Medieval and Jacobite eras, but the Bonar family traced their spiritual lineage back to the Scottish Convenanters of the 1600s. James was born and raised in an old, rambling house in Edinburgh and attended Lady Glenorchy's Church with the rest of his family. He never married but it seems that he was a caring man. When he was twenty, his father died, so he supported and raised his younger brothers and sisters then shared a house with his mother for many years. In time, James trained as a solicitor, when he gained a reputation for refusing to work on Sunday because it was the sabbath day. James worked for a legal firm for many years but he also donated his time to Christian brothers and sisters for free and gave his money to Christian causes and projects. He also found time to become an elder at Lady Glenorchy's Church and had a special place in his heart for charities and missions to seafarers. In the course of time, James' younger brothers Horatio and Andrew

Bonar became ministers, making a name for themselves in Scotland and around the world. Horatio was a poet and a hymnwriter, who originally wrote for the children in his Sunday school class, but discovered that Christian men and women around the world loved the words of his hymns and the reminder to reflect upon "what a friend we have in Jesus". Andrew was involved in mission and revival but is best known for writing the biography of a fellow-Christian and fellow-Scot, Robert Murray M'Cheyne, whose short life and intense faith continue to influence Christians today. James lived a quieter life but was no less committed to Christ or generous to others and it seems that the Bonar brothers remained close throughout their lives. The brothers were all inspired by the Christian heroes of the past and by prayer and they once preached a three-part sermon together: one preached about Christ as Prophet, one preached about Christ as Priest and one preached about Christ as King.

James Hannington

1847 - 1885

James Hannington was a mischievous boy who disliked school, enjoyed collecting things and played all sorts of practical jokes. During one of these “jokes” , involving gunpowder, he accidentally blew the top off one of his own fingers. As a young man he entered his family’s business as a counting house clerk and served as a major in the 1st Sussex Artillery Volunteers. James went to the University of Oxford but he was more interested in boats, rowing and racing on the Thames than studying at the university. When his mother died, however, James thought about life and faith and encountered the wonder of the Gospel. He was ordained and served as a parish priest for seven years. During this time he was a keen evangelist who was known for his temperance and mission work. He also married a young lady called Blanche and had four little children. One day James heard about some Christian missionaries who had been martyred on the shores of Lake Victoria in Africa. Something about this story touched James’ heart and he longed to take their place. His best friends were not surprised by his longing for adventure for Christ and finally, encouraged by his wife, he volunteered to go to Africa as a missionary. It was desperately

hard to leave his wife, little ones and mother-in-law and his first trip was crippled by illness, so he was never really well again, but he was consecrated as a bishop and tried again. He did good work in his African diocese – and, since he still loved collecting things, he collected some local shells of great interest to naturalists – but he wanted to establish a safe route to Lake Victoria for locals and missionaries. Sadly he was oblivious to the politics of the region and was captured and killed before he was forty. James reached the shores of Lake Victoria and he died believing that he had succeeded in opening a new road for the Gospel to Uganda. Some of his last thoughts were scribbled in his diary between his capture and his death: 'Lord, I put myself in Thy hands, I look to Thee alone.' His oldest son was eight years old when James failed to return from Africa but he later served as a missionary to Uganda for almost twenty years. Christians in Uganda cherish James' sacrifice for the Gospel on their behalf to this day.

James Nugent

1822 - 1905

James Nugent was a busy man. He was born to a Catholic family in Liverpool and had eight brothers and sisters. His father was a respectable grocer who paid for James to attend a private school and James divided his time between his father's shop – stocked with boxes of vegetables, sacks of flour and jars of jam – and his own books. His father hoped James would become a successful businessman but James chose to become a Catholic priest. He trained for the priesthood in the English city of Durham and in Rome, in Italy, then returned to Liverpool. James was in his late twenties when he became the curate of St Nicholas' Church in Liverpool and he was appalled by the sickness, poverty and homelessness of the people who filled the great city and lived crowded together in tiny, waterlogged houses or on narrow, freezing streets. James' priestly vocation was rooted in celebrating Mass but he felt compelled to help the people of Liverpool in practical ways too. James started a ragged school for homeless and orphaned children when he discovered that thousands of children in Liverpool had no supper or slept on the city streets every night. He started a technical school for poor boys where they learned how

to be cobblers, tailors, carpenters and printers. He started a home for single mothers and their babies so the women could earn an honest living for themselves and their little ones. James, however, did not work alone. He asked for help from priests and nuns who shared his faith, concern and desire to help. Together they founded a training school for teachers and a school for Catholic children which continues to this day. Later in life James helped families and orphans to emigrate from England to America or Canada, where they had a good chance to live a successful life in a new world, far away from the Liverpool slums. When James died, he was a faithful priest and an old man, who still lived amid the poor people he had given his life to help in the name of Christ.

James the Deacon

Unknown - After 671

Long ago a young and musical monk left his sunny home in Italy and travelled to the misty, rocky isle of Britain. His name was James and he was a deacon: an ordained minister of the church with a special responsibility for preaching and serving. He travelled to the Anglo-Saxon kingdom of Kent. Here the pagan King Ethelbert had been converted to Christianity by his Christian Queen Bertha and an Italian missionary, Augustine, the first Archbishop of Canterbury. Now their daughter, Princess Ethelburga, was travelling north from the gentle hills and woods of Kent to the wild moors and peaks of Northumbria. The princess was a Christian but her future husband, King Edwin, was a pagan. James went with the princess, her ladies-in-waiting and her priest. The journey was long and hard and James was one of the first Christians to preach the Gospel in Northumbria. King Edwin, a thoughtful and wise ruler, became a Christian. Christianity spread from person to person and village to village and it was said that a mother and her baby could walk from sea to sea in safely. Later, when King Edwin was killed in battle, Queen Ethelburga fled to Kent with her children and her priest. James, however, stayed in Northumbria where – faithful but

undismayed – he kept the flickering flame of Christianity alight in the spiritual darkness of the increasingly pagan and violent Northumbria. He sang, preached and served his little group of Christians and, in spite of the danger, more Christians joined his group. And it so happened that, in time, two great missionaries – Aidan and Cuthbert – came to Northumbria and carried the burning torch of Christianity to every corner of the kingdom again. James was at the Synod of Whitby when the new Christian King of Northumbria chose between the old Celtic Church – which dated back to the time of the Romans – and the new Catholic Church. James taught the Northumbrian Christians how to sing psalms and prayers to God and fill their churches with beauty and music. At the end of James' long life, a young monk called Bede wrote a book, full of stories of the Christian faith in England. No one knows for sure, but maybe James told his stories to Bede, the Anglo-Saxon historian. Bede wrote a book called *Historia Ecclesiastica Gentis Anglorum*, which is Latin for "Ecclesiastical History of the English People", which included stories of Ethelburga, Edwin, Aidan and Cuthbert as well as James the Deacon. After that James let himself slip quietly out of history: faithful and undismayed to the end.

Jane Haining

1897 - 1944

Jane Haining was on holiday in Cornwall when WWII was announced over the radio in a prim and proper BBC voice. It was a sunny day of sea, sand and ice cream in Cornwall, but Jane's heart was far away, on the other side of Europe, in Hungary. She was a farmer's daughter from Scotland who grew up in a large, happy and Christian home then worked as a matron at a mission school in Budapest. The mission was to the Jewish community and the school was for the local girls, so most of the girls Jane looked after were Jewish. Standing on the Cornish cliffs and wondering what the war would do to the world, Jane couldn't stop thinking about her girls in Hungary. She carried them in her heart and – like a mother – she thought of their names, faces and personalities as she worried about their future. All over Europe, the Nazi regime was persecuting Jews, so Jane knew that slowly but surely her girls would be touched by the horror of the regime and the tragedy of the war. Quickly Jane packed her suitcase and returned to the school in Budapest. She was ordered to go home – for her own safety – but refused to leave her girls. "If these children need me in days of sunshine," she wrote to the missionary society, at home in Britain,

which ran the mission school, “how much more do they need me in days of darkness?” She stayed even when Hungary was invaded by the German army and she risked her life trying to save as many of the girls as she could, but she was arrested by the Nazi authorities for working with Jews and listening to the BBC programs on a secret radio. Bravely she told her frightened and sobbing girls she would be home for lunch. Instead she was sent to prison then a concentration camp and died in Auschwitz. Her love and sacrifice is remembered to this day.

Jane Sharp

Before 1641 - After 1671

A baby girl was born in the days of the Stuart Kings of England and grew from babyhood to girlhood to womanhood. She is known to history as Jane Sharp. She may have been a Puritan woman of good birth and good education from Shropshire. She probably married and had a daughter. At some point, however, she became a midwife in London and devoted her life to helping mothers and babies through the tricky business of childbirth. She would have learned the art of midwifery by working with an experienced midwife for some time before working on her own, and she was a midwife for thirty years or more. She answered the call for a midwife in sunshine and in snow. She tended mothers of all ages and states of health. She swaddled newborns by daylight and by candlelight. In 1671 she published a book called *The Midwives Book: or the Whole Art of Midwifery Discovered.* In those days childbirth was a perilous undertaking and many mothers and babies did not survive. Midwives were licensed by their parish churches and babies were born at home. Doctors were male and midwives, although female, were uneducated and sometimes inexperienced too. *The Midwives Book* was revolutionary because it was written by ab educated

woman, an experienced midwife and an excellent writer, and because it was written for women. Jane was passionate about midwifery which she called “doubtless one of the most useful and necessary of all Arts for the being and well-being of Mankind”. She wrote that she prayed for God’s help as she wrote. She sympathised with the desire for a child, traced childbirth, motherhood and midwifery back to the women of the Bible and celebrated “the works of the Lord” in the design of the male and female bodies, the miracle of pregnancy and the wonder of birth. A newborn baby, she said, must be touched “very tenderly”, wrapped in soft clothes and laid in a cradle gently. It is thought that Jane’s book encouraged midwives to be more professional and encouraged doctors to take them more seriously. To this day midwives are respected members of the medical profession. Jane – answering the call for a midwife, tending labouring mothers and swaddling newborn babies – could never have imagined that her little book would have helped so many midwives, mothers and babies around the world.

Jocelin of Wells

Unknown - 1242

Jocelin was a royal administrator and church politician for most of his life and in 1215 he was one of the barons who obliged King John to sign the Magna Carta and assent to the idea that the king should respect the law of his kingdom. When Jocelin became Bishop of Wells, the cathedral and the choir school were already hundreds of years old, but Jocelin found plenty to do anyway. He built part of the current cathedral and supported the choir school. When he died, he asked to be buried in the quire of the cathedral, where the choristers from the school still sing Evensong every day. Jocelin also made peace between the rival dioceses of Wells and Glastonbury. He ensured that fairs, markets and businesses prospered in Somerset so the local people were busy, content and secure. At this time – or so the story goes – there was a fierce wyrm which worried the villagers of Dinder like a naughty and troublesome dog. *Wyrm* is an Old English word for "dragon" and the villagers of Dinder were understandably worried that this particular wyrm (or dragon) was going to eat their children and livestock. Jocelin, however, refused to be intimidated. He took a sword and a horse and led a little party of men-at-arms out of Wells

towards Dinder. The men all wanted to be the brave fellow who killed the wyrm but Jocelin told them to wait while he rode on alone. Thankfully for the local villagers – but sadly for the wyrm – Jocelin brandished his sword and killed the creature. From that day forward the villagers of Dinder were safe and Jocelin was celebrated as the bishop who slayed the wyrm and saved his people. The story was told to children and grandchildren and Jocelin was remembered. Many years later, in the days of King Edward III, a monk and writer called Ranulf Higden wrote a massive book of history and theology called *Polychronicon.* It is preserved in the library of Eton College. In *Polychronicon* Ranulf Higden recorded the story of Bishop Jocelin and the wyrm of Dinder. Every fifty years, Jocelin's wyrm-slaying adventure is re-enacted by a left-handed clergyman, for fear of the wyrm awakening and returning. And to this day, not a mile and a half from Dinder, the little hamlet of Worminster shelters in a valley between the hills of Worminster Down and Worminster Sleight.

John and Lucy Hutchinson

1615 - 1664 and 1620 - 1681

It is said that a young lawyer from Lincoln's Inn, John Hutchinson, fell in love with his future wife when he looked through her Latin notebooks. At that time Lucy Apsley was translating an epic poem from Latin into English. John was so impressed with the idea of this educated and cultured young lady that he made haste to win her heart. Lucy, who was born in the Tower of London when her father was the Lieutenant of the Tower, received a boy's education of Latin, literature and maths. She loved reading, teased her friends for liking dolls and composed poems and songs for fun. Her family were trying to arrange a great marriage for her when she heard of John's interest. She was a sensible girl, but when she met John, she felt an unusual liking for the young lawyer and thought he was so handsome that no one could help falling in love with him at first sight. John and Lucy not only shared a love of books but a love for Christ and it wasn't long before they were engaged. On the morning of the day they should have married, Lucy got smallpox. She almost died, but John didn't care that his bride's pretty face was dreadfully scarred. John and Lucy got married as soon as she was well enough to go to church and the marriage was more than happy,

in spite of the fact that John and Lucy were swept up in the turmoil of the English Civil War. Lucy's closest brother was a Royalist, but John was a Parliamentarian, so Lucy committed herself to Parliament's cause too. All through the war John fought and Lucy supported her husband, raised their many children and tended sick and wounded soldiers. John was reluctantly involved in the trial of King Charles I, because he prayerfully decided it was God's will, but he later regretted his involvement. He was arrested when King Charles II returned to England. Lucy worked to ensure that he wasn't executed, but he had a sensitive conscience, so he wasn't entirely grateful. Later John was arrested on another petty charge, put his trust in God and died in prison. Lucy was heartbroken, but she also put her trust in God. Later she wrote a biography of her husband and a memoir of their life together, as well as other essays, poems and memoirs.

John Bethune

1751 - 1815

John Bethune was born on the misty Isle of Skye near the Scottish coast. It was said that his father was a Jacobite who fought for Bonnie Prince Charlie at the Battle of Culluden and his grandfather was a loyal and courteous Scotsman who, although he was no Jacobite, nonetheless risked his life to help the fugitive prince. In spite of the fact that he was a descendant of Scottish lairds, John was a poor boy, who attended King's College Aberdeen with the help of a scholarship. The Jacobite heroine of Skye, Flora MacDonald, went to America and wrote letters to family and friends on Skye about the wonders of the new world. Times were hard in Scotland in those days. As a young man, therefore, John was ordained, went to the American colonies and became the minister of a church in North Carolina. It wasn't long, however, before the American Revolution changed everything. John was a Scotsman through and through: a man of the Highlands and Islands and a speaker of Scotts Gaelic. In spite of this, however, he was a Loyalist during the American Revolution and supported King George III. It was dangerous to be a Loyalist amid a lot of Patriots who wanted America to be a free country, but John resolutely

served as the chaplain of the North Carolina Royal Militia and the 1st Battalion of the Royal Highland Emigrants. At the Battle of Moores Creek Bridge in 1776, amid the smoke, bullets and blood of the war, he was captured by the Patriots. When he was free again, he went to Canada, where he served the 2nd Battalion of the Royal Highland Emigrants. He worked with the Scottish soldiers in black berets, red coats and blue and green tartan kilts by praying and preaching in English and Gaelic, marrying soldiers to their wartime sweethearts and comforting the weary, injured and brokenhearted. Later, when peace returned, John married a French-Canadian girl called Véronique Waddens and had a family. He spent the rest of his life as a minister in Canada and worked in very cordial harmony with the priests and pastors of other denominations. He somehow managed to be very good friends with the local Catholic priest while warning his parishioners to flee the man's Catholic doctrines. He was known as a Loyalist – and a truly loyal man – for the rest of his life.

John Coleridge Patteson

1827 - 1871

John Coleridge Patteson, Bishop of Melanesia, was probably the only bishop at that time who spoke twenty-three South Sea languages. He liked to arrived on one of the many South Sea Islands of his diocese without making a fuss. He pulled his boat onto the beach and walked around, looking at wildlife and talking to people, with a big hat on his head, his shirt sleeves and trouser legs rolled up and his feet bare. John, however, was a Devon boy from England and he was a long way from home. He was raised in a Christian home by parents who helped him overcome a lazy streak and a fiery temper. He was educated at the University of Oxford and completed the Grand Tour of Europe. He wasn't very academic but loved cricket – he played for the university – and languages all his life. He was ordained as a priest in Exeter Cathedral and went to the South Seas as a missionary. John founded a college for local boys and in time he was consecrated Bishop of Melanesia. He was overwhelmed by the immensity of the task, but accepted it humbly and wholeheartedly. He had a big heart, because he somehow or other managed to love his enormous diocese of islands, which were scattered across almost two thousand miles

of the Pacific Ocean. He also loved the Melanesian people. Many South Sea islanders, however, were hurt and suspicious because of "blackbirding" – the stealing of local children by white slave traders – and some missionaries died of poisonous arrow wounds. John was horrified by blackbirding and worked to stop it in his diocese. He persisted in kindness and swam from his boat to the islands with his top hat full of presents. He learned and remembered people's names and the languages of the islands. But then, while he was still young, he was murdered on the island of Nukapu by one of the Melanesian people. No one knows why but perhaps, because he was a white man, it was in revenge for blackbirding victims. His death created a public outcry and the British Navy tried to stop blackbirding forever. Many years later the sister of John's murderer was the first Christian of Nukapu. To this day John's home diocese of Exeter and his ministerial diocese of Melanesia have a strong and cordial friendship.

John Gerard

1564 - 1637

John Gerard was a Catholic priest who loved adventure and risk. His life of adventure began when he was a little boy and his father was arrested for plotting to free Mary Queen of Scots – the Catholic rival of the Protestant Queen Elizabeth I – from prison. Later, when his father was free from prison, John was sent to study at Exeter College which is part of the University of Oxford. As a young man, however, he got into trouble for refusing to take Communion in a Protestant church. His tutor followed him away from university, became a Catholic himself and taught John and his brother at home. After that John was educated in Europe and eventually he became a priest and a Jesuit. Finally, although it was dangerous, he returned to England. He was tall, handsome and dashing. He pretended to be a worldly man – interested in fashion and gambling – but in fact he risked his life to minister to the faithful but persecuted Catholics of England. At this time it was treason for an Englishman to serve as a Catholic priest in England, but John continued his ministry in spite of the terrible risk. He was completely and utterly convinced about the rightness of his faith and his ministry. He was also a brave and dynamic man. His example encouraged many Catholics and also

many Protestants who were inspired to convert to Catholicism – and even become priests themselves – in spite of the fact that converting was illegal. John travelled from house to house to say Mass and once, when he was arrested and imprisoned, he turned his prison cell into a tiny chapel where he said Mass every day and where Catholics visited him regularly to take Communion. Later he was moved to the Tower of London and treated very badly. With the help of brave and faithful Catholics, however, he escaped by breaking through a stone wall and crawling hand-over-hand along a rope from the prison to a boat. In the middle, he was so tired and weak, he almost fell from the rope into the River Thames below, but he hung on, kept going and finally reached the boat. He continued his ministry in England for another eight years before escaping to Rome and writing the story of his adventures.

John Rainolds

1549 - 1607

Not many people knew it, until he died, but John Rainolds was a man who loved geography and maps as well as Christ. He was born into a Devonshire family of Catholics at a time when it was dangerous to be a Catholic. It was also dangerous to be a Puritan. It was, in fact, dangerous to be anything but a normal Protestant and member of the Church of England. John was sent to study at the University of Oxford when he was a little chap of eight and lived with an uncle who later died in prison for his Catholic faith. John read and studied, wrote and researched and learned something new and interesting every day. He was made a probationary research Fellow at seventeen and made a regular research Fellow at nineteen when he graduated with his bachelor's degree. He was made a lecturer of Greek when he graduated with his master's degree. At some time – no one knows when or why – John stopped being a Catholic and became not only a Protestant, but a Puritan, who was intense and serious about his faith and wanted the Church of England to be "pure" in what it taught and how it worshipped. Along the way John became a priest and Doctor of Divinity. No one knows for sure, but some people think John had the great idea for

North
East
West
South

a new Bible in English called the King James Bible, when he and some other priests and scholars went to Hampton Court Palace for a Royal Audience. They suggested the great idea of the new Bible to King James I and he loved it! John was one of the translators of the Old Testament prophets and it was said that he and his fellow translators met in his university lodgings. He was so committed to the translation of the King James Bible that he never missed a meeting, even when he was ill and in immense pain, when he was carried to the meetings. He was working on the translation until the day of his death. He left two thousand books in his library. They reflected his love of theology, politics and geography. They included books like *Britannia* and *Descriptions of Americae* and manuscripts about India. He also left a collection of maps, drawn by hand on vellum and parchment and decorated with diagrams and pictures, of different parts of the world – England, Europe, America, Africa and Asia – which he loved studying and trying to understand.

John Smith

1790 - 1824

John Smith was known as "The Demerara Martyr". At that time, William Wilberforce had convinced the British government to abolish the British Slave Trade, but he was still fighting to abolish slavery and emancipate slaves. Demerara is a place in the West Indies, as well as the name of the sugar produced there, which represented everything Wilberforce hated about slavery. As for John Smith, he was an orphan from Northamptonshire, who became a baker. He sweated to knead flour and water into a smooth, silky dough then sweated again as he pushed and pulled loaves in and out of hot ovens. People ate his bread and he knew he was doing an honest, useful job, but he also knew there was more for him in life. John got married, got ordained as a minister and volunteered to be a missionary in what is now Guyana. It was a beautiful but volatile part of the world: full of lush foliage, exotic flowers and wonderful creatures like hummingbirds and sloths. But it was always bubbling with anger and resentment because of slavery. Here John threw his heart and soul into pastoring a little congregation of former and freed slaves at Bethel Chapel in the midst of the sugar plantations. People loved his preaching and before long people who were still

slaves were risking their lives to attend his church too. John was unfailingly generous and encouraged his congregation to work hard and care for their families. At that time, however, the price of sugar was falling and the plantation owners were forcing the labourers to work harder than ever. One slave man, Quamina, was a carpenter and a deacon in the chapel. His wife was ill and he wasn't able to care for her. She died while he was at work and he was so sad and angry that he got involved in a slave rebellion. Rumours came and went. Between ten and twelve thousand slaves were armed and dangerous and the rebellion was cruelly stopped and terribly punished. The plantation owners accused John of starting the rebellion or of encouraging it, at least, which was just as bad. He was arrested and sentenced to death. Word came from England that he was to be released, but it came too late, because John had already died in his dark, damp prison. His death, however, helped Wilberforce and his friends abolish slavery throughout the British Empire in 1833.

Joseph Anning and Mary Anning

1796 - 1849 and 1799 - 1847

Joseph Anning was walking along the beach at Lyme when he noticed a fossil emerging from the ragged edge of the crumbling cliff. He told his sister, Mary, who went to see it too. The sun shone and the salty sea wind whipped at her hair, the ends of her shawl and the hem of her dress. But there was the fossil and it wasn't an ordinary ammonite or belemnite! It took Joseph and Mary months to release it from the cliff and clean it from the sand and earth of thousands of years. The fossil was huge and magnificent. By then Joseph and Mary – and everyone else in Lyme – realised it was the fossilised skull of a monster. And then Mary found the rest of the skeleton too! The Anning family were committed Christians and the children learned to read and write at the chapel Sunday School. Their father was a carpenter, but times were hard and money was tight, so he collected fossils to sell to tourists. Later he taught Joseph and Mary where to find them, which ones to keep and how to clean them. The children collected fossils when they were little and when their father died, leaving them poor and worried, Joseph learned a trade but Mary found fossils for her mother to sell. The fossil of the monster belonged to an ancient and extinct marine

reptile called a ichthyosaur. Later Mary found the fossilised skeleton of a plesiosaurus and a pterodactyl. They were bought by collectors and museums. Suddenly everyone was interested them and the mysterious creatures they represented. Educated people thought it was embarrassing that they had been found by geologists and paleontologists who were bright, curious and lively, but uneducated, with thick West Country accents and hands which were rough from work. Joseph and Mary, however, just kept finding fossils. No one knows exactly what Joseph thought about fossils. Mary, however, thought long and hard about God, Scripture and fossils, accepted the mysteriousness of the fossils and maintained her deep faith. Joseph and Mary were always poor and neither of them lived to be old. Joseph got married and had five sons. Mary, however, was usually to be found at home copying religious quotations into her diary or on the beach at the foot of the cliffs in Lyme, busy in all weathers, discovering new fossils.

Joseph Harrald

1849 - 1912

The great preacher of the Victorian era, Charles Haddon Spurgeon, called Joseph Harrald his "armour-bearer". Joseph was an East Anglian boy and the son of an artisan basket maker and carpenter. His parents were Christians and he committed his life to Christ at a young age. He grew up teaching Sunday Schools, distributing tracts and preaching. He was a good student and as a young man he went to study at Spurgeon's College in London. At the end of his studies he was ordained and became the minister of a Baptist church. He also married a young lady called Lydia and became the father of four little children, including a little girl, Lily. Joseph wanted to go to India as a missionary, but Spurgeon invited him to be his private secretary. It was a very different call to a very different life, but Joseph thoughtfully and prayerfully decided it was the will of God. Joseph managed appointments and letters for Spurgeon, recorded his sermons, helped him to write some of his famous works like *The Treasury of David*, supported him in his pastoral work and occasionally killed insects for him. When Spurgeon visited the South of France for his health and well-being, Joseph went too, as his secretary and friend. He read to Spurgeon, walked with

Spurgeon and wrote to Spurgeon's wife, Susannah, with news and updates when Spurgeon was too ill to write. Joseph had a deep faith and a good sense of humour, but he was also a faithful husband, father and friend, who suffered two great blows when his wife died in 1882 and his employer and friend, Spurgeon, died in 1892. It was Joseph – busy, efficient and perhaps rather unimaginative – who saw a heavenly vision of angels when Spurgeon died and who comforted Mrs Spurgeon with the idea that Spurgeon was already preaching the Gospel to the saints and angels in heaven. Later Joseph continued to work for Mrs Spurgeon. Together they prepared Spurgeon's biography for publication, managed his legacy of books and sermons and ran Mrs Spurgeon's book fund for poor ministers. Joseph, Spurgeons's "armour-bearer" to the very end, was responsible for the immense collection of Spurgeon's sermons. He had recorded most of them in shorthand but now he prepared them for publication in longhand. He was revising one last sermon when he died. By then he was a Baptist minister in Sussex and he left his money to his daughter, Lily, who was a missionary in Africa.

Josephine Butler

1828 - 1906

Josephine Butler was a gentle but passionate and tough Christian woman. She was happily married with a large family. One night, however, her little daughter, Evangeline, died in the middle of a childish game and Josephine's sorrow made it impossible for her not to try to help other suffering women. Josephine had been educated at home by a man who raised his sons and daughters as equals. He involved Josephine in his battle against slavery and later she visited Ireland during the Potato Famine. She struggled to understand how a loving God could allow evil, but instead of thinking that He was harsh and unloving, she realised that her own compassionate and urgent love for the lost and hurting of the world was "as a drop of water to the ocean of His love". At that time the poorest women in England, who earned money for themselves and their children in terrible and tragic ways, were despised and rejected rather than helped. Everyone knew that what they did was wrong. Josephine, however, realised that the women didn't want to do what they did. They were simply desperate and willing to do *anything* to feed and clothe their children and they were trapped in the consequences of their actions. It was a hopeless situation

because, in spite of all their sacrifice and suffering, these poor women still struggled to earn enough money for food and clothing. Their children often went barefoot because they didn't have any shoes. They couldn't go to school, either, so they grew up to be poor and desperate too. No one seemed to care and Josephine, fully believing that "God and one woman make a majority", appealed to Christians – especially women and mothers – all over England to help the poorest women. At first people were offended by Josephine for publicly discussing things which were considered shameful. Gradually, however, people began to realise that Josephine was right and started to help the poorest women. Members of Parliament made laws to protect all women and provide food, clothing and education for all children. Josephine wanted men to respect women as she believed Christ did and she went on to champion education and Votes for Women. She refused to stop helping women and once said, "I am in earnest … and *I will be heard*."

Kate Edger Evans

1857 - 1935

Kate Edger was a little girl when she sailed around the world from England to New Zealand because her father, a Baptist minister, was appointed as a minister to accompany a group of emigrants to the British colony. He took his family and Kate spent the rest of her life in New Zealand. Reverend Edger educated Kate and her sisters at home and got permission for her to study with the top class of boys at Aukland College and Grammar School. Later he supported her application for a bachelor's degree from the University of New Zealand. Cautiously, Kate stated her age and her qualifications, but did not mention the fact that she was a girl. She was accepted and studied mathematics and Latin. When she graduated, in 1877, she was thought to be the first woman in the British Empire to earn a bachelor's degree. The Bishop of Aukland gave her a white camellia in honour of what he called her "unpretending excellence". Kate, not at all daunted, went on to study for a master's degree and graduated in 1882. She became a teacher and the headmistress of a girls' school and taught a vast range of subjects from English Literature to Mathematics and Singing to Latin. On her thirty-third birthday, Kate married a Congregational minister from Wales,

William Evans. Soon she became the mother of three sons. Kate was devoted to her husband and sons, but housework wasn't among Kate's many joys or strengths. She was honest about this, so she employed someone to help with her domestic chores. For at least some of her married life, while her sons were still little, Kate was responsible for earning the family income. At this time she supported her husband's ministry by working full time to run a small and private girls' school from their house. Later she supported his ministry in other ways: reading in church, preaching from time to time, running the Sunday School, singing in the choir and learning to play the church organ for services when she was over fifty years old. She also supported Votes for Women, temperance and the protection of women and children from violence. Kate once said, "It is too soon yet for a complete answer to be given to this question, but thousands of university women are proving by their lives that it has not unfitted them for home-making, the noblest sphere of women's work."

Laura Ridding

1849 - 1939

Lady Laura Elizabeth Ridding was, in almost every way, the most proper of proper Victorian ladies, but she was also a charming and confident leader and speaker who could encourage and motivate others. She was raised in a devout and lively Christian home in the Anglican tradition and grew into a strong-minded women, with a wonderful sense of humour, who did not stand any nonsense. Her personal faith in Christ was deep and loving and she longed for Christ to call her to some special work for Him. In 1876, when she was twenty-seven, she married the headmaster of Winchester College. George Ridding was a serious clergyman and widower who was over twenty years older than Laura. The couple had known each other for years, but Laura had not been romantically interested for almost as long, until she came to see and understand him in a new and loving light. Laura had some very serious and sweet ideals about the traditional role of a wife and shared a loving and happy marriage with George. For a number of busy and content years, the couple lived in Winchester, where George led the school and Laura mothered the schoolboys. The loss of some little babies of their own was a great sorrow and Laura – who longed to be a mother – noted sadly but submissively that the joy of children was

not given to them by God. In the course of time, however, George was invited to become the Bishop of Nottingham and Laura moved with him to Nottingham. She approached her role as the bishop's wife thoughtfully and generously and devoted her time to serving the people of the diocese. She had a special concern for women from all walks of life and joined organisations to help young girls, working women and busy mothers. In 1894, when women were not yet allowed to vote, she stood for the role of a local councillor, was voted into office and became, not only a councillor, but the guardian of Southwell Workhouse. Laura viewed her guardian role as a motherly responsibility for the women, children and babies within the workhouse. She was desperately concerned for them and worked to get them things like basic underwear and good food. Laura was not a militant suffragette but she was a firm supporter of women's suffrage and right to vote. She desired, as the Liverpool branch of the Church League for Women's Suffrage said, "to show what Our Lord has done for women" and this was reflected in her whole life.

Laurence Chaderton

Between 1536 and 1539 - 1640

Once, in Cambridge, there was a man who planted trees. He was called Laurence Chaderton and he was a university scholar who, for years, preferred hunting and hawking to studying. He never grew out of sport, but enjoyed wrestling, archery and tennis all his life. He went to the University of Cambridge in his twenties and was almost killed in a Town and Gown riot while trying to rescue his best friend. He also became a Protestant. Laurence was the youngest of three Catholic brothers and his father gave him a choice between his family and his new perspective on Christianity. Sad at heart, but convinced that he was right, Laurence chose his Protestant faith in Christ. He eventually became a serious but gracious Puritan, who truly loved the Reformed doctrine of the Protestant church, but was a "quiet and obedient" member of the Church of England in the tradition of what was later fondly called "the old conformity". Meanwhile he finally developed an interest in learning and became a tutor at the University of Cambridge. Later he helped to found Emmanuel College and was its master for many years. Laurence was ordained as a deacon in the Church of England in his thirties. He was thought to be a good preacher and his

congregation begged him to "preach on" when he was tired and thought he'd finished! He got married in his forties. He and his wife, Cecilia, were married at a double ceremony with her sister. At one point the priest confused the names of the brides. Anxiously Laurence exclaimed, "No, no! It is Cecilia I want!" He and Cecilia had a daughter called Elizabeth and were happy together for years. Ultimately, when Laurence was in his sixties, he joined the team of translators who worked on the English version of the Book of Psalms for the King James Bible. They are, to this day, some of the most familiar and beloved words in the Bible. Laurence, however, was also a great lover of nature and studied botany for fun all his days. He planted trees all over Cambridge and watched them grow. Laurence enjoyed robust good health all his life and died, as one of the most respected and beloved men in Cambridge, when he was over a hundred years old. He lived for so long, in fact, that he watched his trees grow from tiny saplings to mighty trees whose graceful branches and green leaves seemed to touch the clear sky above the University of Cambridge.

Lilian Bader

1918 - 2015

It was during the dark days of WWI that a baby girl was born to a black man from Barbados and an Irish woman in England. The little girl was called Lilian and baptised in the Catholic tradition of her mother's family. When she was nine, she was orphaned and sent to a convent, where she lived until she was twenty. Lilian was pretty, clever and friendly, with a gorgeous smile and a good sense of humour, but being a black girl in England at that time was hard. When WWII started, Lilian wanted to join the Armed Forces and fight for Britain, but she struggled to be accepted by the recruitment officers because of the colour of her skin. She was asked to leave the NAAFI, although her commanding officer liked her and shared both her Irish ancestry and her Catholic faith, because her skin was dark. Lilian refused to give up and kept trying until, finally, she was accepted as a member of the Woman's Auxiliary Air Force by the RAF. Lilian was the only black girl among lots of white girls but she cheered up, on her first day, when someone said she looked smart in her new uniform. She worked hard to pass her Instrument Repairer training course and was one of the first women in Britain to qualify as an Aircraftwoman First Class. Later, because

climbing in and out of aeroplanes in a skirt suit was impractical, she was one of the first women in Britain to wear battledress. By the end of the war Lilian had been promoted to Acting Corporal. Meanwhile, when she was in her mid-twenties and the war was still raging, Lilian was introduced to a handsome young black tank driver called Ramsay Bader who, like Lilian, was of mixed race heritage. The two of them fell in love and got married at Corpus Christi Catholic Church. Because of the war, they had a plain cake with no icing or decorations, but Lilian carried a beautiful bouquet of flowers. Later she became the mother of two little boys and then, when they were old enough to go to school, she went to university and trained to be a teacher. She was always pleased and proud of the fact that she was one of three generations of her family to serve Britain in the Armed Forces.

Lilias Trotter

1853 - 1928

Lilias Trotter was a young lady who painted all day long. She loved swirling her paintbrush through paint – cobalt blue, cadmium yellow, rose madder – and across paper – crisp and white – and the pictures she created were beautiful and true. One day the famous artist and philosopher, John Ruskin, said she could be a great painter. Lilias was thrilled, but after a few days of excitement, she knew she had to make a choice which almost broke her heart. Lilias was from a happy and luxurious home and her parents had encouraged her love of nature and gift for painting since she was a little girl. She met Ruskin in Venice and he became her teacher, mentor and friend. He believed women couldn't paint as well as men, but Lilias proved him wrong. He was delighted and said she could be "the greatest living painter" if – and only if – she gave her entire life to painting. But Lilias couldn't do that. She was an artist, but she was a Christian too. And she loved Christ more than anything. Because she wanted to share His love with others, she attended conferences about faith and holiness and ran a street mission in London for the poorest of poor women and girls. And so Lilias made her choice. She turned her back on an artistic career

and threw herself into her mission work, first in London and later in Algeria, loving people for Christ in very different worlds. Lilias was in her mid-thirties when she went to Algeria and she was a missionary in that beautiful country for the rest of her life. She travelled for days in the hot and sandy desert to visit wandering Arab communities with the Gospel of Christ. She never wavered in her commitment to beauty and truth and she developed a respectful and theological approach to mission. She took her paintbox and paintbrushes with her to Algeria and captured the blue sky, the yellow and red sand and all the gorgeous colours of the wilderness flowers. Lilias lived with the constant ache of her desire to paint more and better, but she loved Christ and she loved the country and people of Algeria more than painting, so she regretted nothing. Love filled her heart and overflowed to everything and everyone around her. Once Lilias wrote, “I have been thinking lately what a work for God it is, just loving people.”

Lily O'Hanlon

1900s

One day in 1951 Dr Lily M. O'Hanlon picked up her medical bag and walked across the Himalayan Mountains from India to Nepal. It all began in 1936 when Lily was serving as a medical missionary in India and felt that God was calling her to serve in the neighbouring country of Nepal. At the time the Nepalise border was closed to foreigners and the Nepalise government hated Christianity. For fifteen years, Lily worked in India, waiting and praying for the opportunity to serve God in Nepal. She ran a medical dispensary on the Indian side of the border and worked with both Indian and Nepalise people in the border villages among the foothills of the Himalayas. She tended wounds, treated sickness and delivered babies. It was good work for God and the local people He loved, but Lily couldn't forget Nepal anymore than she could forgot the mountains that towered over her little dispensary. When people asked if she was going to start a hospital in India, she shook her head, then boldly said she was going to start a hospital in Nepal. People were doubtful, but Lily never lost faith in the promises of God. Many times over the years she looked up at the mountains, prayed for Nepal and asked, "How long, oh Lord, how long?" And

then, in 1951, there was a revolution in Nepal and King Tribhuvan opened the Nepalise border to foreigners. Together Lily, five other women – including an English doctor, an English nurse and a Nepali woman – and four Nepali men walked across the Himalayan Mountains into Nepal. Lily and her faithful team founded a little hospital in Pokhara "at the foot of Fishtail Mountain", as she later told the story, first in bamboo huts, then in aluminium shelters and finally in specially built and equipped hospital buildings. The hospital was called "The Shining Hospital" because the aluminium huts shone in the sun. The name stuck and today there are three Shining Hospitals in Nepal where people are loved, served and healed in the name of Christ. Lily never stopped praying for Nepal, the Nepali people and the work of loving them for Christ. She would surely be delighted to know that the work she started in Nepal continues to this day through the International Nepal Fellowship.

Lucius Cary

1609 or 1610 - 1643

Lucius Cary was born in the little town of Burford among the rolling wolds and grazing sheep of Oxfordshire. He was destined to be loved and respected by all who knew him, but in spite of being a man of peace, he was to die in battle before he was forty. In the meantime, he was raised in England and Ireland, then studied French and Latin at Trinity College Dublin and fought a duel. He also married a young lady, Lettice, who was beautiful but poor. His father was furious. Lucius tried to mend the rift, but to no avail, so he took his little family to Holland for a while before returning to England and settling in a country house called Great Tew, near Burford and Oxford, which he inherited from his grandfather. It wasn't long before he inherited the title of Viscount Falkland from his father too. Lucius was a small and unimposing man, but he had a great mind and a warm heart and was known for his integrity and seriousness of purpose. He became part of a literary and philosophical group that came and went from the University of Oxford and gathered at Great Tew. He and his closest friends discussed the issues of the day and the realities of their faith. It was a turbulent time for both the church and the government and the

affairs of the two were hopelessly intertwined. Lucius, an Anglican who resisted the Archbishop of Canterbury's oppression of Puritans, was renowned for uniting faith with reason. He became a Member of Parliament and spoke against the tyranny of the throne, but aligned himself with King Charles I when war broke out between King and Parliament. He worked for peace and believed with all his heart that it was possible, so he was devastated by the outbreak of the English Civil War. He joined a cavalry regiment and fought more bravely and recklessly than necessary because, although he was a man of peace who hated the violence of war, he did not want to be a coward. He died at the Battle of Naseby when he rode at a blockade of enemy musketeers on his own. Some of his friends thought this was an act of heroism and others thought it was an act of despair. Some Anglicans still consider him one of the best and brightest theologians of his age.

Lucius of Britain

100s

It was said by the storytellers of old that there lived a British chieftain or king called Lucius of Britain. For thousands of years the British people had lived in villages with their families and tribes. Their homes had mud walls and thatched roofs, their communities were surrounded by prickly fences and their roads were wandering tracks across the hills and through the woods. They grew crops, raised animals and – wearing blue paint – fought their enemies in fierce battles. But then the Romans invaded Britain. Straight stone roads criss-crossed the countryside between towns full of houses, shops and bath-houses as well as forums where markets were held, basilicas where administration was managed and temples were a host of Roman deities were worshipped. Some of the British people embraced the Roman ways and others rejected them and continued to live as they always had and always would. Lucius, so the story goes, was a noble chieftain whose tribe went back into the mists of time. He was a strong man who rode horses, used weapons like knives, bows and arrows and hunted wild animals for food. He was also a wise man who cared for his family and his tribe. One day Lucius heard an interesting story and

wondered if it was true. He was curious and so, after a lot of thinking, he wrote a letter. He sent it to a Christian priest called Eleutherus in Rome. Lucius said he wanted to be a Christian and asked for guidance. Eleutherus was glad to help and sent a Christian missionary to Britain. Lucius listened to the stories about Jesus and was baptised as a Christian. His wife, children and tribe all became Christians too. Supposedly they lived peacefully and quietly as Christians for hundreds of years. The story of Lucius of Britain was first recorded in a book called *Liber Pontificalis* or "The Book of the Popes" and later included by the Anglo-Saxon historian, Bede, in a book called *Historia Ecclesiastica Gentis Anglorum* or "The Ecclesiastical History of the English People". It was told and retold – over a thousand years later – during the unsettled days of the English Reformation. By then, of course, the stories about Jesus had been shared between grandfathers and mothers and brothers and sisters and friends until hundreds and thousands of people people knew and loved the same stories and the same Lord as Lucius of Britain.

Mabel Barker

1889 - 1978

Once, in Loughborough, there lived a girl called Mabel Elizabeth Barker. Her father was a coal merchant and a preacher at Swan Street Methodist Chapel where the family worshipped every Sunday. Her mother made their house in Derby Square into a home. Mabel and her little brother, Frank, attended local schools and Mabel was good at sewing and PE. Gradually she grew from a little girl with pigtails who wore dresses and pinafores into a young lady with long dark hair and big dark eyes who wore lace blouses and long skirts. She was a quiet, thoughtful girl who was responsible and what her teachers called "ladylike". When she was sixteen, she decided to be a teacher. She was also interested in First Aid, so she earned certificates from St John's Ambulance in First Aid and Home Nursing. In 1913 Mabel got a job at Church Gate Girls' School in Loughborough. A year later WWI started and Mabel volunteered as a VAD (Voluntary Aid Detachment) nurse at Loughborough General Hospital Military Wards. Many of the VAD nurses were young, pretty and enjoying their first taste of independence and usefulness. The soldiers called them Very Adorable Darlings. But the nurses weren't just having fun, they

were helping to win the war. At first the VADs were only allowed to dust wards, make tea and roll bandages. When WWI ended, however, they were trusted to wash and dress the patients and bandage their wounds. Mabel worked as a teacher all day and then, after work, she left the school and cycled – with her pinned-up hair and her dress blowing in the breeze – across the town to the hospital where she worked as a nurse all evening. She gave over five thousand hours of her time to the hospital between October 1914 and February 1919. She kept an autograph book and collected messages and pictures of soldiers. The chances are that she remembered "her soldiers" until the day she died. Mabel was twenty-nine by the end of the war and she, like many girls of her generation, never married because so many men had died in the war. She lived a quiet life teaching and keeping house for her brother. In her old age she was cared for by her cousins who saved her little suitcase containing her VAD uniform and her autograph book and – with it – her story. For many years her cousins continued to love and remember her as "the most wonderful person".

Malcolm and Margaret of Scotland

About 1031 - 1093 and About 1045 - 1093

Once, on a wild and stormy night, a little boat was tossed by the wind and the waves of the North Sea. Inside the boat an Anglo-Saxon princess of England, Margaret, watched and waited for dawn with her ladies-in-waiting. She had been raised in England but now she was forced to flee into exile. Her great uncle, King Edward the Confessor, had died and her brother, King Harold, had been killed at the Battle of Hastings. The little boat was supposed to take Margaret and her ladies-in-waiting to safety in Europe, but with an almighty crash and a terrifying lurch, it was shipwrecked. And there was Margaret, as stuck as the little boat, on the wild coast of Scotland. The dawn of a new day, however, brought help and hope. King Malcolm of Scotland, a prince and a warrior who had fought his way to the Scottish throne, took pity on Margaret and promised that she would be safe at the Scottish court. He was a big, rough man who could not read or write and was not very interested in Christianity, but he fell in love with gentle, educated, devout Margaret, so in the course of time he begged her to be his wife. She eventually consented and came to love him too. Malcolm and Margaret's marriage was known to be very happy. Margaret, who

became known as "The Pearl of Scotland", made the Scottish palaces into lovely and comfortable homes and raised the eight children she and Malcolm had together. She fed orphans with food from her own table and she worked to reform the Scottish church by introducing the Latin Mass and making Sunday a sabbath day of rest. Malcolm, fascinated by her religious books, had them decorated for her with gold, silver and jewels. Margaret read Scripture to Malcolm and it was said that gradually, in time, he changed and imitated Margaret's goodness and gentleness in his own way. Malcolm, however, was still a warlike king and one dark day he was killed in battle. When Margaret died, nine days later, it was said that she died of grief for Malcolm. The King and Queen of Scotland were buried side by side before the altar in Dunfirmline Abbey. One of their sons, the saintly David, became King of Scotland and one of their daughters, the good Edith, became Queen Consort of England.

Margaret of England

Unknown - 1192

In the days of barons and outlaws, when Christianity was full of mystery, Margaret of England travelled all over Europe. Women didn't travel a lot in those days. Usually they stayed at home keeping house and raising children: important tasks, to be sure, but ones that needed a lot of love and time and didn't give wanderlust a chance. Margaret, however, was an English girl who was born, for reasons which history has forgotten, in Hungary. Perhaps this is why, even when she was back at home amid the hills, woods and villages of England, she wanted to travel. Maybe, when she was a little girl, she wondered what was over the green hill and on the other side of the thick wood and wished she could follow the road wherever it led. And maybe the yearning to travel grew until it was impossible to ignore. When she grew up, Margaret became a pilgrim, a person who travelled to the holy sites of Christianity to pray. She took her mother and together they travelled all over the muddy, rutted roads of Europe. Sometimes they travelled alone, but often they travelled with bands of other pilgrims for company and safety. By day they walked or jogged along in carts or on horses. By night they gathered around fires and shared suppers under the

stars or in cheerful, noisy inns. They shared stories, hopes and prayers too. They prayed at the holy sites and collected the sights, sounds and smells like treasures. Finally Margaret and her mother settled in a little house in the rocky town of Bethlehem, in the Holy Land, where they lived simple, holy lives of prayer and poverty like the Christian women of the early church. Later, when her mother had died, Margaret became a nun in a French convent. But her head and heart were full and rich for the rest of her life with the memories of everything she had experienced in her travels.

Margaret Ward

About 1550 - 1588

Margaret Ward was a servant girl with a big heart. It probably got her into trouble many times during her short life. But it didn't stop her wanting to help when she heard that a Catholic priest, Father Watson, was being imprisoned and mistreated in a local prison. Margaret was a country girl from the North of England, but she served a fine lady in London. She was overwhelmed with compassion for the priest and fury at his gaolers and tormentors. Somehow she got permission to visit the priest. The guards were suspicious and searched her, but found nothing worrying in her basket, so let her into the prison to visit Father Watson and out again later. She took food, blankets and hope into the prison and came and went so often that the guards started nodding and smiling when they saw her and stopped searching her and her basket. This was what Margaret had been waiting for. She smuggled a rope into prison and told Father Watson about the clever, risky plan she had made. At the dead of night, the priest escaped from his prison window, then climbed down the rope to freedom. Sadly he hurt himself and left the tell-tale rope hanging from his window. Margaret was waiting to help, but the boatman who had

promised to row the priest along the River Thames to safety had vanished, so Margaret and Father Watson was stranded. Margaret found another, more trustworthy, boatman called John Roche who was willing to risk his life by helping the priest. Quickly Father Watson and John Roche swapped clothes. By then, however, the rope in the window had been spotted by the guards. With a grateful heart, the priest escaped to safety, but Margaret and the boatman were caught. Margaret refused to tell anyone where Father Watson was hidden. She knew she would die for her courageous and kind deed but she admitted in court – without any hint of regretting her courage or her kindness – that she had indeed helped a good man to escape and live another day to serve Christ.

Marianne Sykes Thornton

1765 - 1815

In the days of powdered wigs and buckled shoes, in the city of Hull, a baby girl was born. Her hair was red and name was Marianne. She had five brothers, a little spaniel and a flowery arbour in the garden which she called her very own. The Sykes and Wilberforce children ran in and out of each other's homes every day with books, toys and dogs and William Wilberforce, who later became a famous politician and abolitionist, thought of Marianne as another sister. She was sent to learn music, dancing and French at Mrs Lattafiere's School in Derby and when she came home, she was a young lady, ready to attend parties and balls and get married. At twenty-five, however, Marianne was still very unmarried and went with her brother to Buxton. The mineral waters disagreed with her – her brother said there was nothing the matter with her but lowness of spirits anyway – but William Wilberforce was there with his cousin, Henry Thornton, a banker, reformer and Member of Parliament. Henry spoke seriously to Marianne about the state of her soul and was delighted when she began to enjoy a close and loving relationship with Christ. By then Henry had dined with Marianne and walked her home from church so often that their friendship was

the talk of the town, but Henry was a confirmed bachelor, who wasn't ready to commit to love and marriage. He returned to London with Wilberforce where the cousins shared a house they called "the chummery" and tried to change the world. Marianne took long walks on the Yorkshire Moors, helped her friends when they had babies and started some charity schools. Five years later she got a letter from Henry Thornton proposing marriage, not for affection, but for lots of practical and religious reasons. Marianne, hurt and offended, said she'd rather not marry under the circumstances. Wilberforce cheerfully interfered, however, so Marianne happily became Mrs Thornton three months later and a mother one year later. Henry and Marianne had nine children – including four girls called Marianne, Lucy, Isabella and Sophia – and raised all of them in a loving, happy home which was cheerfully, unselfconsciously Christian. Marianne loved politics as well as Henry, so she encouraged his campaigns, supported his projects and celebrated his victories. She also tried to start an orphanage for abandoned babies, gave tea parties for poor and weary women and wrote hundreds of letters which networked their enormous collection of family and friends together. Henry and Marianne both died of consumption in 1815 and left their children to the care of family friends. For nineteen years, however, the two of them were blissfully happy and their home was full of sunshine.

Mary Fillis

Between 1576 and 1578 - Unknown

Once, in the days of swords and ruffs and farthingales, a little girl travelled from Morocco to England. Her early life is a mystery but it is thought that her father was an artisan and she came to England, when she was six years old, with an English merchant. She and some other Africans were the servants of the merchant and the merchant was connected to the Earl of Leicester – a favourite courtier of Queen Elizabeth I. The differences between hot, colourful Morocco and cold, grey England were huge and the little girl, who was called Mary in England, must have missed her homeland. But she grew up and worked for a seamstress in London. Here, in a little shop amid the narrow streets full of bustle and noise, she learned to earn her own living. Wealthy people at that time wore gorgeous clothes made of coloured wool and silk which were embroidered and decorated with jewels. The underneath layers were made of fine cloth with careful stitching too. And the costumes were finished with lace-edged ruffs made of the finest fabric with the most delicate and precise stitching. Mary must have had keen eyes, careful fingers and good taste. When she was twenty, Mary – "now taking hold of some faith in Jesus Christ" –

was baptised. The priest said she answered the traditional questions about her faith “very Christian like” and recited the Lord’s Prayer and the articles of the Christian faith “decently” and well. She was supported at the ceremony by her English friends who were all upstanding members of the local community. The rest of Mary’s life is as mysterious as the beginning. She was in London when ambassadors from her home country came to negotiate a treaty with her adopted country against their common enemy of Spain – and maybe she even helped to make some of the clothes the courtiers wore – but history doesn’t tell any more of her secrets. All it says for sure is that she was here and she chose to become part of the Christian story in England.

Mary Sumner

1828 - 1921

Mary Heywood was a cultured and quiet young woman of deep faith who went to Rome to study music. There she met a serious young man, called George Sumner, who wanted to be a vicar. The couple were married when Mary was nineteen. Not long afterwards George became a vicar and Mary became a vicar's wife. She also became the mother of three children: Margaret, Louise and Heywood. Together they lived in a tiny village in Hampshire. Mary saw her home life and her husband's church as the world in which God wanted her to love and honour Him. She made the vicarage into a cosy home and helped with music and Sunday School in the village church. When her eldest daughter, Margaret, became a mother – and Mary became a grandmother – things changed for her forever. Mary looked at the young mother and the tiny baby snuggled in Margaret's arms. Mary's heart filled with love for her daughter and grandchild and she remembered how overwhelmed she had felt when she became a mother and how she had longed for comfort and support in raising her children. In those days, people from different walks of life didn't socialise as equals, but Mary realised that mothers from all walks of life loved their children

and wanted the best for them, so they all needed encouragement. Boldly Mary called a meeting for all the mothers in the village. Rich and poor, educated and uneducated, young and old – from Broad Street, Mill Hill and Ladywell Lane – they gathered in her drawing room. Mary was so nervous that her husband had to lead the first meeting, but she led the next meeting. Over cups of tea and pieces of cake, the Mother's Union came into being, with the purpose of encouraging all mothers in the vocation of motherhood. With a little bit of help from the Bishop of Winchester and Queen Victoria, it spread around Britain and it still encourages thousands of mothers to this day. Mary left a prayer which characterised her entire life: "All this day, O Lord, let me touch as many lives as possible for thee; and every life I touch, do thou by thy spirit quicken, whether through the word I speak, the prayer I breathe, or the life I live. Amen."

Mary Teresa Brück

1925 - 2008

Máire Teresa Conway grew up with numbers in her head and stars in her eyes. She was born in Ireland, had seven little brothers and sisters and went to a convent school where her faith grew alongside her studies. She shone at maths, science and music – all about numbers – and used to wrangle over the piano with her brothers because she liked the classical music of Liszt and Chopin and they liked ragtime. She left school to study physics at University College Dublin and research solar physics at the University of Edinburgh. She earned her PhD and went back to work in Ireland at the Dunsink Observatory, where she was called Dr Mary Conway. Here, too, she met and married the love of her life: a widowed astronomer from Germany called Hermann Brück who had two children. Together they made a family of four, then Mary had three babies of her own, so they became a family of seven. Later, Mary moved to Edinburgh with her family, because her husband was appointed Astronomer Royal. Here, while her husband transformed the Royal Observatory into a research centre for astronomers from around the world, Dr Mary Brück – as she was now called – made a home, raised her children and became a lecturer at the University

of Edinburgh. Over the years she researched the numbers, brightnesses and colours of stars in the Magellanic Clouds because she wanted to understand how these nearby galaxies worked. She wanted to share her work with everyone who might be interested in astronomy. Later, with her heart still among the stars, she became an astronomy historian with a special interest in brave and gifted women astronomers. To the end of her days Mary remained loved and respected for her deep and intelligent faith which she cherished throughout her life, her care for other people, her ethical standards, her academic rigour and the enormous sense of fun she brought to her entire life … as well as her endless fascination, not just with numbers, but with stars.

Miles and Sibyl de Gloucester

Unknown - 1143 and About 1100 - After 1143

It was King Henry I who arranged the marriage between Miles de Gloucester and Sybil de Neufmarché. Miles was raised to think and fight like a man and a baron. He was a horseman and a swordsman. His honour and his sword, however, were pledged to the service of the king. Sybil was raised to be a wife and a mother. She learned to pray and sew. Her dowry was all the lands, money and titles of her Saxon and Norman ancestors, the title of "Lady of Brecknock" and the royal lineage of the Welsh kings. The marriage was made by Royal Decree and in the course of time Miles and Sybil became the parents of eight children. It was not long, however, before unhappiness and unrest came to England. King Henry I died and his daughter Matilda fought his nephew Stephen for the throne. The days of war were so terrible that men said Christ and His saints slept. Miles initially supported Stephen, but later supported Matilda and became "a constant friend" to her cause, which he believed was just. He served both of them as Constable of England. He also gave money to support Llanthony Priory in the heart of the Black Mountains of Wales and helped it move to safety in Gloucestershire in England. Here he and Sybil endowed it with tithes, chapels and

land. Sibyl, meanwhile, was a loyal wife who managed her husband's households and estates, and a good mother who raised their children to be healthy, loyal and religious. One snowy Christmas Eve, Miles went hunting, but tragedy struck when he was accidentally killed by a stray arrow in a state of excommunication due to an argument with a local bishop. Sybil, apparently heartbroken, embraced a new life devoted to Christ at Llanthony Secunda Priory, the religious house she and Miles had enriched together, where she found comfort and hope. Miles and Sybil's son, Roger, harried the local church for excommunicating Miles until the last years of his own life. Then he founded a religious house of his own on the spot where Miles died. Their daughter, Margaret de Hereford, served as Constable of England after Miles. She was also a generous patroness of various religious houses and never forgot her parents or brothers and sisters but hoped and prayed that they would be reunited in heaven.

Morwenna of Cornwall

500s

It was said, in the days when the saints of Britain lived their faith and worked their miracles, that Brychan was a Welsh king who had at least four children. Some people, indeed, said he married three times and had as many as twenty-five children! One of his daughters, however, was the saintly Morwenna. She had a heart that burned with love for Christ and a strong desire to share her faith with others. She studied and trained to work for Christ in Ireland and one day, when she was ready, she loaded a little boat with leather bottles of water, woven caskets of food and wooden boxes of supplies. Morwenna pushed her little boat into the sea, waded through the waves that ran up and down the beach and raised the sail to catch the wind. Bravely Morwenna sailed away from the green valleys and misty mountains of Wales. She was willing to go wherever God led and she trusted that He would guide the waves under her keel and the wind in her sails. The tide pulled her little boat this way and that way and the seabirds flew and called over her head. In the distance she saw a new land of rocky cliffs and green moors. She landed in a tiny cove on the coast of Cornwall. Here she settled among the local people, a rugged, warm-hearted

people of land and sea who worked in mines and boats. She shared her faith and soon some of the local people shared her desire for a church building where they could worship Christ. Morwenna carried stones one by one up a steep path from the cove below to the headland. Once she stopped to rest and a spring of fresh, sweet water bubbled up from the ground to refresh her weary body. The local people were so impressed by this miracle that they built the church on the very spot. Morwenna taught and worshipped in Cornwall for the rest of her days and was loved for her kindness and generosity to everyone. Her brother Nectan, who lived and ministered nearby in Devon, was with her when she died and raised her up for one last glimpse of Wales in the distance. The tiny village of Morwenstow – the name means "Morwenna's Holy Place" – still nestles among the hills above the cliffs in Cornwall. Mowenna is the patron saint of the village church. And nearby, hidden among the yellow primroses and green ferns, it is said that the fresh water of her miraculous spring still bubbles and sings over the Cornish rocks.

Myles Standish

About 1584 - 1656

Myles Standish was sometimes called Captain Shrimp or "the little chimney that smokes". His friends, however, trusted him completely and recalled his humility, loyalty and sacrifice for far longer than they remembered his short stature or hasty words. In 1620 he sailed for America with the Pilgrim Fathers aboard the *Mayflower*. The Pilgrim Fathers were very strict Puritans who wanted to live a quiet life and be free from controlling bishops and interfering kings. Myles, however, was not a Puritan. No one is exactly sure who he was but he may have been the son of a landed family in the North of England who were Catholics at a time when it was illegal. He became a soldier in Holland and it was here that he encountered the Pilgrim Fathers. He was employed to go to America and protect them with his fists, his sword and his musket. He did this and more. He was not, it seems, a good soldier but he was a faithful friend and loyal guard. During the first winter in America, when he remained alive and healthy, he tended the sick and dying – including his first wife, Rose – and William Bradford said he comforted and strengthened everyone who was ill. Myles' friendship with William Bradford, the governor of the community,

lasted for years. He also made friends with an Indian man called Hobbomock and they remained friends for the rest of their lives too. Most notably, however, he remained best of friends with John Alden when the two men fell in love with the same woman. One of their descendants, an American poet called Henry Wadsworth Longfellow, immortalised Myles in a long poem called *The Courtship of Miles Standish* which he based on a family tradition. Myles, Longfellow thought, wanted to marry Priscilla Mullins but she wanted to marry John Alden. Ultimately Myles married another pilgrim girl who came to America, Barbara. Their son Alexander married John and Priscilla's daughter Sarah and the descendants of both couples are alive and well in America to this day. Myles signed the Mayflower Compact "in the Presence of God" before he and his Puritan friends left the *Mayflower*. In spite of that, however, he never joined the Pilgrim church in America. He was, however, unswerving present. He attended every church service and his friends felt safe and secure knowing that he was on guard against every danger. He was beloved by them, they considered that the Lord had sent him to them and when he died they said he had "fallen asleep in the Lord". He left a personal library of Bibles and theological books and his sons and grandsons became the leaders of the Pilgrim church in time to come.

Nansi Griffiths

1776 - 1805

Once, in a stone farmhouse called Dolwar Fechan in Wales, there lived a girl who was christened Ann Thomas but called Nansi. She was the fifth of six children – and the youngest girl – and in time, her siblings grew up and left home, but Nansi lived at Dolwar Fechan all her life. The farmhouse was surrounded by hills, trees and streams of water. An ancient saint called Melangell was still celebrated nearby for her goodness and her kindness to a hunted hare. Nansi's father was a farmer and a churchwarden, so Nansi was raised in the Church of England. The whole family were committed to living a Christian life, even the dog, who followed Mr Thomas to the parish church every Sunday morning and sat under the pew during the service. Occasionally, if Mr Thomas wasn't able to go to church, the dog went anyway. It was an age of great Christian revival in Britain and one by one the Thomas family began to take their faith more seriously. For a long time, Nansi didn't, but laughed and teased her family and friends who became too deep and very serious in their faith. When Nansi was eighteen, however, her mother died, she became the mistress of the family home and her brothers encouraged her to take her faith more

seriously too. She joined the Methodist Church and immersed herself in reading the Bible, praying and expressing her faith in Christ through poetry. Her poems, spoken in Welsh, were a heartfelt expression of her most personal and precious feelings. Her love for Christ was fresh and trusting:

All I need through surging waters,
All I need through raging fire;
O! my soul, to cling for ever,
Cling to him, my life's desire.

Nansi recited her poems to her maid, Ruth, as the two women worked around the house and farm. Later Nansi married Thomas Griffiths – a local farmer and an elder in her new church – and had a baby girl. Sadly Nansi and her daughter died within a few weeks. Ruth missed Nansi and recited her poems to her husband. He was a local minister who made a careful record of all Nansi's poems. Eventually they were compiled into twenty-nine hymns and many of them were translated into English. They are sung and beloved to this day.

Ninette de Valois

1898 - 2001

Ninette de Valois saw a ballet called *The Sleeping Beauty* when she was a little girl and she never outgrew the magic of *barre* exercises, *pointe* shoes and Tchaikovsky's music. She was born in County Wicklow, Ireland, as Edris Stamus. She saw another girl dance and knew that she, too, had to dance. And Edris did dance – in the country house in Ireland where she was born then in Kent where she lived with her grandmother then in London and all over England. It is said the first dance she ever learned was an Irish jig but she trained as a professional dancer at the Lila Field Academy for Children and joined Sergei Diaghileve's Ballet Russes with dancers like the famous Alicia Markova. Like her friends, Edris chose a beautiful foreign name – Ninette de Valois – which was printed on theatre programs when she danced, but she yearned to start an English company of ballerinas. She never forgot *The Sleeping Beauty* and she refused to believed that only French, Italian and Russian woman could be ballerinas. Finally she started a ballet company which was based in the Sadler's Wells Theatre in London. It toured to entertain the troops during WWII and after

the war it was invited to become the regular ballet company at Covent Garden Opera House. The first ballet Ninette de Valois staged at Covent Garden was, of course, *The Sleeping Beauty*. Thereafter she was known as “Madame” to generations of dancers – as well as generations of readers who read ballet story books – and made ballet a fixture in English society with her quiet but strong creativity and intelligence and what the ballet experts called her “attention to narrative” and “responsiveness to music”. She kept her private life private but she was, in fact, very deeply attached to her Irish heritage. She was raised in a Christian home and remained a quiet but faithful Christian all her life. She was also married for over fifty years to a doctor and was known, locally, as “the doctor’s wife”. By people who love ballet today, however, she is still remembered as a fairy godmother in the world of English and Irish ballet.

Octavia Hill

1838 - 1912

One day, in the year that Queen Victoria was crowned, a baby girl was born. She was her father's eighth daughter so, naturally, he looked at his baby girl and called her Octavia Hill because Octavia is the feminine form of the Latin words "the eighth". She grew into a woman who believed passionately in helping people help themselves, but giving them lots of beauty and nature along the way. Octavia's childhood was comfortable and secure until her father lost his money and his mental health. Her mother, who had been a governess and writer before her marriage, matter-of-factly went to work to support her large family. She was, in turn, encouraged and supported by her father – Octavia's grandfather – who was a social philanthropist and reformer and became a father figure for Octavia. She was frightened by the grim poverty of her new home and never forgot the financial insecurity of those days but she, too, went to work as a secretary and teacher. Later she supported very young girls who were desperately poor and worked as toymakers while attending a charity school. Octavia desperately wanted to help the girls and their families and at this time she made friends with Christians who were social activists with big ideas

about making the world a better place for everyone. Octavia was baptised and confirmed in the Church of England and started a life's work of providing better housing for the poor and needy. At this time there weren't any health and safety regulations about how houses were built and how many people could live in them so the poorest people in society paid a lot of money to live in tiny houses without proper heating or drainage. Sometimes ten or twelve people would live squashed into one room of a damp and tumbledown house. Octavia's work was always practical and useful but she was inspired by the beauty-loving John Ruskin, an artist and reformer, who believed that everyone needed the beauty of nature as much as they needed food and housing. Octavia was deeply committed to the idea of rights – like education and freedom to vote – for women but for the rest of her life she worked to give the poorest people affordable, pleasant and safe housing and grass, trees and wild open spaces. Today she is most often remembered for her other big work: helping to found the National Trust.

Philip Sydney and Mary Herbert

1554 - 1586 and 1561 - 1621

Philip and Mary Sydney grew up in the ancient and rambling manor house of Penshurst Place in Kent with their five brothers and sisters. They studied literature and languages together, then Philip studied at the University of Oxford and Mary attended Queen Elizabeth I at the royal court and learned embroidery, music and other ladylike subjects. At eighteen, Philip became a Member of Parliament and a diplomat. At sixteen, Mary became a bride and a countess. Philip was in France when, on St Bartholomew's Eve, the French Protestant Huguenot community in Paris was attacked with sword and fire by a Catholic mob. Philip – who was generous, impulsive and romantic – watched the terrible scene in horror. He was transformed, literally overnight, from an idealistic Protestant to a militant Protestant. Back at home in England, he became a courtier and a poet and he had a number of Catholic friends, but he did not forget the Protestant church in Europe. Mary was a courtier, wife and mother who enjoyed archery and sailing and had a private laboratory where she invented invisible ink. She loved Philip's poems. A lady-in-waiting inspired a sonnet but Philip wrote his longest poem for Mary and she called him "a merry maker" of

poems and jokes. She was also a gifted poet and she polished her talent and her work until her poetry sparkled. Eventually Philip went to Europe to fight Catholic Spaniards in Protestant Holland. He was a heroic and reckless soldier who shared his armour with another soldier then died of a battle wound. It is said that the last thing he did was give his drinking water to another wounded man. He was mourned by many including his wife, his best friend Fulke Greville and – of course – Mary. She had already lost her baby girl to illness and she was devastated to lose her beloved brother to war, but in the midst of her sadness, she resolved to finish his translation of the Book of Psalms. She revised his poetry and composed over a hundred psalms on her own. She pored over the Bible and the works of translators and theologians, including texts in Latin, Greek and Hebrew. She used an enormous variety of poetic forms and verbal imagery that expressed her understanding of the Psalms and captured her experience of life and faith as a Protestant, a woman and a courtier. Philip and Mary's choice of words was original, bold and moving and it took readers by surprise at the time, but *The Sydney Psalter* is still read and loved. Psalm 52 rings true through the centuries to this day:

My trust in his true love
Truly attending,
Shall never thence remove,
Never see ending.

Polly Newton

About 1728 - 1790

When Polly and John were tiny children, their mothers hoped they would grow up and marry someday, but such things cannot be made to happen. Polly met John for the first time when they were teenagers. At the time she was a good girl of fourteen and he was a careless youth of seventeen, with many years of rebellion and trouble before him, but this meeting was the beginning of a long and lasting romance. Polly prayed earnestly and faithfully for John during his young adult years. He was sent to sea by his seafaring father, to keep him out of trouble, but he was wild and rebellious on board ship and was terribly punished before he submitted to authority. He was a white slave in Africa before he escaped and became the captain of a slave ship which collected Africans from the Ivory Coast and carried them, against their will, across the Atlantic Ocean to the West Indies. The boats were crowded and full of disease and the Africans were sold as slaves for plantations which, at that time, produced sugar and rum for England. The men who worked on the slave ships were rough and tough and John became rougher and tougher than ever. Back at home in England, meanwhile, Polly refused to believe that he was a lost cause. She

prayed and prayed and prayed and many miles away, in the middle of a terrible storm, John turned to faith in Christ. Safe and sound, John was determined to be a good Christian and prove himself to Polly, who accepted his heart and hand in marriage. She gave him her whole heart in return and their love was unbroken and undismayed throughout their marriage. Polly was a sailor's wife for some time and then – when John left the sea and the slave trade and became a Church of England priest – she was a minister's wife. She kept house and supported his parish ministry in every way. Together they shared the pain of being unable to have children of their own and the joy of adopting their nieces. Finally Polly – who had always cared for John – accepted his tender loving care as she lay ill and dying. The heartbroken John, who is famous for writing the famous hymn *Amazing Grace*, said that Polly was the most great and lasting influence on his spiritual life and all he did for Christ.

Priscilla Buxton Johnston

1808 - 1852

One day in 1833 or thereabouts, when women were not allowed to enter the public galleries of the Houses of Parliament to hear debates, Priscilla Buxton made her way to a ventilation shaft above the House of Commons. She knew this spot well. Here, if she listened very hard, she could hear her father, Sir Thomas Foxwell Buxton, speaking to the Members of Parliament in the House of Commons far below. At this time the British Slave Trade had been abolished – it was, in fact, abolished the year before Priscilla was born – but British slavery had not been abolished. Slavery was illegal in Britain but not in the British colonies. Hundreds of people in Britain were rich because they owned estates and slaves in the West Indies and hundreds of men, women and children from Africa suffered under British slavery. William Wilberforce, who had worked so hard and so long to abolish the British Slave Trade, had entrusted this new battle to Priscilla's father. He fought in the House of Commons and Priscilla – horrified, offended and saddened by slavery – fought at his side in his study. As her father's special assistant, Priscilla helped to research and write his abolition reports and parliamentary speeches, then went to the Houses of

Parliament to hear him speak through the ventilation shaft. Her father founded the Anti-Slavery Society, but only men could belong, so Priscilla helped to found and lead the London Female Anti-Slavery Society. In 1833 Priscilla helped to organise a petition against slavery which was signed by one hundred and eighty-seven thousand women. It was so big that two men had to lift and carry it into the House of Commons. Some Members of Parliament laughed but Priscilla didn't care. She continued her work for her father and helped to organise an educational mission to Africa. At the age of twenty-six, Priscilla married a Member of Parliament called Andrew Johnston. He was ten years older than Priscilla and worked with her father, but they were both committed Christians and uncompromising abolitionists. They got married at Trinity Church in Marylebone on the day that British slavery was abolished and slaves were freed throughout the British colonies. Priscilla died quite young but not before she and her husband had a cheerful family of six children – Andrew, Euphemia, Foxwell, Sarah Maria, Priscilla Hannah and Catherine Isabel – and divided their time between London and Scotland.

Reasonable Blackman

Before 1579 - After 1592

In 1561 someone gave Queen Elizabeth I a pair of silk stockings. It's said that she was delighted and exclaimed, "I like silk stockings well; they are pleasant, fine and delicate. Henceforth I shall wear no more cloth stockings." The queen and all the ladies in waiting at the royal court wanted silk stockings to wear and this was good news for an honest Londoner from Africa, called Reasonable Blackman, who lived and worked in a humble street to the south of the River Thames. In this part of London, called Southwark, people jostled each other in dark, narrow, cobbled streets full of rubbish. Merchants and pedlars hawked their wares at the top of their lungs. Musicians played their instruments on street corners for a few coins. Beggars pushed and shoved in gutters and doorways and asked wealthy pedestrians for money. Nearby there were the noisy, rollicking theatres where William Shakespeare's plays were performed for the first time. It wasn't the ideal place to run a business and raise a family, but it was cheaper than it would have been north of the River Thames. So here, near London Bridge, Reasonable Blackman wove silk thread – as delicate and precious as the thread of a spider's web – into laces and ribbons and

stockings. He and his wife, an English girl, had three children and had them christened in St Olave's Church: Edward, Edmund and Jane. Sadly Edmund and Jane died of the plague while they were children and were buried in the churchyard. Later Edward married a local girl and became a silk weaver like his father. But then Reasonable Blackman slips out of history. He leaves only a little bit of his story for us to know today: he was a good weaver, he earned a good income, he was a husband, he was a father who promised to raise his children as Christians and buried them, when they died, in the churchyard and he confessed the Christian faith. No one knows for sure, but it's possible that his laces, ribbons and stockings were worn by courtiers at the royal court, maybe even by Queen Elizabeth I.

Robert Adkins

1626 - 1685

Robert Adkins was born in Chard in Somerset. His father wanted him to go into business, but Robert had set his heart on being a preacher of the Gospel, so his father sent him to study in Oxford. Its dreaming spires were a world away from the green fields and blue hills of the West Country, but Robert settled down and worked hard at Wadham College, which is part of the University of Oxford. He eventually became a Fellow and was honoured for his academic achievements. He strode around the cream-coloured buildings of the college, built around a grassy quadrangle, with books in his arms, learning in his head and faith in his heart. Finally, at the city church of St Mary where Cranmer, Latimer and Ridley had all been tried for heresy and condemned to death a century before, Robert preached his first sermon. He was small and looked very young, so the congregation refused to take him seriously at first, but dismissed him as “just a boy”. He preached so earnestly and so well, however, that in the end the congregation took him very seriously and so did Oliver Cromwell. In fact, Oliver Cromwell appointed Robert as a chaplain, although he did not stay in that post for long. Instead, he worked as a parish priest, preaching good

sermons full of solid doctrine and giving his parishioners so much care and conversation that they all wanted to come to church! Robert ended up in Exeter in Devon and here, in 1662, he was ejected from the Church of England during "The Great Ejection". At that time all Church of England clergymen were required to swear allegiance to the Act of Uniformity. For Puritans – who were very strict Protestants – it was impossible to swear allegiance without compromising their convictions about what was good and right before God. Around a thousand clergymen like Robert were "ejected" from the Church of England on St Bartholomew's Day in 1662. Faithful Puritan clergymen mourned "to see how the shepherds are scattered" but cheered each other on for refusing "to change with the times". An English church, distinct from and dissenting from the Church of England, came into being. And in a little church in Exeter Robert said, "Let him never be accounted a sound Christian that doth not fear God and honour the king." Earnestly, as he preached one last sermon, he said, "We will do anything for his majesty but sin. We will hazard anything for him but our souls."

Robert le Converse

Before 1245 - After 1301

In the days of the barons, when Simon de Montfort fought King Henry III for the rights of England and the English people, the king had a servant called Robert le Converse. It was an era of treachery and unrest. The king was a gentle and yielding man and in the midst of battles and charters, promises made and promises broken, he trusted Robert and called him his "beloved servant". Robert was a Jewish man who had converted to Christianity and perhaps this is why he came to the attention of the king, who was interested in and supportive of Jews, especially when they converted to Christianity. At this time Jews and Christians lived and worshipped side by side in England but ignorance and superstition in the Christian community inspired some horrible outbreaks of violence against the Jewish community. As a Jew, Robert prayed in Hebrew, read the *Torah* in the synagogue and observed *shabbat* on Saturday. His Hebrew name, the details of his life in the Jewish community and the reasons why he converted to Christianity are forgotten. Maybe he came to believe in Christ or maybe he wanted to be part of the Christian community and the English society. For whatever reason, however, he took the English name of Robert, served the king and

became part of the Christian story in England. As a Christian, he prayed in Latin, heard the Gospels read in church and attended Mass on Sunday. Robert served the king as a sergeant-at-arms, one of the servants or soldiers who was closest to him, most trusted to protect him from anyone who approached him with treason in mind. At some point he was dismissed from the royal household in disgrace but it was not long before he was was forgiven and restored to his old position. The king's "beloved servant" could not be spared for long and lived to serve his son, King Edward I, in due course. Robert was married to Sibil and they lived in the parish of St Sepulche in London where they raised their children in a little house within walking distance of both St Paul's Cathedral and the Great Synagogue in Old Jewry. Later, their son John identified himself as "a convert of London", as if he was proud of his Jewish heritage or his Christian conversion or both and he, too, was a sergeant-at-arms to the kings of England.

Robert Williams

1500s

Robert Williams was a shepherd who worked for Master Latimer of Gloucestershire in the Tudor era. In those days London was the only city in England and most people lived in the countryside rather than the towns. The life of a shepherd, then as now, was shaped by the needs of his sheep. In the autumn, while the farmers were ploughing their fields, the shepherds were examining their flocks and deciding which sheep to keep for breeding and which to sell for eating. Male and female sheep nibbled grass together over Christmas and after a long, dark winter a new generation of lambs was born in the spring. It was the busiest time of the year as the shepherds worked all day and slept near the expectant mothers at night to help the lambs into the world. The lambs grew through the spring, the sheep were sheared in the summer and in the autumn everything started again. In the Tudor era, when the English Reformation was changing everything in church and society, many poor men and women learned to read so that they could read the Bible in English. It was being printed – legally and illegally for rich and for poor – and distributed all over England. Robert Williams was probably a weather-beaten man with the rough

hands, rosy cheeks and searching eyes of every good shepherd. He could read and write and he had a burning desire to read the Bible in English. Officially only rich and educated people were allowed to read the Bible but he didn't care. And one day, when he was watching his sheep on Saintbury Hill as he was used to doing in all weathers, he wrote in the front of another book, "At Oxford, the year 1546, bought down to Saintbury by John Darbye, price 14*d*, when I keep Mr Latimer's sheep. I bought this book when the Testament was abrogated, that shepherds might not read it. I pray God amend that blindness. Writ by Robert Williams, keeping sheep upon Saintbury Hill, 1546." Hopefully he got to read the Bible in English someday.

Roger Martyn

About 1527 - 1615

In the days when farming sheep and selling wool made England rich, it made the Martyn family of Long Melford in Suffolk rich too. One of their precious possessions was a prayer book, written by hand and illuminated with paint and gold. In time a baby boy was born and christened Roger Martyn. He was raised, like his father and grandfather, in the wool trade. And, for the first ten years of Roger's life, everything in England was the same as it had been for hundreds of years. The year was marked by the seasons and the sheep: spring for lambing, summer for shearing, autumn for butchering and winter for resting. It was full of feast days and holy days when the stories of Christ and saints were remembered and celebrated by merchants, shepherds and beggars together. The village priests processed around the village green with candles and bells, and there were feasts and bonfires. In the church, which was full of statues, candles and incense, the priests led the congregation in celebrating Mass in Latin every day. When Roger was ten, however, everything started to change. Monasteries and convents – the communities where monks and nuns prayed and worked, and which were schools and hospitals too – were closed. Feast days and

holy days were cancelled and people were told to work instead of pray or celebrate. Statues of saints were taken out of churches and services were said in English not Latin. Once, when a statue of Christ on the cross was thrown out of the church, Roger took it home and hid it in his own house. He grew up and trained to be a lawyer in London, then got married and raised a family of his own in Long Melford. Roger was still a young man when statues, candles and incense were put back in churches and Mass was celebrated in Latin again. Lovingly he helped restore the Long Melford church. He was a church warden and his heart was happy until everything changed again. This time the things he loved about church were banished forever. Roger was sad at heart, but he was faithful to his understanding of Christianity for the rest of his life. He recorded his memories of statues, processions and bonfires for Christ in words on paper, so he and those who came after him wouldn't forget anything.

Rose de Burford

Unknown - 1329

Once the streets of London ran higgledy-piggledly from the countryside to the River Thames and St Paul's Cathedral rose like a guardian angel over the homes and businesses built in its shadow. In those days a little girl was born to a wealthy wool and spice merchant. She was called Rose in honour of Mary the Mother of Christ – whose emblem was a rose – and she grew up surrounded by sacks of wool and barrels of spices. She learned to pray, sew and cook like every other little girl in England, but she learned more: how to read and write, add and subtract. Rose was fascinated by her father's business: by the wool of the Ryeland, Cotswold and Lincoln sheep that left England and the spices – with names like pepper, cinnamon and ginger – from exotic foreign lands which came to England. When she grew up, Rose married her father's business partner, John de Burford. Together they had a girl called Katherine and a boy called James. Tragedy struck when John died and Rose was left as a widow with two children to support. She took everything she had learned about business from her father and her husband and kept their wool and spice trade going. She also ran an embroidery business. King Edward II ordered a robe for a

priest from Rose and she embroidered it so beautifully with coral that the queen sent it to the pope in Rome instead. Rose managed her business concerns sensibly and provided well for her family. She even bought a country house in Kent. She was a religious woman and wanted to do something for the church and the good of her soul. Before she died, she had enough money to build a chapel on the south side of the Church of St Thomas the Apostle, where Christians prayed until the Great Fire of London in 1666.

Rose Hickman

1526 - 1613

It was in 1610 or thereabouts that a very old lady picked up a quill pen, dipped it in a little bottle of ink and started to write. She covered about forty-five pages of parchment with her handwriting and the story of her long and adventurous life. In her little book she wrote what she called "certain old stories recorded by an aged gentlewoman a little before her death to be perused by her children and posterity". Rose was born as Rose Lok and died as Rose Throckmorton, but she spent most of her life as Rose Hickman. Her father was a London merchant who rose to be an alderman of the city, a knight and a courtier in the royal household of King Henry VIII. He traded in wool, linen, silk, as well as little haberdashery accessories like needles, thread, pins and buttons, but he also smuggled Bibles and prayerbooks into England for Queen Anne Boleyn. Rose lived quietly at home with her eighteen brothers and sisters at a house called The Sign of the Padlock. She recalled, however, that her mother used to secretly read books about the Protestant form of Christianity to Rose and her little sisters. The secret books obviously made a great impression upon Rose because she was a faithful Protestant – almost a strict Puritan – for the

rest of her life. Rose may have been a silkwoman in her own right, but when she was sixteen, she married a merchant called Anthony Hickman and eventually she became the mother of seven children. The couple interacted with Protestants from all over Europe and during the reign of Catholic Queen Mary I, when Protestants were persecuted, Rose's brother and husband were imprisoned for their faith. Rose later remembered that when she gave birth to a baby, she wanted her little one baptised and welcomed into the Christian church as soon as possible, but there was no Protestant priest to perform the ceremony. Rose allowed a Catholic priest to baptise her baby, but when he called for salt during the Catholic ceremony, Rose gave him a little bag of sugar. In this way she felt she was able to compromise between her Protestant convictions and the safety of her family. Later, Rose's family fled from England to Belgium for safety, but eventually, in the reign of Protestant Queen Elizabeth I, they returned to England. Later, when Anthony died, Rose was married again then widowed again. She lived with her son and grandchildren in the North of England – near the home of the Pilgrim Fathers – for the rest of her days. It was here that she wrote the story of her life so it would not be forgotten.

Ruth from Madras

1800s

In the sun-drenched, spice-scented land of India there lived a young woman called Ruth. She came from Madras and during the days of Queen Victoria she became the *ayah* – the name for an Indian nursemaid – to the Rolandson children from England. Colonel Rolandson of the 12th Madras Infantry was a soldier in the British Army and Mrs Rolandson and their children probably lived in a white bungalow which was cool and shady in the hot weather. The house would have been a little bit of England in India and Ruth was one of many Indian servants who helped to keep the Rolandson family happy and healthy in their home from home. But Ruth was a beloved nursemaid and when the Rolandson family went back to England, Ruth went too, to help the children as they travelled around the world to their new home. The children probably held her hand, tugged her *sari* for attention and asked a thousand questions as they travelled from India – via the Indian Ocean, the Suez Canal, the Mediterranean Sea – to Europe. Finally, as they crossed the English Channel, they watched the tall, white cliffs of Dover loom out of the mist and went home to a big house in the Lansdown area of Cheltenham. Cheltenham, a spa town where people used to

drink the mineral-rich waters for their health, was a centre for Indian culture in Britain. Everyone, it seemed, had a personal or professional connection to India. English and Indian people mingled in the town. A school for boys kept a record of school leavers who had gone to India and been eaten by tigers, and a school for girls was run by the survivor of an Indian mutiny which she and her baby daughter had only just escaped alive. And here, one lovely Sunday in 1882, Ruth was baptised at Christchurch. She was a long way from home, but she chose to become part of the Christian story in England. She was baptised at the same time as her youngest charge. Miss Julia Rolandson was baptised by the vicar of Christchurch in English, and Ruth was baptised by Reverend Robert Pargiter in the Tamil language. Colonel and Mrs Rolandson and the rest of the children probably smiled and nodded while Rev Pargiter asked, “Do you come to Christ, the way, the truth and the life?” and Ruth said, “I come to Christ.” The sun shone, the bells rang and Ruth celebrated a new beginning in her story.

Sally Lunn

1600s

Once, so the story goes, a young girl called Solange Luyon was persecuted in France for her Protestant faith. French Protestants at that time were known as Huguenots and many fled persecution and war by going to England or to Canada and America in the new world. Sometime in the 1680s, Solange Luyon came to England, where everyone called her Sally Lunn. In the underground kitchen of an old house in Lilliput Alley, at the heart of the golden-stoned city of Bath, Sally worked as a baker's maid. Here, mixing flour, kneading dough and shaping loaves in a tiny space with a hot fire, she made a French delicacy: buns which were a cross between cake and bread. Sally was young and far from home and the work was hard and relentless. Often she pushed her hair out of her eyes with the back of her hand and left a smudge of flour on her nose. Sometimes the heat of the flames scorched her festival-bread buns. Most of the time, however, the magic of ingredients, heat and time worked. Sally pulled hundreds of fluffy buns with golden crusts out of the bread oven. The buns were delicious, hot from the brick oven or toasted over the fire, with cheese or jam. At first Sally sold her sweet wares in the streets around Bath Abbey. She wore a clean

apron and carried the buns into the fresh air in a covered basket. Cheerfully she called, “Come and buy my sweet buns!” The rich people of Bath loved her festival-bread buns and soon Sally sold them in a tea shop above the basement kitchen in Lilliput Alley. The oldest recipes for Sally’s famous buns, written in spidery handwriting in faded ink on stained paper, call for the finest flour and richest milk as well as yeast, sugar, butter and eggs. Sally stayed in England where she made and sold her buns for over thirty years. Sally Lunn Bunns, made to her secret recipe, can still be found in Bath today.

Sheth Ghulam Hyder

Unknown - 1823

Long ago, before the days of the British Raj in India, Persian was spoken in India. It was an ancient and courtly language, but it became the language of the people, which united Indians. It was recorded in beautifully written and gorgeously illuminated books of prayer, history, story, poetry and essays. The men who read and wrote Persian in India were cultured and educated. One of these men was called Sheth Ghulam Hyder. In the early 1800s he travelled around the world from Bengal in India to the East India College at Hailey, in Hertfordshire, near London in England. It was an incredible journey. The wind filled the canvas sails of the wooden ship and carried him across the Indian Ocean, around the Cape of Good Hope and the Ivory Coast then north past the Mediterranean Sea, across the Bay of Biscay and into the English Channel. Finally, in England, Sheth was appointed to the post of Persian Writing Master at the East India College, where he taught Persian to the British boys destined to become the civil servants of the British Empire. At that time, the East India Company was laying the foundations of the British Raj in India, but Sheth cannot have imagined that the Queen of England would someday be

called the Empress of India. He was presumably eager to share his love of his language and literature with the boys at the college. He was paid two hundred pounds a year and considered a professional man. The East India College was in the Church of England parish of Great Amwell but there was also a chapel at the college. Maybe it was here that Sheth encountered Christianity for the first time. In the course of time he chose to become a Christian. Later he married Rose Slocomb, the daughter of a local school master, with whom he had four children. Sheth was ill and poor when he died, the East India Company was not generous to his widow and children and at least one of his sons returned to India. Today the East India Company is a thing of the past and Haileybury College is an independent school for boys and girls. Sheth, however, is remembered for his excellence in Persian, his epic journey from India to England and the fact that he became part of the Christian story in this country.

Susannah Spurgeon

1832 - 1903

Susannah Thompson was raised in a Christian home but felt her faith grow uncertain in her late teens and early twenties. One day, some friends invited her to attend a London church with them and hear a new preacher called Charles Haddon Spurgeon. He was a young man in his late teens who was already the pastor of a tiny chapel in Cambridgeshire where he was called “the boy preacher of the fens”. Susannah was a fashionable and pretty London girl and she was amused and scornful about the preacher’s unsophisticated appearance and way of speaking. What she couldn’t doubt – or forget – was the sincerity and wisdom of his sermon. He soon became the pastor of that London church and she went to hear him preach regularly. Her faith revived and she was baptised. One day, when they were at the Crystal Palace with friends, Charles asked Susannah, “Do you ever pray for him who is to be your husband?” Charles and Susannah soon fell in love and married. On many evenings, Susannah read sermons and prayers to her tired husband or waited alone for him to return home from church preaching and pastoral visiting. Initially, she resented the loss of his attention and time, but he encouraged her to understand it as a sacrifice for the

Lord. Eventually this made her smile, instead of cry, whenever they said goodbye. Once, when Charles was struggling to write a particular sermon, Susannah woke in the middle of the night and realised that her weary husband was preaching in his sleep. She made a note of the text and his key points and gave them back to him in the morning just before he went to church! In time, Susannah became the mother of twin boys, but she couldn't have any more children and she struggled with illness and pain for the rest of her life. At this time, she had a special sense of Jesus' care and fellowship. Once, when Charles asked her if she wanted anything, Susannah laughed and said she'd like a piping bullfinch and an opal ring. Strangely, both of these uncommon gifts were given to her, which she understood as a token of the Lord's love for her. She worried that she was failing Charles, because she couldn't support his public work, but she was his secret source of strength even when she couldn't leave her bed. From here, helped by friends, she started a charity which collected and posted thousands of books and sermons to poor ministers who couldn't afford resources for their own study and work. Later she supported Charles' fight against the fashion of reading the Bible as literature rather than Scripture. She was at his side when he whispered his last words: "Oh … I have had a blessed time with my Lord." After Charles' death, Susannah compiled his autobiography from his diaries, letters and notes, as well as writing a devotional book of her own which reflects her deep, loving and unshakable faith in God.

Susanna Whatman

1753 - 1814

Susanna Bosanquet was born into a Huguenot family of religious refugees from France. Over fifty years after they arrived in England, when they had made their fortunes as merchants and bankers, Susanna was raised in a manor house in Essex. Her mother died when she was fifteen, so Susanna kept house for her father and five little sisters. Nine years later, Susanna married James Whatman and became the mistress of his country house, Vinters. He was a successful papermaker and an important man who became High Sheriff of Kent before he was thirty, but like Susanna, he had already experienced sorrow. His first wife, Sarah, had died and left him with two tiny girls: five-year-old Camilla and two-year-old Letitia. Susanna became their mother and gave them a brother called James. As well as running her nursery and raising her children, Susanna managed her household and servants. She ensured that her maids knew how to keep the household linen fresh and ordered, when to close the window shutters of each room to stop the sun spoiling the pictures and why they had to clean the furniture and carpets a certain way. Once, when she was away from home, she wrote, "This is glorious weather for hay making but

sadly *hot* for being in London. I hope the sun is kept from the pictures …" But Susanna was a kind and generous mistress. Once she sent a letter home with a scrap of fabric for her maids' new dresses. She wrote, "It is a finer one than I should have given them, but it is *so pretty* that if they *fell in love* with it as I did, I should be tempted to take it." She wrote the details of her housekeeping arrangements in a little book. Her husband died young and Susanna's health wasn't good, so she gave her housekeeping book to her daughter-in-law when she became the new mistress of Vinters. However Susanna, writing in her old age, confessed, "My trust in Providence is unbounded. I have not the most distant doubt that everything is working together for the best ultimately …" Later, in the year of her death, Susanna left two guineas to the Society for Promoting Christian Knowledge. But her lasting legacy was her home and her housekeeping book.

Thomas Birch Freeman

1809 - 1890

Thomas Birch Freeman was the son of an African gardener and an English housekeeper. He lost his father as a young child but came to faith in Christ as a boy, after teasing the local cobbler, who introduced him to the Gospel. Thomas became a gardener like his father and worked for a baronet. The house was large and imposing, but Thomas was busy in the garden, where he worked with seeds, plants and soil. Day by day he nurtured living things through every season and every weather. In his spare time, Thomas collected a small library of books, studied and visited the famous Kew Gardens in London. He learnt the Latin names for his beloved plants and became an accomplished botanist. Thomas was also a convicted non-conformist Christian rather than a member of the Church of England and his employer forced him to choose between his faith and his job. Thomas could have kept the job he loved and the wage he needed and he might have risen to the role of head gardener, if only he had been willing to join the Church of England, but he believed that the church should be independent from the state and he loved the Methodist chapels and ways of worship. Thomas left his job and the garden and became a missionary to Africa. He

established and ran a mission station in Ghana in spite of formidable obstacles and suffering. He got married and his wife died within a year or two – and this happened not once but twice! Thomas was not good with money and exceeded his budget, so at one point he had to retire for a few years to work, to repay his debts and regain his honour. However, after enduring this sorrow and embarrassment, Thomas got married again and he and his third wife had four children. In time Thomas became a beloved and successful missionary – serving, however he was needed, as a Methodist preacher, school teacher and informal doctor – who was deeply and sincerely mourned when he died. In spite of all these responsibilities, however, Thomas loved plants to the end of his life. He was fascinated by the native plants of Ghana. He corresponded with gardeners and scholars at Kew Gardens about the fauna and flowers he discovered and identified, including the intriguing *Synsepalum dulcificum* or “miracle plant”, which makes sour tastes sweet.

Thomas Clark

1775 - 1859

Thomas Clark was a Canterbury shoemaker who had music running through his heart and his fingertips. It was said that he was born with a natural love of music, because he never had a music lesson in his life, but he was one of the biggest composers of West Gallery Music in his generation. In those days country churches and non-conformist chapels – which were independent from the Church of England – didn't have organs. People still wanted to sing hymns anyway, of course, so they made their own music. People who could sing or play a musical instrument – and were used to singing and playing together at May Days, Harvest Festivals and barn dances – gathered in the west gallery of the church or chapel and made music during services. The music was usually joyful and a bit raucous as the notes of recorders, violins, flutes, cellos and bassoons mingled. Thomas wrote a huge quantity of West Gallery Music for chapels in and around Canterbury during his eighty-four years of life. Sometimes when he was sitting at his workbench and lapstone – making or mending shoes with leather, knife and hammer – a tune would come to him and he would jump to his feet and scribble it on a scrap of paper. Sometimes he was woken

from sleep by a tune and he would scramble out of bed, fumble to light a candle and write the bare bones of the tune down before going back to sleep. Later he would write the melody in more detail and write the harmony too. He wrote pieces of music with names like *Almighty God, who through Thy only begotten Son* (for a prayer from the *Book of Common Prayer*) and *Awake up my glory, awake lute and harp* (for a Psalm) as well as *Cranbrook* which is still used today: prayers and hymns, psalms and anthems which were unique but beautiful and bursting with life.

Thomas Coram

About 1668 - 1751

Thomas Coram was born in Lyme Regis and it was almost as if he had salty sea water running through his veins. Every night, as a little boy, he fell asleep to the sound of the waves swishing back and forth along the beach. He knew every mood of the sea and loved the way the sun glinted on it during the summer calms and the way the waves crashed and roared during the winter storms. His mother died when he was three and when he was eleven his father, a master mariner, sent him to sea. Later Thomas was apprenticed to a shipwright and went to America where he built ships and married an American girl with whom he built a life. Over the years he built a lighthouse, founded a library – starting with the *Book of Common Prayer* – and worked as a missionary to Native Americans. He was an unusual missionary, at that time, because he believed in education – especially for girls! Eventually Thomas and his wife moved home to England and here, as he went about his business, Thomas noticed something that broke his heart. He grew up without his mother and he and his wife weren't able to have any children of their own, but in bawdy and bustling London terribly poor mothers were forced to abandon their tiny babies in the streets, where they

The Foundling Hospital

died. Thomas – a tough sailor who could shout and swear in spite of his faith in Christ – knew he had to do something. For nineteen years he battered through criticism and opposition to establish a Foundling Hospital where mothers could leave babies they couldn't afford to raise. Eventually in 1739, after countless petitions had been signed, a Royal Charter was granted and the "hospital" was established "for the maintenance and education of exposed and destitute young children". Every abandoned and homeless baby was christened and named and Thomas hoped that every one of them would grow into a good Christian and useful member of society. He was poor when he died because he had given all his money to the Foundling Hospital. To this day it has helped more than twenty-five thousand children find a hopeful future in life.

Thomas Fairfax

1612 - 1671

During the days of the English Civil War there was a Christian nobleman who was called "Black Tom" because of his dark eyes and long, wild dark hair. His real name was Thomas Fairfax and he was a Cambridge-educated Yorkshireman who fought for Parliament during the Civil War. He didn't want to fight against King Charles I in the Civil War and worked as hard as he could, for as long as he could, for peace between the Royalists and Parliamentarians. In the end, though, war became inevitable and Fairfax fought for Parliament and freedom for everyone. Thomas wasn't a great politician, but he was an excellent soldier: sometimes ruthless, but always fair. He became a general and trained the rag-tag Parliamentarian army of soldiers, volunteers and boys into a fighting force. The soldiers admired and trusted Thomas and followed his deep faith, daring sword and flying hair into battle and forward on to victory again and again and again. Men said he was brave and lucky, but in time the army rallied around the charismatic and uncompromising Oliver Cromwell, who came to embody the Parliamentarian cause. Thomas, however, was still one of the most reliable Parliamentarians. He was such a good, honest man, in

fact, that his great enemy, King Charles, I said, “The general is a man of honour, and keeps his word which he had pledged to me.” Thomas never wanted King Charles I to be executed and he refused to help with the king’s mock trial or to sign his death warrant. He begged for mercy for the king, but no one would listen. Thomas had fought for freedom and honour, not tyranny, so he retired to his country estate in Yorkshire during the Commonwealth of Oliver Cromwell. Later he helped with the Restoration of King Charles II. When he died, Thomas left a beautifully-written collection of Psalms he had translated into English, as well as some bad poetry and a heartbroken *Elogy on my deare Wife*. He always said he went to war against the king because his “judgement was for the Parliament as the king and kingdom’s great and safest council”. His life, in his own version of Psalm 1, could be described as:

> … by the runing streames the well sett tree
> His fruit in season yeild, the just shall be …

Thomas Gambier Parry

1816 - 1888

Thomas Gambier Parry was a man who unashamedly and wholeheartedly loved beautiful and sacred things. He inherited a fortune made in the East India Company, earned a degree from the University of Cambridge, bought a country house, married a sweet girl and had twelve children. He was a man of deep faith and intellectual curiosity who embraced a traditional kind of Christianity popularised by the Oxford Movement, and gave lots of money to charity. He was also a man of great suffering who was orphaned when he was a little boy, watched four of his beloved children die as babies and lost his first wife to illness. Later Thomas remarried and eight of his children lived to adulthood. But through it all Thomas continued to seek the beautiful and sacred things in life. He travelled around Europe and collected a gorgeous range of art. He was especially fascinated by religious art from the Renaissance. He wrote a book in which he said that religious art is "to adorn not walls alone but minds, with thoughts of what is highest, noblest, loveliest, that the blessed God has spread along the path of life, to lead them upward to Himself". But it wasn't enough for Thomas to look at and write about beauty and faith and other

people's art. He was, himself, an artist who mixed his own paints and developed his own style. In his thirties, after the death of his oldest children and first wife, Thomas built a church: the Holy Innocents Church in Highnam in Gloucestershire. He invested a lot of love and money in the church and decorated it with stone carvings and stained glass. He designed and painted the wall frescos himself and used the village people as models for his picture of the Palm Sunday procession of Jesus, His disciples and the pilgrims into Jerusalem. In old clothes, daubed with paint, a gentleman with a beard and a pair of kind but sad eyes – who was known as Mr Gambier Parry of Highnam Court – worked for hours to create a beautiful and sacred place where he hoped Christ would be worshipped, especially by children, for years to come.

Thomas of Oxford

Before 1386 - After 1427

For many years, in a workshop in the university city of Oxford, Thomas of Oxford – or Thomas Glazier – worked with glass, paint and lead to create works of art in stained glass. After a long apprenticeship, when he learned everything there was to know about the art of the glazier and the artist from a master glazier, he became a glazier in his own right. In those days the windows of chapels, churches and cathedrals were filled with stained glass depicting heroes and heroines from the Bible and saints from the history of the church. Thomas bought glass in thin, flat sheets. He designed his windows by drawing a full-sized plan or *vidimus* – Latin for "we have seen" – in charcoal on a wooden table. He used a hot iron to soften the glass and a grozing iron to chip and crimp the glass into the right shapes for the different elements of the picture. Some of the glass was the right colour. Some of it needed painting and Thomas used handmade paints and natural brushes to add details and suggest texture, light and shadow. When all the glass was ready, Thomas assembled the pieces of the picture on the *vidimus,* joined them together with lead and soldered it so the glass and the lead were stuck together forever. Once Thomas designed

and made twenty-three panes of glass for the east window of New College in Oxford. Then, a few years later, he designed and made forty-five panes of glass for the east window of Winchester College in Winchester. It is thought that he also created stained glass windows for Merton College in Oxford as well as St Mary the Virgin of Thenford in Northamptonshire and Winchester Cathedral in Hampshire among many other places of worship. Thomas worked with architects, builders, labourers and craftsmen and became known for his beautiful designs and his good work. The sun still shines through the glass in his windows and illuminates Adam with his spade, Eve with her spindle and St Christopher dressed for travel. Moreover, in a corner of the east window of New College in Oxford, a little man of stained glass still kneels in prayer. He has a little beard and wears a long robe. His hands are folded and his eyes are lifted to heaven. It seems that one day Thomas created a little self-portrait and left it there, in the window of the college, praying forevermore.

Thomas Percival

1740 - 1804

One of Thomas Percival's favourite things to do, when he was a young boy, was to read the medical books in his uncle's library. Thomas, who grew up to be a devout Christian and committed doctor, was born in Lancashire and orphaned at the age of three, so he was raised by his older sister. He went to a grammar school, where he excelled in classical and theological studies, but he wanted to be a doctor like his uncle. Although Thomas was a Christian, he wasn't a member of the Church of England. In those days, that meant he couldn't go to the great universities in Oxford or Cambridge. Instead, as soon as he was old enough, he went to study medicine at the University of Edinburgh in Scotland and the University of Leyden in Holland. Thomas earned his MD degree, which qualified him as a doctor, when he was twenty-five and later that year he became a member of the Royal Society in London. Eventually he became a member of the Royal Society of Edinburgh too. Thomas was an experienced and mature doctor when he developed a code of conduct for doctors to use when treating patients. He distributed it in a pamphlet in 1794. He expanded it and published it as a book in 1803. Books in those days almost

always had long titles and Thomas's book was called *Medical Ethics; or a Code of Institutes and Precepts, Adapted to the Professional Conduct of Physicians and Surgeons*. It was the first book to discuss and suggest medical ethics, meaning not just a code of conduct, but a set of values for doctors. Any and every doctor could refer to it if they weren't sure whether something in their medical practice was right or wrong. It made the best and right thing clear in moments of personal confusion or professional conflict. Thomas' book emphasised the importance of personal integrity and honour. It also advocated an holistic approach to patient care. Thomas went on to help found the first Board of Health in Manchester. His code of conduct for doctors was ultimately adopted by America, Canada and Australia as well as Britain. Thomas was married and in his spare time he advocated for better working conditions and shorter working hours for children in factories. His book, meanwhile, could be found on the bookshelves of many doctors – just like the books he had read in his uncle's library when he was a boy.

Walter de Lud-Auk

1300s - 1400s

Sir Walter de Lud-Auk was, according to the storytellers of old, a fine and upstanding man with strong muscles and white hair. His sword was pledged to King Henry V but his heart was pledged to Christ. He was a knight bound to serve his king and country, a landowner obligated to manage his hand and peasants and a householder responsible for leading his house, family and servants in the way they should go. He was also the guardian of his little granddaughter – a tiny girl called Alice. Somehow this good man, Walter, encountered the teaching of a rebel priest and scholar from the University of Oxford called John Wycliffe. Wycliffe taught that Christ, not traditions of the Catholic Church, was the only way to God and he translated the Bible into English for all men and women to read. Walter became convinced that what Wycliffe said about Christ and the Bible was true. At the time the Catholic Church was the only church in England and it was considered heretical to practice Christianity in any other way. Walter nonetheless gathered a group of people called Lollards who, like him, believed Wycliffe's fresh and exciting teachings. The little church met in a mysterious and secret chasm near a rocky ridge in

Staffordshire. The chasm was tall and narrow and full of shadows – it's said, to this day, that the sun only just reaches the bottom of the chasm at the height of the summer. The walls, covered with bright green mosses and curly green ferns, twist and turn and touch the sky. But here the rebel Christians gathered and worshipped God. Tragedy struck, however, when the king's soldiers broke into the chasm. The forester guarding the entrance couldn't stop them and they swarmed into the chasm. Walter's granddaughter Alice – who was eighteen and tall, slender and beautiful and sang like a little bird – was wounded by a bolt from a crossbow. She fell and took her last breath in her grandfather's arms. Walter had loved and raised Alice since she was a baby. Now he and the forester carried her body outside the chasm for burial under the protecting branches of an oak tree. Finally Walter led his Lollard friends in surrendering to the soldiers and the king. He resisted pleas to escape and allowed himself to be taken to London. Some members of the little church were imprisoned and others were pardoned and released. It was said that Walter – whose heart never really left the secret chasm, his Lollard friends or his beloved granddaughter – died in prison. To this day, in Staffordshire, people remember Walter and Alice when they visit the rocky chasm called "Lud's Church".

Walter Tull

1888 - 1918

One day a little boy called Walter wore a small suit and a cloth cap and posed for a family photograph. He was the son of a black carpenter from Barbados – his grandparents were born into slavery – and an English woman. For the first years of his life he played with the other children in the streets around his home in Folkstone. But the happy days ended when his parents died. The family were staunch Methodists and the local minister arranged for Walter and his brother Edward to go to a London orphanage, run by the Methodist Church, where he was taught religion and given an education and a start in a line of work. He also learned how to play football. Life wasn't easy for black men and women in England and Walter battled prejudice and discrimination. He got a job in a print shop and dreamed of working in a newspaper office, but became a professional footballer almost by accident. He was playing in a friendly match when he was spotted by a talent scout, so he played for Tottenham Hotspur and Northampton Town. Sometimes people shouted insults about his race while he was playing, but Walter ignored them, playing his best and letting what the sports reporters called "his clever footwork" speak for itself. His faith was active,

no-nonsense and focused on society. When WWI started, he joined up to fight at once, because he felt it was right to fight for his country rather than because he wanted to be a soldier. He joined the Football Battalion – the 17th Battalion of the Middlesex Regiment – and suffered from shell shock but returned, when he was better, to fight at the Battle of the Somme. Walter become an officer in the British Army even though black men weren't, technically, allowed to hold such high rank. It is thought that this was partly because of the respect and care he showed to the men under him as well as the officers over him. At this time he was mentioned in dispatches for "gallantry and coolness". He was beloved by his men, so when he was shot and killed shortly before Armistice Day, they risked their lives in a doomed effort to rescue his body. One of his fellow officers wrote to Walter's brother that he had lost a friend and said, "I hope that those who remain may be as true and faithful as he." Although it was never granted – possibly because of his race – Walter was recommended for a Military Cross for his bravery and gallantry.

William and Alice Harpur

About 1496 - 1574 and Unknown - 1569

Once, in the county town of Bedford, there lived a humble but thoughtful and obliging young man called William Harpur. He attended the Mill Lane school run by the monks of Newnham Priory and trained as a tailor like his father. Later he married a young lady called Alice, went to London and became a Merchant Tailor. In time he became an alderman and on Michaelmas Day in 1561 he became the Mayor of London. It seems that William was raised in the Catholic faith and became an alderman during the reign of the Catholic Queen Mary I. At this time he encountered a group of Protestants condemned to die for their faith. He tried to reason and trick them into recanting their "heresy" and saving their lives, but they refused and died. William was understandably distressed by this incident. He served as Mayor of London during the reign of Protestant Queen Elizabeth I although he was probably still a loyal and discrete Catholic. While he was mayor, however, St Paul's Cathedral caught fire, its roof was destroyed and William worked carefully and zealously with the Protestant people of London to raise the money for the restoration. He is remembered for being good, wise and diligent as well as generous. Alice, who

managed their household, table and servants, is remembered for being affectionate, kind and noble. They are buried in St Paul's Church in Bedford – William is buried in the chancel, near the altar, by his special request before dying – and remembered by a pair of brass plaques in the Trinity Chapel. Their good works, however, continue. William and Alice had a lot of money but no children and it seems that they wanted to do something to help others. William's school had been closed at the Dissolution of the Monasteries so together he and Alice endowed a grammar school for thirty boys in Bedford and provided money so that "poore chylders" (poor children) would be "nurrysshed and enformed" (nurtured and informed). They also provided money for dowries for "porre maydes" or girls of Bedford as well as "almes to the poor". Their generosity was supported by the land they owned, which is still identifiable as "the Bedford bounds", in London. The Harpur Trust still manages William and Alice's legacy and uses it to support excellent education and meet all sorts of needs in Bedford to this day.

William Herschel and Caroline Herschel

1738 - 1822 and 1750 - 1848

Once, in a tall, thin house in Bath, a brother and sister startled their neighbours with bangs, explosions and other mysterious noises while they built telescopes to study the night sky. It all began in Germany when a little boy called William Herschel stared up, up, up into the darkness to look for stars. William's grandfather was thought to be a committed Jew but William's father was a nominal Christian and a court musician. William grew up, became a musician and moved to England, but he never lost his love for the beauty and mystery of the night sky. He joined Charles Avison's orchestra, worked as a church organist and settled in Bath. Eventually William's little sister, Caroline, came to England to keep house for her scientific brother. He was good at making music, manipulating notes or numbers and plotting stars, but he was terrible at managing servants, housework and meals. Caroline cheerfully managed those things and reminded him to eat and sleep too. She was a bright, curious girl with a lovely singing voice, who longed to be beautiful and beloved, but lived with the fact that her face was scarred and her body was stunted from a childhood illness. Caroline craved learning and independence and adored William

because he gave her sympathy, support and a real home. She earned her living by singing until she, too, became fascinated by the night sky. William, who noticed the glory of God in everything he saw through his telescope, devoted his life to tracking stars and trying to understand the mysteries of the heavens. He studied what he thought was a comet and discovered that it was the planet of Uranus. It was the first planet anyone had discovered for hundreds – or maybe even thousands – of years and William was invited to join the Royal Society. He went on to build the biggest telescope in the world at that time, study the Milky Way and receive more honours before he died, but he remained a loving, generous and humble man, awed and touched by the wonders of God in the universe. For fifty years or more, even when William got married and didn't need her domestic help anymore, Caroline – who called herself "a hunter of comets" – worked at her brother's side to find and map stars. She also became an astronomer in her own right, however, who discovered eight comets and three nebulae and was given an honoury membership of the Royal Astronomical Society. At the end of her life she returned to Germany where she rediscovered her love for singing her favourite hymns when she was alone with her faith, her memories and the stars.

William Howard Campbell

1859 - 1910

William Howard Campbell was a missionary who loved Christ but also loved literature, botany and sport. As a boy in Ireland, the eldest of nine brothers and sisters, he was fascinated by birds and moths and created a private museum of nature specimens with his brothers. Later he attended the University of Edinburgh and here he studied arts, theology and medicine, learnt Sanskrit – an ancient and venerable Indian language – and played tennis, cricket, rugby, football and any other sport that was going. He was the rugby champion of the university, but later he was ordained, joined the London Mission Society and went to India as a missionary. Here he married a girl called Elizabeth, had four sons and grieved when one of them died of a tropical disease. As a missionary, William started churches and provided gentle support for the local people. He sympathised with their concerns and worked for their good. One time he brought people together to resolve an issue with a local dam before the wall was breached and the area was flooded. Another time he wrote a series of articles to attract and direct much-needed food and medicine during a famine. William made a habit of gathering the local people together for tennis and cricket

matches too! William also developed linguistic and translation projects, became an expert on the local dialect of Telegu and helped to revise the Telegu Bible. He wrote a number of religious books with titles like *Grounds for Belief in a Personal God* and a political critique of the British government in India called *The Truth About the Government of India*. William's great love, however, was still natural history. He joined the Bombay Natural History Society, became an expert on the local plants, birds and moths and identified around seventy new species of moth. Unfortunately, due to the habits of his era, he collected specimens of what he observed. He also contributed long lists of botanical names and translations to a Telegu dictionary and grammar. Towards the end of his life, William was offered a place as the principle of a theological college in India, but he died, while still quite young, before he was able to take his post. He was in Italy at the time, trying to rest and recover, but no doubt fascinated by the natural beauty and unique wildlife of the area at the same time.

William Keble Martin

1877 - 1969

One quiet evening, when the Devon hills were bathed in the golden light of the setting sun, William Keble Martin hurried towards the railway station. His busy Sunday of church services and parish work was behind him now and he wanted to catch a train which would whisk him away for a day or so in the countryside where he could study and paint flowers for the book of flora and fauna which he was writing. The train was puffing as William ran along the platform, jumped into an empty carriage and sank back against the leather seats. The guard whistled, the driver nodded and with a whistle the train pulled away. At the vicar's side, his leather satchel was full of natural history books, his sketchbook, pencils, paintbrushes and paintbox. Many years before, when he was a boy, William had became fascinated by wildlife while growing up in Devon. He recalled a happy childhood in the Christian tradition. One of his ancestors was a Knight of the Garter and another relation was John Keble, who sparked the Oxford Movement in the Church of England, but William's father was a country vicar, his mother was a headmaster's daughter and he had four brothers and four sisters. In those days he climbed a tree to see a nest of red

squirrel kits and swam while kingfishers dipped and dived around him in the water of the river. Later William studied Greek and Botany at the University of Oxford then became a dedicated vicar with a heart for prayer and visiting the sick. He worked for many years in a series of poverty-stricken parishes in the North of England, which he called his “mission field”, but he found time, now and then, to draw pictures of flowers. He served as an army chaplain during WWI and after the war he and his family – he was married twice and had five children – moved to a rural parish in Devon. Here he served as a vicar until he was in his seventies. William was used to being busy in the North, but happy to have more time in the South West, so he developed his love of botany and his talent for identifying, grouping and illustrating flowers and foliage. For years, around Sunday sermons and parish work, he caught trains to various parts of England where he thought he might find a new specimen. William was a gentle, humble man with twinkling blue eyes who authored a beautiful book about English botany, called *The Concise British Flora in Colour*, when he was eighty-eight.

Zechariah and Mary Taft

1772 - 1848 and 1772 - 1851

Zechariah Taft was the Methodist minister of Cherry Street Chapel in Birmingham and Mary Barritt was a farmer's daughter from Lancashire. The couple got married in 1802 and became the parents of two daughters called Jane and Eliza. In 1825 Zechariah – a stocky man with a plain face, a serious expression and a tiny hint of a smile – wrote a book called *Biographical Sketches of the Lives and Public Ministry of Various Holy Women.* In it he noted, "It is worthy of remark that those females that are most active in the church, are in general those of the highest order in religious attainments, especially in communion with God, and conformity to Him." It was an unusual thing for a man to say at the time but Zechariah had been supporting his wife and other women preachers for many years by then and he never regretted his words. It seems that history remembers very little else about Zechariah, but perhaps he wanted it to be that way, because he was first and foremost Mary's closest friend, greatest fan and staunchest ally. At that time the Methodist movement was considered rather revolutionary for its emphasis on revival, faith and holiness. Mary was considered very subversive because she believed God was calling her to preach.

Being both devout and determined, she obeyed and preached in churches, barns and fields. As a result it is thought that hundreds or maybe even thousands of people came to faith in Christ. As another result, however, Mary's father forced her to choose between her home and family and her involvement in the Methodist movement. Mary promptly chose the Methodist movement and was more or less homeless until she married Zechariah. The Methodist movement, however, threatened to expel her for disorderliness. Mary said it was more important to obey God than man and she was supported by a respectable minister who said, "It is at peril of your soul that you meddle with Mary Barritt; God is with her and fruit is appearing wherever she goes." It was said that she preached "with masculine eloquence and womanly tenderness". Once, when it started raining while she was preaching, she prayed for it to stop and it did so. Mary continued to preached with Zechariah's support for the rest of their lives as, together, they proclaimed the grace of God.

How beautiful are the arms which have embraced Christ,
the hands which have touched Christ,
the eyes which have gazed upon Christ,
the lips which have spoken with Christ,
the feet which have followed Christ.
How beautiful are the hands
which have worked the works of Christ,
the feet which treading in His footsteps
have gone about doing good,
the lips which have spread abroad His Name,
the lives which have been counted loss for Him.

(Christina Rossetti)

Chronological Reading Order

Read the stories in chronological order to get a glimpse of the big story of Christianity in the British Isles.

Lucius of Britain

Brendan the Navigator

Morwenna of Cornwall

Edwin and Ethelburga of Northumbria

James the Deacon

Chad of Mercia

Eadfrith of Lindisfarne

Bega

Edmund the Martyr

Ethelflaed of Mercia

Edith of Wilton

Malcolm and Margaret of Scotland

Caradog of St Davids

Miles and Sibyl de Gloucester

Margaret of England

Bartholomew of Farne

Jocelin of Wells

Robert le Converse

Geoffrey Luttrell

Rose de Burford

Thomas of Oxford

Walter de Lud-Auk

Elizabeth the Daughter of Rabbi Moses

Anne Bulkeley

Christopher Trychay

William and Alice Harpur

Robert Williams

Roger Martyn

Rose Hickman

Alice Driver

Laurence Chaderton

John Rainolds

Francis Taylor

Margaret Ward

Philip Sydney and Mary Herbert

John Gerard

Mary Fillis

Reasonable Blackman

Myles Standish

Adrian Batten

Brilliana Harley

Elizabeth Tilley Howland

Lucius Cary

Thomas Fairfax

John and Lucy Hutchinson

Ann Fanshawe

Robert Adkins

David Lestourgeon

Jane Sharp

Sally Lunn

Agnes Wilson

Elizabeth Elstob

Thomas Coram

Gilbert White

Polly Newton

William Herschel and Caroline Herschel

Thomas Percival

Esther de Berdt Reed

John Bethune

Susanna Whatman

Marianne Sykes Thornton

Fanny Coker

David Thompson

Zechariah and Mary Taft

Thomas Clark

Nansi Griffiths

Barbara Wilberforce

John Smith

Billy Bray

Joseph Anning and Mary Anning

Sheth Ghulam Hyder

James Bonar

Deborah Levy Alexander

James and Elizabeth Finn

Priscilla Buxton Johnston

Fanny Kemble

Thomas Birch Freeman

Anthony Trollope

Thomas Gambier Parry

James Nugent

Georgiana Liddell

David Richards

Alfred Edersheim

Elizabeth Wilson

John Coleridge Patteson

Josephine Butler

Mary Sumner

Susannah Spurgeon

George and Grace Stott

Octavia Hill

Charles Taylor

Charlotte Mason

Isabella Gilmore

Agnes Lewis and Margaret Gibson

James Hannington

Laura Ridding

Helen Gladstone

Joseph Harrald

Lilias Trotter

Ellen Lakshmi Goreh

Henry Tidmarsh

Kate Edger Evans

Albert Mahomet

Ruth from Madras

William Howard Campbell

Etta Lemon

C. T. Studd

Edith Brown

Edward Wilson

Isabella Pringle

William Keble Martin

Ivy Williams

Christopher Chavasse and Noel Chavasse

Frank Foley

Walter Tull

Mabel Barker

Dorothy Garrod

Cicely Mary Barker

Jane Haining

Ninette de Valois

Dorothy Dennison

Lily O’Hanlon

Charles Fraser-Smith

Lilian Bader

Mary Teresa Brück

Topic Index

Read the stories about men and women
or places and topics of special interest.

Cicely Mary Barker

Eadfrith of Lindisfarne

Edith of Wilton

Edward Wilson

Georgiana Liddell

Henry Tidmarsh

Lilias Trotter

Thomas Gambier Parry

William Keble Martin

Artisan Crafts

David Lestourgeon

John Smith

Mary Fillis

Sally Lunn

Thomas of Oxford

Reasonable Blackman

Black Britons

Fanny Coker

Lillian Bader

Mary Fillis

Reasonable Blackman

Thomas Birch Freeman

Walter Tull

Business

Francis Taylor

Reasonable Blackman

Rose de Burford

Rose Hickman

Sally Lunn

Cornwall

Billy Bray

Morwenna of Cornwall

Education

Charles Taylor

Charlotte Mason

David Richards

Elizabeth Elstob

Helen Gladstone

Mabel Barker

Sheth Ghulam Hyder

William and Alice Harpur

French Huguenots

David Lestourgeon

Esther de Berdt Reed

Sally Lunn

Susanna Whatman

Housewives and Homemakers

Barbara Wilberforce

James and Elizabeth Finn

Kate Edger Evans

Malcolm and Margaret of Scotland

Marianne Sykes Thornton

Mary Sumner

Susannah Spurgeon

Susanna Whatman

Indian Britons

Albert Mahomet

Ellen Lakshmi Goreh

Ruth from Madras

Sheth Ghulam Hyder

Ireland

Bega

Brendan the Navigator

Francis Taylor

Mary Teresa Brück

Ninette de Valois

William Howard Campbell

Jewish Believers

Alfred Edersheim

Deborah Levy Alexander

Elizabeth the Daughter of Rabbi Moses

Robert le Converse

William Herschel and Caroline Herschel

Knights

Christopher Chavasse and Noel Chavasse

Geoffrey Luttrell

Walter de Lud-Auk

William Keble Martin

Law

Ivy Williams

James Bonar

John and Lucy Hutchinson

Roger Martyn

Linguistics

Agnes Lewis and Margaret Gibson

Charles Taylor

Elizabeth Elstob

James and Elizabeth Finn

John Coleridge Patteson

John Rainolds

Laurence Chaderton

Sheth Ghulam Hyder

Martyrs

Alice Driver

Edmund the Martyr

Francis Taylor

James Hannington

John Coleridge Patteson

John Smith

Margaret Ward

Medicine

Christopher Chavasse and Noel Chavasse

Edith Brown

Edward Wilson

Isabella Gilmore

Isabella Pringle

Jane Sharp

Lily O'Hanlon

Mabel Barker

Thomas Percival

Mission

Alfred Edersheim

Chad of Mercia

Charles Fraser Smith

Deborah Levy Alexander

Edith Brown

Ellen Lakshmi Goreh

George and Grace Stott

Isabella Pringle

James Hannington

Jane Haining

John Coleridge Patteson

Lilias Trotter

Lily O'Hanlon

Morwenna of Cornwall

Thomas Birch Freeman

Thomas Coram

William Howard Campbell

Music

Adrian Batten

David Richards

Caradog of St Davids

James the Deacon

Mary Sumner

Thomas Clark

William Herschel and Caroline Herschel

Nature

Bartholomew of Farne

Cicely Mary Barker

Edward Wilson

Etta Lemon

Gilbert White

Laurence Chaderton

Lilias Trotter

Octavia Hill

Thomas Birch Freeman

William Howard Campbell

William Keble Martin

Outstandingly Happy Marriages

Ann Fanshawe

Barbara Wilberforce

Charles Taylor

Deborah Levy Alexander

Edwin and Ethelburga of Northumbria

James and Elizabeth Finn

John and Lucy Hutchinson

Laura Ridding

Laurence Chaderton

Malcolm and Margaret of Scotland

Marianne Sykes Thornton

Polly Newton

Susannah Spurgeon

Thomas Gambier Parry

Royalty

Bega

Edith of Wilton

Edmund the Martyr

Edwin and Ethelburger of Northumbria

Ethelflaed of Mercia

Malcolm and Margaret of Scotland

Morwenna of Cornwall

Scientists

Dorothy Garrod

Edward Wilson

Joseph Anning and Mary Anning

Mary Teresa Brück

William Herschel and Caroline Herschel

Scotland

Agnes Lewis and Margaret Gibson

Agnes Wilson

George and Grace Stott

Isabella Pringle

James Bonar

Jane Haining

John Bethune

Malcolm and Margaret of Scotland

Severe Health Challenges

Charlotte Mason

Cicely Mary Barker

George and Grace Stott

Gilbert White

Ivy Williams

Susannah Spurgeon

William Herschel and Caroline Herschel

Sport

Christopher Chavasse and Noel Chavasse

C.T. Studd

John Coleridge Patteson

Laurence Chaderton

Walter Tull

William Howard Campbell

Stage

Fanny Kemble

Ninette de Valois

Travel

Agnes Lewis and Margaret Gibson

David Thompson

Fanny Kemble

Georgiana Liddell

James and Elizabeth Finn

Joseph Harrald

Margaret of England

Wales

Caradog of St Davids

Charlotte Mason

David Richards

David Thompson

Miles and Sibyl de Gloucester

Morwenna of Cornwall

Nansi Griffiths

WWI and WWII

Charles Fraser-Smith

Christopher Chavasse and Noel Chavasse

Dorothy Dennison

Etta Lemon

Lilian Bader

Mabel Barker

Walter Tull

William Keble Martin

Writers

Albert Mahomet

Ann Fanshawe

Anthony Trollope

Christopher Trychay

Cicely Mary Barker

Dorothy Dennison

Fanny Kemble

Georgiana Liddell

Gilbert White

Jane Sharp

John and Lucy Hutchinson

Lily O’Hanlon

Philip Sydney and Mary Herbert

Rose Hickman

Susannah Spurgeon

Susanna Whatman

William Howard Campbell

Your Warriors, Saints and Dreamers

Who do you know who is a warrior, a saint and a dreamer
and who inspires you to be a warrior, a saint or a dreamer too?
You might be thinking of a relation, a friend
or someone you know and like to think about because
they're interesting or inspiring in some way.

Write their stories or draw their pictures below.

Name:

Story:

Name:

Story:

Name:

Story:

Name:

Story:

Name:

Story:

Name:

Story:

Name:

Story:

Author's Note

Dear Reader,

I hope you love this little book of stories about warriors, saints and dreamers as much as I do!

Because I enjoy knowing a bit of "the story behind the story", I thought you might like to know how this book came into being, starting with the fact that I read stories about Christians in history when I was a little girl. I always wanted to write a big book of stories (with pictures) about Christians in history to share with others, but I thought it was an old-fashioned idea, so I did not try for a long time.

The fact that people enjoy *Goodnight Stories for Rebel Girls* by Elena Favilli and Francesca Cavello and other similar books – including, for example, *100 Adventurous Stories for Brave Boys* by Glenn Hascall or *100 Extraordinary Stories for Courageous Girls* by Jean Fischer for Christian boys and girls – encouraged me to think people might enjoy *Warriors, Saints and Dreamers* too.

I wrote the book bit by bit over five or ten years or more and illustrated it too. For any factual, interpretive or technical errors, I wholeheartedly apologise. I wrote a few more stories this last Christmas because they are just too good not to share and I hope you think so too!

A book like this is always going to reflect the interests of the author and his or her interpretation of records. I am a storyteller, not an historian, so this is reflected in the stories in this book too. There are so many stories to tell that choosing the ones for this book was endlessly challenging, but one of the things I like about this selection is that it shows how many different and interesting things Christians have done with their lives through history, which you can see at a glance in the (in-exhaustive) index.

I am still encouraged and influenced by the stories of great Christian men and women, but many of their stories have already been told hundreds of times, so I decided to write about people whose stories are less well known. I wanted to write about men and women who lived faithful, quiet, unfamous lives, because we live in a celebrity culture, but these stories show us that we don't need to be celebrities: we just need to be faithful. I also chose to write about people whose achievements are well respected but whose faith is little known and rarely celebrated. Also, lastly, I wanted to write about Christians from multiple orthodox traditions – including both Catholics and Protestants – and I wanted to include people who were part of the Christian story but whose faith may have been a part of life (rather than the whole of life) or a bit of a struggle for some reason.

I have written about men and women who were part of the Christian story in the British Isles because this is my culture. I have never wanted to appropriate or misrepresent the stories of other cultures. I do encourage you, however, to seek the (often very wonderful) stories of Christians in other cultures around the world.

It has been a special concern of mine, from the beginning, to write – if possible – with the blessing of anyone who might have personal or family memories of the people in this book. A special note of thanks is due to the families of Christopher Chavasse and Noel

Chavasse, Edith Brown, Edward Wilson, Etta Lemon, Isabella Gilmore, Henry Tidmarsh, Mable Barker, Mary Teresa Brück and Walter Tull, the biographers of Frank Foley and Lilian Bader and the organisations connected to Agnes Lewis and Margaret Gibson, Charles Taylor, Edith Brown, George and Grace Stott, Isabella Gilmore, Ivy Williams, Lilias Trotter, Ninette de Valois, Octavia Hill and Sally Lunn. You know who you are – thank you so much for answering my emails, sharing your memories, photographs and ideas and reading my drafts, then making invaluable suggestions for improvement.

Regarding Dorothy Dennison, Lily O'Hanlon and William Keble Martin, I have drawn upon material which they shared in *The Worldover Book for Girls* by Dorothy Dennison, *At the Foot of Fishtale Mountain* by Lily M. O'Hanlon and *Over the Hills …* by William Keble Martin. Regarding Laura Ridding, I have drawn upon her autobiography manuscript which is quoted in *Lady Laura Ridding (1849-1939): the life and service of a bishop's wife*, a 2003 PhD thesis by Hannah Baud with the University of Gloucestershire, publicly available online.

Regarding Cicely Mary Barker, C.T. Studd, Dorothy Garrod, Helen Gladstone, Isabella Pringle and Jane Haining, I have drawn upon material which is abundantly and readily available to the public in printed books and online. This is what I have done for all the stories earlier in history too, and I believe that all quotations are in the public domain. I would be delighted to hear from you if you find the story of someone you remember personally in this book.

A personal note of thanks is due to others too. My thoughts about the story of the ordinary people of the British Isles was shaped by two of Professor Michael Wood's documentary films: *The Story of England* and *The Great British Story*. Thank you to Penny, who emailed back and forth with me about "the beautiful ordinary" as long ago as 2013. Thank you to Bishop Martin, who encouraged me to tell the stories of some of the many faithful, quiet, unfamous souls one beautiful but ordinary day at “the cathedral”. Thank you to Reverend Bernard and Catherine, for living the lives of loyal and unsung warriors, saints and dreamers with us in our parish for seven good years. Thank you, most of all, to my darling family for living with many hundreds of lists, stories and pictures of warriors, saints and dreamers for years … and years … and years, for finding many wonderful souls to include in the book, for bringing order out of chaos, for keeping me writing, drawing and hoping and for helping me to make this book a reality. Thank you all so much for so much more than I can say.

All of the warriors, saints and dreamers in this book were once as alive as you and I are now. I hope I have told their stories truthfully and with all due love and respect. I hope each and every one of them encourages you, too, to live your own story and your own faith in Christ as a warrior, a saint and a dreamer.

Best wishes,
Elizabeth Allen
Candlemas 2024

Printed in Great Britain
by Amazon

43203770R00239